WARREN GETLER
AND BOB BREWER

the Sentinel

ONE MAN'S QUEST TO FIND THE

HIDDEN TREASURE OF THE CONFEDERACY

SIMON & SCHUSTER

NEW YORK LONDON TORONTO SYDNEY SINGAPORE

Simon & Schuster
Rockefeller Center
1230 Avenue of the Americas
New York, NY 10020

For information regarding special discounts for bulk purchases,
please contact Simon & Schuster Special Sales at
1-800-456-6798 or business@simonandschuster.com

Designed by Karolina Harris

Manufactured in the United States of America
10   9   8   7   6   5   4   3   2   1

Library of Congress Cataloging-in-Publication Data

Getler, Warren
Shadow of the sentinel : one man's quest to find the hidden treasure of the Confederacy /
Warren Getler and Bob Brewer.
p.   cm.
Includes bibliographical references (p.   ) and index.
ISBN 0-7432-1968-6
1. United States—History—Civil War, 1861–1865—Antiquities. 2. Confederate States of
America—Antiquities. 3. Southern States—Antiquities. 4. West (U.S.)—Antiquities.
5. Treasure-trove—Southern States. 6. Treasure-trove—West (U.S.) 7. Knights of the Golden
Circle—History. 8. Secret societies—Confederate States of America—History—19th century.
9. United States—History—Civil War, 1861–1865—Underground movements.
I. Brewer, Bob. II. Title.

E646.5.G48   2003
973.7´13—dc21   2002044586

For map and photograph credits, please see page 304.

Acknowledgments

WE'D like to thank the many sources of information and intellectual inspiration who made this book possible, experts from a multitude of professions—history, cartography, cryptography, genealogy, theology, geophysics, geology, mathematics, numismatics and treasure-hunting. They are too numerous to mention in full. The same must be said of the authors of relevant books and manuscripts, stretching back to the mid-1850s, who revealed disparate pieces of the puzzle. Their thought-provoking markers served as guideposts as we made our way through the encrypted trail left behind by the secretive Knights of the Golden Circle.

We owe much gratitude to our editor, Bob Bender, for grasping the size and scope of the enigma surrounding the KGC and its hidden gold. Bob's enthusiasm for the subject—and its implications for historical discourse—inspired us throughout the writing. It was with the help of Bob's long experience that we were able to strike a fair and, we hope, engaging balance between historical analysis and adventure tale. Thanks to his assistant, Johanna Li, for helping us marshal the various visual components of the book.

We are also highly appreciative of the support from our literary agents, Matt Bialer and Robert Gottlieb of Trident Media, who stood behind this complex and provocative project at an early stage. Matt's sage advice at the proposal phase kept us rightly focused as we—an unlikely duo—hit the New York publishing circuit.

Others who provided helpful comments and suggestions throughout include: Michael Getler, Bob Whitcomb, Ayfer Jafri, John Buffalo, Betsy Stahl and Cari-Esta Albert.

Those providing much appreciated assistance in our research of primary and secondary sources include: Dave Kelly of the Library of Congress's main reading room, James Flatness, of the geography and maps division, and John Sellers and his colleagues in the manuscripts division; Nick Sheets, of the special collections division at Georgetown University's Lauinger Memorial Library; Fain McDaniel, Commanche County Museum in Commanche, Texas; Ana Lash, Hayden Public Library, Hayden, Arizona; and Paul and Joan Tainter, Freemont, Nebraska.

Among those who contributed directly to the telling of the KGC story in Arkansas, providing invaluable help through personal insights, photos, memorabilia, documents and other pages from the past: Bob and Wanda Tilley, lifelong friends and neighbors of Bob and Linda Brewer; Don Fretz, a treasure hunter and lifelong friend of Bob's; Don and Jeff Ashcraft, grandson and great-grandson of W. D. Ashcraft; Bud Ashcraft, nephew of W. D. Ashcraft; Dave and Jack Brewer, Bob's brothers; and local history buff Mitchell Cogburn.

Also deserving thanks and credit for their insight into the KGC: John London, a KGC researcher and treasure hunter from Texas; Bud Hardcastle, a respected KGC authority and Jesse James researcher from Oklahoma; Stan Vickery, a KGC researcher and treasure hunter from Louisiana; Richard Scott from Texas, who provided valued assistance in field research; sisters Jo Anne and Ceci Gillespie, of Oklahoma, on whose property much KGC history is in evidence and for whose diligent research and warm hospitality we are especially grateful; Steve Wilson, author of *Oklahoma Treasures and Treasure Tales*; and, for his unquestionable knowledge about the KGC's money trail, Michael Griffith, a junior-high school history teacher from Oklahoma.

In Arizona we'd like to thank a handful of people for their wisdom, documents and other invaluable information: Ellie Gardner, president, Heart Mountain Project, Apache Junction; Brian MacLeod, vice-president, Heart Mountain Project; and Bob Schoose, owner, Goldfield's Ghost Town, Apache Junction.

And ample credit is due those who have helped Bob with his Ouachita Treasure Consulting "Golden Circle Research" in other parts of the country, uncovering signs of KGC buried treasure from coast to coast.

Credit is also due genealogists Barbara Fulton and Barbara Lucas.

We thank DeLorme, *www.delorme.com,* for its cooperation and assistance, particularly topographical maps generated by TOPO USA® Ver. 3.0, 4.0, copyright © DeLorme, Yarmouth, Maine. TOPO USA® software has greatly simplified our treasure-hunting map work.

We'd like to acknowledge Dr. Alan Witten, professor of geophysics at the University of Oklahoma; as well as Dan Woods, geophysicist with Digital Magnetotelluric Technologies, and independent geological consultant Jim Rose for their scientific insights into magnetometry.

Finally, a word of appreciation must go to those universities that have provided a wonderful service in digitizing centuries-old magazines, journals and books and then making those documents available via the "Making of America" series on the Internet. This service, funded by the Andrew W. Mellon Foundation, has enabled researchers like us to dig for obscure yet vitally important nineteenth-century references, such as those for the Knights of the Golden Circle, by using keyword searches. Without this keystroke ability, some of the source material uncovered in this book—and the relationship of that information to what was generally known to be in the public domain—might never have surfaced.

William M. Wiley, KGC sentinel

For my wife, Linda, for her patience, support and assistance in our many years of arduous, often frustrating and always dangerous work.

And for the Brushy Valley mountaineers who, through example, taught me the meaning of sacrifice, dedication and hard work. Whatever their mission in life, they did it well without complaint and took their secret to the grave.

—BOB BREWER

For Juli. Were it not for her devotion and shared love of history and adventure, the path might never have been clear.

And for my parents, who provided a compass.

—WARREN GETLER

Contents

Preface

THIS book is the product of a five-year collaborative effort between Bob Brewer—a self-educated Arkansas mountainman, amateur historian and treasure hunter—and a Washington, D.C.–based investigative journalist. It is the story of how one man's obsession to uncover family secrets in the backwoods of Polk County, Arkansas, led him to discover not only buried treasure but buried—and troubling—pieces of America's past.

For Bob, following decades of intensive fieldwork and archival research, it was a matter of "getting the story out," for others to ponder. As for myself, I was intrigued by the scope and layered complexity of this all-but-unknown chapter in American history. After getting past my initial skepticism by observing Bob's method on the trail and by jointly mining the archives, I realized that I had stumbled upon one of the rare untold stories of hidden power and intrigue.

We both knew that the ramifications of this story were large. In pursuing the mystery surrounding the Knights of the Golden Circle, or KGC, we hoped that readers might at least take away the thought that truth, in recorded history, lies just below the surface.

Our foremost goal was to provide an authentic, accurate and plausible account of a chilling, unseen segment of Americana—the KGC, with its vast underground grid of wealth, its historic ties to Scottish Rite Freemasonry and its allusions to European Knights Templar traditions.

The KGC, we demonstrate, existed not only during the Civil War but for decades thereafter. It included many powerful men of the times—

politicians and outlaws, statesmen and generals—and some ordinary citizens as well. Its leadership, which took the organization fully underground in 1864, was fiercely determined that the American South would somehow, someday, prove victorious in a Second War of Rebellion. Toward that tomorrow, the KGC put in place a vast and extraordinarily ingenious network of underground caches of arms and money—much of it stolen U.S. payroll.

The Knights of the Golden Circle was a secret society with members sworn to blood oaths, and it left virtually no written records. As a result, we rely on some limited primary material but are forced to work largely with circumstantial evidence—symbolism, place names, odd turns of event—in an interpretive, analytical framework. Of course, errors of fact are ours alone.

As noncredentialed authors of an investigative history, we recognized our limitations going into such uncharted terrain as this book covers. With the hope of provoking debate and stimulating further exploration of the subject, we decided to plug on.

On a personal level, Bob's investigation into the inexplicable behavior of some of his forebears and his subsequent journey into the world of hunting for Rebel gold has produced rich insights into the idiosyncratic treasure-hunting community.

Stretched finances, badly strained relations with family and friends, accusations of being mad, private-property and public-land issues, run-ins with armed interlopers and bruised emotions from betrayal have all been part of the mix. No less so the constant support and forbearance of his closest family and colleagues.

Ultimately, Bob's search for treasure has become a mere touchstone in his larger quest for truth—a half-century-long probe into the activities of beloved relatives and their unswerving devotion to an obscure cause.

What this book does not do is pass judgment on the nature of the hidden system unveiled. Nor does it attempt to provide concrete, final answers as to why the underground grid of secreted wealth exists (or why it may still be guarded in places). In addition, we are unable to fully explain what might be behind startling parallels to a similar phenomenon—geometric grids possibly tied to treasure—in Europe. We would prefer that curious readers analyze, synthesize, chew over the possibilities and then turn to other sources. Ours is only one interpretation of an extraordinary sequence of discoveries.

The book is intended as a measured, deliberate journey into the subtle: into subtle signs that go unnoticed, into subtle associations that go unacknowledged. Only the understated, persistent approach, over many years, could have rendered a glimpse into the mind-boggling forms of communication behind an organizing force like that of the clandestine KGC.

We tip our hats to others who have touched on this arcane, controversial topic. We believe there is something here that goes beyond "tantalizing possibilities." When gold repeatedly is found through decipherment of coded maps, etched carvings and buried metallic clues, logic says there is a system behind it.

WARREN GETLER

October 2002

The Effigy

T H E effigy twisted on a thin steel wire.

When Bob Brewer brought his Jeep to a full stop, he could see that the headless figure hung precisely over the spot where he had walked the day before. It was dressed in blue jeans and a sweatshirt. And it was riddled with bullet holes. The dummy's torso was stuffed with rocks, and it slumped forward in a deadweight slouch—nearly snapping the sapling from which it dangled. There were other ominous changes to the landscape, as well. Tree trunks surrounding the spot had been spray-painted with inverted crosses. A stack of spent rifle shell cases, piled on the boxes that had held them, lay nearby. A trail of yarn, tied to the back of the effigy, led to the pile of used ammunition . . . in case anyone missed the connection.

Twenty-four hours earlier, on a crisp October morning in 1993, Bob and a friend had arrived at the remote site along a dirt trail in Arkansas's Ouachita Mountains. They had brought along an old topographical map of the region, a metal detector and a camera for the purpose at hand: to find and record clues leading to what Bob suspected were buried caches of treasure. It was not a farfetched suspicion. The experienced treasure sleuth had previously unearthed caches of Civil War–era gold and silver coins not far from the site, and he had reason to believe that this area was linked to those sites. Over the course of that first day, the two men had discovered and photographed numerous buried clues: rusted plow points and other pieces of metal that served as geographic pointers. The location of the buried directional markers had been carefully recorded on a grid to ensure the correct orientation of each piece, which was then reburied. It was a system that had yielded results in the past and which Bob was steadily improving. As Bob and his friend had headed back to camp that night, he felt sure that he was close to finding something big.

When the men returned the next day with a third treasure-hunting friend, they quickly realized that their plans would have to change.[1] They agreed to notify the police about the overnight transformation of their site. When a deputy sheriff and a U.S. deputy marshal for the Forest Service arrived, the officers asked a few questions, took photos of the effigy and removed it—carrying it off as if it were a cadaver.[2] As Bob looked on, he wondered about the decision he'd made to pursue a decades-old mystery deep in the Arkansas timberlands.

The Education of a Confederate Code-Breaker

THE backwoods that surround Hatfield, Arkansas, are thick, nearly opaque in places, and vast. Towering pines and hardwoods crowd steep mountain slopes, their canopies eclipsing much of the sun's rays. On the north-facing ridges, where the giant hardwoods cluster, only the rare splash of sunlight reaches the damp forest soil. This shadowed environment, spiked with its treacherous crags, can seem uninviting—even menacing—for those who come from beyond the rugged hill country of west-central Arkansas. But for those native to the hills, the natural shroud helps keep things private, elemental, protected.

That is why, despite their sometimes unforgiving topography, the Ouachita Mountains have attracted frontier-minded people for millennia. Abundant elk and bison herds lured primitive hunter-gatherers some ten thousand years ago. Prospects of finding gold and silver deposits in Paleozoic-aged veins of quartz charmed Spanish explorer Hernando de Soto into the region in the 1500s, while ample beavers and minks attracted French trappers in the following centuries. The French gave the mountains their name, from the local Quapaw Indian phrase, "Wash-a-taw," which means "good hunting grounds." Settlers from Kentucky, Tennessee and surrounding areas began arriving in substantial numbers in the 1830s. Homesteading in a land with limited agrarian potential, these robust Scots-Irish mountaineers carved out a hardscrabble existence.

With settlement came the stagecoach. This, in turn, pulled in the outlaw gangs, which used this great Southern range—stretching east to west from Little Rock to Atoka, Oklahoma—as a springboard for some of their dramatic raids. Jesse James was reported to have ridden through the Ouachita hills following a stagecoach robbery near Hot Springs, Arkansas, in 1874. Then, the ill-defined border area between frontier Arkansas and the Indian Nations territory to the west was a haven for every fugitive from justice, giving rise to the maxim, "There is no law west of Little Rock, and no God west of Fort Smith."

It was these images of the untamed woods that captured the imagination of nine-year-old Bob Brewer, back in 1949. Tiny Hatfield—population 300—had been home to generations of Brewers before him. Many of his forebears had figured in the growing wave of westward migration from Kentucky in the mid- to late-1800s. Most, like his paternal grandfather, William Brewer, a Kentucky-born teacher turned cotton farmer who would become mayor of the town, decided to stay in Hatfield for most of their adult lives. Bob's father, Landon, sought adventure for a time beyond the timbered hills, but, in the end, succumbed to the pull of the Ouachitas.

In 1949, after a long career as a naval officer, capped by several years at war in the Pacific, forty-one-year-old Landon Brewer moved his family to the bluffs of Arkansas's Polk County from his latest posting on the outskirts of San Diego, California. It was time, he sensed, to return to the interior, to the soil, after a two-decade hiatus. For Bob, who loved reading Jack London, Mark Twain and tales of outlaws and treasure, the Arkansas hill country held out enormous possibilities. And none too soon. Life as a Navy brat on the fringes of the city had long lost its luster.

Young Bob swiftly embraced the surrounding Ouachitas. The pristine two-million-acre forest of red oaks, white oaks, beeches, hickories, maples, hollies, shortleaf pines and Eastern red cedars seemed a boundless playground. Life was suddenly distilled to its simple pleasures and truths. Whatever light penetrated the thick foliage was good enough for him; whatever steep trail let him navigate two-thousand-foot elevations was just added sport. The same could be said for dodging rattlesnakes, copperheads and the occasional feral hog. Ticks, chiggers and poison oak abounded, but Bob regarded them as minor nuisances.

To Bob, the mountains and the dense deciduous forest were not the least bit threatening. They were inviting, nourishing—clear streams teeming with fish; seasonal yields of hickory nuts, black walnuts, wild

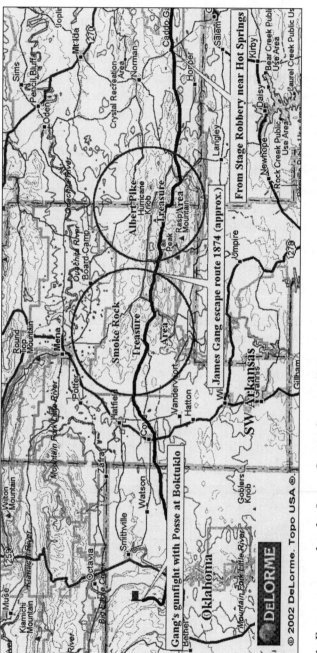

1. Escape route taken by James Gang after an alleged September, 1874, Hot Springs, Arkansas, robbery.

huckleberries, blackberries, cherries and muscadine. The Ouachitas, he
sensed, were materially and spiritually tied to his parents' backwoods
past. A child who had known his father only as an infrequent visitor during the war years and his mother as a dutiful career Navy wife, Bob
began to grasp what his parents had meant by settling down and "going
home." It was a phrase that he had heard many times.

When Landon and Zetta Brewer finally bought an old two-story
farmhouse in the rolling hills around Six Mile Creek near Hatfield, they
made a pact to leave the transient lifestyle of a twenty-year military
career behind. They knew there would be a period of adjustment for
their three sons and their daughter in downshifting to a thumbnail town
with little more than a school, a few churches, a couple of stores and a
post office. Still, the rustic Arkansas backcountry near the headwaters of
the Ouachita River would offer a simple, unencumbered existence that
would set their kids on the right path.

*2. Close-up topographic map of Polk County, west-central Arkansas, show-
ing Ouachita range and the towns of Hatfield and Cove, along with Smoke
Rock Mountain, Six Mile Creek and other landmarks central to Bob
Brewer's upbringing in the wooded hill country.*

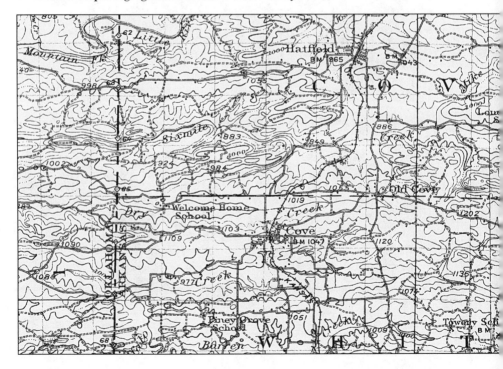

But the woods that blanket the Ouachitas have their own special temptations and distractions. It was only a matter of months before Bob's simple life would become very complex.

In the rugged mountains along the Oklahoma border, which include the better-known Ozarks to the north and the Ouachitas to the south, kin can run as thick as the trees. Extended families, with a bewildering number of relatives residing within a few miles of each other, are common. After the Brewers' arrival in Hatfield nearly a hundred cousins, aunts, uncles and friends showed up for a reunion. Afterward, Bob barely could put faces to names, except for two imposing figures, forty-year-old Odis Ashcraft and Odis's spry, seventy-four-year-old father, William Daniel Ashcraft, whom everybody, including the Brewers, called "Grandpa." Both "Uncle Ode" (the husband of Landon's sister, Bessie) and "Grandpa" Will Ashcraft had taken a special liking to Bob and his brothers the few times that the Brewers had visited Hatfield during Landon's military service. The feeling was reciprocated by the Brewer boys, who saw in these tough, lean, laconic woodsmen the personification of the mountaineer.

Grandpa Ashcraft was a powerful and revered figure, both in the family and within the tight-knit Hatfield community.[1] Having arrived in the

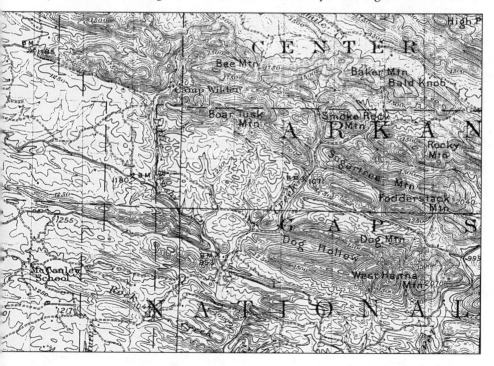

valley in 1907, Kentucky-born W. D. Ashcraft spent his early years raising livestock and helping transform Hatfield into the cattle- and hog-trading center for Polk County. He also trapped and hunted, selling some of the furs. During the Depression, he was known to have distributed freshly killed game to families struggling to put food on the table. And there were rumors of moonshine being made in the hills.

Later in life, Grandpa's occupation was not so easily defined or understood. W. D. Ashcraft took to the woods nearly every day on horseback, from sunup to sundown and sometimes through the night, with his well-oiled rifle tucked neatly into his saddle scabbard. On one occasion, he went off knowing full well that his pregnant wife, Delia, had gone into labor at home, delivering one of the couple's thirteen children. "You little, short-legged sonofabitch! You just get on your horse and leave me with all of your kids!" she had screamed, but to absolutely no effect, family members recall.

The ostensible mission behind such outings was "hunting cows," as Grandpa would explain to family and as he would often note in his diary.[2] Bob, for one, thought this odd because he had seldom seen significant numbers of cattle on his great-uncle's property. He would discover as an adult what Grandpa Ashcraft meant.

Grandpa's diary, Bob would later learn, contained two unusual entries: "Found cow in cave" followed by the next day's "Stayed home." As a boy, Bob had no way of knowing that "cow" might have been shorthand for "cowan," an old Masonic term for "intruder."[3] And while there had been rumors around the region for decades that Will Ashcraft may have killed a man or two, Bob would not become aware of them until he was well into his adult years.

Grandpa's family lived an austere, subsistence existence—through mid-century—in a pre–Civil War log cabin lit by kerosene lamps and devoid of plumbing, some ten miles from the Brewer farm. But no one within the Ashcraft clan ever seemed to complain, even though the small cabin—with its more than a dozen inhabitants—had but one or two windows and only a few beds. The Ashcrafts were self-sufficient and always seemed to have whatever basic food supplies—garden-grown vegetables and fruit, salted pork, wild hog, deer, squirrel and raccoon—and clothing they needed. Drinking water came from a spring next to the cabin. Heat was provided by a mud-and-stone fireplace and a wood-burning stove. The real mystery for the family at large was the grizzled mountaineer's orthodox devotion to the woods: he was hardly ever at home.

For Bob and his brothers, visits to the rustic cabin along Brushy Creek and to Uncle Ode's house nearby were limited to weekends during the school year. But after school let out in May, and the crops were planted, the Brewer boys' visits extended into weeks at a time. Now that the family had reestablished roots in the Brushy Valley, there would be plenty of time to learn the ways of the mountains: logging, prospecting, hunting, trapping, fishing and horsemanship.

Within days of school's shuttering for summer in 1950, Bob, his older brother Jack and his younger brother Dave climbed onto Uncle Ode's wagon for a logging haul far into Brushy Creek's interior. Grandpa, in the front seat, handed Bob the reins, and the youngster quickly took command while Odis looked on from the rear.

The idea of steering a mule-drawn wagon across mountain trails was so exciting that Bob almost missed Grandpa's casually spoken words. "Bobby, see that ol' beech, there along the creek?" the old man said, pointing to a sturdy tree with soft, dapple-gray bark and dark green almond-shaped leaves. "That's a treasure tree. It's got carvings on it that tell where money is buried." Bob, his eyebrows arched, stared intently at his great-uncle, seeking elaboration. All he got was a stern gaze from the old man. As the wagon rolled on, Will Ashcraft pointed toward a narrow hollow abutting Brushy Creek. "That's where a Mexican is buried. Somebody found him messing where he shouldn't have been messing and shot him." This time, Bob pressed him with questions, but the mountaineer would say no more. He simply told the Brewer boys to jump out of the wagon and get busy with the log-splitting job ahead. W. D. Ashcraft had a reputation for being more than demanding—he was outright tough.

In the silent moments that followed—and they were silent, for the Ouachitas are a place where youth show respect for elders and do not ask many questions—something began to stir within Bob's head. What had Grandpa been talking about? The woodsman's words were deliberate, premeditated, meant to sink in. And they did just that. The education of a Confederate code-breaker had begun.

During the next few months, the theme of buried treasure filtered through Bob's new life in the Arkansas forests. References to hidden gold were sporadic, always oblique and never satisfying. He sometimes overheard talk of "mining claims" among the Ashcrafts and two of their neighbors, brothers Isom and Ed Avants, descendants of John Avants, who had moved into the Brushy Creek valley right after the Civil War.[4] And he sometimes observed mysterious visitors talking with Grandpa or Uncle Odis—rugged men who would unravel tattered topographic maps on the hood of a truck and ask the Ashcrafts for help in finding certain spots.

Then there was Grandpa's padlocked chest in the cabin's kitchen. Bob would sit atop the chest and read the old man's complete collection of *National Geographic* magazines. Once, he asked Delia Ashcraft what was inside. "That's Grandpa's. I don't ask and you shouldn't either," she scolded. (It would take another fifty years before Bob would learn of the contents.)

In his forest ramblings—whether helping Ode on logging excursions, collecting firewood, hunting game, or exploring old mine shafts—Bob occasionally stumbled across what by then he recognized as treasure signs. Over time, a menagerie of inscribed animal figures—horses, snakes, turtles, birds, turkey tracks—and a collection of cryptic lettering, dates and other abstract engravings revealed themselves on beech bark or rock faces along faint forest trails. Between bites of homemade biscuits with eggs and ham—his usual lunchtime meal when working the hills—he would ask Ode about the obscure, coded guideposts. But Ode would just offhandedly confirm that what Bob had observed were in fact encrypted treasure markers and not idle graffiti.

It was as if a scavenger hunt had been laid out but no one had explained its rules or purpose. Yet Bob knew that it was not a joke, a tease, a gimmick. It had to do with family: Grandpa and Ode were aware of some dark mystery, while Landon Brewer, who had a warm relationship with his sister Bessie and his brother-in-law, seemed detached from, if not completely ignorant of, the intrigue.

Bob, who conversed little with his taciturn father, decided that it was best to keep his knowledge of the woods and its secrets to himself. The challenge was to absorb more, however, and whenever, he could. If the opportunity presented itself to take a break from schoolwork and the demanding chores around the farm, he would head off on foot or horseback to Aunt Bessie and Uncle Ode's place on Brushy Creek. His aunt would have her biscuits, jams and fresh goat's milk at the ready, and Ode invariably would offer up some entertaining enterprise outdoors. Odis Ashcraft had no children of his own, but he loved kids. Over time he made the Brewer boys, particularly the irrepressibly curious Bob, feel like his own sons. There was one other thing, Bob sensed: Ode was testing him.

The test was not whether he would become a true mountaineer. That was all but assured. Ode, a logger by profession, quickly discovered that Bob had a keen and growing knowledge of the trees and plants in the forest, their value to the logging industry, their medicinal properties and their place in the ecosystem. (Little did Odis know that Bob already had read a prized set of *Compton's Encyclopedia,* nearly cover to cover.) Like all local kids working summer jobs in timber, Bob could pump out his share of stave bolts, those narrow pieces of wood that form the sides of a barrel. He also had shown his mettle as an assured horseman and a clean shot with his .22 rifle. The test, Bob intuited, was how well he could absorb knowledge about the signs that he had seen in the forest and then explain the puzzle they presented.

Bob vaguely perceived that he was undergoing a slow initiation into a hidden world. Every time he tried to quicken the pace, to ask probative questions, he hit a wall and was forced to slow down. But over the years a pattern began to emerge in which Ode, acknowledging Bob's persistence, would let on a little more each time. He would describe certain signposts—grafted tree limbs, axe slices or "blazes" on tree trunks, rock piles laid out in subtle geometric patterns—and challenge the youngster to find these on the trails.

One morning, while spearfishing in a remote bend of Brushy Creek with his brothers, Bob was startled to see Odis ride up on his stallion, "Rebel." Without prompting, Ode abruptly pointed his rifle toward a steep ridge. "Boys," he intoned, "there's more money buried on that mountain than all of you could spend in a lifetime." Bob, now in his early teens and feeling cocky, replied: "Then why don't you just go dig it up, Uncle Ode! We could sure use it." Odis paused before he responded. "Because it belongs to someone else and nobody can touch it," he replied, coolly. He dismounted and asked the boys to follow him to a holly tree along the bank. The tree had a snake figure and various other symbols neatly carved into its bark. "Someday, perhaps one of you will learn how to read these signs and know where that money is," he said cryptically, and departed.

For the first time, Bob realized that a lot of money was involved and that perhaps it was still being watched. The whole idea was confusing and confounding. It didn't seem to make sense: people living at near poverty levels and leaving treasure—and apparently lots of it—buried in the ground!

Several months later, Uncle Ode flashed annoyance when the Brewer boys once again got ahead of the backwoods pace that the older men practiced. Jack had returned to Ode's house from a brisk November squirrel hunt with news that he had found a rock carving of a rising sun that looked "like half the Japanese flag." He had discovered the deep-cut engraving, which had odd lettering next to it, on a ledge partly overgrown with moss and lichen. Odis looked up from the meal he was eating as Jack went on about his find, but Bob could see that his brother's tale about the sunrise symbol had unsettled their uncle. "Well Jack, I guess you found that gold," Ode barked. "Now why don't you go dig it up and share it with us all."

On another occasion, while out squirrel hunting, Bob had tripped over the rusted remnants of a partly unearthed Wells Fargo strongbox.[5] The spot lay deep in the woods, along a remote trail allegedly taken by Jesse James after robbing the Hot Springs stage. When Bob ran to show the corroded iron frame to Odis, the logger brusquely told the boy to put the rusted strongbox back where he found it. Odis then grabbed the rusted frame and hung it on a tree limb next to the spot. Bob and his brothers never saw the old money box again.

This pattern of baiting the Brewer boys—Bob most of all—and then swatting them down when they overreached would repeat itself over the next year. Bob took his unspoken initiation in stride; it was a chess game of sorts, and he was in the realm of a master, who, in turn, was son of a master boardsman. Yet whatever obscure wisdom was being imparted, and for whatever purpose, came to an abrupt halt in May 1955, when Odis was killed in a freak timber accident.

A thirty-foot Yellow Boy pine had smashed the logger's skull. Moments before, Odis had been talking with seventeen-year-old Jack Brewer, who was helping measure pines to be cut into poles for construction. A heavy chain saw—a technological innovation that was replacing the seven-foot crosscut saws pulled by a man on each end—had made short work of the tall pines.[6] But the noisy saw had prevented Odis from hearing the sound of a falling precut tree that had been lodged precariously against another. The irony of a modern saw snuffing out the life of a woodsman so devoted to the past was not lost on Bob and his brothers, who were devastated by the passing of Ode, as was all of the Brushy Creek community.

Odis's death brought other changes to the rhythm of life in the Arkansas backwoods that year. Grandpa Ashcraft's favorite son (of five) and apparent successor was gone. Soon, the old mountaineer's health began to crumble. His regular outings, which could last several days at a time, stopped altogether. Will Ashcraft had finally slowed down. He and Delia abandoned the old cabin they had lived in since 1910 and moved closer to Hatfield. The weathered outdoorsman who had always trod his own secret path now sought the company of others, particularly Bob. The change in Grandpa's behavior was obvious to the teenager, who sensed that he was being groomed as a surrogate Odis, a replacement on some kind of mission. It seemed to be linked to some type of vigil: watching over the Brushy Creek valley.

About a year after Odis's passing, Grandpa began asking Bob to accompany him on trips back to the cabin, to check on the old place. The old-timer had been commuting daily by Ford tractor, which he treated as if it were a horse, yelling "whoa" at it when he wanted to stop. In between odd jobs—cutting tall weeds around the adjacent smokehouse and fixing up the large barn—Grandpa would recount to Bob the history of the frontier cabin. He explained how its foot-thick hand-hewn logs had been tightly dovetailed, using no nails. He also related how Jesse James had paid more than one visit in the previous century. (The cabin was located on the James gang's escape route from the Hot Springs robbery.)[7] Further, he told of an ex-Confederate soldier, William Martin Wiley, from Van Zandt County, Texas, who had occupied a crude windowless hut on the Cossatot River nearby until his death at nearly one hundred in 1930.[8] Bill Wiley was a tall, charismatic, long-haired, mustachioed pioneer who could play the fiddle with the same hair-trigger precision as he could shoot. He and Grandpa were the closest of friends, the old man explained. The two loved the woods; they knew its trails like no one else, and they marked them with their axe blades, accordingly. Both men "worked the mines," and both were expert trackers and marksmen.

Bob figured that there must be some connection among Jesse James, the Confederacy and solitary-minded men staking mining claims after the Civil War. But he had no idea at the time that bits of a vast conspiracy were being revealed.

Over time, Bob's visits with his great-uncle became less frequent, as demands of high school and then, in his senior year, National Guard duty kept him occupied. Around the time he graduated from Hatfield High School in 1958, a rumor circulated that all who were recently on active duty in the state's Guard unit would be drafted into the regular Army. Weighing his options, Bob decided to follow in his father's footsteps. He joined the Navy in June of that year.

When he broke the news to Grandpa that he had signed up and would be shipping out soon, he saw that the old man was hurt. It was, in fact, the first time that he had seen emotion creep over the face of the stoic mountaineer. No further words were exchanged. Bob began what would be a twenty-year career in the Navy, and he would not see the old man again for two years.

During a brief home leave in 1961 with his new wife, Linda, Bob asked his father for a loan to buy a car. Landon Brewer, hit by hard times, could not spare the money and suggested that Bob speak to W. D. Ashcraft about some credit. Grandpa, thrilled to see Bob again, said that if he wanted cash, it would take a "day or so to dig it up." Bob told him that he needed money for a family car and promised to repay on time with interest. The old man suggested that a check would suffice and immediately presented one. Bob, good to his word, repaid the loan with interest a little over a year later and looked forward to seeing more of the old-timer. But infrequent breaks from military duty over the next few years offered little time to visit with his parents and the Ashcrafts. After one last brief meeting, he departed for the first of two tours in Vietnam. He would never see W. D. Ashcraft again.

Bob flew in over two hundred missions in Navy helicopters and fixed-wing aircraft in Vietnam. He received the Air Medal with four flight/strike awards, the Commendation Medal with combat "V" and other citations for his role in supporting the Navy's riverine forces in the Mekong Delta. During those years of combat, thoughts of the Arkansas hill country remained distant. But Will Ashcraft had cast a long shadow.

News of the old man's death at ninety-four in 1971—a few months after Bob's return from Southeast Asia but before he could get home on leave—hit him hard. The loss of his mentor—a larger-than-life figure, in turn avuncular and remote—had left a mark. So did the fact that Grandpa's potent secrets—the rumors of treasure and the people behind it—went with him to his grave in Six Mile Cemetery, where a handful of Confederate soldiers lie buried on the adjacent hill. The one heirloom that would come Bob's way was Bill Wiley's old 1899 Savage 25-35-caliber rifle. Wiley had passed it to Grandpa, who, in turn, had given it to Uncle Ode. Ode's wife, Bessie, had promised it to Bob.

Bob Brewer's decision to leave a successful Navy career and return to tiny Hatfield, to launch a quest that would shed light on Grandpa and Uncle Ode's secrets, seemed preordained. He knew, even at this early stage, that he had no choice but to unravel a mystery that had been thrust at him. It was a mystery that would turn out to be far bigger and far older than he could have ever imagined at the time. And it was one that would require him to immerse himself first in the history of his native Arkansas hill town and then in the history of the United States at its most turbulent time, the Civil War.

Knights of the Golden Circle

THE Knights of the Golden Circle, or KGC, was the most powerful subversive organization ever to operate within the United States. It helped rip America apart in the Civil War. And it stealthily planned a Second War of Secession years after the surrender at Appomattox.

The KGC's strategists planned the firing of the opening salvos against Fort Sumter on April 12, 1861; one of its members, Cherokee chief Stand Watie, was the last Confederate general to surrender, on June 23, 1865. In between these milestones, the KGC carried out extensive guerrilla-warfare—including terrorism against civilian populations—on behalf of the Confederacy. And the secret order probably played a hidden hand in the April 14, 1865, assassination of President Abraham Lincoln by rogue agent John Wilkes Booth. The war's formal end in the spring of 1865 notwithstanding, the KGC's underground and seditious activities would continue well into the 1900s.

Yet few Americans today have ever heard of the KGC, whose rank-and-file membership may have swelled to several hundred thousand during the Civil War, according to U.S. intelligence estimates at the time.[1] No mainstream history book has been devoted to the subject; few accounts of the Civil War even mention the Knights of the Golden Circle, much less its covert efforts aimed at demoralizing the North.[2] None records its existence after 1864.

The KGC, according to the scant references in today's textbooks and encyclopedias, was a secret pro-South political society that was mostly active in the North and quietly dissolved *before* the end of the war. In fact, the clandestine paramilitary order functioned first in the South and only later in the North. It was a potent, long-lived Confederate underground army, with a cross-border command structure, unconventional fighting and espionage tactics, secret code and a complex system of buried financial assets. Relegated to a skimpy footnote in America's bloodiest conflict, the *postwar* KGC falls off the pages altogether, leaving a void in the annals of the nation's uncertain and painful transition from division to reunion.

The core hidden KGC was a truly "secret" society—one that left very little written record and whose members swore blood oaths of silence. This, in part, explains why so little has been revealed about a group of zealots that not only helped foment a "War for Southern Independence" but, following the July 1863 defeats at Gettysburg and Vicksburg, took the Rebel cause underground with gold, silver and arms aplenty to fight again. To understand the KGC is to appreciate that the Confederacy did not simply die in 1865. It hid, for decades. The South's behind-the-scenes power elite resorted to oral commands, coded missives, encrypted photographs and treasure maps—passed on from generation to generation—in preparation for another war.

The Snapshot View

The limited historic literature on the Knights of the Golden Circle yields a blurred and misleadingly simple snapshot of the organization. Missing are the historical and ideological roots—the KGC's legs, so to speak, stretching back to early-nineteenth-century America and perhaps much earlier in Europe—as well as its outstretched arms, its reach into Reconstruction and then into the twentieth century. Also absent from the record are the names of its hidden command, its "inner sanctum," with its powerful Masonic ties. Most of all, the ill-defined image misses the KGC's central strategy: to maintain a powerful, hidden base of politico-military operations in the American Deep South, no matter the outcome of the Civil War itself, and with ample treasure to finance them.

First, the established history. Most popular references depict the KGC as a militant pro-slavery, pro-secession movement that surfaced with some fanfare in the mid- to late-1850s. Its self-anointed leader in the run-up to the Civil War was George W. L. Bickley, a Virginia-born eccentric of questionable character who ran his recruiting operations initially out of Cincinnati and then later from Louisiana, Texas and Alabama before returning to the Midwest.

Whatever Bickley's personal shortcomings—he was often accused of being an unsavory character of limited financial integrity—the self-styled KGC promoter was a master propagandist. At a minimum, he knew how to play the politicized editorial boards of the pro-South newspapers to obtain positive coverage of his organization's controversial aims and to help demonize Lincoln and the "abolitionists."

According to one historian, whose work focused on the frothy mix of secret societies bubbling up during the Civil War period, pro-Union editorial writers in turn deliberately exaggerated the threat of the KGC to create a political bogeyman for pro-Union candidates in Midwest gubernatorial and Congressional elections. Historian Frank Klement, in his *Dark Lanterns: Secret Political Societies, Conspiracies, and Treason Trials in the Civil War,* called reports of KGC activity little more than "rumors" and myths.[3] These reports, Klement writes, were based on nationalism, wartime propaganda and career-enhancing efforts of local politicians and Union military authorities. Nevertheless, Klement's book cites numerous official documents of the period that warn that the KGC posed an ominous threat to the Union.

The KGC's chief prewar aim in the North was to generate popular underground support for the secessionist cause among pro-slavery and "states' rights" sympathizers above the Mason-Dixon line, in the Midwest and in the border states of Kentucky and Missouri.[4] California, which had entered the Union as a free state, was also a key target for subversive KGC operations. The reasons for targeting the Bear State were obvious: gold and other mineral resources, shipping routes and a large Southern-sympathizing population in various parts of the state.[5]

More fundamentally, the KGC called for the creation of a geographic "Golden Circle"—an independent political and economic zone to include the southern and border states, Mexico, Central America and Cuba. At the productive center of this "circular" Southern Empire, with a radius of 1,200 miles extending from Havana through the Gulf of Mexico and the Caribbean, would be a slave-based, agrarian society. Plantations producing cotton, tobacco, sugar, indigo and coffee would power its economic engine. This Southern slave empire would attract investment from Europe, build an extensive rail network (with links westward to California that would make the West depend more on the South than on the North) and develop some manufacturing capacity—

thus becoming a competitive self-sufficient trading zone. The acquisition of new territories south of the border would maintain the balance of power in Congress between free and slave states until the South could secede to establish full independence. Or so the vision, as articulated by Bickley, promised.[6]

The secret order's immediate task was to incite rebellion—to "fire the Southern Heart"—through its "castles," its local cells or chapters spread across the South, North and border states. Tens of thousands of supporters from a cross-section of society (doctors, judges, craftsmen, editors, lawyers, clergymen, laborers, etc.) were reported to have taken secret oaths and joined such castles. For a fee of $1, $5 or $10, for the first three degrees of initiation, respectively, as well as payment of a pro-rated property tax, initiates became rank-and-file members.

Yet, the vast majority of KGC initiates into the "lower degrees" of indoctrination were probably unaware of the full scope of the Southern leadership's ruthless plan for cementing secession.[7] Many of the Northern members were merely opposed to prosecuting a war against the South, and later opposed President Lincoln's perceived heavy-handedness on the home front during 1862–63. The president's call for Congress to provide authority to suspend the writ of *habeas corpus* (the requirement that the government bring charges against those that it arrests) and a subsequent wave of seemingly arbitrary arrests of alleged Southern sympathizers in Indiana and Ohio provoked sharp outcries. These acts, derided by KGC agitators as the new U.S. "despotism," served as rallying points for proliferating KGC castles in the region.[8]

The consensus history also maintains that the KGC, during the latter half of the Civil War, functioned primarily as a political fifth column in the North and Midwest with the aim of weakening the Union's resolve and thus its prospects for total victory. Known as Copperheads or Peace Democrats, these Northern-based associates of the secret order were tasked toward war's end with undermining the fabric of society in the Old Northwest (today's Ohio Valley/Midwest), and thus opening up a new front for the South. According to Klement and others, these operatives were supposed to stir up trouble before congressional, gubernatorial and presidential elections in Ohio, Indiana, Illinois and Iowa; interfere with the draft (launched in March 1863); encourage desertion; provide intelligence; smuggle supplies; assassinate U.S. military and state government officials; and eventually generate fear about rumored general uprisings at a time when war fatigue had taken root.[9]

Ultimately, the KGC and its derivative "political" offshoots—the Order of American Knights (1863) and the Sons of Liberty (1864)—were accused by Republican governors in the region and by pro-Union editorial writers of attempting to carve out a "Northwest Confederacy" that would close forces with the rebel army and the Confederate States of America.[10] Confederate Gen. John Hunt Morgan's bold but abortive raid north of the Ohio River into Indiana and Ohio in July 1863—precisely when local newspapers had speculated about a so-called Copperhead-sponsored insurrection—provided some evidence for that thesis.[11]

According to the consensus history, the failure of those "Northwest" raids to achieve their intended results sent the KGC into rapid decline and eventual oblivion by 1864. Standing in the way of success were a number of factors: effective counter-espionage measures; decisive troop deployments; preemptive arrests; and seizure of arms ordered by pro-Union governors and Union military officials assigned to the region.[12] Some historians, like Klement, argued that the feared organizing capacity of the KGC and Copperheads was overblown to begin with, fanned by Republican jingoism, and that the overall mission was doomed to fail.

The KGC's nominal public "leaders"—Bickley, Sons of Liberty head Clement L. Vallandigham and the Order of American Knights' Phineas C. Wright—were all at some point arrested and thrown into jail for their seditious activities, along with numerous other KGC associates or affiliated operatives.

It was through the capture of Bickley and his wife later in July 1863, while traveling in Indiana after the failed Northern Uprising, that a number of revealing KGC documents and artifacts came to light. These included an 1859 handbook, *Rules, Regulations and Principles of the K.G.C.*, most likely penned by Bickley. Also seized were a KGC cipher (written inside a pocket-sized prayer book), the order's "great seal" insignia, as well as an assortment of medals and pins. The documents and regalia—found either in Bickley's suitcase at the time of his arrest or in the undergarments of his wife, who was searched by a female detective—are on file at the National Archives. They form the basis of much of what has been written about the traitorous secret order. (Historians have overlooked a revealing reference in one of the primary source documents found in Bickley's possession. A card containing nineteen items of the KGC's principles describes a key fraternal hand signal used to indicate KGC membership. It calls, in code, for placing the index finger against the thumb to make a circle. "A golden circle, encasing a dark or

iron hand clasped on a scroll; whole [sic] to be about the size of a dime."
Numerous tintypes and photographs of leading secessionists and, later,
Confederates, reveal this KGC signal being given.)

Bickley, who languished in federal prisons for months after the war
(all the while denying involvement in the KGC and its treasonous plots),
was questioned by federal agents about possible complicity in the assassination of President Lincoln. The nominal KGC leader vehemently dis-
claimed any role in the murder of the president, who had received
multiple direct communications from U.S. military intelligence in the last
two years of his life about the personal danger posed by the KGC.[13]

An emotionally and physically drained Bickley died two years later in
Baltimore, a free man never formally charged with a crime. With Bickley's imprisonment, the established history of the KGC comes to an
abrupt end.

The problems with the above conventional view of the Knights of the
Golden Circle are manifold. First, as often occurs with personality-
driven history or journalism, it attaches far too much weight to a high-
profile individual—in this case, the front man, Bickley. No doubt,
Bickley's grandstanding drew significant press attention and dispropor-
tionately elevated his persona through North and South alike in the
antebellum and early war years. But in the end, Bickley—who got off to
a questionable start by organizing a failed raid into Mexico in 1860—
was a crank. Although well-acquainted with the symbolism, rituals and
grand designs of a mysterious political underground movement, he was
someone unequipped to lead the KGC. He was, at best, a pamphleteer,
or, in today's parlance, a marketer, for the organization.

Whether sanctioned by the true powers behind the KGC or not, Bickley brought to public light the rough outline of the cabal's broad political
agenda. An early anti-KGC exposé, appearing in the May 1862 issue of
Continental Monthly, aptly described Bickley's propagandist role:
"George Bickley [is] a miserable quack and 'confidence man,' a person
long familiarly spoken of by the press as a mere Jeremy Diddler, but who
has been a useful tool to shrewder men in managing for them this precious order." The essay's author pointed out that building state-to-state
momentum for secession was a mission for powerful—albeit hidden—
political machinery, and not the province of a single man:

The prompt and vigorous action of the whole Secession movement, by
which states with a majority attached to the Union were hurled, scarce

knowing how, into rebellion, would never have been accomplished save by a long established and perfectly drilled organization. It is not enough to sway millions that the leaders simply know what to do, or that they have the power to do it. There must be *organization* and *subordination,* if only to control the independent action of demagogues and of selfish politicians, who abound in the South, as elsewhere. Had the existence of the K.G.C. never been revealed, the historian would have detected it by its results, and been compelled in fairness to admit that it was admirably instituted to fulfill its ends, evil as they were, and that its work was well done.[14]

An earlier exposé, in the same magazine in January 1862, makes the case that the KGC's sole mission, going back to presecessionist drumbeating from South Carolina in the mid-1830s, was always the dissolution of the Union and the establishment of a Southern Empire. It asserts that these twin goals were foisted upon an unwitting, and moreover *unwilling,* public in the South by a clique of wealthy plantation owners. "And it was solely by means of its secret but powerful machinery, that the Southern States were plunged into revolution, in defiance of the will of their voting population," it postulates.[15]

Front men such as Bickley and Vallandigham (the latter having legitimate credentials and a real following as a former prominent congressman from Ohio) offered certain benefits for the concealed, well-oiled machine. They not only provided a populist link to the citizenry but also insulated the KGC's true leadership from damage. If trouble came, as it inevitably did, how convenient to have charismatic front men languish in jail. The burden of association with a hidden traitorous organization would lie squarely on their shoulders, and theirs alone.

Historian I. Winslow Ayer, author of *The Great North-Western Conspiracy,* captured the essence of this strategy when he wrote in 1865 that the KGC's leaders "put forward the most irresponsible persons at their command, as the mouthpieces and official representatives of the Order, to the end that if detected, the theory of *crazy, powerless fools,* could be wielded upon public sentiment by an undisturbed partisan press, to save the scheme from thorough investigation and development by the authorities."[16] Moreover, if the front men were arrested and emerged looking like martyrs to Southern sympathizers—as in the case of Vallandigham—all the better. Lincoln, a shrewd reader of hinterland sentiment, or, as he put it, "fire in the rear," was clever enough to minimize the political fallout in the fragile Midwest by reducing Vallandigham's sentence to banishment to the South, as historian James McPherson has noted.[17]

Furthermore, the base of operations of the front men provided value. Their proselytizing in such cities as Cincinnati and St. Louis made it *appear* that the KGC was fundamentally a Northern, Western or Northwestern movement. While the Union made all-out efforts to penetrate the so-called Northwestern Conspiracy (and in the process made it seem that bringing this clandestine group to heel meant an end to the KGC nationwide), the KGC's Southern bastions of power—Charleston, New Orleans, Montgomery, Richmond and finally Nashville and Canton (Texas)—stayed out of range of Lincoln administration agents during the war.[18]

This is not to say that the efforts of Bickley and Vallandigham were deliberate red herrings. The KGC's core leadership knew that the efforts of a Northern-based branch (supported by communiqués transmitted by covert agents and by coded messages placed in Northern newspapers) could enlist new recruits, weaken Northern public resolve for total victory and possibly lead to a coordinated movement (between uniformed Rebel forces from the South and nonuniformed fifth column KGC recruits from the North) to open up a Northern front. As it turned out, Vallandigham campaigned openly and aggressively in public speeches for an abrupt, negotiated end to the war that would leave the South's independent slave-holding republic intact. At the least, the Northern branch could stir up enough internal dissent in Ohio, Indiana, Illinois and Iowa—all suffering from weak economies—to thwart Lincoln's chances of reelection in 1864. And, even if Lincoln were to be reelected, a stepped up KGC campaign of terrorism and subversion might convince a weary Union that the war might not be worth the cost in lives and matériel.

Stirring up a sense of panic and chaos in the North clearly was the unspoken reason for the brutal antidraft riot in New York City in July 1863, which, after three days, left hundreds, mostly blacks, dead in the streets.[19] Some believe the KGC was behind this bloody event. According to Benson Lossing's social history from the late 1800s, the carefully organized "riot" had begun with the destruction of telegraph wires extending out of the city. After uttering cries against the draft, the mostly Irish mob, fueled by the KGC's plotting and invectives, yelled:

"Down with the Abolitionists, down with the nigger, Hurrah for Jeff Davis." . . . This riot seems to have been only an irregular manifestation of an organized outbreak in New York City simultaneously with a similar insurrection projected in some western cities. But the draft went on in spite of all opposition; and the Knights of the Golden Circle and the Peace Faction were discomfited.[20]

Ultimately, even if all else failed with political agitation and paramilitary operations in the North and West, a key component of the KGC's North/South strategy would remain intact: the move *underground,* via widely dispersed cells in the South, to prepare for a second Civil War.

Timing was critical. The KGC's leadership had seen the writing on the wall during that eventful month of July 1863. In those critical few weeks, first Gettysburg and then Vicksburg—the Confederacy's vital stronghold on the Mississippi—fell. KGC leaders immediately recognized that the South, after suffering such devastating battlefield defeats, could no longer expect British or French intervention on their side. Such intervention, they knew, had always been dependent on convincing London and Paris that the South ultimately would prevail in its bid for independence.[21]

The KGC elite realized that the South had insufficient capital, matériel and troops to prosecute the war alone without European assistance, particularly after giving up key logistical advantages along the Mississippi. Better, they reasoned, to take firm steps to build the resources and command structure *below ground* for a renewed fight on more equal footing, at a time of their choosing and with an emphasis on guerrilla warfare. Focusing government agents, newspaper columnists and academic historians on such cranks as Bickley gave the KGC convenient cover while it plotted to go below surface on its home turf. This enormous enterprise was undertaken late in the war, and all but escaped scrutiny.

4 Coming Home: A Gold-Filled Legacy

THE phrase "Knights of the Golden Circle" meant nothing to Bob Brewer in 1977, the year that he moved his young family to Hatfield after a nineteen-year career in the Navy. It would take another sixteen years before "KGC" entered his vocabulary. Once he had resettled in the Arkansas hill country, a powerful desire to solve the mystery of Grandpa's deep-woods excursions—and their links to possible treasure—was never far from his mind. In fact, in that small Polk County mountain town, where everyone seemed to know each other, the topic of hidden treasure was all but unavoidable.

Bob spent the first year at home unwinding, adjusting to the pace of civilian life. He put his modest savings toward fixing up a small ranch that he and Linda had purchased a few miles from town. It felt good having stretches of free time, the first since his youth.

But, notwithstanding the buffer of a military pension, he also recognized that with three young boys to feed and a daughter going off to college, he had to enter the civilian workforce. To troll for job leads and catch up with old acquaintances, he would drive to McLain's, the coffee shop on the edge of town, where burly men from the timber and trucking industries would gather for breakfast. Much of the conversation centered on the hunting season, the mills and local politics. Almost invariably, amid the din, someone would slip in a line or two about hunting treasure, "Spanish gold," to be specific.

It struck Bob as odd just how much treasure talk there was. Some of the conversationalists—locals such as Art Akins and George Icke—were self-avowed, full-time "treasure hunters." Others claimed to do their "coin shooting" for sport in their free time. No one claimed outright to have found hidden caches. Yet many spoke of having uncovered mysterious "Spanish treasure" signs in the surrounding mountains.

Bob could only grin. Among the many vague descriptions of such signs from these well-meaning men—all of whom claimed to know more than they actually did—he would occasionally hear a precise account of one of the carved symbols that he had seen with Grandpa and Ode. When told about carvings that were unfamiliar, he carefully would sketch them on loose pieces of paper. If a location was given (and there was an implicit level of trust among these mountain men), he would head to the woods to investigate. On several occasions, he concluded, the tree- or rock-face engravings fit a pattern: the same knowing hand or hands had created them. That knowledge he quietly kept to himself. In his study at home, he began incorporating each field report into a master, color-coded topographical layout of the Brushy Creek area near Smoke Rock Mountain.

He recognized a certain irony in all this seemingly haphazard talk about "lost Spanish treasure" in landlocked Arkansas. He had just arrived from the Florida Keys, his last Navy posting, where an effort had been under way to find the sunken Spanish galleon, *Nuestra Señora de Atocha,* and its reputed millions. During his "twilight tour" at Naval Air Station Boca Chica, Bob occasionally had bumped into high-profile treasure hunter Mel Fisher at local establishments in nearby Key West. He learned that Fisher's treasure-hunting team was focused, well-equipped and maintained a *systematic* approach to finding its target. At some point, Bob speculated, Fisher was going to find the mother lode in the shallow waters off the Keys. (Fisher did just that with the *Atocha,* in 1985, for a total recovery estimated at more than $400 million in gold coin, ingots, jewels and gems. In the process, Fisher lost a son, a daughter-in-law and another diver to a freak salvage-boat accident.)

In their last encounter in Key West in 1976, Bob had told the veteran offshore treasure hunter that as a boy growing up in the Ouachitas he had been shown treasure markings. When Fisher asked about the origin of the rumored land treasure, Bob said that he didn't know but that it might be Spanish. (At the time, Bob had no way of knowing that Fisher would wind up on the same trail, fifteen years later, near Smoke Rock, on property owned by a daughter of Grandpa Ashcraft. A gold "mining" company, called Equity AU and financed in part by Fisher, would leave a hole ten feet long, five feet wide and eight feet deep a quarter-mile east of where Will Ashcraft had pointed out the beech tree with the "treasure signs" to Bob. The area, in fact, was thick with treasure markings and near the spot where Grandpa had staked some of his mining claims. After Fisher died of cancer in 1998, the short-lived Equity AU mining operations in the Ouachitas ceased.)

Grandpa and Uncle Ode never spoke about Spanish gold. So when Hatfield locals at McLain's gabbed loosely about sixteenth-century Spaniards having to hide their loot in the hills from marauding Indians, Bob chalked it up to plausible chatter. But, he figured, it could just as easily amount to mere myth. Whatever the stories' merits, he recalled how Grandpa had referred to a "Mexican" getting killed for "snooping around" not far from the Ashcraft cabin, in an area with numerous treasure markings. Was this "Mexican" actually a Spaniard, and did he ever exist?

The questions nagged Bob. So he set out to talk with the one person in town who, he thought, could shed some light: William Hicks, a former neighbor, retired preacher and friend of Will Ashcraft. When asked about the Mexican's murder, the octogenarian chuckled: "My grandfather loaned Tandy Hatfield the gun that he used." Hicks also said that young Tandy—one of several sons of John Hatfield, an early homesteader with Confederate roots—had been arrested for the fatal shooting, jailed and then, mysteriously, vanished. There was plenty of speculation, Hicks added, that a local conspiracy had freed Tandy and that he had lived quietly on a mountainside above Brushy Creek, some twelve miles from Hatfield, for years.

Bob thanked the old man and set out to confirm his account in the county court records in nearby Mena and then in newspaper archives in Little Rock, three hours away. The court records revealed an 1884 indictment for first-degree murder against T. A. Hatfield, but there were no follow-up documents as to the outcome of the indictment.[1] Moreover, Bob could find no trial record, no punishment record or even a death certificate for the murder suspect. In Little Rock, he came across a July 18, 1884, article in the *Fort Smith Elevator*.[2] It described how, in early 1884, an "old Mexican or Spaniard" had arrived in Brushy Valley via Texarkana with an old map of the area. The map reportedly delineated local "mines." The man, going by the name "Vannetta," used the information provided by the map to find a vertical shaft said to have hidden gold bullion inside. Vannetta reportedly recovered buried tools in the shaft, but, the article said, "nothing was done at the time toward developing" the search for the bullion. Vannetta then reportedly returned to the area in early July, seeking other trails for other mines, where he met his fate. The Fort Smith newspaper said: "Some week or two ago, this old Spaniard was delving on one of his claims, and it proved to have been homesteaded, and he was shot and killed." The young fugitive, Tandy Hatfield, was later arrested and jailed in Dallas, Arkansas, the old county seat of Polk County, it noted.

Bob found the century-old article fascinating. Parts of the story seemed to fit with what Grandpa had told him, on that first logging trip into the mountains. But what was the real motive behind the killing? What, if anything, was Tandy Hatfield trying to protect from Vannetta? Was Vannetta truly Spanish, he wondered. The name did not sound Spanish, and Linda, his wife of Mexican heritage, agreed.

Then, what about these "mining claims," in that area of Brushy Creek, near the Hatfields and the Ashcrafts? He scoured mining records stored at the Polk County courthouse and found that Grandpa, indeed, held extensive claims in precisely the same sector, running into the mid-1950s.[3] Some of the claims appeared to be related to the same dank, abandoned tunnels and shafts that veined Smoke Rock mountain—unsafe excavations that he had been warned to stay away from as a boy.

Most perplexing was that, despite persistent talk and effort expended on "Spanish" gold mines (and there were lots of abandoned "diggings" in the area), there never seemed to have been any authenticated amount of gold discovered. A state geologist contacted by Bob reported that there had *never* been any substantial quantity of gold mined in Arkansas.[4] Manganese, for hardening steel, had been quarried extensively in the 1930s and 1940s in Polk County, but not precious metals.

It was all very confusing: the local papers from the mid-1880s through early 1900s had reported sporadic gold strikes by newcomers.[5] Bob began to suspect these stories were apocryphal. He guessed that a "staged" gold rush in Polk County might have been promoted before 1900—perhaps as a smokescreen for some other purpose, one related to treasure.

A conversation he later had with Hatfield's postmaster, Jim Harris, bolstered his hypothesis. The postman's father, Tutt, owned the local general-supply store in Hatfield in the early part of the century. During the 1930s and 1940s, Tutt Harris regularly sold groceries and mining supplies to a perennial, albeit mysterious, visitor to town, William Chambers Dobson. Born in nearby Cove, Arkansas, in 1866, Bill Dobson was a close friend and associate of Will and Odis Ashcraft. He would arrive each year, beginning in April or ·May, from his home in Coolidge, Arizona.[6]

After picking up rations of salt pork, pinto beans, loaves of bread and sticks of dynamite at Tutt Harris & Son, Dobson would gather up a paid crew of five young locals and work his and Grandpa's mining claims along the trails and creeks near Smoke Rock. (Joe Dobson, Bill's son and an all-star pitcher for the Boston Red Sox during the 1940s, visited his father in his Hatfield "mining" operation, causing quite a stir in the local barbershop and other parts of town.)

Dobson stayed in a miner's shack that had been built by Bill Wiley in the late 1800s or early 1900s. But Dobson's main interest was not exactly mining, in the traditional sense; it was something to do with buried treasure. Tutt Harris and others, for instance, had observed Dobson carrying around a "waybill," or what to them looked like a coded treasure map. On the one occasion that young Jim Harris visited the site, he noticed the overweight Dobson taking readings with a compass. He observed the old man wandering up the creek bed unaccompanied, while the rest of the crew dug into the side of the mountain. Jim recalled Dobson telling him that they were looking for a "vein of gold that runs all the way to Arizona." Moreover, this mysterious transient figure who hired local teenagers to dig holes deep into mountainsides had another puzzling habit: after the young men had dug to a certain depth, he invariably would pull them off the shaft and move them somewhere else. No one ever knew for sure what they were looking for. It was almost as if Dobson knew how deep something was buried and abruptly stopped the digging—presumably to finish it later, alone, after the heavy lifting had been completed.

Dobson died suddenly, in June 1946, of a heart attack. He was found collapsed in a creek bed just a few hundred yards from the spot where Vannetta was said to have been killed. On his death certificate, his profession was listed as "mining, prospecting."[7]

Such leads—nineteenth-century newspaper clippings, court documents, mining claims and oral histories about mysterious men like Vannetta, Hatfield and Dobson—were intriguing. But they did not yield a coherent picture, a clear historical context, from which Bob could devise a plan to solve Grandpa's riddle. To crack the code, he knew that he would have to pursue two tracks: archival and "grass-roots" field research, the latter involving hands-on exploration of clues on the surface and in the shallow underground.

Although he had done some weekend metal detecting, most recently with his teenage boys in the Florida Keys, he now was gearing up for something wholly different. This was to be a *systematic* hunt combining technology, instinct and a rough sense of direction provided by the abstract carvings in the forest.

Bob relished the idea. Yet, after a year with no formal job and with his nest egg from his time in the Navy gradually being depleted, he knew he had to put family first. Luckily, he landed a moderately well-paid job as a state apiary inspector in early 1978: it would take him along every backwoods trail in the region and provide an opportunity to search for further clues.

As a boy, Bob had learned a few tricks from Uncle Ode about harvesting honey from wild bees. In setting up the ranch in Hatfield, he decided to try his hand at running some commercial hives. A state apiary inspector who came by to examine the bees for disease and parasites mentioned that he was planning to resign in a few weeks and suggested that Bob look into applying. Upon hearing that the position offered flexible hours during nine months of season-based work each year, Bob shot over to Little Rock and soon was locating, registering and inspecting hives for two adjoining counties, Polk and Scott. But backwoods folk from distant areas were not greeting him with open arms when he came to inspect their bees.

In certain assigned inspection areas, parts of which happened to be monitored by the local police as marijuana-growing terrain, "beehive" owners were downright unwelcoming. The occasional hostile reaction, he thought, may have stemmed from his volunteering as a reserve police officer for the Mena Police Department. As it turned out, a nasty confrontation with an armed local near Nella, Arkansas, persuaded him to resign the following year. But he did so with mixed feelings, for the job had provided a little cash and some valuable visual leads from the field.

What most intrigued him was the discovery, along these distant western-Arkansas trails, of treasure markings similar to the ones surrounding Hatfield. If the Spanish had been depositing gold and silver caches in what is now Arkansas, they had spread their hoards over large distances.

To help resolve the markings' origins, he bought a few self-published books about so-called Spanish treasure and treasure signs, nearly all of which he found to be somewhat dubious in their assertions. Nevertheless, he saw a certain overlap between several symbols illustrated in the books and those that he had observed in the woods.

Bob—a committed do-it-yourselfer—wanted to decipher the signs that he had observed and meticulously recorded. By now, his inventory of carved hieroglyphics ran the gamut from countless letters and numbers with odd flourishes, to crosses and crescent moons, to bizarre stick-figure depictions of animals: snakes, birds, turtles (including one laying eggs), horses, mules and deer. These were almost always laid out in groupings, seldom singularly. Most were at eye level of a person standing or riding horseback.

From these etched tableaus, he knew there were messages to be discerned. He inferred that the key indicators were for distance and direction. Others, he surmised, indicated numerical compass headings and perhaps even the outline of topographical features in the immediate area. What appeared to be, say, the carved letter *Y* could actually be the confluence of two streams.

Bob wandered wherever his intuition would take him. There were innumerable false leads and cold trails, but for every ten of those, there was a payoff of sorts. He would carry along a U.S. Geological Survey topographic map and mark the location of every treasure sign—tree carvings, rock carvings, rock piles—that he discovered. Back in his study, he would sketch the various encrypted signposts, along with their relative positions and orientations, on yellow legal pads.

Rather quickly, he realized that the mysterious symbols extended along distinct tangents, sometimes for miles on end. He speculated that they were directional markers for some kind of linear, geometric grid. The grid appeared to be anchored in physical features of the Brushy Creek countryside, as there were clusters of carvings in the area. Distinct lines, it seemed, radiated from Smoke Rock Mountain, the rugged expanse where Grandpa had spent much of his time away from home.

But where did it all lead? Through simple trial and error, Bob tried to determine the gauges for surveying distances that he believed the clues indicated. Turning to his small library of Spanish treasure books, he resolved to experiment with historic Spanish distance measurements. These ranged from varas (30–35 inches) to statute leagues (2⅛ miles). Armed with his compass and topo maps, he would pace off along directionals that he assumed the tree carvings indicated. But the only results— over months of slogging through poison oak–infested forest along these transit lines—were blisters, tick bites and added confusion. The symbols did not correspond to the Spanish metrics. Chagrined, he began to question whether he was, in fact, dealing with Spanish treasure—or treasure of any kind.

It was a stressful period. Bob no longer had the freedom to immerse himself in the hunt. Over the past six months, he had spent so much time on the treasure trail that obligations around the ranch had gone wanting. Linda expressed growing concern that his focus on uncovering Grandpa's mystery was becoming a financial liability. Their daughter, Brenda, was at college, and Bob still had not replaced his bee inspector job. And there was a flicker of heat from the outside. Some relatives in town and friends of Linda's at church let it be known that they thought Bob was wasting good time and may even have gone "a bit crazy" with his meanderings in the mountains. "Why do you let him do that, running off to the woods?" was a constant question thrown at Linda, and it pained Bob.

Things turned his way in February 1979, when the job of utilities superintendent was tossed in his lap. The town's utilities supervisor had left abruptly, leaving Hatfield without anyone to oversee water supply operations during a fierce winter storm that had frozen the well controls. An elderly woman who had known Bob as a teenager and recognized his mechanical skills urged the mayor to call him. Within a few hours, the town got its water supply back, and Bob had a full-time job. The money was decent and the hours flexible. He enjoyed the work and soon became involved with the design, construction and operation of an environmentally friendly wastewater-treatment plant.

Hatfield's state-of-the-art facility received state and regional media recognition, sparking a visit by then-Governor Bill Clinton (who, due to politicking in town, never kept his appointment to tour the plant with Bob). Bob soon received numerous out-of-town job offers, including assistant to the director of the Arkansas Department of Pollution Control and Ecology. But, to pursue his life passion, he elected to stay in Hatfield. With the exception of a brief stint as director of public works in a small, southern Texas town in the mid-1980s (where he quickly grew tired of local government politics interfering with the job), he remained in Hatfield with its mysterious surrounding forests. With his children now well into their adult lives, his military pension—combined with income from occasional cattle and timber sales and from intermittent contract jobs—would be enough to keep Linda and himself comfortable while he explored the treasure trail.

In the late 1980s, Bob's investigation took a new turn. He began to realize that the clues around Brushy Creek and Smoke Rock Mountain were not limited to carvings on trees but in some cases included the *shape* of certain trees.

Walking along indicated directional lines, he began to notice that select trees—almost exclusively red and white oaks—had a pattern of grafted limbs or oddly shaped trunks which, he thought, could not be naturally occurring. Some had grown into the shape of football uprights; others looked like half-finished scaffolding, with perfectly vertical limbs sprouting off perfectly horizontal branches. Some took the shape of *T*s or crosses. It appeared as if nineteenth-century pioneers had snapped the trunks of saplings and tied them into right-angled contortions, using twine that would disintegrate. By now these were no mere landmarks but giant sculptured signposts, or, in some cases, neat rifle sights—showing a traveler that his compass bearing was correct as it sliced through the center of the marker tree. Other contorted oaks had large bent-knee knobs knitted into their trunks—providing a waist-high "this way" indicator.

He wondered if his imagination were running wild. But the pattern was uncanny. If only Uncle Ode were around to explain, he thought, recalling how his mentor had grafted fruit trees.

By far the most fascinating "treasure" tree in Brushy Valley was the "map tree," the big beech singled out by Grandpa and Ode back in 1950, near where the Mexican had been killed. Bob had rediscovered the inscribed tree in the early 1980s by following a line indicated by one of the odd bent oaks in the area. Upon his return from Texas, he had spent months trying to decipher the beech's weird cluster of signs and symbols.

Anchored at the base of Smoke Rock, it was pocked with sixty-five inscriptions—a cross, a bell, a heart, a legless horse or mule, a legless bird, a priest-like figure and a host of letters, symbols and numbers. The challenge was in seeing in this naïve indigenous "art" a sophisticated coded message.

The beech, to Bob, was the starting point. Certainly, there were other marked trees nearby, but this one, because of its complexity, drew him in. Some of its signs were fully visible; others were covered with moss and lichen, which had to be delicately removed with a wire brush. Several engravings had been stretched or otherwise distorted by the tree's growth. Nonetheless, over many years, the carvings remained legible, particularly if outlined lightly in chalk.

(The bark of the North American beech, *Fagus grandifolia,* is unusual among temperate-climate trees. Its original tissue replenishes itself externally, producing the telltale smooth outer surface of the species; in contrast to the fissured bark of, say, oaks, which produce new bark tissue deeper inside the tree.[8] Hence, the relative abundance of old inscriptions on beech bark.)

The name Odis Ashcraft—juxtaposed with the date "1924"—was carved into the beech, as Bob discovered one morning while brushing away the moss. From that startling moment, he knew that this tree "tablet" probably held important keys for unlocking the puzzle that had preoccupied him for so long. The bark engravings, inscribed as they were on a long-lived beech, were no idle graffiti. They conveyed something esoteric, arcane, perhaps spiritual. At the top of the inscription, more than four feet above the ground, was the lettering *1st Thess 2:3*. Slightly below and on the opposite side of the trunk were the inscribed initials *J.A.S.*, surrounded by three dots arranged in a triangle.

Bob at first did not know what to make of these, but he came around to thinking that they might be Biblical references, in keeping with the priest-like figure centrally carved into the bark. Turning to his King James Bible at home, he tried First Thessalonians, chapter two, verse three. The passage speaks of exhortations being true. As for *J.A.S.* and the three dots, he guessed at "James, chapter three, verse three"—which speaks of turning a horse around by its bit.

The tree "tablet" seemed to suggest focusing on the prominent legless-horse figure, while the biblical references appeared to allude to the animal's direction. The trick, he guessed, was to turn the horse around and to know that this new direction of the turned animal was true. The horse's image was unusual because it had no legs and had one ear pointing down. If the image were reversed, the drooping ear would point east to a spot on the ground. The telltale ear of the "stationary" horse provided a directional line. Twenty yards from the tree, in an easterly direction as indicated by the ear of the reversed horse, lay a large depression in the forest floor, covered with brush.

Bob would never know whether the person who dug the pit had recovered a large cache or had merely excavated a large hole. But whatever initial disappointment he felt on discovering the dry pit was surpassed by a buoyant confidence that his interpretations of key aspects of the Map Tree had been on track. He renamed the beech the Bible Tree.

The trick now was to deduce additional directional lines leading from the tree, to sift out distinct compass headings from its explosion of symbolism. He scrutinized each carving for any suggestion of geographic headings. Several seemed to indicate a northeast direction: a fancy number 7, with a scythe-like tail, seemed to point that way. And, amid the scrambled letters, he noticed that *NE* seemed to have been carved as a distinct pair in an area not far from the upturned tail of the 7.

With compass in hand, Bob headed into almost impenetrable vegetation along a line to the northeast, as indicated by the 7's fish-tail. At just under half a mile, he made a series of discoveries. A large number 7, about the length of a man's arm, had been chipped into a rockface with a pick or chisel! The full length of the 7 was visible as a shadow figure under the bright sun. Not far from the 7 was a vault-like chamber, about eight feet on a side. Above the vault and to the right was a large carved symbol in the shape of a three-toed turkey track, whose middle toe pointed directly to the vault. The track had been partly defaced by someone, apparently years ago. Climbing into the vault, Bob could see that the man-made chamber connected to a waterlogged tunnel going off to one side and that a narrow entrance tunnel, coming up from the creek below, had collapsed.

Exiting from the vault, he felt confident that the Bible Tree had directed him to the spot. He realized that it was the same creek bed that Grandpa had said was the final resting place of the mischievous Mexican. He wondered how much of a coincidence it had been for Grandpa to have pointed out both the Bible Tree and the site of the Mexican's undoing during that first outing, nearly forty years ago.

Back at his study, Bob charted his discovery on his topo map. Using dividers to obtain pinpoint accuracy in calculating distance, he could see that he had walked exactly three-eighths of a mile to the 7 rock-face carving from the 7 engraving on the Bible Tree. On several prior occasions, he had noted that he seemed to have traveled a certain distance between signs measured in precise one-eighth-mile units. The trip from the Bible Tree to the seemingly important vault made him wonder: Could the measurements be indicated in furlongs, a standard legal gauge for American surveying calculated in eighths of a mile, or 660 feet? The "Spanish hypothesis" seemed to be fading fast.

Returning to other trees with distance indicators, he satisfied himself that the American surveyor system of measurement was being used. He found that he could predict the distance at which a clue was likely to be found along an indicated line. By early 1990, he began to find markers systematically. Typically, the clues were carved in tree bark or chiseled in stone outcroppings. But the symbolic signposts could also take the form of strategically placed rocks or groupings of rocks. The stone markers were often shaped like an elongated diamond or trowel; some resembled large arrowheads, and some even looked like a boot.

Moreover, Bob began to realize that the rusted "junk" metal that he occasionally discovered with his metal detector while walking lines could hold some significance for the overall geometric grid. Until this point, he had discounted all such seemingly random findings: horseshoes, muleshoes, plowpoints, pick and axe heads, wagon and stove parts. He had assumed that the "stuff" had been lost or deliberately tossed by miners or woodsmen working in the area long ago. But was it really junk? No, the pattern was too consistent, too linear, in fact, to be a coincidence.

He eventually concluded that constellations of abandoned spare parts had been placed at calculated distances and then buried four to six inches underground. That depth of burial, he realized, was just enough for concealment but within range of a magnetic-compass needle to mark the ferrous target below the surface.

(Those individuals who created an underground money grid—perhaps a century or more ago—obviously owned no metal detectors or other electronic devices for remote sensing. All they had in their employ was the basic needle compass or a similarly functioning instrument, known as a Spanish dip needle. The horizontally rotating magnetic needle of the compass or the vertically seesawing Spanish dip needle would orient itself to the induced magnetic field produced by the buried iron object—the container for the gold and silver coins, bullion, jewels and the like—in the shallow underground.

The science behind the venerable compass, the less-well-known Spanish dip needle and today's prosaic but reliable electronic magnetometers and metal detectors is fairly straightforward. Yet it takes a little explaining to relate this science to the task of finding treasure.

All magnets have two poles, commonly referred to as north and south. With any two magnets, like poles repel and opposite poles attract. Thus, a north pole of one magnet is attracted to the south pole of a second.

A powerful magnet exists within Earth's core, created by flows of molten iron. The presence of this giant subsurface magnet is detected by a compass.

A compass, in its brilliant simplicity, is nothing more than a bar magnet balanced on a pivot, such that the magnet is free to rotate. Since like poles of magnets repel and opposite poles attract, the south pole of the compass is attracted to the north pole of the Earth's core magnet.

The Earth's magnet occupies a relatively small volume in the planet's core. Consequently its magnetic poles do not extend to what are called Earth's true geographic north and south poles. The result is that Earth's magnetic north pole deviates from its geographic north pole, over time and from different locations. Nevertheless, under most circumstances, the magnet of a compass points true north, and this elementary tool can be used for land, sea and air navigation by those who know how to adjust for the deviation.

Because of the powerful magnet lying inside the Earth's core, all ferromagnetic objects—those containing iron, nickel or cobalt—lying on the Earth's surface will become "induced" magnets and thus detectable to some degree by a compass. Recall how a paper clip in the proximity of an actual magnet starts to behave like a magnet itself. The object becomes "magnetized" when near a magnet, or technically speaking, it transforms into an "induced" magnet whose magnetic strength is proportional to the distance from the actual magnet.

Moving from a paper clip to a buried iron washpot full of coins or an iron safe stuffed with jewels, the principle is the same. These buried iron containers have absorbed some of the magnetism of the Earth's core magnet. When a hand-held compass passes over these substantial "induced" magnets, the compass needle will react by pivoting sharply to this sudden, proximate magnetic force attracting or repelling it.

Hence, in the pre–metal-detector years of outlawry, those burying substantial caches risked never recovering their gold or silver [nonferrous metals] unless the caches were marked by signs or code on the surface or were buried in ferrous containers [iron washpots, safes, strongboxes, milk cans]. They would also need to be buried near the surface, for small stashes such as a glass jar full of coins capped by a ferrous lid would provide only a weak signal. The rusted lid could completely oxidize, leaving an even weaker signal. That is why heavy iron parts—from old stoves, wagons, field tools—were deployed just under the surface as unseen markers for actual treasure or crucial clues buried deeper. Their magnetic field, undetectable to the eye, would send the compass awhirl. Moreover, the buried rusted relics might have a distinct pointed part that, in turn, would provide a topographical heading to follow.

But it was not that easy to find treasure with compass in hand. The treasure hunter would need to stand on top of the target and then crouch down low with the compass and hope that the object was not buried too deeply. With each doubling of the distance between the compass as a sensor and the ferrous target, the detectable magnetic force decreases by a factor of eight.

Today's treasure hunter has better and affordable tools at his or her disposal. A magnetometer, like a compass, is an instrument that measures magnetic force. But, electrically powered and programmed, it is far more sensitive and powerful than the rudimentary, centuries-old compass. With a magnetometer, a treasure hunter can detect much smaller magnetic objects, and items lodged at greater depths. Still, like a compass, it can only find ferrous objects.

A metal detector, also electrically powered, detects all metals, not just ferrous objects. It does so by broadcasting a weak radio wave [far weaker than those emitted by a radio station] that is then reflected by buried metal objects. The metal detector monitors rebounding signals, which appear as a movement of a dial or as an audible alarm, indicating the presence of nearby metal. The larger, or the shallower, the metal object, the greater the interference to be monitored. Yet, since radio waves do not penetrate very deeply into the ground, metal detectors are limited to sensing and locating only shallow objects. There are other challenges as well. Soil conditions can wreak havoc: iron-rich soil or sediment covered by iron-laden rocks can create an impossible blur when looking for specific targets.)

Such were the considerations as Bob tried to comprehend both the mechanics of the elaborate grid system before him and the nature of what he was looking for.

Not only did the buried metal clues lie on indicated lines; more important, they also seemed to mark where two lines crossed. And there was another facet to consider. If the distances indicated thus far were in furlongs, what other American surveyor measurements might have been used in the system? Among the buried junk that he had found were random short links of chain and iron rods. If these were being used to indicate distance, could they not metaphorically represent surveyor gauges for linear measurement, known as chains (66 feet) and rods (16½ feet), where 40 rods would equal 1 furlong, and 8 furlongs would equal one statute mile (5,280 feet)?[9]

Bob began to grasp the ingenuity, the enormity of the puzzle. In the distribution of the carved clues and buried markers, there seemed to be a hidden logic, a symbolic language, a cunning intelligence to it all. These boys were surveyors, he thought to himself. The hunt was becoming intoxicating.

When Bob told Linda that the scattered metal parts might not have been junk after all, she was not convinced. She was pleased for Bob and his new enthusiasm, but she still wondered what the real facts were and whether any treasure were actually involved. Bob had been saying "Spanish" treasure for more than a decade, and now, in the early 1990s, he was saying that it wasn't Spanish. And what last week had been junk was now something useful.

She was at a loss as to why he had nothing to show for his painstaking detective work except a bunch of withered metal scrap and weird-shaped rocks. She had several female friends whose husbands had been avid treasure hunters: to a man, they left their families poorer for the effort, never seeming to turn up much—in fact, anything at all—on the trail. She was also concerned for the safety of her husband, who, with failing eyesight, continued to venture out every day amid the deadly snakes and the treacherous crags. Still, the patient soft-spoken Sunday school teacher had not lost faith in Bob's ability to succeed at whatever he started. She marveled at his mental discipline, his inquisitiveness, his ability to concentrate on an abstract, inscrutable puzzle for impossibly long stretches. Most of all, she marveled at his ability to disregard all detractors and doubters.

Hearing Linda's concern and acknowledging her forbearance over all these years, Bob reassured her that if he ever reached the point where it was obvious to both that he was not making progress, he would quit. And then he went back to work on his maps.

Rather than sit home and worry, Linda started accompanying Bob more often. She loved the exercise of traversing the mountains. But most of all she craved the opportunity to spend more free time with her husband, whose renewed enthusiasm was infectious. In a matter of weeks, she became adept at spotting clues, working off Bob's leads.

Now, with a partner in tow, Bob's rate of discovery of buried clues climbed exponentially. Linda, in turn, showed signs of becoming hooked on the hunt, watching the system of interconnected clues play itself out. Still, she harbored doubts that all his efforts would ever yield a substantial return, intellectual or financial.

One April day in 1991, Bob's hunt took him to an intriguing marker-filled area, where several lines appeared to cross. There, at a thickly wooded spot along a creek bank, he noticed some large odd-shaped rocks that looked out of place. Moreover, one of the surrounding trees—a maple—had a subtle vertical line cut into its bark. He recognized it as a "blaze," a trail marker crafted by the sharp edge of a woodsman's axe. That was the clincher, the subtle signal that the surrounding stones on the forest floor were clues.

Because it was already dusk, he decided to head home and return the following day with Linda, who could provide a welcome second set of eyes. Vigilance was critical. It was well into snake season, and the timber rattlers, copperheads and water moccasins were energetically sloughing off hibernation. While he routinely carried a large .44 Magnum revolver loaded with snake shot, the weapon would not do much good if his eyes were focused exclusively on the clues at hand. The holstered gun also interfered with the operation of his metal detector, constantly requiring him to remove his gunbelt. As the site had looked promising, he decided to lose no time and return early the next day with his new detector. The device was capable of finding deeper targets, such as caches, rather than just smaller objects on the surface or just below.

Soon after sunrise the next morning, with Linda at his side, Bob surveyed the base of the "blazed" tree, but his detector emitted no signal. He then aligned himself with the north-pointing tip of a large arrow-shaped rock, which lay a few feet from the blazed maple. He followed that line from the pointed rock across the creek, some twenty feet away. On the other bank, about fifteen feet from the creek bed, the detector sounded.

Excitedly, he probed with a shovel and hit metal, about four inches deep. Reaching into the hole, he pulled up an old axe head and marked its precise southwest orientation on his topo. While washing off the axe head in the creek, he noticed that it had a small notch chipped in its blade. Recalling how other buried metal clues had similar grooves or notches, he thought that the grooves might represent surveyor's distance markers.

Which one, though? Walking southwest, back across the creek, precisely one chain—sixty-six feet—he came to a large, shoebox-shaped rock. Searching behind the rectangular boulder, he detected part of a buried metal singletree, a device used in harnessing horses. Noting the precise orientation of the object's rounded tip, he took a compass heading. It pointed in the direction of the maple—providing a line that completed the third leg of a triangle. Bob held the detector low to the ground as he paced slowly in the southeasterly direction indicated by the singletree. Some twenty feet along that bearing, the detector swung to its maximum reading.

As Bob started probing with the shovel, he realized that the object was buried deeper than usual. He carefully dug through the soft, loamy soil. At about eighteen inches, the shovel struck something that he knew was neither metal nor rock. Dropping to his knees, he reached into the hole and felt smooth glass. He groped again, this time retrieving a patina-coated, pint-sized fruit jar with his trembling hands. It was filled with gold and silver coins.

The system had worked.

The signs and the lines had led to treasure. In that brilliant second of discovery, Bob experienced a serene, indescribable calm. Intuitively, he knew that this breakthrough was no mere coincidence. Geometry, geography, navigation, cryptanalysis, intuition and raw persistence had meshed to bring him to this tiny spot in a vast wilderness.

In that wonderful moment, he sensed that he had only just begun to unlock the code.

Wiping the sweat from below the rim of his felt Stetson hat, he bowed his head and for a while was at a loss for words. He stood up, slowly, still unable to speak. He twirled the heavy glass container in his large palm, letting the sunshine bounce off the lustrous coins inside. "It's gold," he said softly to Linda, who ran over to hug him. He held her close as she took in what had happened. "Oh my goodness. Oh my goodness, honey! It looks so nice!" she blurted, her face now wet with tears. Her slight frame trembled and Bob looked at her, concerned. She laughed, and, with a kiss, reassured him: "Well, at least now I know you're not crazy."

At this first major milestone in his odyssey, Bob felt dizzy and disoriented. Steadying his stocky five-foot-ten, two hundred twenty pound frame, he walked the cache to the nearby stream to rinse off the coins. Then he called out the dates and denominations of each washed coin. They were all U.S. Mint—nothing even remotely resembling Spanish pieces-of-eight. "Five dollar gold piece, 1866. Twenty dollar gold piece, 1854. Ten dollar gold, 1845," and on and on. The tally: over $400 face value in gold coins (which, in today's numismatic terms would be some 50 to 70 times that amount, depending on rarity and age), and around $60 face value in silver dollars (or a numismatic multiple of some 15 to 30 times that amount, depending on rarity and age), plus loose change.

All were minted between 1802 and 1889. The date on the bottom of the jar: June 1903.

"This is outlaw money," Bob exclaimed. "And those funny signs got us to it."

Those "funny signs," in fact, were the coded inscriptions of the Knights of the Golden Circle and their post–Civil War adherents.

5

The KGC:
The Hidden History

THE only official document even to hint that the KGC, and thus a shadow Confederacy, may have gone underground in the Deep South in the final phase of the war is the Holt Report, on file at the Library of Congress.[1] The 14,000-word submission to U.S. Secretary of War Edwin M. Stanton, dated October 8, 1864, provides the most detailed account of the KGC. Entitled "A Western Conspiracy in Aid of the Southern Rebellion," it is based upon Union intelligence from Ohio, Illinois, Indiana, Michigan, Wisconsin and the border states of Missouri and Kentucky, but not from the South itself.

Written by the highest-ranking officer in the military-justice system at the time, Judge Advocate Gen. Joseph Holt, the report makes several trenchant points and describes the KGC as the "echo and faithful ally" of the Confederacy.

Holt begins by acknowledging the existence of the KGC, "chiefly military in its character." He asserts that as many as 500,000 Northerners were KGC members and estimates that as many as 340,000 men were trained and equipped for mobilization.[2] No mention is made of the number of possible inductees in the South.

The report emphasizes that the order promoted an individual's "absolute right" to own slaves as private property and a state's right to resist "coercion" from federal authorities.[3] It goes on to point a finger squarely at the KGC for precipitating fratricidal conflict on American soil, noting that the subversive society's "detestable plotting culminated in open rebellion and bloody Civil War."[4]

Holt concludes his report with the admonition: "Judea produced but one Judas Iscariot, and Rome, from the sinks of her demoralization, produced but one Cataline, and yet, as events prove, there has arisen together in our land an entire brood of such traitors, all animated by the same patricidal spirit, and all struggling with the same relentless malignity for the dismemberment of our Union."[5]

But by far Holt's most intriguing comment appears near the end of the document. It is this: "A citizen, captured by a guerrilla band in Kentucky last summer, records the fact that the establishment of a new Confederacy as the deliberate purpose of the Western people was boastfully asserted by these outlaws, who also assured their prisoner that in the event of such establishment, there would be a greater rebellion than ever! Lastly, it is claimed that the new Confederacy is already organized; that it has a 'provisional government,' officers, departments, bureaus, etc. in secret operation."[6]

With that provocative lead, the snapshot view of the KGC might have been blown up, magnified to reveal the secret order's full colors. It never was. History missed it, perhaps precisely because the KGC was so effective at concealing its real plans, its motivations, its intentions. Still, a reasonable attempt can be made to provide the fuller, true picture of the KGC—based on what is largely circumstantial evidence that plausibly links key players, places and organizations in a convincing, interpretive framework.

None of the individuals described below acknowledged membership in the core KGC. To do so, according to the rare anonymous or pseudonymous-insider historical accounts that exist, would have been suicidal.

The KGC's Power Brokers

Charleston was the crucible. The aristocratic coastal city, in whose busy harbor the Civil War would commence, spawned the KGC in its embryonic, nameless form in the 1830s. Two powerful social forces led to the formation of the secret organization.

The first of these influences was the nullification/states' rights/secession movement led by the formidable South Carolina statesman, aristocrat and pro-slavery ideologue, John C. Calhoun. The second was the establishment by the Scottish Rite of Freemasonry of a national Supreme Council in Charleston in May 1801.[7]

What possibly could have served as a common thread between these two camps: one a radical political movement, the other an age-old, semi-secret fraternal order with European roots?

The answer lies, in part, in a shared and passionate belief in rugged individualism (that is, at least for the white majority population at the time) and in the conviction that there is no higher good than individual freedom triumphing over a central, despotic authority. Essayist Robert Penn Warren, in his famous rumination, *The Legacy of the Civil War*, noted that one of the prime sources of "self-division" leading up to the War Between the States "was the *universalist* conception of freedom based on natural law, inherited from the Revolution."[8] Both secessionist and Masonic forces centered in Charleston saw Jeffersonian principles of "popular sovereignty" (essentially letting ultimate political power reside with individuals as a check on strong central government) as a radiant guiding light, although each followed that light in its own way.

Calhoun was the nation's leading advocate of states' rights and its essential corollaries, the right to own slaves and to transport them as human chattel into the territories of the United States. His vision of America, shared with many others of his social class, was the "eighteenth-century agrarianism of a stable planter society," as one historian noted.[9]

Scottish Rite Freemasonry stressed an individual's intellectual, scholarly and political freedom. Such is a legacy, perhaps, of what many believe is Freemasonry's historical association with the medieval Knights Templar and that powerful French-based secret order's flight from persecution by King Philip IV of France (who was not only jealous of the order's growing influence but owed financial debts to the Knights) and the Roman Catholic Church of French-born Pope Clement V (who, under pressure from King Philip, turned on the former crusaders).[10] It will never be known if there is a direct link between these soldier monks, known as "Templars" (from Knights of the Temple), and subsequent "Freemasons," or whether early Freemasonry merely modeled itself after certain real or perceived Templar traditions, rituals and customs.[11]

Some researchers believe that the persecuted monk warriors (excommunicated by Clement V in 1312) originally took refuge in Scotland and England,[12] hiding within the stone-mason guilds, hence the provenance of the name "Mason." That "Masonic" link between the United Kingdom—

particularly Scotland—and the Continent likely further developed when two Scottish Masons living in exile in Paris in the early 1700s, Charles Radclyffe and Andrew Michael Ramsay, sparked a surge of interest in Freemasonry in France. All of this, in some combination, may have engendered the term Scottish Rite. No firm evidence exists, however, as to the true origin or meaning of the phrase, first used at the beginning of the nineteenth century.[13] In any event, the early Freemasons, or, as some would have it, the neo-Templars, would find themselves repeatedly at odds with the Vatican, which they saw as an incorrigible foe of free thinking and civil liberties.

Beyond any philosophical affinity, old-line Scottish Rite Freemasonry provided an organizational structure for the underground states' rights/secessionist movement that would become the KGC. The Rite promoted democracy and democratic values, at least rhetorically. But it built its own governing structure pyramidally, with its select "Supreme Council" members at the top, in command of the most valued information and highly guarded secrets. The Rite, to be sure, pursued a universalist base, yet one overseen by an enlightened elite. With its ascending ritualistic degrees of initiation (a winnowing-out process), code words, tacit understandings, secret geometry and cryptic symbolism, this complex order of Masonry provided an ideal basis for the KGC to establish a hidden politico-military network. Moreover, the Scottish Rite's chief headquarters in Charleston and its northern headquarters in New York, established in 1813, provided an ideal axis for a subversive organization seeking to expand its power nationwide.

In the volatile political mix that stirred in antebellum Charleston, these two forceful sociopolitical influences of secessionism and Scottish Rite Freemasonry became intertwined in the parlors and meeting rooms. Nowhere was this more potently felt than within the redbrick building on the corner of Church and Broad streets in Charleston—headquarters of the Scottish Rite's Mother Supreme Council of the World.

(The two-hundred-year-old Scottish Rite, the largest modern Freemasonic organization, is very much in existence today, with its world headquarters—The House of the Temple—now located on Sixteenth Street in Washington, D.C., not far from the White House. According to its literature, the Rite functions as an intellectual and philanthropic fraternity, with its initiates pursuing a goal of self-improvement and a commitment to voluntarism, public health and public education.)[14]

As civil war approached, the Scottish Rite, although supposedly nondenominational and nonpolitical, found it increasingly difficult to deny harboring strong pro-Confederate tendencies and affiliations among its core leadership. One of the issues its Supreme Council would find hardest to explain, after war broke out, was the destruction by fire of all its internal documents from its founding in 1801 to 1860. Some observers have asserted that the records were deliberately destroyed to obliterate a treasonous, pro-Confederate paper trail involving key members of the Scottish Rite's leadership. "The Charleston Supreme Council destroyed its proceedings, for more than a half century. From 1801 to 1860, no records exist," wrote the former president of Wheaton College and Masonic critic, Jonathan Blanchard, in 1882. "Those records covered the period of Nullification and the rise of the Rebellion, and were doubtless ghastly with treason, with attempts to burn down Northern cities, and poison inhabitants; for such things were attempted."[15]

Who, then, were the key players behind these two powerful social forces?

John C. Calhoun emerged as the intellectual father of the KGC, and a number of Civil War–era commentators describe him as such.[16] He was so inspirational for the pro-slavery secret society that KGC members initially used "Nuohlac"—Calhoun spelled backwards—as their password.[17] A brilliant orator and debater, he stood apart as the Southern Rights advocate who held the respect of even his toughest foes in Washington. In addition to representing South Carolina as a distinguished congressman and senator, Calhoun would ably serve the nation in various high-level positions, twice as vice president, and as secretary of war and secretary of state, before his death in 1850.

Calhoun did not start off as a Southern separatist and states' rights advocate. As a young congressman, he had campaigned hard for a strong national response to Britain's invasion in 1812 and for strong nationwide economic initiatives, including a national bank, for years after the War of 1812. But, as a plantation owner and son of a South Carolina farmer, he also was extremely devoted to Southern interests, namely the protection of the South's slave-based economy. An owner of dozens of slaves himself, Calhoun described the relations between whites and blacks in slaveholding states in the 1830s as not an evil but "a good—a positive good."

Eventually, two perceived threats to the South's economy and "way of life" emerged—the federal tariffs of 1824–1832 and Northern-based abolitionism. In their wake, Calhoun took up the cause of resisting (nullifying) the will of Congress by a single state. Later, he would foment a movement toward the ultimate act of rebellion: secession.

Secession, Calhoun emphasized, should be considered only as a last resort to secure sovereignty that resided with the states as the agents for their respective populations. A state, he argued, could rightfully and legally withdraw its consent from an oppressive federal government only if that government was perceived to have overstepped its constitutionally delegated powers. Such a government would then become an "intruder" that rightfully had to be "expelled."

Although Calhoun expressed hope that a Union-preserving compromise could be reached merely by demonstrating a *unified* Southern threat of secession, he recognized that the slavery issue could lead, inexorably, to disunion. Over time, his pro-secessionist bent would only grow stronger in light of what he saw as a Northern tidal wave of abolitionist agitation and legislation.

Under the political and intellectual influence of Calhoun, deep political fault lines ran through antebellum Charleston and other Southern cities, creating a fertile environment in which secret societies could germinate. The first slavery-expansionist associations to sprout from this environment were the so-called Southern Rights Clubs. Direct precursors of the Knights of the Golden Circle, these hidden "clubs" emerged in Charleston around 1835. "About the close of the year 1834, there were to be found, in Charleston, New Orleans, and some other Southern cities, a few politicians who earnestly desired the re-establishment of the African slave trade and the acquisition of new slave territory," writes the anonymous author of an important exposé, *An Authentic Exposition of the K.G.C., Knights of the Golden Circle; or, A History of Secession from 1834 to 1861.*[18] The booklet, published in 1861 as one of the few "insider" documents tracing the origins of the KGC, points out that these conclaves were more than social gatherings: they provided a subversive secessionist infrastructure in the Cotton South. Building that infrastructure would be a coterie of leaders from the 10 percent of Southern society that comprised its plantation-owning aristocracy.

Such infrastructure required clear lines of communication and command, as well as geographic demarcation. So, these Southern Rights Clubs used secret passwords, recognition handshakes, initiation rites and other rituals that were hardly distinguishable from those used by the Masonic fraternity and its Charleston-based Supreme Council. "These men formed themselves into secret juntos, which, without any particular form or ritual, were called SRCs (Southern Rights Clubs). They had certain signs of recognition, by which they made themselves known to each other, and met weekly, semi-weekly, or otherwise, as the cause which they labored to promote seemed to demand," the unnamed author of the *Exposition* writes.[19] The author goes on to note that the name "Knights of the Golden Circle" did not surface publicly until some twenty years later, in 1855.

The cause being promoted behind closed doors was the establishment of "The Golden Circle"—the imperial expansion of the Southern slave economy, which required both new slaves and new territory. International prohibitions against the slave trade notwithstanding, the Southern Rights Clubs clandestinely sent out "slaver" ships to Africa between 1834 and 1844. These voyages met with mixed results. Numerous slave ships were captured by British and U.S. naval vessels on patrol off West Africa. But others successfully reached secret ports in Louisiana, Mississippi and Florida with their illicit cargo, according to the *Exposition* and other accounts.[20] The Ashburn Treaty of 1842, committing both Britain and the United States to enforce maritime efforts to suppress the slave trade, made the SRCs' overseas slave trafficking ever more complicated. The importation of slaves—mostly via Cuba—would continue right up until the Civil War. But, by the mid-1840s, the SRCs' focus shifted largely to slave-oriented territorial expansion to the south, under the rubric "filibustering."

The United States' 1846–48 war with Mexico—which yielded New Mexico (then comprising much of modern-day Arizona) and California—encouraged the SRCs to look for new targets further south, in Central America and Cuba. Leading the charge on the Cuban front was a high-ranking Scottish Rite Mason and hero from the Mexican-American War, Maj. Gen. John A. Quitman, who later became governor of Mississippi.[21]

A transplanted New Yorker who would marry into a wealthy plantation-owning family and move to Natchez, Mississippi, Quitman was a pivotal player in the early KGC and its march toward secession. Symbolism provides a trail. A famous portrait of Quitman astride his stallion during the Mexican War reveals a telltale emblem: on the lower-left corner of his equestrian blanket can be seen a five-pointed star floating above a crescent moon—two of the key symbols of the KGC.[22] That precise symbolic juxtaposition—of the star poised above an upturned crescent moon—can be seen in an illustration of a secret lynching within a

KGC castle in a revelatory book on the Knights of the Golden Circle, dated 1864 and written under a pseudonym.[23]

As both skilled lawyer and owner of several plantations with more than four hundred slaves, Quitman emerged as an early and ardent defender of slaveholders' rights and states' rights. Not surprisingly, he rapidly became a leading protégé of Calhoun. In short order, the Mexican War veteran carried Calhoun's secessionist torch beyond Carolina into his adopted state of Mississippi, where he also built a major beachhead for Scottish Rite Freemasonry, beginning in 1830. There, the pro-slavery firebrand would serve as the state's highest-ranking Mason for many years and would also play a prominent national Freemasonic role as a thirty-third-degree Scottish Rite Mason on the Rite's Supreme Council in Charleston, beginning in 1848.[24] This occurred precisely when he began plotting his slavery-expansionist strategy on the "filibustering" front. Not coincidentally, the borders of the Scottish Rite's southern jurisdiction were greatly expanded soon after the Mexican War to include the new territories of New Mexico and California. Such a move surely would have involved Quitman's influence as a Scottish Rite Supreme Council member.[25]

As a leader of a zealous pro-slavery camp and a mysterious Southern-based fraternal society, Quitman found himself in a position of considerable influence at mid-century. He was not one to stand idle. Within Mississippi social and political circles, he created States' Rights Associations that operated on a countywide and statewide basis.[26] Calhoun and other national figures were invited to attend some of these meetings. The core mission was promoting the belief—so boldly pronounced by Calhoun—that there did not exist a consolidated "perpetual" Union but rather a voluntary confederation of sovereign states. These conventions often conducted their most important business—discussions of slavery expansion in the territories and, ultimately, the forming of a "free Southern government"—in secret committee. But occasionally, these discussions would be floated publicly, most certainly to prepare the Southern masses for the idea of secession and the need to face the growing "threat" of Northern "abolitionist" aggression.

In late 1849, with President Zachary Taylor calling for the admittance of California and New Mexico as free-states, Quitman and other pro-slavery leaders called for a slave state convention in Nashville. Then, after becoming Mississippi's governor, in early 1850, Quitman floated the idea of Mississippi and South Carolina seceding simultaneously from the Union. He soon called for a special session of the Mississippi legislature to that effect. But, when a southern convention opened the following June in Nashville and failed to inspire much support for rebellion, the secessionist impulse faded. It was a movement ten years ahead of its time. Yet it set the stage for the subsequent insurrection that would divide and then batter the nation.

Taking his cue from Calhoun, Quitman took an aggressive stand not only on states' rights but also on the issue of slavery's expansion into new territories, the proximate cause for the Civil War. During the Mexican War, the major general had proposed the complete annexation of Mexico, not just the northern part (where the terrain did not lend itself to plantation farming). After that war, Quitman went so far as to threaten to march a pro-slavery army into New Mexico from Texas to ensure its slave-state status.

Not surprisingly, Quitman rapidly became a prime target of the Taylor administration. Zack Taylor was a slaveowner but, as president, forcefully stood against slavery's expansion into the territories.[27] He had a demonstrative personality and could only be pushed so far. It was Taylor who had Quitman, a national war hero, and a handful of other slavery-expansionist southerners indicted in 1850 by a federal grand jury in New Orleans. The alleged crime: involvement in planning a failed military raid on Spanish-owned Cuba. As it turned out, all key members of the failed raid, including its organizer, American-based Cuban exile Narciso Lopez, were Masons and believed to be members of a KGC precursor, the Order of the Lone Star, based in New Orleans and east Texas.[28] Due to a series of hung juries on the charge of their having violated the 1818 Neutrality Law, Quitman and his alleged co-conspirators eventually were absolved of all charges by the Justice Department. Coincidentally, after the Quitman-Lopez indictment in 1850, Quitman's nemesis on the national stage, President Taylor, died suddenly under peculiar circumstances: the president, according to the official record, had eaten a bad batch of cherries.

Significantly, the lawyer who had been hired by the government to prosecute Quitman (and then hand-pick the jurors) on the Cuba case was New Orleans attorney Judah P. Benjamin. The former Charleston native was subsequently elected senator from Louisiana and appointed secretary of war and then secretary of state of the Confederacy. He later would appear to play a key role in the upper echelons of the KGC, during the Civil War and its immediate aftermath, in the areas of intelligence gathering and procuring funding for secret missions.

It is in this period, in the early- to mid-1850s, that Quitman and a clique of other hard-core secessionists moved to ensure that the KGC's underground recruitment and propaganda network expanded well beyond its Charleston-based anchor and its early Southern moorings in Natchez and New Orleans. By this time, a "firing of the Southern Heart" had been partially achieved in the Deep South by staging regional semi-open assemblies—variably referred to as States Rights Associations, Southern Rights Conventions and Southern Commercial Conventions.[29] Such conclaves trumpeted the need for a vigorous defense of Southern rights and for an increasingly competitive Southern economy. At critical moments, these table-thumping meetings could be called on to whip up emotion—at elections—for secession and territorial expansion.

Still, Quitman and others recognized that the South's secessionist plan lacked an effective, locally based army of militant supporters that could be called on to mobilize quickly. This was to become the purview of the successor group to the imperialist Southern Rights Clubs—the Knights of the Golden Circle. Quitman, with his ample political, military and Scottish Rite fraternal connections, was uniquely equipped to lead this underground mobilization until his sudden death in 1858. According to authoritative reports, the KGC could call on 100,000 trained and armed men by late 1860.[30]

Quitman's service in the Mexican War had led to his connection to Caleb Cushing, another suspected leading light of the KGC. Like Quitman, Cushing had served as a volunteer officer in the war (although, unlike Quitman, he never saw action). A scion of one of the wealthiest pro-British shipping families of Newburyport, Massachusetts, Cushing was also a high-ranking Freemason and, like Quitman, harbored strong secessionist and slavery-expansionist sentiments.[31] (When Cuban separatist Lopez began plotting his Masonic, pro-slavery revolution against Spanish Cuba, he first turned to Cushing and then Quitman as potential sponsors.[32] A newspaper editorial in 1860 accused Cushing of admiring slavery so much that he all but believed the "normal condition" of poor people everywhere was "that of slavery.")[33] Like Quitman, Cushing was a prominent player in Democratic Party circles, who could, in turn, parlay this political clout behind the scenes for the KGC. According to the insightful 1861 *Exposition of the Knights of the Golden Circle*, "a certain Mr. C——, of Massachusetts," and "a Mr. V——, of Ohio," were "said to be about the only reliable members of the Order claimed among the prominent Northern politicians."[34] The unnamed well-informed author of the exposé was referring, ostensibly, to Caleb Cushing (former congressman of Massachusetts) and Clement Vallandigham (former congressman of Ohio).

In 1851, Cushing joined Quitman and another powerful friend from the Mexican War, Jefferson Davis, in promoting yet a fourth war veteran and friend, Franklin Pierce, as the Democratic Party's candidate for president. Cushing would later serve in the Pierce cabinet, as attorney general, alongside Davis as secretary of war—both men subsequently bending the Pierce administration's domestic and foreign policy toward their slavery-expansionist, KGC point of view. Pierce, a virtual nobody in Washington prior to his election, would be accused soon after the outbreak of the Civil War of direct involvement with the KGC.[35] (It would not be the last time that suspected top-ranking members of the Knights of the Golden Circle would serve in high-level cabinet positions and have a major impact. Under the administration of President James Buchanan that followed, Treasury Secretary Howell Cobb and Secretary of War John B. Floyd reportedly played seditious roles—redirecting federal funds and arms into Southern hands—for the KGC on the eve of the Civil War.)[36]

Where Quitman had taken up the Southern aristocrats' torch from Calhoun, Cushing would serve as a master conspirator operating backstage for a decade or more before the Civil War.[37] His subversive efforts would have far-reaching impact on both sides of the Mason-Dixon line. His role as a secessionist-minded KGC agitator is particularly intriguing, given his long association with numerous radical abolitionists (some of whom promoted *Northern* secession and disunion as a price for being rid of slavery) in the prewar years. Among high-profile New Englanders in Cushing's social circle was the anti-slavery fanatic and newspaper publisher, William Lloyd Garrison.

Perhaps, as some have speculated, Cushing's hidden sociopolitical agenda was broader than just Southern secession—perhaps, in fact, his main objective was fomenting *disunion,* specifically the disintegration of the American Republic over the predictably divisive issue of slavery. If so, he may have had powerful European interests backing such an objective. An anonymous column in the March 30, 1861, edition of *Vanity Fair* alludes to such a scenario. It mentions by name several vitriolic "Fire-eater" secessionists, but does not mention Cushing, who preferred quiet, backroom intrigues:

Of all the reptiles with which this country is cursed, the Blowing Viper is the worst. It is confined to no section, but is a native of all. The most deadly specimens belong to the North and South. They are called Abolitionists and Secessionists. The former is known by his seeing all things through a dark medium; a great smoked glass is continually before his eyes, and every object that he beholds through it becomes the long-lived denizen of Africa or, in the vernacular, the Everlasting Nigger. . . . The reptile is undoubtedly honest in his delusion, but he should be crushed, notwithstanding. The Secession viper is of a different breed, and is continually casting his skin. He was warmed into life by a political madman, named John C. Calhoun, who christened him Nullifier. He became a Democrat, and running for Congress, wormed himself into a thousand fat offices, and became the bosom friend of Floyd, Thompson, Wigfall and Toombs, and other blowing vipers. He affects to hate the abolitionist, which is odd, considering that he helps him in his dirty work of Disunion. He should be crushed at once, or at least confined to the Cotton States, in whose slime he was bred. Put your heels on him. Let him be Anathema Maranatha.[38]

Cushing was able to orchestrate his disunionist grand strategy with the help of two key colleagues, each of whom would rise with his steerage to key positions within both Confederate circles and that of the elite inner circle of Scottish Rite Masonry in Charleston: Albert Pike and John C. Breckinridge.

Cushing and Pike, longstanding friends from Massachusetts, shared much in common beyond a passion for the Southern cause. They both spent their youth in Newburyport, Massachusetts; were accepted by Harvard (Pike declining to attend out of an inability to pay enrollment fees); served as military officers in the Mexican War; developed reputations as talented, peripatetic lawyers, linguists and writers; joined advanced-degree Freemasonry; transferred their political allegiance from the Whigs to states' rights Democrats; and demonstrated multifaceted talents. (Both were extremely adept at mathematics, for instance, and Pike was an accomplished poet and a reputable musician. Pike, in fact, wrote the lyrics to the Confederate version of "Dixie," the war anthem of the South.)

In the 1830s, Pike distinguished himself as an editor of the *Arkansas Advocate* and as a lawyer in private practice in Little Rock. But it was through Cushing's political patronage that he was able to develop a political machine in Arkansas by the 1840s.[39] A large, heavily bearded man with dark, thick, flowing hair and brooding eyes, he was an imposing, shrewd and generally brilliant character in his own right. Northern commentators, including those writing in *Continental Monthly* in the early Civil War, fingered "brutal and arrogant" Pike—in contrast to the "miserable quack" George Bickley—as the dark genius behind the Masonic-influenced, hidden Confederacy, the KGC.[40]

Pike, born the same year as Abraham Lincoln, combined elements from three important aspects of his life: membership in Scottish Rite Freemasonry; political experience with the Whigs and then with the short-lived anti-immigration, anti-black, anti-Catholic Know-Nothings, followed by the Democratic Party; and, finally, legal and Masonic connections with the Cherokee and other Nations in Indian Territory (what is now Oklahoma) across the border from Arkansas.

With unprecedented speed, Pike rose through the higher ranks of the Scottish Rite, and eventually wrote its key manifesto, *Morals and Dogma*. He had first become a Masonic brother in 1850 in Little Rock, where he was initiated under the three "Blue Lodge" degrees of common—otherwise known as "symbolic" or "craft"—Masonry. (These neophyte degrees—Entered Apprentice, Fellow Craft and Master Mason—are stepping-stones to the higher degrees in the two main forms or "appendant" systems of American Masonry: the Scottish Rite and York Rite. Most Masons today only participate in these lower, common degrees of initiation in the fraternity and, unlike those initiated into the advanced degrees, have no special knowledge of tightly held secrets or ancient mysteries.) After advancing through the basic degrees, Pike quickly received, by 1853, all ten additional degrees of the York Rite, with its strong early-American roots in New England. The top degree for a York Rite Mason happens to be that of "Knight Templar."

Later that year, brother "Knight Templar" Pike switched his fraternal focus to the Scottish Rite, with its progressive thirty-three degrees, exotic rituals, symbol of the double-headed eagle, and twin credos of "from chaos, order" and "liberty, equality and fraternity."[41] Formally, the Ancient and Accepted Scottish Rite of Freemasonry confers twenty-nine higher degrees—including that of "Knight Kadosh"—up to the rank of thirty-second degree for those over twenty-one years of age. It ultimately confers a final, thirty-third, degree as an honorary title on a select few. Members of the Scottish Rite Supreme Council are thirty-third-degree Masons.

The Scottish Rite's origins in America are not entirely clear. Basic or "craft" Freemasonry (involving the lower degrees) had already established public lodges in the American colonies, chiefly in Philadelphia and Boston, by the 1730s. The higher-degree Scottish Rite is believed to have migrated to American shores in the second half of the eighteenth century, most likely from France and the French West Indies colony of Santo Domingo.[42] (Recall, many Scottish Masons had fled to France during political and social unrest in the seventeenth and eighteenth centuries, hence the name Scottish Rite, according to some Masonic authorities. It is possible that the Rite also was influenced by certain German [Bavaria- and Frankfurt-based] Freemasonic strands emerging in the late eighteenth century.)

By the late 1700s, the Rite had established its strongest beachheads in the South, in New Orleans and Charleston, both cities a popular refuge for French Protestants (Huguenots). Charleston also had a large, socially prominent Jewish population, whose representation on the Rite's Supreme Council was second to that of the Huguenots. Around the same time, the Rite had established footholds in New York City, Albany, Philadelphia and Boston. Its core centers would coalesce around Charleston and New York by the early 1800s.

Pike, who would emerge as the world's most powerful Freemason, joined the Scottish Rite in Charleston in March 1853. He revised its rituals between 1855 and 1857 and became a thirty-third-degree member later that year. Elected to the Supreme Council of the Scottish Rite's Southern Jurisdiction in July 1858, he ultimately became its Sovereign Grand Commander, in January 1859. (Pike would hold the supreme position until his death, in 1891. Highly revered by the Scottish Rite, he is interred in the House of the Temple headquarters in Washington, D.C.) Coincidentally, Pike's confirmation as a Supreme Council member came a few days after the mysterious death—possibly the result of a slow-acting poison—of prominent Supreme Council member John A. Quitman in Mississippi.

The enigmatic six-foot-two, three-hundred-pound Masonic scholar from Little Rock had become the intellectual *sine qua non* of the inner temple of the powerful fraternal order. That said, neither the Supreme Council (Southern Jurisdiction) nor Pike as its Sovereign Grand Commander spoke for all Freemasonry or controlled all Masons. Although influential, the Scottish Rite and its elite could not dictate rules or policy for regional or state Grand Lodges of common, or craft, Freemasonry scattered throughout the nation.

Recognizing the limits of his new authority, Pike wasted no time reorganizing the Scottish Rite. No small part of this included the destruction of records. Pike is quoted in the Scottish Rite Southern Jurisdiction's chronicles as saying that all of the organization's records that are not "worthy of preservation" should be "committed to the flames."[43] He then quickly moved to consolidate control over a recalcitrant regional lodge in New Orleans. That achieved, he embarked on a grander strategy: to widen the Scottish Rite's popularity in the South and West through a revised, more alluring set of rituals. This he carried out by culling choice bits from Jewish mysticism, medieval Christian sects and even alchemy in the process of revising the initiation rites.[44]

Pike expanded the Supreme Council itself, from nine to thirty-three members, with representation from across the South, that is, from the budding Confederacy. In an April 2, 1861, address to a Supreme Council session in New Orleans, he avowed: "There is a world of significance in the fact, that this Body, which only a few short months ago was the Supreme Council, in name, for the Southern, and, in fact, for the Southern and Western Jurisdiction of the United States of America, is now the Supreme Council . . . for the Confederate States of America."[45] He went on to assert that "the convulsions which rock the outer world, severing the bonds that have heretofore tied State to State, and creating new Republics, do not shake the firm foundations of our Masonic governments and institutions." As it turned out, the long-existing dividing line between the "Northern Jurisdiction" and "Southern Jurisdiction" of the Scottish Rite would mirror the future demarcation lines between the Union, Confederacy and border states. That is, the New York–based "Northern Jurisdiction" would be neatly defined as east of the Mississippi, north of the Ohio, south of the St. Lawrence, and west of the Atlantic—precisely the settled area outside the Confederacy.

An unabashed apologist for slavery, Pike also saw to it that key supporters of the Southern cause were corralled into the Supreme Council's ranks by the fall of 1859. Most significant among his appointments to the Council in 1859 was that of Kentuckian John C. Breckinridge, who then was vice president of the United States under James Buchanan.[46]

With the onset of the Civil War, Breckinridge headed to the battlefield as a major general in the Confederate Army and then, near war's end, was called to serve under Jefferson Davis as the Confederacy's secretary of war. Like Quitman, Cushing and Pike, Breckinridge was a veteran of the Mexican War and a Scottish Rite Mason. A slaveholder, Breckinridge endorsed the doctrine of states' rights and limited federal sovereignty (his paternal grandfather, John Breckinridge of Kentucky, had been a major promoter of that doctrine with his friend and colleague, Thomas Jefferson). He did not, however, at least publicly within the uncommitted border state of Kentucky, champion secession until very late in the game. His private views might have been far less moderate.

Breckinridge, according to the pseudonymous author of *Narrative of Edmund Wright*, was a member of the Knights of the Golden Circle. The aristocratic vice president would "flaunt the emblems of treason under the nose of an imbecile president (Buchanan)," observes the author, who adds:

> John C. Breckinridge was, and still is, one of the great lights of the K.G.C. He is indebted to the Order for his nomination at Cincinnati on the Buchanan ticket, and for subsequent political advancement. While Breckinridge was vice-president of the United States, he publicly wore, in the City of Washington, the emblematic jewelry of this traitorous Order—thus shamelessly parading his treason to the Government of which he was one of the principal officers.[47]

Another damning charge against Breckinridge comes from the *New York World*'s editorial of June 1862, as quoted in Henry Conkling's (1864) *An Inside View of the Rebellion:*

> In the dark days of 1860, we had the imbecile and false-hearted Buchanan at the head of the Government; the incompetent and perfidious Cobb was ruining the public credit. The thief Floyd was transferring the public arms to the Southern States. . . . The Senate was presided over by the traitor Breckinridge and both houses of Congress swarmed with secessionists.[48]

Breckinridge would play a central role in delivering the KGC's most important prewar goal: ensuring the election of Abraham Lincoln as a "justification" for secession. The 1860 National Democratic Convention in Charleston, chaired by none other than Pike's New England mentor, Caleb Cushing, had ended in bitter acrimony and without an unchallenged front-runner candidate. Consequently, Breckinridge was put forward in a rump convention in Baltimore as a southern Democratic alternative candidate (supporting slavery's extension into the territories) to northern Democratic leader Stephen Douglas. This unprecedented move—of dividing the party in the run-up to the election—split the Democratic Party ticket at the polls and handed Lincoln, who was committed to preventing the spread of slavery, a sufficient margin in the Electoral College to take the four-party election. (Lincoln received only 40 percent of the popular vote, followed by Breckinridge and the others.)

In the election's wake, seven Deep South states seceded, from December 1860 to February 1861. It would take the firing on Fort Sumter several months later to spark the secession of the Upper South slave states. That final act toward precipitating full secession and Civil War was led by Confederate Maj. Gen. Pierre G. T. Beauregard of Louisiana, a Scottish Rite Freemason. According to *Edmund Wright,* Beauregard had tried to establish a KGC castle at West Point.[49]

But Breckinridge was not Pike's only key antebellum appointment to the Scottish Rite's Supreme Council. Howell Cobb of Georgia, the U.S. secretary of the treasury under Buchanan, was also named to the expanded thirty-three-member body.[50] This, like the Breckinridge appointment, helped bolster the KGC–Scottish Rite nexus and solidify the Council's representation beyond the confines of Charleston's city limits. Cobb, a former governor of Georgia and son of a wealthy plantation owner, came late to the secessionist table, at least in his public pronouncements. After Lincoln's election, he became an uncompromising secessionist and an eventual candidate for the presidency of the Confederacy. During his tenure in the Buchanan cabinet, Cobb was believed to have aided the KGC by helping funnel funds out of the U.S. Treasury on the eve of the Civil War.[51] Cobb, perhaps the most powerful member of Buchanan's cabinet, would, like Pike and Breckinridge, become a Confederate general.

Perhaps Pike's biggest pre–Civil War coup—and one that certainly contributed to his initial postwar exclusion from presidential amnesty—was recruiting the Cherokee and other Indian nations to the Confederate and KGC cause.[52] As the chief Scottish Rite Mason in Arkansas in the 1850s, Pike had included Indian Territory in the Arkansas "Grand Consistory of the Thirty-Second Degree" under his direct control. He then went on to establish numerous Scottish Rite lodges among the various displaced tribes living in Indian Territory. Moreover, on the eve of the Civil War, Pike initiated several tribal leaders into the advanced thirty-second degree of the Rite. One of these high-level initiates, a Cherokee leader from Little Rock, Elias Boudinot, was invited to serve as secretary of the Arkansas Secession Convention in March 1861.

Pike had long been fascinated by Native American culture. Polyglot that he was, the expatriate New Englander eventually learned how to communicate with members of the Western Nations in their native tongues (complementing his fluent French and working knowledge of Greek, Latin, Hebrew and Sanskrit). Before settling in Arkansas in 1832, Pike had traveled as a member of a trading party through what is now New Mexico, Texas and Oklahoma—meeting Choctaw, Cherokee, Creeks, Chickasaw and Seminole along the way. Once established in Arkansas, he developed an abiding affinity for the so-called Five Civilized Tribes, an estimated fifty thousand Native Americans forced by the U.S. government into Indian Territory from homelands in the East. He would regularly embark on camping and hunting excursions with tribe members; and, as a bar-certified lawyer by 1835, he began to focus his Little Rock–based practice on advocating Indian rights before Congress.

In particular, Pike pressed for federal payment of claims due for Indian lands that had been confiscated earlier in the nineteenth century. He obtained a six-figure settlement for the Creeks and went on to win other important suits and financial rewards for the aggrieved tribes. In securing one of those payments—$500,000 for the Choctaw—Pike obtained Vice President Breckinridge's backing to let him name members of the Senate conference committee deciding the fate of the payment.[53] Breckinridge, at the time, had recently been named a member of the Scottish Rite Supreme Council by Pike.

Successful lobbying for slave-holding Indian tribes proved lucrative for Pike, and it helped the KGC and the Confederacy on many levels. First, he would earn substantial fees (paid mostly in gold coin) that could be put toward future unnamed causes. As biographer Robert L. Duncan noted: "One of the still unsolved mysteries in the life of Albert Pike concerns the $190,000 received" for his prosecution of the Indian claims.[54] "For the times, this was a staggering fortune, and there is no record that Pike invested it or paid off debts with it."

Second, Pike would win the enduring respect and admiration of several Indian nations (for whom he acted as paymaster in disbursing hundreds of thousands of dollars in gold-coin payments) that would later side with the Confederacy. Such an alliance, bolstered by trained Indian cavalry units, would provide a buffer against Union use of Indian Territory as a staging ground for raids against his adopted home of Arkansas and its huge Confederate neighbor, Texas.

Finally, Pike would secure an important position within the Confederacy. Beginning in March 1861, he would be appointed Confederate commissioner to the Indian tribes, then commander of the Department of Indian Territory, and, ultimately, brigadier general in charge of Indian troops fighting for the Confederate States of America. (As it turned out, an untested Brigadier General Pike would be harshly criticized for the mismanagement of his Native American brigade at the March 1862 battle of Pea Ridge, Arkansas. This high-level censure—over accusations of scalping and mutilations by his troops—contributed to his resignation from the Rebel army in late 1862, after little more than a year of service. Pike, who quickly condemned the scalpings, somehow managed to avoid court-martial over the Confederate debacle at Pea Ridge, perhaps through the good offices of his friend, Jefferson Davis.)

Despite personal setbacks in his official role in the Confederate Army, Pike cemented a broad strategic alliance—and long-lasting friendships— with important elements from each of the Five Civilized Tribes. Once again, the KGC's cryptic symbols provide a marker. An article in the August 29, 1861 edition of the *Arkansas True Democrat* describes Pike's presentation of two symbolic flags to the principal chiefs of the Creeks and Seminoles.[55] The "Confederate" flags comprised "a *crescent* and a *red star* [italics added] in a green union and upright bars of red and white for the Creeks, and the same for the Seminoles, with the exception of diagonal bars," the article said.

In pro-slavery alliance treaties undertaken for the Confederacy, Pike secured for the tribes significant autonomy and economic rights far beyond what the Nations had enjoyed from Washington. These alliances, still secretly active after the war in federal no-man's land (that is, in Indian Territory, which remained virtually lawless for decades), would play an important role for the postwar KGC.

Pike's alliance with Chief Stand Watie was crucial. A "Confederate" Cherokee leader who would fight under CSA officers Pike, Thomas Hindman, Benjamin McCulloch and Sterling Price, Watie emerged as a feared hit-and-run cavalry raider in Indian Territory, Arkansas, Missouri and Texas. The hard-charging warrior would become a brigadier general in 1864, making him the only Native American to achieve the rank of general in the Confederate Army. It was during that year that Watie executed two stunningly successful raids—the capturing of the federal supply steamship *J. R. Williams* on the Arkansas River in June; and, a few months later, the seizing of a Union supply train carrying an estimated $1.5 million worth of matériel. These bold ambushes of federal convoys would foreshadow the postwar KGC's activities. Small coincidence that Price, Watie's highly respected Confederate Army commander, was, according to the 1864 Holt Report, the KGC's operational leader on the trans-Mississippi Western front.[56]

Through Pike, Watie had become a thirty-second-degree Scottish Rite Mason just before the outbreak of hostilities. As war approached, the mixed-blood Cherokee leader signaled his readiness to join the Rebel ranks far beyond any other Indian Nation leader. His early, staunchly pro-South position had challenged the majority will of the full-blood "Pin" Cherokees under the leadership of Chief John Ross, who initially sought to remain neutral and to protect Cherokee sovereignty. Following a series of Confederate victories at the beginning of the war, the entire Cherokee nation under Ross signed an alliance treaty with the Confederacy, thereby joining, in October 1861, the other four Civilized Tribes in the secessionist cause. Those treaties maintained that Indian troops were to be used only to defend Indian Territory itself. However, to Pike's consternation, that would not be the case: Confederate Indian troops were soon deployed outside the territory's borders, by orders from Richmond.

Significantly, Watie's minority faction of Cherokees—mostly wealthy, educated, English-speaking slave owners who had intermarried with southern, mostly Scots, whites—had readily adopted the name "Knights of the Golden Circle" by March 1861. No doubt, this southern, pro-slavery Cherokee army—the Cherokee Mounted Rifles—was a direct product of Pike's handmaiden role.

When Watie, a veteran of more than twenty major battles, belatedly surrendered in late June 1865, in the Choctaw capital of Doaksville along the Arkansas border of Indian Territory, his Indian Brigade had no arms and munitions. Had Watie hidden his braves' guns, bullets and cash in the underground depositories of the Knights of the Golden Circle? Indian Territory, as it turned out, would serve as a prime burial ground for KGC caches.[57]

Pike—through Scottish Rite connections in Charleston, Little Rock, Washington, Louisville, New Orleans, Nashville, Atlanta, Natchez and Indian Territory—had established a powerful, hidden network of KGC operatives. While a dispersed network of discreet partisans was a necessary condition for success, it was not sufficient. He needed to build a secret organizational infrastructure that allowed for ultimate impact with maximum command, control and communication capabilities. This he achieved through a Masonic-based ritual of initiation.

After resigning from the Confederate Army, Pike sequestered himself in a remote part of the Ouachita Mountains, called Greasy Cove, in west-central Arkansas. There, in a two-storied house along the Little Missouri River, he maintained a hermit-like existence with his extensive library, beginning in the spring of 1863. Ostensibly, he had retreated from society to continue the revision of the Scottish Rite rituals. Could it be that he was devising a greater, more carefully considered plan for the KGC and its budding underground network of hidden depositories?

Various local legends existed at the time (and continue to this day) about what Pike was doing in the cabin next to Little Missouri Falls. Rumors swirled about a substantial amount of gold that he supposedly had brought with him. Whether at the hands of Union marauders or simply of greedy interlopers, Pike's place eventually became the target of a raid. "Believing he had a trunk full of gold hidden there, the marauders laid plans to rob and kill him," writes Pike biographer Walter Lee Brown.[58] "But Pike was warned, so the story goes, by a neighbor's son and managed to escape in the dead of the night with his money and most of his valuable papers and books." Pike is said to have paid his informants, friends from nearby Caddo Gap, with a handful of gold coins before fleeing in a horse-drawn buggy.

If Pike's real mission in Greasy Cove was to develop new codes and protocols for the inner temple of the KGC, it might have been in response to damaging exposés that had started to appear in the pro-Union press by late 1861.[59] No doubt, the secret order's tried-and-tested subversion methods were still largely intact and troublesome to the North: they simply may have required new types of camouflage in the later and, for the South, more desperate stages of the war. As the author of *Narrative of Edmund Wright* observed in 1864: "Who conveys in untranslatable cipher or cunningly devised hieroglyphics information to our Southern foe of our plans and movements?"[60] With Pike at work refining "new" rituals for his beloved Scottish Rite, could he not also have been overlaying those new rituals—codes, hieroglyphics, passwords, grips, insignia and organizational structure—on the highly transmutable KGC?

If one knows where to look, numerous overlaps can be found between the abstruse symbols and language of the super-secret KGC and those of the Scottish Rite. The KGC seal as discovered among Bickley's possessions consists of a Maltese cross with an eight-pointed gold star affixed in the center, all circumscribed by a narrow golden circle adorned with sixteen small points. That badge compares closely with the far more ornate "Scottish Rite jewel belonging to [the Rite's] Grand Commander, Albert Pike," with the exception of the "jewel's" inner star being a bit larger and having nine points, and its outer circle taking the form of a snake biting its tail.[61] The author of *Narrative of Edmund Wright* observed a Confederate officer wearing the KGC seal into battle at Antietam: "Among the marks of his rank, there sparkled a strange jewel, a golden serpent coiled in a circle, and crested with jet enamel. The eyes of the serpent were formed of beautiful diamonds, that fired and sparkled with every movement of the wearer. The ornament conveys no riddle. . . . The coil was a golden circle. What more simple: Knight of the Golden Circle!"[62] A fiery image of a "Golden Serpent" figures prominently in the dark, closeted initiation ceremony of the KGC, as do human skeletons, according to the narrative in *Edmund Wright*.[63]

And there are other parallels between KGC symbolism and that of advanced-degree Freemasonry. The circle on the floor of the Masonic lodge is replicated on the floors of the KGC castle; the skull-and-bones designation of a Master Mason ("a brother to pirates and corsairs") appears as one of the most widely observed KGC symbols in the literature; the term "chivalry," a lofty epithet at the time for members of the KGC, most likely derives from Knights Templar associations within the Scottish Rite. Then there are the KGC's symbols of the five-pointed star, the crescent moon and the radiant sun. All figure prominently in a "Masonic Chart of the Scottish Rite," dated 1874, on display at the Scottish Rite Museum of Our National Heritage, in Lexington, Massachusetts.[64] Atop the enormous bronze doors leading into the Scottish Rite's Southern Jurisdiction headquarters in Washington sits an ornate sunburst sculpture.

The author of the revealing 1861 *Exposition*, which contains a vivid illustration of the radiant sun and other key symbols adorning the interior of a KGC castle, described the symbols he encountered inside:

> The symbols were a large bronzed crescent, or new moon, set with fifteen stars; a large temple, under the dome of which shone a beautiful representation of the noon-day sun, and around the corona of which were fixed fifteen stars. To these were added the skull and cross-bones. Now for the language of the symbols: The crescent represents the growing Southern Confederacy; the temple, with its glowing sun and fifteen stars, foreshadows the glorious "sunny South" under the benign influence of a fully

matured Southern Government, extending its borders through Cuba, Mexico and Central and South America; the skull and cross-bones signify death to all "Abolitionists" and opposers of Southern Independence.[65]

For Pike and others at the pinnacle of the KGC's pyramid-shaped organizational structure, Scottish Rite Freemasonry offered the KGC more than a matrix of relationships, rituals and symbols. Importantly, it provided a tiered power structure that rigorously channeled information and ensured fierce loyalty, both among rank-and-file and higher-degree Scottish Rite fraternal brothers. In such a conspiracy, the fully informed elite could pass instructions on to cells of obedient, ill-informed foot soldiers. As Thomas P. Kettell, author of the 1866 *History of the Great Rebellion,* observed: "the Knights of the Golden Circle, having for its primary object the extension and defense of slavery, was organized; and several degrees, as in the Masonic order, were open to the aspirant for high rank in it. To the initiated of the highest rank only was the whole plot revealed, and the others, with but an imperfect idea of its purposes, were employed to further its designs."[66] Adds I. Winslow Ayer, author of *The Great North-Western Conspiracy,* written around the same time: "Upon this ingenious plan the vast body and mass of the Order simply held the relation of probationary membership, until they were rendered competent through the educational capacity of the society, to advance into full fellowship with its diabolical design."[67]

Such observations must not be taken to mean that all Masons active in the Civil War flocked to the Confederacy and the KGC. In fact, some three hundred generals or high-ranking officers were Masons—some Union, some Confederate. What is significant is that the advanced form of selective Masonry known as the Ancient and Accepted Scottish Rite, particularly its Southern Jurisdiction's Supreme Council under Pike, moved away from its apolitical role and toward engagement with pro-South ideals and pro-South political and military figures. Ultimately, it moved into engagement with the underground Confederate Army, the KGC, and may well have been the controlling body.

On the other hand, lower-degree or "Blue Lodge" Masonry took pains before the outbreak of the war to remain nonpartisan and to plead on a local level to preserve the Union—as Masonic historian Allen E. Roberts points out in his *House Undivided: The Story of Freemasonry and the Civil War.*[68]

By late 1863, the designs of Pike and the KGC were twofold: to continue to strive for Southern independence by helping to defeat the North on the battlefield, and to prepare, simultaneously, for a future conflagration, post–Abraham Lincoln, if they lost the rebellion then under way.

Yet, Lincoln—the presidential candidate whose election the KGC had secretly supported as a tripwire for secession—had proved himself a most worthy political and military opponent. With victories secured by his generals at Gettysburg and Vicksburg—and with considerable advantages in matériel, a national banking network, nearly $500 million in federally guaranteed greenbacks, mass-assembly production and rail-based logistical lines of supply and communication—Lincoln stood to win not only another victory at the polls but also an outright victory in the trenches.

As a visionary leader whose primary goals were to preserve the Union and then, later, to improve the Union by abolishing slavery, Lincoln seemed to recognize the challenge posed by the KGC and its terrorism and subversion. Certainly, the beleaguered president had been warned early and directly. Here, some early correspondence is revealing. In the Abraham Lincoln Papers at the Library of Congress can be found three prescient letters. The first, dated April 18, 1861, is from Robert Bethell, a Philadelphia resident and friend of Lincoln's secretary of war, Simon Cameron:

> Allow me to suggest to your excellency the propriety of using a portion of the secret service money placed at your disposal to discover the parties connected with a secret Society called the Knights of the Golden Circle. There are strong suspicions of their existence in this City—I am informed Wm B Mann Esqr. District Attorney of this City entertains the like opinions with myself as the existence of such a combination among us . . .[69]

Several months later, Lincoln received a lengthy letter from expatriate Samuel T. Glover warning of KGC plans to absorb a long-unstable and vulnerable Mexico—as well as "the whole of Central and parts of South America"—to expand a "slavocracy."[70] Glover urged Lincoln to make a strong stand against such a plot. Then, on April 9, 1862, the president received a personal letter from Union army officer Thomas Ewing, who charged that "strong doubts are entertained about [General George B.] McClellan's loyalty." The letter from Ewing, who avers that McClellan is "either false or strangely incompetent" on the battlefield, raises the startling possibility that Lincoln's top commander, the head of the Army of the Potomac, was a KGC inductee:

> I have lately heard a report, for some time current in Cincinnati, that [William L.] Yancey, while there in the fall of 1860, inducted McClellan a Knight of the Golden Circle—This may be true, or not; but if true it explains fully what was otherwise inexplicable—namely his persistent inaction—the knowledge by the enemy in advance of every contemplated movement, and at last, his generous permission to the enemy to abandon Manassas & retire to a better line of defence, without the loss of even a baggage wagon . . .[71]

Moreover, the author of the 1861 *Exposition* had described the seriousness of the KGC threat in those early months of the conflict: "The designs of the order . . . threaten not only the subsequent ruin and destruction of the American Republic but menace the happiness and well-being of every neighborhood north of Mason and Dixon's line. . . ."[72] The unnamed scribe went on to warn that America's democratically elected form of government was threatened by seditious men attempting to replace it with an oligarchy run by plantation owners, a fact few history books have emphasized in describing the North-South divide: "The American Government is now threatened by an enemy far more dangerous than any it has hitherto contended with. All the foreign powers of the world combined would not be so much to be dreaded as the internal foe we now have to contend with."[73]

Lincoln would take numerous dramatic measures to uphold the supremacy of the Constitution. These included the arrests of more than fifteen thousand civilians—part of a coordinated effort to snuff out the KGC in the North. While these actions surely helped to achieve ultimate Union victory on the battlefield, they may not have been enough to protect the president's life. Francis Wilson put it well in his 1929 analysis, *John Wilkes Booth: Fact and Fiction of Lincoln's Assassination:*

> As was proved, Lincoln was capable of taking care of the Nation: the Nation however, was culpably weak in taking care of him. Lincoln was a fatalist and felt it useless to guard against something that must happen. This helped him readily to disregard things in connection with his personal safety. He would go about from the White House to the War Office at

night, or to the Soldiers' Home, close to Washington, with but a single guard and quite often unaccompanied.[74]

Lincoln's politico-military countermeasures certainly were not enough to eradicate the KGC, which had gone completely underground by the end of 1863. In one of the most prescient—and most overlooked— examinations of the political landscape of the period, the author of the 1861 *Exposition* prophesied the bloody end of the Lincoln era some *four years* ahead of the first assassination of an American president:

> Members of the Inner Temple of the Knights of the Golden Circle are to be scattered all through Missouri, Kentucky, Virginia and Maryland, for the purpose of harassing and injuring the friends and soldiers of the Union in every way they can. If they can use poison successfully, they will do it . . . if they can, by false statements, so direct the movements of the United States troops as to cause them loss or defeat, they will do that. . . . But one thing above all others, some one of them is to distinguish himself for—if he can, that is—the assassination of the 'Abolition' President.[75]

John Wilkes Booth, a popular Shakespearean actor from Maryland, took up the challenge. Booth reportedly became a KGC initiate in the fall of 1860 in a "castle" in Baltimore. According to *The Great Conspiracy,* a richly detailed albeit anonymous account from 1866, the high-strung thespian took the vows of the KGC in a room adorned with portraits of Confederate leaders Jefferson Davis and Stephen Douglas, and a bust of John C. Calhoun.[76] There, according to the book's opening pages, the zealous Confederate sympathizer swore to "risk all to help Southern Independence," as well as to end "Yankee domination" and to "resort to all means, underneath the canopy of the heavens, to carry out these ends."[77] Booth, who had plotted to abduct Abraham Lincoln before his 1861 inauguration and then again to kidnap the president in March and early April 1865, most likely planned and carried out the assassination on his own initiative with the support of a handful of paid followers.

It is possible that Booth—whose only formal role for his beloved "secesh" cause was running quinine and other medicines behind enemy lines—acted at the request or silent encouragement of others far more powerful than he in a general plot to destabilize the government in Washington during the final phases of the war. The anonymous author of *The Great Conspiracy* tells of a KGC meeting in Richmond in early 1865 that Booth allegedly attended. Booth was a Richmond resident at the time, a fairly well-known member of the city's theater company. While in that Richmond castle meeting, and without ever identifying himself, Booth reportedly spoke about a mortal blow to Lincoln being planned. The head of the KGC cell took no position other than to say that if such a "daring deed" were to happen and its perpetrator were to escape uninjured, then the KGC would need to "treat him as a friend and brother" and "extend all possible facilities" for safe passage.[78]

Izola Forrester, who claimed to be Booth's granddaughter, quotes family associates as saying that the president's assassin was a member of the KGC castle in Baltimore.[79] Forrester, in her well-researched *This One Mad Act* exposé of 1937, makes the following dramatic comment in the preface: " . . . after forty years of ceaseless research to find new material and verify reports and rumors, I have come to the following conclusions . . . *that Lincoln's assassination was instigated by men high in the order of the Knights of the Golden Circle, said to have been a branch of Freemasonry, flourishing in the North as well as in the South.*" [Italics added.][80]

A staunch supporter of slavery and the Confederate cause (although never one to take up the Rebel uniform), Booth positively did *not* act alone when he mortally wounded Lincoln at Ford's Theater, just after ten o'clock on the evening of April 14, 1865. Numerous articles, essays and books have been written on just who was behind the Lincoln assassination and what their motives might have been. One of the best-researched recent volumes, *Come Retribution: The Confederate Secret Service and the Assassination of Abraham Lincoln,* sets out the case for direct Confederate government support of the Lincoln assassination plot, primarily through Booth's links to senior Confederate secret service agents operating from Canada.[81] Somewhere along the line, Booth's mission changed from kidnapping Lincoln and using him as supreme bargaining leverage (for prisoner exchange and/or strategic goals) to murdering the president. But whether Booth made that decision himself may never be known.

Judah P. Benjamin, who late in the war served as Confederate spymaster, is believed to have funneled funds to a bank used by Booth in Montreal before the assassination. Earlier in the war, according to a leading Confederate political figure from Virginia, Alexander Hugh Holmes Stuart, Benjamin had placed a deposit equivalent to three million British pounds-sterling in a London bank for use by KGC operatives in Canada.[82] U.S. Secretary of State William Henry Seward, following the assassination and the coordinated attempt on his own life, reportedly said that he believed that Booth and his direct accomplice, John Surratt, had conferred with Benjamin about the plot.[83] Seward believed that Benjamin had encouraged and subsidized the plan but had not discussed it with any other member of the Confederate cabinet. Whether or not it was an acknowledgment by Benjamin of complicity, the former U.S. Senator from Louisiana was the only high-level Confederate exile not to return to the United States after the war: he elected to spend his remaining years as a high-paid lawyer in London. Before his flight from Richmond with Jefferson Davis, John C. Breckinridge and other ranking members of the Confederate government, Benjamin reportedly burned all documents related to the Confederacy's secret service—and, most likely, its KGC and "Copperhead" links, including, one could imagine, those to Booth.[84]

Solving the Lincoln conspiracy is not the purpose, or within the scope, of this book. Suffice it to say that some federal government insiders believed that Booth and his small band of Lincoln-assassination co-conspirators were KGC operatives. How else to explain that official Washington turned immediately to Maj. Henry Lawrence Burnett to prosecute the "co-conspirators" tied to the assassination plot, four of whom were hanged. At their trial in military court, in which Judge Advocate General Joseph Holt (author of the Holt Report on the KGC) presided as chief judge, the defendants were repeatedly probed about their knowledge and possible involvement in the Knights of the Golden Circle by Burnett, who by then had been promoted to colonel.

Burnett hitherto had been a little-known lawyer in the Union army. But his life would change late in the war when he was assigned to lead the government's case in two high-profile treason trials involving alleged KGC members, the first in Indianapolis and the second in Cincinnati. He was making closing arguments as judge advocate in the Cincinnati trial against Confederate spy and KGC operative Thomas Hines (in absentia) and associated squads from bases in Canada when he received the urgent call to investigate the murder of the president.[85]

For his part, Burnett, who ultimately would be promoted to major general, had won convictions against KGC subversives in the earlier treason trials. His success at the Lincoln trial seemed preordained, at least when it came to the lesser bit players in the conspiracy. It should be noted that Jefferson Davis (who had been labeled a KGC member, despite his comparatively moderate stance on secession, in various exposés during the war) was also named one of ten co-conspirators in the Lincoln murder plot. The same was true of the mysterious George Sanders: a former colleague of Caleb Cushing in the Pierce administration and comrade of Hines in running KGC operations in Canada. Historian James D. Horan depicts Sanders as one who seemed to be "pulling wires . . . to manipulate the actions of the Confederate agents."[86] Sanders, prior to the war, had been the leader of the territorial-expansionist "Young America" movement, which attracted the likes of Pike and Bickley and was allied with European radical movements led by Giuseppe Mazzini.

More than 135 years after Lincoln's murder, the notion that a Confederate underground may have facilitated the assassination plot is gaining support. In his recently published *Blood on the Moon: The Assassination of Abraham Lincoln*, Lincoln biographer Edward Steers, Jr. observes:

> Booth also benefited greatly from the Confederate leadership in Richmond. Whether he was an agent of that leadership or simply a beneficiary can be debated. But in putting together his plans to strike at Lincoln, Booth was aided by key members of the Confederate underground at every step. After [Lincoln's] capture turned to assassination, that same Confederate apparatus used all of its resources to help Booth in his attempt to escape. If it had not been for key members of the Confederate underground, Booth would never have made his way as far as he did or for as long as he did.[87]

The Postwar KGC

With Lee's surrender and Lincoln's murder coming in quick succession in the spring of 1865, the country would hold its collective breath. The fog of war would linger for several more months before the traumatized nation began to make tentative steps toward reconciliation and reunion.

Yet, despite or perhaps because of such steps, sentiments of revenge and retribution boiled below the Mason-Dixon line. Die-hard rebels within the KGC's highest echelons were determined to see the Confederacy rise again: at the proper time and choosing. For Albert Pike and other "inner sanctum" leaders of the Knights—now in exile in Canada, England or Mexico, with some operating under deep cover in Nashville and elsewhere in the South—there were two burning issues. The first was how to maintain the order's underground operations as the hated Radical Reconstruction regime was imposed; the second was how to protect their hidden hoards of gold, silver and munitions scattered across the South and West.

Pike had a more immediate and personal postwar problem—his status as an American citizen. At war's end, he had been excluded from President Andrew Johnson's general amnesty granted to Confederate soldiers and officials. He also faced an indictment for treason for his responsibility in the scalping-and-mutilation massacre at Pea Ridge. Ultimately, he turned to some well-placed Scottish Rite underlings to help see him through his exclusion from the amnesty rolls.

Certainly, Pike had well-placed friends. As the incoming Supreme Council leader before the outbreak of war, he had appointed a leading Scottish Rite Mason in Washington, D.C., Benjamin French, to the Council. French had served as personal secretary to President Franklin Pierce, and thus was in close contact with Pike's friend, Caleb Cushing, the activist attorney general at the time. A deft Washington operator who had worked the floor of the 1860 Democratic Convention for Cushing, French would later become commissioner of public buildings in Washington. A year after Appomattox, French and a group of other prominent Scottish Rite Masons met with Johnson inside the White House and secured a presidential pardon for Pike, at the same time conferring several advanced Scottish Rite degrees on the president himself.[88] The stage was set for the next phase of KGC inspired subversion.

At this point, it is worth recalling the KGC's modus operandi *during* the war. In the North, where the order was vulnerable to penetration by federal moles, it had operated semi-publicly through front organizations and frontmen, such as Bickley and Vallandigham. These Northern-based above-ground operations provided a protective buffer for the KGC's inner core, operating out of the South, as they did for various clandestine missions in the North and West. An argument can be made that the *postwar* KGC rooted in the Deep South deliberately unleashed the Knights of the Ku Klux Klan (KKK) for the same purposes: to sabotage and distract at the same time. A core goal was to achieve certain out-in-front political ends: the destabilization of Reconstruction through repeated acts of intimidation and terrorism against newly emancipated blacks and

Republican officials. Yet, in the likely event that KKK members got caught, the KGC could remain invisible, that is, logistically and legally out of reach of government troops, prosecutors and the news media. The Klan, with its provocative white-robed regalia, would serve as an expedient militant arm of the KGC but also, longer-term, would act to deflect any potential crackdown on the KGC's continuing subsurface operations, now that the "oppressive" mechanisms of federal government had been "imposed" throughout the former Confederacy.

There can be little doubt that the hidden KGC spawned the original KKK. Ample circumstantial evidence supports this. There is the ever-important symbolic trail and the persistent whiff of a familiar modus operandi. Here a noted scholar of Masonic history, John J. Robinson, writing about the origins of the KKK in his *Born in Blood: The Lost Secrets of Freemasonry*, provides insight:

A few years later, during the War Between the States, Masonic officers and men found themselves facing their Masonic brothers on the other side. There are many Civil War legends of help rendered in response to Masonic signs of distress, but the most significant event happened just after the war was over. Angered by the erosion of their way of life and the enforced growing political power of men who had been their slaves until the war was lost, a group of Southerners decided to fight back by means of a secret society. Many of them were Freemasons, who drew upon their knowledge of Masonic rites to develop a ritualistic infrastructure for the society that was to save the South through the maintenance of white supremacy. They adopted the circle of the lodge as their formal meeting arrangement for members, named their society for it, and demonstrated their educational level by using the Greek word for "circle," which is *kuklos*. The pronunciation and spelling quickly became Ku Klux, and they styled themselves as the Knights of the Ku Klux Klan, as terms of chivalry were introduced into the ritual. The single All-Seeing Eye of Masonry became the Grand Cyclops. There were hand-signals, secret passwords, secret handgrips and recognition signals, even a sacred oath, all adapted from Masonic experience. Some Klansmen even boasted of official connections between the Klan and Freemasonry. A society that had begun as the South's only recourse against the postwar invasion of the South quickly degenerated into something else. Violence took hold, with beatings, lynchings and even torture, so it was decided by the leadership that the Klan should be disbanded. In 1869, the Grand Master and former Confederate cavalry general Nathan Bedford Forrest issued his only General Order, which was for all Klans to disband and disperse. It was too late. The general's order was ignored by many who still smarted under the humiliation of defeat in the war, and what they felt was the even greater humiliation of its aftermath. As the violence grew, and the target for Klan hatred widened in scope from blacks to Jews, to Catholics, to all foreign-born, the talk of the Masonic connection continued. Finally, state Masonic Grand Lodges in both North and South felt called upon to declare publicly their total rejection of the philosophy, the motives, and the actions of the Ku Klux Klan. Nevertheless, a shadow had been cast on Freemasonry. . . .[89]

What Robinson does not mention in his examination of the early Klan era is that the same descriptions largely applied to the long-extant KGC and its Scottish Rite–influenced infrastructure. What link might Albert Pike, head of the Scottish Rite for most of the latter half of the nineteenth century, have had to the original KKK, which functioned from 1865 through the 1870s? (A so-called resurrected Klan emerged in 1915, under a William Joseph Simmons, as an anti-black, anti-Jewish and anti-Catholic nationwide organization.)

In his well-documented biography of Pike, Walter Lee Brown states that there is no evidence that Pike was a member of the KKK. Yet, he writes, "one might reasonably surmise that Pike, considering his strong aversion to the Negro suffrage and his frustration at his own political impotence, would not have stood back from the Klan."[90] No doubt Pike's possible parentage or patronage of the KKK is awkward for the Southern Jurisdiction of the Scottish Rite, today the world's largest Masonic body. Membership and possible leadership of the prewar and wartime KGC is one thing: Charleston was a hotbed of secessionist sentiment and, at the same time, hosted the southern headquarters of the Scottish Rite. So, for the officially apolitical Supreme Council to have linked temporarily with the "South"—as a wartime exigency—could be explained away or, better, quietly ignored. But the question of a direct link between Pike and the post–Civil War, racist and murderous KKK was far more troubling. In a recently published analysis of the KKK's reign of terror, author Philip Dray points out that by 1892, reported lynchings of black Americans were averaging three a week "chiefly in Alabama, Arkansas, Florida, Georgia, Louisiana, Mississippi, South Carolina, Tennessee, Texas and Kentucky."[91]

The modern Scottish Rite has denied that its revered former

Supreme Commander had any involvement whatsoever with the KKK, whether as its founder or—as some have charged—as its chief judicial officer. William Fox, official historian of the Supreme Council and a thirty-third-degree Scottish Rite Freemason, addresses the subject in his recent volume, *Lodge of the Double-Headed Eagle: Two Centuries of Scottish Rite Freemasonry in America's Southern Jurisdiction.* Fox's denial is measured, not categorical. "Whether or not Albert Pike was ever involved with the Klan is a matter of conjecture. . . . Pike never admitted, nor did Forrest ever reveal, that he was a member of the notorious Ku Klux Klan. Many men came forward years later to admit their former involvement in the Klan of early Reconstruction, almost as a proud badge of honor, but Pike never said or intimated a word. He seemingly had nothing to admit because he probably had nothing to hide."[92]

Officially, Pike and his supporters could deny that he was ever a member of the KKK, precisely because of the KKK's deliberate distancing from the true hidden power, the KGC.

Still, Fox seems to be on far less solid ground when he writes: "Pike held no sympathy with nor expressed any sentiment for the Lost Cause myth. . . . Pike, even when portrayed as an authority on fraternal ritual, does not fit the profile of a rabid southern patriot."[93] But, leaving epithets like "rabid" aside, the evidence to the contrary is powerful. Pike, as part-owner and editor-in-chief of the *Memphis Daily Appeal,* wrote the following editorial in the April 16, 1868, edition:

> The disenfranchised people of the South, robbed of all the guarantees of the Constitution . . . can find no protection for property, liberty or life, except in secret association. Not in such association to commit follies and outrages; but for mutual, peaceful, lawful, self-defense. If it were in our power, if it could be effected, we would unite every white man in the South, who is opposed to Negro suffrage, into one great Order of Southern Brotherhood, with an organization complete, active, vigorous, in which a few should execute the concentrated will of all, and whose very existence should be concealed from all but its members.[94]

Pike, between the lines, has laid out what already was long under way: the hidden-government mission of the KGC, with its postwar militant arm, the KKK, serving to "protect" Southern whites from perceived injustices of federal occupation. He would go on to use the bullhorn of the *Appeal*'s editorials to defend the South's "honorable" and "just" decision to secede and would attack the "dishonoring measures of Reconstruction."

After the war, Pike settled in Memphis as a lawyer and newspaper editor. His move followed numerous months in exile in Toronto, Montreal and elsewhere in Canada. He is believed to have associated there with Confederate spy Hines, who had started studying law in Toronto after the war under Confederate exile John C. Breckinridge. Were these studies a smoke screen for the regrouping of the postwar KGC? Hines, notably, would follow Pike to Memphis and serve under him at the *Appeal*. Both Pike and Hines were probably drawn to postwar Memphis by native Tennessean and famed Confederate cavalry officer Nathan Bedford Forrest.

Before the war, Forrest had become a wealthy Memphis-based businessman, as a cotton planter and slave trader. During the war, the dashing officer was deemed by many to be the South's most brilliant tactician. But his wartime legacy would forever be marred by his actions following the April 1864 capture of Fort Pillow, in western Tennessee. There, hundreds of Union troops, most of them black infantrymen, were reportedly massacred—after surrendering—by troops under Forrest's command. While some Southern reports disputed the account—asserting that the black troops were killed defending the outpost or retreating to the nearby Mississippi River—official U.S. charges of "atrocity" and "massacre" stuck.[95]

Given Forrest's racist tendencies, it came as little surprise to official Washington that the decorated former general (a Freemason who undoubtedly was well familiar with arcane symbols and exotic regalia) would be described as the first Grand Wizard of the Klan. But Forrest refused to confirm that status during lengthy congressional hearings on the Klan in 1871.

As to the Invisible Empire's true origins, the consensus history is that a group of six restless ex-Confederates banded together in Pulaski, Tennessee, at the end of 1865 for the "entertaining" purpose of harassing newly liberated blacks. As the intimidating practice of hooded night-riding spread—and eventually led to more sinister violence against people and property throughout the South—greater Klan organization, its leaders decided, was needed. Hence, at a conclave at the Maxwell House in Nashville in 1866, the Klan turned to Forrest as its grand commander, or so the accepted history maintains.

This, however, might be nothing more than a classic KGC cover story. Forrest and other high-ranking KGC members perhaps were behind the semi-public Klan from the beginning and *expected*, if not outright *wanted*, the KKK to become a high-profile target of investigation by federal authorities. The early Klan would achieve certain short-term goals; ultimately, however, it would serve as a smoke screen, a decoy, to let the hidden, postwar KGC remain undetected once the KKK was *declared officially dead* in front of congressional panels.

The plan appeared to work. The federal government, under President Ulysses S. Grant, lost little time in descending upon the Klan: first with federal investigations launched in the late 1860s; then, a few years later, with Congress holding extensive hearings (the largest to date at the time); and, finally, with the enactment of legislation to suppress the Klan in 1871. Here is how Fox, the Scottish Rite historian, summarizes Forrest's bowing out:

> Nathan Bedford Forrest, the renowned Confederate cavalier, had resigned as Imperial Grand Wizard and officially dissolved the Klan by 1869. Forrest spent the rest of his life denouncing the remnants of the Ku Klux Klan he had tried to deactivate once the guerilla tactics had crossed over the proprieties of the order's original purpose (and began damaging, too, Forrest's own business interests in railroads and insurance). Forrest appeared before a congressional hearing in June 1871, revealing very little of the Klan's membership or secrets. In spite of his cagey evasions during the interrogation and testimony, he insisted that the organization was "broken up in 1868, and never existed since that time as an organization and [was] to be no longer countenanced."[96]

The heat was off, as far as external political-military operations were concerned. Pike, as well as Forrest and others at the helm of the postwar KGC, could now pursue the secret order's main postwar priority: the expansion of a nationwide underground network of hidden treasure and arms. Still, the purely political effort of forestalling congressionally mandated political equality for newly freed blacks would continue unabated by duly elected Deep South politicians during Reconstruction and beyond. As Columbia University historian Eric Foner astutely observes in his recently published *Who Owns History?*: "In the 1870s, as the Northern commitment to Reconstruction and the ideal of racial equality waned, Democrats regained control of one Southern state after another.

By 1877, Reconstruction had come to an end, and white supremacy had been restored throughout the old Confederacy."[97]

The KGC's Gold

Pike's mastery of secret Masonic code, its symbolism and sacred geometry (a mathematical paradigm or metaphor based on Pythagorean and Euclidian formulas and ratios) was but one factor that positioned him perfectly to take control of the design—the architectural and topographical blueprints—of the hidden Confederacy's postwar Fort Knox: a geometrically based grid of monumental ingenuity that involved hundreds of secretly coded, underground financial depositories scattered across the South and Southwest. Pike's familiarity with the rugged terrain of Arkansas, Oklahoma, Texas and New Mexico—and his familiarity with the various native cultures there—gave him the personal access that a master mapmaker and financial gatekeeper would require.

The exact sources of the KGC's gold, silver and arms are not known. As noted, some Confederate reserves had been sent by Secretary of State Judah P. Benjamin (a former English subject raised in the British West Indies) to England for safekeeping during the war. In addition, an unknown amount of precious-metal reserves (coins and bullion) may have been shipped abroad from the Confederacy's near-depleted treasury at war's end, to be secretly repatriated to KGC operatives after the war. Several hundred thousand dollars worth of gold coins and bullion, and some lesser amount of silver coins and bars, reportedly was hauled south by train out of Richmond shortly before the fighting stopped, as historian William C. Davis has noted.[98] Some part of this treasure is believed to have been used to pay straggling Confederate troops. The rest may have arrived in safe harbor in London, to be later secured and returned to the KGC by the likes of Benjamin, Breckinridge or others who fled to England after the war. As it happened, one of Benjamin's first stops in London, after a long arduous escape at sea, was an August 1865 visit to the home of Sir Frederick Pollock, lord chief baron of the exchequer (treasury).[99]

Breckinridge, who fled to Cuba via Miami in May 1865, arrived in London around the same time as Benjamin. It is not clear what his motives were, in a subsequent visit, in seeking out Confederate officials —including men, the likes of Benjamin and Sanders, who had some accounting of Confederate funds on reserve in London banks.[100] Was it, as William Davis alludes, meant to secure remaining assets to pay off outstanding Confederate debts? Or perhaps to clear up rumors of financial scandals involving expatriate Confederates? Or, was it wholly different: securing funds for repatriation into KGC coffers back home?

Another possible source of KGC funds after the war was hidden coin and precious-metal reserves from KGC coffers in Toronto, Montreal and Windsor, Canada. Historian McPherson notes that in a "secret session on February 15, 1864, the Confederate Congress appropriated $5 million" for establishing "Canadian-based sabotage operations against the North."[101] Those operations were well under way by late spring 1864.

By war's end, exiled Confederate and KGC cadres operating out of Canada under the seasoned leadership of Jacob Thompson, Clement Clay and Thomas Hines had amassed a treasury estimated at more than $2 million in gold and silver coinage.[102] These funds had been obtained in part from various wartime raids on financial institutions in New England and other parts of the Union. It stands to reason that they eventually may have been smuggled into KGC depositories inside the United States in the years immediately following the war. Moreover, ex-Confederates who fled to Mexico may have hauled some treasure back into the United States via Texas and New Mexico Territory (the latter including most of what today is Arizona).

Additional precious-metal reserves might have come into the KGC's possession from gold- and silver-mining operations owned by ex-Confederates and their sympathizers. California, to be sure, had been a hotbed of KGC agitation, particularly in the Gold Rush territories east of Sacramento. Even if the subversive organization did not own mines outright (some KGC luminaries, including Cushing and Breckinridge, held extensive mining interests in such diverse locations as Mexico, Arizona, New Mexico, California and Minnesota), KGC operatives could have resorted to "high-grading," or pilfering, from mines owned by unfriendly interests.[103] Indeed, stealing from the Union—whether from the U.S. Treasury or from Northern financial institutions, as in the raid on the St. Albans, Vermont, bank in October 1864—was central to KGC tactics before and during the war.

But by far the biggest boost to its postwar coffers likely sprang from its activities in the Wild West. Federal stagecoaches, carrying bank transfers and U.S. Army and other federal payrolls in the form of freshly minted

gold and silver coins, were easy prey to the new Western "outlaws"—
more accurately, to KGC "Knights Gallant" marauding the open plains
and mountain ranges. Their modus operandi had been spelled out by the
author of the 1861 *Exposition,* a self-avowed former KGC initiate:

> Their mission is wherever they wish to go, and their license to take what
> they can, and do as they please, except to injure or violate females or little
> children. By the "Knights Gallant," provisions are to be secured from
> Northwestern States, in case of scarcity in the South, for the Southern
> Army. All the property or money they can obtain in the course of the per-
> ambulations is to be considered Southern wealth.[104]

Among the postwar KGC "Knights Gallant" were war-hardened ex-
members of William Quantrill's guerrilla force, men on horseback who,
like Morgan's raiders in the Northwest, had worn star- and crescent-
moon lapels on their pinned-up brim hats as they had ridden into battle
in Missouri and Kansas. And there were many others who had engaged
in unconventional warfare operations for the Confederacy, much of
those in the trans-Mississippi theater. Some ten months after the war, a
group of ex-Quantrill men—led by Cole Younger—hit the Clay County
Savings Association in Liberty, Missouri. In that audacious daylight raid,
the outlaws took some $70,000 in gold, currency and bonds. In pulling
off the heist, they set a marker for their postwar style of operations.

Still, the most famous KGC outlaw of them all was a thirty-third-
degree Scottish Rite Mason, Jesse Woodson James. A former Rebel guerrilla conducting hit-and-run raids during the Civil War, Jesse W. James
would become the KGC's master field commander. Consider: the James
and Younger brothers never became rich as a gang; they never used the
booty they had stolen for personal gain. So what did they do with their
plunder? The answer, which is only now emerging, is that they systematically buried it—under a masterful grid likely devised by Pike, Cushing
and others. The system employed complex cipher, precision surveyor's
techniques, cryptic Masonic-linked inscriptions on trees and rock faces,
and a handful of bewilderingly coded maps.

The hidden caches had to be protected. They had to be guarded by
lifelong sentinels watching over them. The plan, in order to succeed,
required loyal families dedicating their lives—from generation to generation—to overseeing the treasure. And this at substantial costs and depri-

vations to the sentinels—sworn to absolute secrecy—and their often unknowing families.

As Lee had failed to bring victory to the South in its quest to maintain itself as an independent slave-holding Republic, the KGC itself had failed in its first mission of the war: to undercut the North's will to fight on. At all costs, it could not fail in its second mission: to adequately prepare for a second civil war.

Finally, it should be noted that among the last acts of the peripatetic Albert Pike were his many travels across the American South and West in the 1880s. In 1880, according to Pike biographer Walter Lee Brown, the Scottish Rite leader and former Confederate general embarked from the Scottish Rite's Southern Jurisdiction headquarters in Washington, D.C., on a 7,000-mile journey that took him through Minnesota, Iowa, Kansas, New Mexico, Colorado, Wyoming and Missouri.[105] The following year, Brown notes, Pike traveled over 12,000 miles through the Midwest, as well as to Tennessee, Arkansas, Texas, Louisiana, Mississippi, Alabama, Florida, Georgia, South Carolina, North Carolina and Virginia. Then, in 1882, he ventured to other parts of Florida, Georgia and Alabama, before heading off in the spring of 1883 to New Orleans, El Paso, New Mexico, Arizona and the Pacific Coast, from Los Angeles to San Francisco, and then on to Portland and Seattle. Finally, in the summer of 1885, Pike set out on an extensive trip to Nebraska, Missouri, Wyoming, Utah, Montana, North Dakota, Minnesota and Iowa. At the end of all this travel—ostensibly for the purpose of setting up Scottish Rite lodges—he was left "worn out and sick," according to Brown.[106] He died on April 2, 1891. One has to wonder whether Pike, the mysterious dark genius that he was, was making the rounds on the KGC's underground network of gold: making sure that the inventory was bountiful and manned by responsible sentinels.

Retracing History in the Arkansas Woods

6

WITH his discovery of the jar full of gold and silver coins, Bob Brewer had achieved his first goal: he had proved to himself that there was a rational system, a matrix of coded twists and turns, that linked disparate pieces of a puzzle scattered over many square miles—the solution to which would lead to treasure. But he wondered whether he might just have gotten lucky and stumbled upon an old pioneer's secret stash. That was a possibility, but he could not explain away that the small treasure had been found in the deep woods, directly in the midst of what he had determined to be directional markers. And these coded signposts lay along defined lines, based on compass headings that had started many miles away. Yet he knew that for his hypothesis to be scientifically valid, he had to be able to repeat the result over and over. He was confident that he could recover other, possibly larger, hoards of secret treasure. What he was unsure of was the motives of those who had buried the nineteenth-century gold and silver coins in the Arkansas mountains.

Bob felt it was time to invest in a more advanced metal detector. A friend from town, who happened to be a consultant to a company that produced sophisticated detectors, suggested that he buy a lightweight programmable system that could detect at greater depth and be used in thick brush. Bob's existing detector often proved impossible to use in the thickets of the surrounding mountains. Within days of acquiring his Garrett Master Hunter CXIII, he decided to try the new system at a few suspected cache sites, some of which had proven beyond the scope of his old device.

Topping the list was Jess "Goat" Brown's abandoned property in the wooded hills east of Hatfield. Bob had heard rumors that the eccentric Spanish-American War veteran had buried containers of gold and silver coins. Brown, a recluse and a friend of W. D. Ashcraft, had lived in a small house with an untold number of pet goats along a remote dirt road that led to the Ashcraft cabin. The colorful woodsman, who had been known to loan money to locals and demand repayment in hard currency because it had to be "reburied," died mysteriously in the 1930s. The fallow Brown homestead was decades overgrown, with no trace left of the house but a gnarled fruit-laden apple tree and an overgrown grapevine from the erstwhile orchard.

Armed with his new detecting equipment, Bob returned to the Brown site for a day of cache hunting. He was able to probe beneath the rotted, vine-entangled remains of a trellis. To his amazement, he received a strong bell tone from the detector. Reaching through vines and the disintegrated lattice with his Army entrenching tool, he recovered a pint-sized fruit jar stuffed with U.S. gold and silver coins. The gold coins, dating from 1871 to 1919, were mostly $5 and $10 pieces.

With this, his second find in eight months, he felt elated. But his delight was tempered. He recognized that this recovery was different; it had relied largely on hearsay and better technology, and seemed to have nothing to do with carved signs and symbols. It had to be placed into the seasoned hobbyists' category of lucky strike: the recreational metal detector's recovery of a "posthole bank" containing coins, jewelry or other objects of value at a place of former habitation or work. Still, this second find amounted to more than a few loose coins of recent vintage. The little bit of dizzying self-satisfaction that he allowed himself soon would interfere with his better judgment: he knew that he and Linda should keep the news to themselves, but somehow he could not resist flaunting his success in the face of one of his "competitors."

Soon after his success at Goat Brown's, Bob bumped into another Hatfield treasure hunter, Bob Smith, at McLain's. He had mixed feelings toward Robert L. "Snuffy" Smith. He viewed the older man as the shrewdest of the town's treasure-sleuthing contingent. A few years earlier, Smith had moved to Hatfield from Gillham, Arkansas, thirty miles to the south. Bob, having been introduced to Smith by his trusted lifelong friend, Bob Tilley, had shown the inquisitive newcomer some of the carvings and sites that he had been investigating. Smith reciprocated by offering to sell Bob a used metal detector for a song. Their budding friendship, however, soon hit a snag. Bob had returned to a few of the sites that he had revealed to Smith and noticed that several of the elaborate tree carvings had been defaced. Bob had known about these particular inscriptions since childhood, and their mutilation enraged him. Bringing matters to a head, he also had found several holes dug near the engraved trees. Bob decided that Smith was trying to beat him at his own game, and brazenly. The worst of it, he later learned, was that Smith had been trying to undermine some of Bob's long-standing friendships.

That morning at McLain's—for whatever reason, perhaps to show Smith that he had the upper hand when it came to *finding* treasure—Bob impulsively pulled some of the Goat Brown coins from his pocket. He walked over to Smith, who was sipping coffee at his usual spot, and rolled a few of the gold pieces onto the table. "Got lucky yesterday," he said, nonchalantly. Smith's immediate reaction was surprise, if not shock, and he started nervously rubbing his forefingers together. "Very nice," Smith responded, while fondling the coins. "Did they come from around here?" Bob said that they did and went on to relate how he had found the glass jar buried near the dirt road to Goat Brown's. The man's finger rubbing accelerated, a habit of Smith's whenever talk of gold surfaced. Smith's evident envy gave Bob a rush of satisfaction. In a small town where talk of treasure far exceeds treasure being found, and where the poseurs outnumber the pros ten to one, rivalry exists at the top. Yet, as he left the restaurant that crisp morning in December 1991, Bob knew that he had made a foolish, ego-driven mistake and that he should have kept his find to himself.

From the moment he arrived in Hatfield, Smith proved an enigma. He seemed to be a cagey hound dog hot on a scent—the scent of buried money. He had come to town looking for anyone with information about Avants Mountain. He claimed to have heard of a legendary Spanish treasure or gold mine supposedly located there. That query led to Bob Tilley, one of the oldest surviving descendants of the Avants line in town and a close family friend of the Brewers. Tilley, a former logger and retired Polk County employee, is the great-grandson of John Avants, who, at the Civil War's conclusion, had homesteaded on acreage that came to be known as Avants Mountain, some twenty miles east of Hatfield.

As it turned out, Goat Brown, Will Ashcraft and Isom Avants (John's grandson) were close friends who lived in the Shady-Brushy Creek area along Brushy's main east-west dirt road. Grandpa and Odis Ashcraft occupied the middle ground; Brown lived on the western access point into the valley; and the Avantses on the eastern end. The north and south entrance points, along the other access road, were where W. D. Ashcraft's son, Nooks, and his son-in-law, Dan Lawrence, lived. Any outsider would have had a hard time driving into Brushy Valley and Smoke Rock Mountain undetected. The Ashcrafts were known to pass emergency signals through the hills by blowing through hollowed-out cattle horns—"coon hunting" horns, in the local vernacular.

Smith initially told Tilley that he was a "flea-market" vendor and wanted to detect around the abandoned Avants homestead to find "junk metal." Tilley called Smith's bluff: "You're a treasure hunter and there ain't no Spanish mine on Avants Mountain, period."[1] When Tilley explained that others had come fishing for similar information, the two shared a good laugh. They soon struck up a longer conversation that eventually led to a treasure-hunting partnership and to Smith's buying a small farm near the Tilleys' house on the outskirts of town.

What specifically had drawn Smith to Hatfield in the late 1980s was an article that he had read by a local Hatfield treasure seeker and history buff, George A. Mitchell. In the December 1969 issue of *Frontier Times,* a magazine of Western Americana, Mitchell wrote a piece, "Twin Springs Spanish Gold."[2] The article described a site in the Ouachita National Forest, where a series of old beech trees were inscribed with cryptic carvings: a snake, turtle, crescent moon and a horseshoe among the dozen or so symbols. "The carvings on the beech trees could provide a clue to some serious-minded treasure hunter and perhaps eventually lead him to the resting place of the golden horde [sic]," Mitchell wrote.

The Twin Springs legend, according to Mitchell's article, originated with talk of Spaniards having buried "seven burro loads of precious metal" near the riverbank and near a spring after being attacked by Indians. The legend held that a stranger appeared more than a century later in nearby Shady, Arkansas, at the homestead of John Avants and his seven sons. He was searching for a landmark "twin springs" that would lead him to a "vast amount of treasure." When the Avants family said that they had no idea about the site's whereabouts, the stranger left. But, as Mitchell wrote, some of the Avants sons eventually found the "twin springs" with the inscribed beech bark nearby. Two of John Avants's grandsons—Isom and Ed—eventually showed Mitchell some of the carvings in trees that were still alive. (Mitchell, who had moved to Hatfield in search of treasure himself in the 1960s, died shortly after Bob had arrived with his family from Key West. From the one brief meeting that he had with Mitchell, on a visit in 1975, Bob was impressed with the man's knowledge of the area and of other treasure sites in Texas and Arizona.)

Tilley, a nephew of Isom Avants, had known Bob Brewer since the two were kids. A few years older, Tilley mostly had spent time with Bob's older brother, Jack. But, since Bob's return from military service, the two Bobs had become close friends. They shared an interest in local history, treasure lore and treasure hunting, and they seemed to have a common heritage: Isom Avants and Grandpa Ashcraft were the closest of friends, and partners in some obscure enterprise. That enterprise seemed to be related to "mining," for the old-timers shared numerous "mining claims" in the heart of the Ouachitas.

Because Tilley held a regular weekday job, he and Bob hunted treasure on weekends only. On one outing in late 1989, Tilley told Bob about his new treasure-hunting buddy, Bob Smith, and said that he would like to introduce the newcomer. The "Three Bobs" hit it off, initially, and Bob and Tilley both showed Smith many of the tree signs they had encountered over the years.

Curiously, Smith was all ears and no talk. Other than calling the signs "Spanish," not once did he offer any interpretation about what he had seen and, ultimately, photographed. It was not just his sponge-like behavior that unsettled Bob and Tilley: Smith, on the trail, acted as if he were paranoid. He constantly spoke of people "tailing him," of incessant remote "surveillance" of his outings into the forest. Never would he venture out without his miniature electronic eavesdropping headset. And he always insisted on taking someone else's vehicle because his was "bugged with a tracking device."

The two Hatfield locals did not know what to make of the outsider's rantings and they laughingly brushed them aside. Smith's anxieties, Bob thought at first, could be dismissed as eccentricities and therefore could be overlooked.

But he was not able to ignore Smith's subsequent moves: "backtrailing" by four-wheel drive to the sites, defacing clues, digging around the clue sites and then having the audacity to tell Tilley that he suspected "Brewer" of having done it all!

Bob had begun to sense a bigger problem when he learned from Tilley that Smith was complaining about his bringing along a camera and then a video recorder on the hunt. When Tilley subsequently revealed that

Smith also had been badmouthing Bob about a defaced tree sign, Bob blew his top. What Tilley did not know at that point was that Bob had already confronted Smith about the defaced sign. Smith, of course, had denied any such vandalism. As it was, on his reconnaissance mission back to the site, Bob had seen tracks from Smith's pickup but did not bother to go further in making the point to Smith. He had already sworn off the outsider.

What most disturbed Bob was that Tilley seemed to have come under the schemer's spell. His lifelong friend was snubbing him for the first time. Tilley, in turn, had become so fed up with both Smith's bad-mouthing and Bob's subsequent protestations that he decided to stop treasure hunting with either one. It was around this time that Bob had run into Smith at McLain's and rolled the gold coins in front of his nose.

In the weeks after his encounter with Smith at the coffee shop, Bob invited another lifelong friend, Don Fretz, to go treasure hunting. Although he preferred to cache hunt alone into the Ouachitas, he knew that it was best to have someone along who knew the terrain. Over the next month, he gave Fretz a crash course in interpreting some of the treasure signs and bent-tree formations used as line markers. Fretz proved a quick study. He was grateful for the pointers and hoped that his miserable treasure hunting luck might soon change.

As soon as Smith caught wind of these outings, he made his move. He ingratiated himself with Fretz and repeated what he had done with Tilley: drive a wedge between the two locals using the same self-serving tactics. Before Bob knew it, Fretz and Smith were hunting together, and Bob's old friend would hardly speak to him.[3]

Smith worked fast. Within weeks of learning from Bob about the origins of the Goat Brown stash, he found out everything he could from Hatfield residents about Brown's abandoned property. One had even drawn him a map, showing the general location of a few rocked-up springs on the forested site.

Soon thereafter, Smith approached Fretz at McLain's and asked the experienced local if he could help scout a few trails around the old Jess Brown property. The two headed out, and Fretz found the area with little problem. At the time, Fretz had no idea that Bob had found a jar stuffed with gold coins on the homesite and that Smith knew about the recovery. When Fretz found one of the springs drawn on the local's map, he noticed that a giant bent-knee marker tree was pointing directly at the spot. The disfigured oak was a near copy of one of the deformed trees that Bob recently had shown him. To his astonishment, he saw two other oaks in the distance with unnaturally curved trunks—each pointing a separate marker line toward the spring. He recalled Bob having said that two or, even better, three marked lines converging at a point could indicate a hot zone.

When Fretz activated his metal detector and surveyed along a ten-yard radius from the spring, he received a strong electronic response to the east. The echo, he soon discovered, came from a horse-bridle bit buried just a few inches under the surface. Moving in the direction indicated by the rusted bit, toward the spring, Fretz was wholly unprepared for the loud signal he received a foot behind the waterhole. This was undisturbed, uninhabited territory in the deep woods. No one had been near the place for at least fifty years.

Fretz was all but paralyzed with excitement. He grabbed his shovel and began to dig. Smith, watching from ten yards away, suddenly ran up and grabbed him by the arm. "Hold it. . . . You hear that?" he exclaimed. Fretz, who was hard of hearing, shook his head. "Hear what?" Smith replied: "The car. I heard a door slam. I think we better get out of here. There could be somebody watching us." Fretz was afraid to continue. Just that week, he recalled, Smith had said something about "surveillance." The two left immediately, agreeing to return the next day to dig up what Fretz believed would be his first treasure cache.

When Fretz called up the next day to see if Smith was ready, Smith begged off, citing back pain. There was a litany of other excuses over the next several days. Smith then switched gears altogether, saying that he was tracking down a new, less risky site, over near Avants Mountain. As proof, he produced a waybill that he said had been ripped out from behind the wallpaper in Isom Avants's abandoned home. Then he disappeared for a week.

Fearing the worst, Fretz drove alone to Goat Brown's spring. When he got to the spot where the detector had sounded, he was devastated to see that a hole had been dug and refilled with soil. When he stuck his hand into the pit, he could feel the smooth outline of a small shaft, precisely the size of a tall thin jar, with a round depression at the bottom. He was distraught as he drove to Bob Brewer's ranch to tell his friend about what had happened.

Bob felt for Fretz and barely managed to refrain from blurting out, "Told you so." He and his forlorn friend headed to the site immediately. When he saw the layout, which lay less than a mile from the trellis where he had found his second cache, he thought that it might be part of the same system that had led him and Linda to the axe head and then to the jar filled with gold and silver coins. When Fretz related the whole story—about Smith's hearing a door slam, about his wanting to check out the Avants site and his taking the map from the Avants home—Bob drew several inferences.

The first was that Smith unquestionably could not be trusted. The second was that Smith seemed to know what he was doing. The third was that Smith seemed highly interested in treasure leads associated with Goat Brown, the Ashcrafts and the Avantses. (A subsequent trip to the abandoned Avants house confirmed that the wallpaper had been torn off and that someone had dug fresh holes in the yard and in the exposed cellar beneath the house.)

Was there a connection, Bob began to wonder. Was his own quick-hit recovery of the jar at Goat Brown's abandoned homestead as random a strike as it seemed, or was Jess Brown intimately connected with "the system"? Moreover, was there some kind of geometric grid being defined around Smoke Rock, with Grandpa anchoring the middle, Jess Brown and the Avantses the east-west axis, and other Ashcrafts the north-south axis?

All that Bob reasonably could deduce was that there may have been a group of individuals burying small caches of treasure in the Ouachitas in some seemingly encrypted, widely dispersed pattern. Smith seemed to have had some awareness of the scheme, and he may have been getting richer by that knowledge. Adding insult to injury, Smith showed conspicuous signs of a "lifestyle change" immediately after the incident at Goat Brown's spring, buying all sorts of new home-entertainment equipment and going out to restaurants on a regular basis. And this all after making frequent self-described "business" trips to Dallas. Bob guessed that these trips could have been to cash in gold coins at pawnshops and rare-coin dealerships in the city. Fretz, for his part, managed to swallow his pain, and never directly confronted Smith, though he wanted to throttle him.

During his alienation from Tilley and Fretz—the handiwork of Smith's artful insinuations—Bob had reverted to his lone-wolf style of investigation. He returned to his most valued sources of information: the old-timers in town. In particular, he had sought out a ninety-two-year-old mountaineer, Melvin Mitchell Cogburn, who had been a friend of Bob's father, Landon. The visit paid off. The woodsman—old as

Methuselah, as they say in the Ouachitas—gave him an interesting lead: there could be some truth to a story that gold was buried near the Greasy Cove cabin of Albert Pike along the Little Missouri River. The site was along a tributary of the Ouachita River, just sixteen miles east of Grandpa's cabin and twelve miles east of old Bill Wiley's place.[4]

At the time, Bob knew little about Pike, other than that he was a former Rebel general, who, after resigning from the Confederate Army, had lived a reclusive existence during the latter half of the war in a two-story cabin in Montgomery County, some thirty miles east of Hatfield. The wooded area had been turned into the Albert Pike Recreational Area, part of the Ouachita National Forest, during the early twentieth century.

Cogburn, whose memory was still sharp, recounted how Pike had hired his maternal grandfather, Dick Whisenhunt, to build the cabin—and had paid the local handsomely in gold coin, as he had the previous owners of the property. He also revealed that another relative of his, on a tip from one of Pike's black servants, had planned to raid Pike's property in search of gold rumored to be stockpiled there. When word of the plan leaked out, Pike—forewarned of the raid by a neighbor and Masonic friend—fled in the middle of the night in a horse buggy. Pike departed with a trunk full of books, gold coins and loose clothing that he and his loyal servants had snatched up at the last minute from inside the cabin. According to Cogburn's oral history, Pike had no time to recover any of his buried treasure. When the armed raiders arrived, led by Henry Page Cogburn (Mitchell's great-uncle who, he said, had harbored Unionist sympathies and had switched sides in the middle of the war), they ransacked the house and burned it to the ground. The raiding party found a large iron washpot filled with hundreds of mid-nineteenth-century U.S. gold coins. It had been hidden below a rock used as a doorstep to the cabin: precisely where the robbers had been tipped to look by Pike's servant.

Cogburn had only one thing to add to the colorful account: he believed there was more of Pike's gold buried in the area. Bob, amazed at the old man's lucid recollection of the family lore, heartily thanked him for the local history lesson and the treasure leads.

Back in his study, he immediately began to rummage through boxloads of local historical and treasure-oriented magazines collected at yard sales. There was no mention of Pike in any of the yellowed pages that he reviewed. But he did find something of interest in a copy of *Old West* magazine (owned by the same publisher as *Frontier Times,* where Mitchell's article had appeared). It was an article from the 1970s that recounted how a family living around Greasy Cove in the early 1900s had recovered a buried iron washpot containing $100,000 in gold coins.[5]

The article, "One Black Pot with a Yellow Fortune," had a magical effect. Bob was struck by the subtitle, "All you have to locate is three beech trees in a triangle. Where to look—Montgomery County, Arkansas." The article described carved beech trees in a geometrical formation. He read on: there were carvings (eight arrows and a cross) on each tree, which, the article said, had helped direct a group of four men and a young boy to a common point within the triangle formed by the trees. The site was located a few miles north of Pike's cabin and just south of Little Missouri Falls, on the bank of the river.

"It was either in 1907 or 1908 that we found the gold," wrote Greasy Cove local Arthur Porter, recollecting the incident he experienced as a young boy. "I could see a little of one side of the rusty washpot. It didn't take the men long to expose the entire top. It was covered with an old piece of sheet iron or some kind of sheet metal," Porter recalled in the article. When the group tried to remove the gold-filled washpot—reportedly found with guidance from a smudged waybill—they could not lift it out of the hole because of the weight of the coins inside. Most intriguing to Bob was the article's suggestion that the waybill (reportedly lost in the excitement of the washpot's discovery) had indicated that another washpot, containing perhaps as much as $80,000 in gold coins, was buried in the same area. The second cache apparently had not been recovered, or at least no one had come forward claiming to have found it.

Bob was fascinated. It added up to an uncannily familiar modus operandi: the cryptically carved beech trees, the location near a river, the geometric formations, the use of an iron washpot to contain the coins. Even more telling was the positioning of a large iron sheet—below ground but placed above the deeply buried pot—to ensure that those seeking to recover the money would notice compass gyrations at the correct location. Given what he had learned from Cogburn, Bob could not help but think this was Pike's money: it was in the precise area where Pike had lived. If it were Pike's money—and, as such, money stockpiled underground within a recognizable grid of cryptic symbols—could this suggest that the system was not only "outlaw" but also Confederate?

Bob used an invitation to explore the Pike site as the means to re-launch his friendship with Fretz and Tilley after the Smith affair. In particular, he wanted to prove to the now skeptical Tilley some key points.

First, that he knew what he was doing. Second, that this was not likely Spanish treasure. Third, that it was likely outlaw and possibly Rebel gold. And finally, that their own families may have been involved in its burial and oversight. It was not just a matter of satisfying his own powerful curiosity; he wanted to share his discoveries with trusted friends who could help solve the puzzle and provide some honest feedback. If they each made a little money, all the better.

At this point in his quest, Bob wasn't sure which internal force was predominant: the psychological thrill and financial reward of recovering the gold, or the higher "art" of breaking a bewildering code and revealing some kind of underlying system.

Tilley, tucking a pinch of chewing tobacco into his cheek, said he regretted what had happened with Smith and was glad to be hitting the trail once again with his hometown buddy. As for Bob's theory that Isom Avants may have been involved with all this underground gold, Tilley thought little of it. "Isom was a drinker," and could not be trusted with all that money, he said.

Any further questions about Spanish money and about Bob's ability to interpret the signs to a point on a map were cast aside soon after the three reached the Pike site. Bob quickly located what appeared to be a depression where the washpot likely had been found in 1907, as indicated on the map drawn in the *Old West* article. Only one of the original three beeches still stood near the suspected treasure hole, but Bob and his two friends discovered a range of moss-covered clues in the bark of surrounding beech trees, spread over several square miles in the Little Missouri Valley. (Locals call the old trail along the river from Pike's property upstream to the Little Missouri Falls the "Crowfoot Trail," because so many of the beech trees are inscribed with three-toed bird tracks.)

To Bob's great satisfaction, the beech-bark signs correlated closely to the ones that he had investigated at Smoke Rock. And they were just as complex. On one, carved into a thick sturdy tree with peeling bark, the letters *PIKE* were plainly visible. It had distinct etchings, a snake and a moose among them. Another ancient beech, some distance away, had an ornate carving of a palm tree, capped with a crescent moon overhead. Above, the initials *A.P.* were neatly inscribed. Nearby the scrambled letters *GreawLGO,* topped with the letter *t,* stood out. Recent "graffiti" cluttered the overall image somewhat, but the older, deeply incised carvings were still legible.

Bob obtained a compass bearing off one of the key carvings and then

led the group through the forest on the indicated bearing. Using the subtle tricks that he had developed for following the signs, they arrived at
the first of two spots in the woods where metal clues were buried. He
told Tilley and Fretz to walk along the lines indicated by the respective
buried pointers and then to holler upon reaching the spot where the lines
crossed. After a few minutes of pacing off, Tilley shouted back: "Do you
want me to try to jump across this hole or walk around it?" Fretz and
Tilley were standing on the edge of a three-foot-wide pit, where some
thing sizable seemed to have been excavated a long time ago.

Whether the circular depression was the imprint of the missing second
washpot containing the rumored $80,000 in gold coins could never be
known. Within thirty yards of the hole stood a large beech engraved
with several arrows and other carvings. Tilley was convinced that Bob
was on to something big.

Back home, Tilley phoned his sister to ask if she had any old documents, personal records, or memorabilia of Uncle Isom or other Avants
forebears. Within a few days, he was in possession of a curious heirloom,
whose importance was not immediately clear. It was an encrypted diary, a
"Memorandum" book of Isom Avants, dated 1920. Its lined pages contained the names Avants, W. D. Ashcraft, J. P. Smith and James Blalock,
all locals of the Shady-Brushy Creek region, at the time. Other pages were
filled with various payroll notations. A page in the back contained an odd
spiderweb-like drawing, with concentric circles and sporadic dots within,
next to which was written "Shady, Arkansas, August 23, 1920."

When Tilley showed Bob the fragile diary, Bob was stunned. He had
seen a beech tree not far from Smoke Rock and Isom Avants's home that
had the names "J. Avants W. D. Ashcraft J. P. Smith" inscribed on it, along
with various dates, "1855," "Nov. 22 1910," as well as the outline of a
Winchester rifle. The s in Ashcraft, he recalled, had been carved in the
shape of a question mark. The correlation between this record book—in
which a financial accounting for services rendered was being denoted—
and the beech tree with its coded treasure indicators could not be a simple
coincidence.

Bob had begun to unlock a code, one that hinted at a hidden depository system, not just in his immediate environs but in woods thirty miles
away. By now he was convinced that the treasure caches could be found
with some regularity—by using the patterns of interlocking symbols and
signs, by integrating geometry with geography and land navigation with
topography, by thinking like "them." The joy of the hunt—staying on

track, avoiding the cold trail, solving the mystery of the trails' makers—
had become perhaps more important than finding the gold itself.

To ferret out new information and to see whether, indeed, the trail
extended beyond the borders of Polk, Scott and Montgomery counties of
west-central Arkansas, Bob and Linda produced an hour-long videotape
showing the Bible Tree and its elaborate symbolism. (In the tape, Bob
made multiple references to "Spanish treasure signs," even though by
then he doubted that they were Spanish. He simply did not know what
else to call the inscriptions. He knew, for instance, that the old Spanish
colonialists were not likely to write, "1st Thess"!) Initially, he gave the
hour-long tapes to a few friends. But they quickly became hot commodi-
ties at a handful of treasure-hunting shows attended by the couple in
1993. Within weeks of releasing the Bible Tree video, Bob was inundated
with letters and phone calls. His hunch was right. The signs were everywhere. Bob was amazed at how many treasure buffs from out of state
wrote or called to say that they had seen similar tree or rock carvings,
either on the trail or, in some cases, on their own property. But none of
the respondents—all from the South or Southwest—knew anything
about the origins of the cryptic inscriptions.

One of the more interesting letters arrived in July 1993 from Stan Vickery, an insurance salesman and treasure hunter from Alexandria,
Louisiana. Vickery was fascinated by Bob's interpretation of the Bible
Tree's symbols. He had encountered similar beech etchings in Louisiana
and East Texas, and he commended Bob for having "done his homework."

In a follow-up conversation, Vickery suggested that the two cache
hunters get together, and Bob consented. At Bob's ranch, Vickery
showed him photographs of treasure signs that looked uncannily familiar. Bob certainly was impressed, but all that he volunteered was that the
abstract images appeared part of the same system; to try to interpret
their meaning out of context and without having surveyed the environs
would be premature. The two agreed that they should put their talents
together, and soon thereafter, Vickery invited Bob to join him on a trip to
Ackworth, Georgia, to canvass a site being explored by some treasure-
hunting friends.

Bob, his curiosity piqued by the photos suggesting that the "system"
extended into neighboring Texas and Louisiana, quickly agreed. Weeks
later, he met Vickery in Shreveport, and they headed east for Georgia in
Vickery's pickup. They traded treasure stories the entire way, partly to
kill time and partly to build trust, to gauge the all-important "b.s." fac-

tor that runs rampant in cache-hunter circles. Vickery gave Bob a book
from his bag and said he might want to take a look at it. The book was
*Jesse James Was One of His Names: The Greatest Cover Up in History
by the Famous Outlaw Who Lived 73 Incredible Lives.*[6] In the few minutes he took to leaf through it, Bob was struck by what he read.

His head spun at the sight of carved stick-figures captured in a set of
photos in the book. The first caption read: "Golden Circle treasure
sign." In one photo, he could see the shape of a chiseled turtle figure juxtaposed next to a carved donkey or horse. In another, he could make out
an etched bird astride a man's head. A third showed what looked like a
sunrise symbol, with two turkey tracks and the initials *JJ* (as in "Jesse
James") carved above and the name "Cole Younger" and the date
"1874" below. Chapter 12 started on the facing page. Its title was "The
Knights of the Golden Circle." The chapter began:

> One of the deadliest, wealthiest, most secretive and efficient spy and
> underground organizations in the history of the world was The Knights of
> the Golden Circle, which operated over the globe for sixty-five years
> (1851–1916). . . . Some of the craftiest, finest brains in the South directed
> the activities of the Knights of the Golden Circle. The group was heavy on
> ritual, which was borrowed from the Masonic Lodge. . . .[7]

The clincher, however, came two chapters later, in a startling twenty-
page section entitled "The Fabulous Confederate Treasure Troves." He
read there that at the Civil War's end, with the people of the South starv-
ing and the region in chaos, a hidden Confederacy based in Nashville,
Tennessee, had buried enormous caches of gold, silver and arms for the
South to rise again. The stockpiled caches, ranging from those that could
be dug up by shovel to those that required enormous mechanical lifts,
were hidden in a complex, cross-border depository system. "The symbols are not always arrows, turkey tracks, snakes and birds, but sometimes they are the old Confederate Army Code. Every venture old Jesse's
[James's] organization did was in multiples of 3s, 5s and 7s."[8] The gold
and silver specie and bars said to be buried in the Confederate troves—
stretching from Florida to California—was in the hundreds of millions,
and possibly billions, of dollars in current values, it said.[9]

Bob was silent as a rush of images from his past converged with the
published images in the book: the arrows from Mitchell's "Twin
Springs," the "7" from the Bible Tree leading to the "7" rock carving,

the turkey track near the "Spaniard's" grave site; the many snakes, birds, horses and other animal carvings he had recorded in the Ouachitas. Confederate, indeed. Yet, it was no longer just the possibility of Pike's involvement but that of . . . Jesse James! Suddenly Bob had a tingling sense of how big this treasure conspiracy was.

He wanted to shout, "My God, this is it!" But this time he contained himself and kept quiet. He desperately wanted to stop, read and reread the three-hundred-page book from start to finish; to find out who the authors were and to assess the content's credibility. But that would have to wait until after the mission at hand. "Interesting ideas . . . sounds a lot like what I was discovering," he said casually to Vickery, who nodded. "The photos seem to match," he added.

At the forty-acre site in Georgia—heavily forested hill country northwest of Atlanta—it took but a couple of hours of orientation before Bob realized that the landscape abounded in tree carvings. He had heard that the spot might have been a location for buried "Cherokee" treasure. It lay but a few miles from New Echota—the former Cherokee capital, where in December 1835, Stand Watie, his brother Elias Boudinot and his uncle Major Ridge agreed to move the Cherokee nation west into Indian Territory, without the consent of chief John Ross. Among the symbols depicted in the bark of the local beech were a cavalry boot, a crude figure of a man wearing a crown and a pipe-smoking Indian sporting a feather headdress. Bob also came across a large flat rock that had been inscribed with a turtle figure. Despite encountering such promising signs, the men did not have permission to track lines (indicated by the turtle's head and other directional markers) into adjoining sections of private property. So, the mission ended without getting close to identifying a potential cache-burial site.

That mattered little to Bob, for he had found the "evidence" that he was seeking. The "system" extended across state borders. His Georgia observations made him ever more eager to assay—for both its historical and treasure-hunting value—the apparent gold nugget that he had just encountered in *Jesse James Was One of His Names*. The book contained some outlandish comments and bold assertions about places and times that strained credulity. But, despite his justified skepticism, Bob felt convinced that there was valuable information in its pages. His quest, he knew, had just become exponentially more challenging.

7

Jesse James, KGC Field Commander

THE name Jesse James evokes an unambiguous image in the American psyche: a dashing pistol-packing outlaw in a class of his own. Yet, Jesse James's story is one of *the* great ambiguities in American chronicles. Hundreds of books—from biography to Western Americana—have been written about the secretive bank-, stagecoach- and train-robbing outlaw and his "gang." With but a few exceptions, they plow through the story-line that the "Missouri-born" brothers, Frank and Jesse James, wreaked havoc in the postbellum West for their own criminal and, ultimately, selfish ends.[1] Jesse and his elusive band of hardened ex-Confederate guerrillas may well have targeted "Unionist" banks and railroads. Likewise, they may have eschewed robbing those who made their living off the Southern, trans-Mississippi and trans-Appalachia lands. The Robin Hood image of a handsome good-natured brigand redistributing wealth to the poor—to Southern veterans, widows and orphans—has been widely attached to the traditional Jesse James saga and legend. But in nearly all these accounts, the notorious, sometimes brutal James-Younger gang was in it for *themselves*.

Still, these accounts never adequately answer two central questions. First, if Jesse and Frank James did rob in order to get rich while exacting sweet revenge, what happened to the money? Second, why didn't any of the gang members show signs of increased personal wealth after their unprecedented string of twenty to twenty-five successful hits, amounting to a then-estimated quarter of a million dollars in stolen loot?

Virtually nowhere in the popular history does one encounter this jarring possibility: that Jesse James, America's most famous outlaw, was a masterful *political* operative, plundering and plotting and spreading misinformation not for himself but for a powerful pro-slavery secret society, the Knights of the Golden Circle. (As this book was being prepared to go to press, author and independent historian T. J. Stiles published a well-researched volume, *Jesse James: Last Rebel of the Civil War,* which sets forth the case that Jesse was politically motivated: that he was attempting to keep up the fight for the Confederate cause amid Reconstruction. Stiles focuses his research primarily on the bitterly divided situation in pre– and then post–Civil War Missouri, where James and his cohorts carried out often brutal acts of subversion and revenge: "a cultural and political offensive waged by the defeated rebels to undo the triumph of the Radical Republicans in the Civil War." Stiles makes brief mention of the Knights of the Golden Circle, who, he writes, were rumored to be "preparing to rise" in Missouri in early 1864.)[2]

Such a "revisionist" thesis might go far to explain what could have been the real motive behind the storied armed robberies and murders carried out by Jesse and his clandestine band from as early as 1866 to at least 1881—securing funds for another Civil War. It could explain why all the fabulous wealth reportedly stolen by the everyday criminal enterprise remains almost entirely unaccounted for: it was buried in the coffers of political combatants, in the coded depositories and weapons stockpiles of an underground post-Confederate terrorist network.

In a rare mention in the mainstream media of a long-lived Jesse James, *U.S. News & World Report* noted the following in its July 24, 2000, "Mysteries of History" issue: "Jesse James's Gold: He died in 1882—or maybe he didn't. Some say he lived into the 1900s, burying gold in New Mexico and Texas (to finance a second Civil War in which the South would rise again)."[3]

For 120 years, some have speculated that Jesse James faked his death on April 3, 1882, in St. Joseph, Missouri, and lived for decades under scores of aliases.[4] Could Jesse's "outlaw" career have extended far beyond the sixteen years from 1866 to 1882? Those who believe so say that James was not shot in the back of the head for $10,000 reward money by "turncoat" gang-member Bob Ford. They maintain that James became a field commander and financial overseer of the KGC after he was alleged to have been shot. Having the support of a highly effective underground would certainly have helped in perpetrating the death hoax. It also would have been useful to have a KGC member or sympathizer in the press, both to further the KGC's overall mission and to perpetuate the myth that James was assassinated.

Midwest columnist John Newman Edwards seemed to fit the bill. During the war, he had been an assistant to Brig. Gen. Jo Orville Shelby, a major KGC operative in the trans-Mississippi theater. In a book published in 1867, *Shelby and his men: or the war in the West,* Edwards makes a rare historical reference to the fact that the KGC was operational in the western theater of the Civil War in 1865: "Much reliance, too, was placed, especially by Generals Price and Marmaduke, upon the secret orders of the Knights of the Golden Circle. Periodical installments of these well dressed, sleek looking gentry came among the ragged veterans of four years service, with mysterious books, innumerable signs, grips, signals, passwords. . . ."[5] In the postwar era, it was Edwards who almost single-handedly cultivated the knight-gallant "Robin Hood" image of the James gang through his pandering editorials and columns in the *Kansas City Times* and later in the *St. Louis Dispatch.*[6] In his famous "Chivalry of Crime" column in the *Kansas City Times* on September 29, 1872, Edwards went so far as to refer to men "with the halo of medieval chivalry upon their garments." (The romantic reference may suggest a James gang association with the Knights Templar and the Templar-oriented KGC. It is worth considering whether much of Edwards's prose about the James gang may have been written as a subtext—as cipher—meant to be understood only by the initiated.)

As a result of disinformation and propaganda, the true identity and whereabouts of Jesse James may never be established. The mystery has only deepened over time, with new installments every few decades. Indeed, many self-proclaimed Jesse Jameses came forward in the late nineteenth and early- to mid-twentieth centuries.

The one who created the biggest stir was J. Frank Dalton in the late 1940s. Dalton reportedly died at well over one hundred years of age, on August 15, 1951, in Granbury, Texas, southwest of Fort Worth. A few years earlier, the mustachioed, wrinkled centenarian with flowing white hair, bushy eyebrows and a thick goatee, had given an interview in Lawton, Oklahoma. In a front-page story published May 19, 1948, in the *Lawton Constitution,* he claimed that he was the real Jesse Woodson James and that he had a slew of telltale scars, rope burns, tattoos and living friends to prove it. "JESSE JAMES IS ALIVE! IN LAWTON," blared the banner headline. In an accompanying article by *Constitution* staff writer

Frank O. Hall, Dalton was cited mentioning buried gold "taken from trains and stage coaches," Jesse James "maps" and "a code that wasn't easy to break." The story added:

> Jesse declares that there still are many of those caches untouched by human hands since they were buried years ago, but he is an old man and money no longer means anything to him. Besides, too much blood has been spilled already over the inglorious gold which sets the very blood of mankind racing with greed. Leave it for the individuals who are capable of working out its puzzles and solving the secrets of nature's most severe problems, Jesse confides.

The Lawton "scoop" sparked a wave of interviews in the national media and brought forward an aged, ragtag army of affidavit-signing witnesses. Needless to say, Dalton-James's genealogical claims and his colorful version of post–Civil War history caused a sensation. And, while most of the commentary at the time was highly skeptical, not all of it was dismissive.

The J. Frank Dalton story stands at the center of *Jesse James Was One of His Names*. This controversial book, published in 1975 by Santa Anita Press (Arcadia, Calif.), is filled with tantalizing historical possibilities and a bevy of bold claims. At its core are the propositions that Jesse Woodson James was a post–Civil War leader of the Knights of the Golden Circle and that the KGC's primary goal, after going fully underground, was to prepare for a second civil war. The book—now out of print and highly sought after by treasure hunters, Jesse James fans and Civil War buffs—goes into considerable detail to explain the secret organization's methods. It cites numerous changes during the KGC's postwar evolution. These include owning major businesses—railroads, mining and timber operations, banks, racehorses—as front-company sources of operating revenue.[7]

The accuracy of the account provided by J. Frank Dalton–Jesse James (as disclosed by the book's authors) remains open to investigation. Dalton-James's life is told in *Jesse James Was One of His Names* through the voice of someone going by the name Jesse James III. The latter, whose legal name was Orvus Lee Howk, also went by the name Jesse Lee James and claimed to have been a grandson of Jesse Woodson James. "Jesse Lee James, alias Orvus Lee Howk, spent his lifetime as a detective and bodyguard-confidant-executor for his notorious grandfather," the book states.[8]

The book does not elaborate on the fact that Orvus Lee Howk/Jesse Lee James (who is now deceased) also paraded his said grandfather— who was in a severely enfeebled state, suffering from a broken hip— around at vaudeville-type road shows in the late 1940s. (It is of course entirely possible that Orvus Lee Howk/Jesse Lee James may have been unrelated to J. Frank Dalton by blood, yet may have won the trust and confidence of the old man, who relied on him for daily care and mobility in his later years. Howk, for his part, seemed to have taken a keen interest in the location of the KGC's buried gold, something about which J. Frank Dalton appeared to know a great deal. It is clear from the book that the two men traveled great distances to scores of states.)

Writing as Jesse Lee James, Howk first wrote about Jesse James in *Jesse James and the Lost Cause*, published in 1961 by Pageant Press of New York. Fourteen years later, Howk teamed with journalist Del Schrader, from the now defunct *Los Angeles Herald Examiner*, to coauthor *Jesse James Was One of His Names*. In this book the two authors state categorically that J. Frank Dalton was Jesse Woodson James, who, they assert, was born in Kentucky on April 17, 1844 (as opposed to the traditional September 5, 1847, birthdate and the Centerville, Clay County, Missouri birthplace). As such, the authors note, J. Frank Dalton/Jesse Woodson James lived to the ripe age of 107. Their intentionally provocative book sparked immediate controversy. Some critics insisted unequivocally that Jesse was killed in 1882; others charged that many of the book's core assertions strained credulity; still others criticized fast-and-loose chronologies, misplaced geography, poor spelling and awkward grammar.

It is impossible to tell how much independent research Schrader, now deceased, undertook. He notes that his own forebears had some positive personal encounters with Jesse Woodson James. He makes no skeptical rejoinders: he merely conveys the story that Dalton-James allegedly told to Howk.[9] The authors say that they relied on diaries, correspondence, affidavits and photographs of Dalton-James to patch together the (in parts) compelling volume.[10]

It is not possible to evaluate every bald unproven assertion or the sum of assertions in *Jesse James Was One of His Names*. But it *is* both possible and worthwhile to highlight some of the more tantalizing claims in the text, particularly as they relate to the Knights of the Golden Circle. To do so, one has to assume that the text is written in symbolic narrative, interspersing potentially factual passages among hyperbole and outlandish dross.

The authors emphasize the robust sense of humor of the man who they claim was America's most wanted outlaw.[11] At one point, they note that "Colonel" J. Frank Dalton deliberately threw out "whoppers" to journalists in the post-Lawton media feeding frenzy. By doing so, Dalton-James was able to keep much of the history, the players and the victims of the KGC in a confused blur. It was all part, perhaps, of a strategy of disinformation and obfuscation, with select, key messages covertly getting through to the initiated. "For instance, Jesse told the Lawton reporters that . . . at the age of 67 he enlisted in the Canadian army and fought four years in Europe. . . . But Jesse hadn't done these things—he was merely covering up for old compadres still alive," they write.[12]

If Dalton-James had thrown up a few fanciful smoke screens in 1948, his view apparently changed in the three years before his death in 1951. In the opening pages of their 1975 book, Schrader and Howk explain: "Why write the book at all? It was old Jesse's deathbed wish that the 'record be set straight once and for all.' There are many kernels of history and hitherto unknown facts, which may encourage better historians of this day to run down additional information."[13] Schrader and his coauthor say that the KGC had voted in 1916 to "seal its records for 50 years," or at least to wait until the last known Confederate soldier had died (believed to be in 1959).[14]

Thus, the path was clear by the mid-1960s to expose segments of overlooked episodes in U.S. history. Schrader and Howk caution, however, that living descendants of Confederate and KGC associates of Jesse Woodson James "don't take kindly to revealing exact directions on how to open the many Confederate depositories scattered across the land."[15]

They also make clear that their mysterious biography is not meant to be a paean to Jesse James: "This book was certainly not written to whitewash old Jesse W. James activities. Old Jesse may have rationalized many of his crimes against humanity as being for The Cause (the Confederate Underground) but he was not without his own principles. He had great administrative ability. He was a man of compassion, [and] demanded and received a fanatical loyalty."[16] Ultimately, Schrader and Howk set out to answer this question, unequivocally: "Did Jesse command a 'gang,' or as chief of the Knights of the Golden Circle, did he direct the activities of the Confederate Underground Army, which was preparing for a Second Civil War?"[17]

The latter view gained some currency in a small, well-researched nonfiction paperback published in 2000. Ralph P. Ganis, author of *Uncom-*

mon Men: A Secret Network of Jesse James Revealed, combines circumstantial evidence from coded photographs and various oral histories to make the case that Jesse and his gang operated in North Carolina and Tennessee after the Civil War with a "secret network of ex-Confederates."[18] That network, Ganis posits, was most likely the KGC. He relies heavily on a photograph, taken in Nashville in 1879, of Jesse and Frank James and other workers in front of the Mocker Barrel Factory. Several of those photographed are giving suspected KGC-membership hand signals. Significantly, Ganis notes that historians have thought Jesse James–KGC connections to be "too elusive to find."[19] He does not mention the possibility that Jesse may have faked his death and lived well into the twentieth century.

The following are among the key points that James (Howk) and Schrader made more than a quarter of a century ago—some obviously central, some seemingly obscure—as they relate to Jesse James and the Knights of the Golden Circle. That so many of the assertions highlighted below seem to flow from the perspective of a KGC insider would seem to bolster the book's credibility. Consider: if J. Frank Dalton were a mere crank and if Del Schrader and Orvus Lee Howk were mere dupes, then at least one of them and perhaps all three certainly possessed an amazingly vivid and detailed sense of much-neglected, or deliberately concealed, chapters in U.S. history. But there is a larger point to the ever-controversial *Jesse James Was One of His Names:* it has to be assessed within the context of the KGC's pattern of disguise, deception and coded subtext.

1. Two Jesse Jameses: First Cousins, Jesse Woodson James and Jesse Robert "Dingus" James.

One of the most important assertions in *Jesse James Was One of His Names* is that history failed to realize that there were two Jesse Jameses, one from Kentucky and one from Missouri, who were first cousins and comrades-in-arms.[20] History—the book avers—has focused on the Missouri-born outlaw, Jesse Robert James. The latter's postwar KGC exploits were secondary to those of his slightly shorter but broader-shouldered, wider-faced, Kentucky-born cousin, Jesse Woodson James. Adding to the confusion, each Jesse had a brother who went by the name Frank. All four—the two Jesses and the two Franks—were active in the operations of the KGC after the war and earlier had fought with different units of the Confederacy. Moreover, all four Jameses moved through the KGC's headquarters in Nashville during the mid-1870s. The book says the KGC maintained its postwar headquarters in Nashville from 1865 to 1884.[21] It is not clear whether the four men also gathered as a group, post-1884, in Canton, Texas, and Colorado Springs, Colorado, the said successor KGC headquarters.

According to the book, *after the war* Jesse Woodson James led operations aimed at seizing federal assets in Indian Territory (Oklahoma), Arkansas, Texas, as well as in New Mexico Territory, Colorado, Wyoming Territory and other areas in the Far West. He was also active in Mexico and in the Deep South. The postwar Missouri Jesse James, for his part, operated chiefly out of Missouri, Kansas, Nebraska, Iowa and Kentucky, along with his brother Frank, Bud Dalton and others.

Jesse Woodson James, who became the head of the inner sanctum of the Knights of the Golden Circle, and his older brother, ex-Confederate Army surgeon Dr. Sylvester Franklin James, were the sons of Capt. George James and Mollie Dalton of Scott County, Kentucky, according to Schrader and Howk.[22] Jesse Woodson, *during the war,* operated mostly in Virginia, the Carolinas, Tennessee, Kentucky and the Deep South (only once connecting with Quantrill's guerrillas in Kansas, and occasionally making forays into Oklahoma Territory, Arkansas and Texas).[23] In the final two years of the war, he raided Union supply wagons, boats and trains. "We'd go behind the Yankee lines, capture and bury Union payrolls, figuring unpaid soldiers would become demoralized. And we'd grab and run with medicines, blankets, guns, ammunition, quinine . . . horseshoes, nails, sugar, hams . . . ," Dalton-James is quoted as saying.[24]

These trans-Mississippi raids were sometimes made in conjunction with Choctaw and Chickasaw Indians, KGC allies in the region. The Indian cavalry troops, under Col. Tandy Walker, fought alongside generals John S. Marmaduke, Joseph O. Shelby, and Samuel B. Maxey—all under the overall command of Maj. Gen. Sterling Price. (Recall: Price was identified as the KGC's Western commander by the U.S. government in the 1864 Holt report.) Following a successful raid on a Union payroll and supply wagon train, at Poison Springs, Arkansas, Jesse and his Choctaw and Chickasaw fighters buried a Union Army pay chest packed with gold and silver coins at Wild Cat Bluff, near Centerpoint, Arkansas, according to Dalton-James.[25]

After his wounds had healed at the end of the Civil War, Kentucky-born Jesse Woodson threw himself headlong into KGC operations, according to

Schrader and Howk. Among his first assignments, in 1867, was a rescue mission inside Mexico. The task was to extract Confederate general Jo Shelby and his Missouri cavalrymen, who, rather than surrender after Appomattox, had crossed the Rio Grande in July 1865 to seek refuge and to prop up the faltering regime of Emperor Maximilian, an apparent KGC ally.[26] A multimillion-dollar award, according to Dalton-James, was later granted by Maximilian to Jesse James for his efforts. That money, in the form of gold coins minted by Maximilian in Mexico, allegedly was hauled by Jesse Woodson James and his KGC cohorts into Texas and parts of Indian Territory. The KGC soon thereafter appointed Jesse W. James comptroller general of all its funds, a steppingstone to his becoming the secret order's top field commander, write Schrader and Howk.[27]

Still, to ensure adequate cover to run a super-secret underground, Jesse James would need to be declared legally dead. This, according to Schrader and Howk, he accomplished on April 3, 1882, in St. Joseph, Missouri, first by bumping off rival Charlie Bigelow, who bore a resemblance, and then by placing the cadaver of Bigelow in the casket that was displayed at the "Jesse James" funeral in nearby Kearney.[28] Missouri governor Thomas T. Crittenden, said to be a lifelong friend of Kentucky Jesse, was in on the plan from the beginning—having been bought off, the authors say, long before by the KGC. There was never any doubt, they write, that Crittenden would grant a full and unconditional pardon to Bob and Charley Ford after the two brothers were sentenced to hang for the "murder" of Jesse James.[29] The two Fords may have been involved in a well-scripted murder . . . that of Bigelow!

It seems that the Jameses, and others in the upper ranks of the KGC, were masters, even geniuses, of deceit. If this death hoax were true, it would mean that Jesse Woodson James—and a fairly lengthy list of co-conspirators—pulled off a triple coup de grace. First, he terminated the life of an annoying rival (who reportedly had been using his name in various robberies). Second, he used the body of his rival as a fill-in at "his" funeral. Third, he made the world believe not only that he was officially dead but that the person buried in Kearney, Missouri, was the one and only Jesse James, the one born there on September 5, 1847.

The name Jesse Robert James never surfaced. The legally dead and interred outlaw was known to the world as Jesse Woodson James—so said the tombstone and so said the paperwork. Moreover, the Schrader-Howk book asserts that a black colleague of Jesse Woodson James, a loyal confidant and cook named John Trammell, commemorated the

hoax (including the murder of Bigelow, in which he was said to participate) by burying several etched bricks.[30] Whether apocryphal or not (the
bricks were eventually dug up in 1966 and written up, with photos, in
the St. Joseph, Missouri, newspaper), the images inscribed are telling.
"[One] brick contained an image of a Spanish dagger, the numerals
'777,' the letters 'KGC' and 'JJ'. Of course, KGC and JJ stood for the
Knights of the Golden Circle and Jesse James," Schrader and Howk
vouch. Trammell died at the age of 118, and outlived J. Frank Dalton to
become one of the oldest living Americans at the time. Trammell was the
subject of a November 8, 1954, front-page article in the Colorado
Springs *Gazette-Telegraph* entitled "116-Year-Old Jesse James Gang's
Cook Visits Region." It describes Trammell as a "confidante of Jesse
James" and a subject of a scientific research project into twenty-five of
the oldest people in the world. In the article, Trammell describes himself
as a general handyman of the "rebel" James gang after the Civil War.
The article states: "One big reason why he came here was to show Jesse
James III of Manitou Springs, a great grandson of the famed Jesse, the
location of two caches of gold coins, gold and silver bullion which the
original Jesse reportedly buried in the Ute Pass area in 1876."

Jesse Robert "Dingus" James and his brother Alexander Franklin
James, this "revisionist" theory holds, had operated during the war as
much feared bushwhacking guerrillas in Missouri and Kansas. They
fought Unionist Kansas "Jayhawkers" on the so-called Western Border
of the conflict gripping the nation. Their commanders were the infamous
guerrilla cavalry leader and head of the KGC's Knights of the Iron Hand,
William Clarke Quantrill, and Capt. "Bloody Bill" Anderson. At their
side was Missouri-born Thomas Coleman Younger.[31] Sons of the Rev.
Robert James (brother of Capt. George James who was the father of the
other Jesse and Frank James) and Zerelda Cole, the Missouri Jesse and
Frank Jameses secretly kept in close contact with their Kentucky first
cousins, both during the war as Confederates and following the four-
year conflict as KGC commanders, according to Schrader and Howk.[32]

In a telling passage, Howk describes a reunion between Jesse Woodson James and Jesse Robert "Dingus" James that was arranged in Pen-
sacola, Florida. Howk said that he had walked up to "Dingus," gave
him a silver dollar and said: "Turkey tracks." Then, handing over
another silver dollar, he added: "Seen a turtle go by my friend?" The
response was immediate: "Nope, I ain't seen a turtle, but I know you're
from The Organization—where's Jesse?"[33]

Nowhere do the authors explain the symbolic meaning of "turkey tracks" or "turtle," but they are among the most important pictorial indicators of buried Confederate or KGC treasure.

The book's authors argue that the two sets of James brothers deliberately sowed confusion about the "real" Jesse James and his whereabouts. "The two Jesse Jameses and the two Frank Jameses were not about to set the record straight. The two sets of 'composites' were working fine for them in their secret work. All four were unreconstructed Confederates. All four felt their mission in life was to help the South rise again."[34]

Two Jesse Jameses—operating in different places at the same time and for the same cause—is a powerful concept. Numerous chroniclers of the mainstream Jesse James story (that he died in 1882, was the Missouri-born son of Robert and Zerelda, and went to the grave in Missouri as a mere bandit) have been unable to explain how nearly simultaneous robberies attributed to Jesse could have occurred over vast distances. Consider: there was the four-man holdup of the Tishomingo Savings Bank in Corinth, Mississippi, in which some $10,000 in funds and jewelry was stolen on December 8, 1874; then came the five-man train heist the next day of an estimated $30,000 to $60,000 from the Kansas Pacific Railroad, some six hundred miles away in Muncie, Kansas. Surely these could not have been pulled off by the same Jesse James! Even if Jesse and his gang had hopped on a train in Corinth and ridden by rail to Muncie, they could not have made it: train travel averaged a mere twenty-five miles per hour, with frequent whistle stops. As James historian William Settle noted in a respected 1966 biography: "Friends of the Jameses and Youngers often pointed out the incongruity of charging them with both the Corinth and Muncie robberies. Yet it is entirely possible that the leaders had separated and that some of the gang were in Mississippi and others in Kansas at the same time."[35] Settle does not consider the possibility of there being two Jesse Jameses, first cousins and outlaws both.

Confusion over a Jesse doppelgänger—or, possibly, the presence of Jesse Woodson James in one place and Jesse Robert James in another—would arise repeatedly in history books and local lore. In his recent volume, *Frank and Jesse James: The Story Behind the Legend,* author Ted Yeatman notes that Jesse James, using the alias Mr. Howard, was sighted along with his younger friend, Brushy Bill "Billy the Kid" Roberts, in 1877 in Las Vegas, New Mexico Territory, by a Dr. Henry Hoyt.[36] Hoyt, who later became the chief surgeon of the U.S. Army, wrote in his memoirs that Howard had a missing fingertip on his left hand. The latter observation—significant because of its specificity and because it came from a medical professional—fits the exact description of a telltale physical characteristic attributed to Dalton-James in the Schrader-Howk book.

Yeatman (who does not subscribe to the J. Frank Dalton scenario) notes that it cannot be ascertained whether Jesse James had traveled to the Far West from what he believes was James's base in Tennessee. But Schrader and Howk write that Jesse Woodson James operated chiefly in the Far West for much of the post–Civil War period.

The Hoyt observation is also significant in that the alias reportedly used by the alleged Jesse, "Mr. Howard," shows up as one of the seventy-two aliases listed in *Jesse James Was One of His Names*.[37] In addition to Charles Howard, John Davis Howard, and Col. J. Frank Dalton, the aliases included Roy Hewitt, D. H. Moffat and a range of others. Moreover, Jesse Woodson James and other members of the post-war KGC could have assumed the identities of living or recently deceased U.S. citizens, all part of a strategy to constantly move about undetected through the use of disguise and subterfuge.

2. Jesse Woodson James was a thirty-third-degree Mason.[38]

This statement by Schrader and Howk suggests a direct Jesse James connection to the Supreme Council of the Southern Jurisdiction of the Scottish Rite in Charleston: only those selected by the Supreme Council could attain this highest honorary degree within U.S. Freemasonry. Could this then imply a secret link to Albert Pike, the Supreme Council's Sovereign Grand Commander at the time, who gets no mention in *Jesse James Was One of His Names*?

In a related vein, the book oddly notes that a few members of the KGC's Inner Sanctum were "members of the Rosicrucians," and that Jesse James was also interested in alchemy.[39] Why would a Wild West "outlaw" be interested in something so esoteric, indeed, so Old World?

Perhaps, once again, there is an Albert Pike connection. As Scottish Rite historian William Fox observed about Pike: "The organizing premise of the Pike rituals of the Scottish Rite and his *Morals and Dogma*, was according to [Scottish Rite researcher] Rex Hutchins, 'religious cross-fertilization,' so that knowledge of the ancients, whether from Jewish mysticism, Christian Platonism, or medieval hermeticism and alchemy (nourished specifically by a seventeenth-century sect of German mystics called Rosicrucians), was funneled into Freemasonry 'along many diverse paths.' "[40]

The Rosicrucians, whose chief symbol is a cross with a red rose at its center, put considerable store in the ways of the Knights Templar and their mystical and cabalistic traditions. They have been associated with European Freemasonry and an underground sociopolitical movement supporting intellectual freedom (one in direct opposition to the Roman Catholic Church). In addition to a philosophical worldview grounded in mathematics and science, the Rosicrucians of the Enlightenment also tended to value insights from alchemy and astrology.[41] Centuries later, Albert Pike is reported to have traveled to a world Rosicrucian conference in Paris *during the Civil War*, attended by France's Napoleon III and other European luminaries.[42]

3. A Habit of Going into the Woods Alone.

Schrader and Howk briefly mention that "Jesse had a life-long peculiarity of going into the woods or a canyon alone to think things out."[43] Was this perhaps far less "peculiar" than it seemed? Could it suggest that Jesse was deciphering KGC code inscribed in the trees, in caves or on exposed bluffs, or that he was perhaps creating new signposts for buried KGC treasure? The authors ask: "[Did] Jesse go romping about the country in invisible, astral form, keeping his eye on the vast post–Civil War Confederate Underground and his own vast financial empire?"

4. Signs of KGC Treasure.

Coauthor Howk writes that he is often asked if there are any Knights of the Golden Circle records in existence. "Only a handful," he replies. But, he adds, "there are Confederate signs, often confused for Indian markings, on rocks throughout the West, South and Midwest."[44] "JJ," he says, is the most obvious, for "Jesse James," while others include images of animals and numeric code.[45]

5. Locations of KGC Treasures.

In the book's two key chapters, "The Knights of the Golden Circle" and "The Fabulous Confederate Treasure Troves," J. Frank Dalton's professed revelations to Howk provide vague locations for the supposed KGC caches of gold, silver and arms. Dalton never says "X" marks the spot for any given area. But he does disclose that most caches are buried near cattle trails, waterways, railroad rights-of-way, livery stables, stagecoach stations, smelters and old mills.[46] Most of the troves, Dalton-James says, were buried in Oklahoma, Texas, Colorado, Montana, Wyoming, South Dakota, California, New Mexico, Arizona, Nevada, Georgia, Florida, the Carolinas, Missouri, Iowa, Illinois, Ohio and the Northwest.[47] A coded list of about one hundred sites from some eight states is provided, with the KGC's assigned name (including such vivid flourishes as "Fat Man's Greed Treasure" and "Fat Man's Misery Treasure") and, in some cases, the face value of the KGC treasure allegedly buried.[48]

Howk notes that some of the caches are relatively small. Some were buried in metal milk cans, as reportedly was the case when several hundred thousand dollars in KGC treasure—including double-eagle gold coins—was found in the 1960s near Troy, Ohio, by a great-grandson of a former KGC associate of Jesse James.[49] But the bulk of the KGC money and arms is buried in elaborate, deep underground vaults or chambers, some of which, Dalton-James said, were booby-trapped: "The old Confederate Underground agents employed both engineers and geologists. . . . The Golden Circle spared no expense in burying its gold. It employed the best engineers and the most modern equipment available."[50] Many of these professionals, including surveyors and those expert in building tunnels, were recruited from Germany, Austria, France and Italy, Howk (a.k.a. Jesse Lee James) explains in an earlier book, *Jesse James and the Lost Cause*.[51] To recover any of these large treasures would require significant manpower, machinery and, in those cases where the money is buried on public land, a "fight . . . through a maze of federal and state government red tape."[52]

6. Building—and Protecting—the Depositories.

Dalton-James explains through his intermediary, Howk, that much of the depository excavation (the digging of underground vaults and bunkers to conceal the KGC's gold, silver and arms) was done under the cover of "mining" companies. Once the large subterranean infrastructures were created, an above-ground protective sentinel system was established.

Mining companies also employed a network of agents to report "unusual activities" [near the site]. The Confederate Underground was busy sinking shafts for caches, and this could pass for "mining." Golden Circle agents were merciless, and many a "snooper" was tracked down and killed before

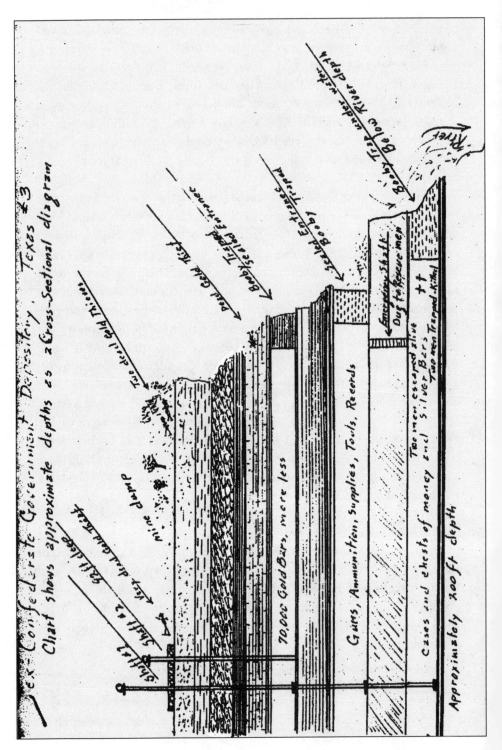

Confederate Government Depository, Texas #3
Chart shows approximate depths as a Cross-Sectional diagram

Shaft #1 per Gold Back

Shaft #2 per Gold Back

True decoil Gold Thieves

mine dump

Decoil Gold Kist

Booby/sealed Entrance
Trapped Entrance

sealed Booby
Entrance Trapped

Booby Trap below River depth
Below River depth

River

Emergency Shaft
Dug to Rescue men

70,000 Gold Bars, more less

Guns, Ammunition, Supplies, Tools, Records

Two men escaped alive
Two men Trapped Killed
Silver Bars

Cases and chests of money and Silver Bars

Approximately 200 ft depth

he could file a report. "Shoot—and ask questions later," was Colonel James' standing order to his secret operatives. Another order was, "Better to kill a man than be sorry." On rare occasions a Golden Circle agent would violate his blood oath and attempt to slip back and recover some of the buried loot. The man was invariably shot because Jesse kept a concealed guard around a new cache for generally a month. After that it was periodically inspected to see if it had been tampered with.[53]

Jesse Woodson James, according to the book, dipped into the caches on three or four occasions during his lifetime. Howk, for his part, says that he personally was tempted to uncover some of the money. He once investigated a cache site in south-central Oklahoma, north of Dallas, with a said $8 million face value in buried loot. The indicated clues on site were "two large boulders, side by side," which, ultimately, he failed to find. He gave up the thought of going back a second time after being pestered repeatedly by a greedy friend. "I told my friends I was calling off the hunt and returning to Dallas. I thought of all the blood that had been shed by those old Southerners to steal the gold and the sweat they'd expended to cache it away. This greenhorn had killed any desire I had to retrieve the trove."[54]

7. Jesse's "Key" to the Treasures.
Perhaps the most intriguing passage in the book is the following:

On his 100th birthday in 1944, old Jesse told his closest relatives, "There are no free and easy Confederate treasures, any that an amateur or tenderfoot could locate and dig out on a weekend. He'd need a hell of a lot of inside information. There is a 'key' to Confederate treasure troves. In 1916 we sealed our Golden Circle records for fifty years. So in 1966—I will be long gone—it won't belong to anybody. I will leave the 'key' to my grandson Lee Howk (Jesse James III). There are no written records of the caches, just signs and symbols, but Lee will have the 'key'—that I assure you."[55]

Not another word is mentioned about the "key."

3. Cross-sectional diagram, from a Howk letter, showing a typical deep-burial KGC depository, in this case in Texas. If large depositories exist—those containing perhaps hundreds of millions of dollars worth of gold specie and bullion bars—then they are likely to be well-engineered feats of workmanship, involving 30- to 40-foot shafts, ventilation ducts, booby traps and more.

8. The KGC: A Highly Efficient, Often Brutal, Underground.

Schrader and Howk's book, based on the latter's account of Dalton-James's rendition of the Knights of the Golden Circle story, indicates that the KGC's leadership was a well-organized, hidden Confederate cabinet. As mentioned, the secret order's headquarters were later moved to Texas, and subsequently to Colorado, after Jesse Woodson James—under his new assumed identities—took control around 1883–84. The order employed blood oaths, cryptic passwords and handshakes among its co-conspirators, and used cipher, signs and symbols to communicate.[56] It was all-male: women were kept in the dark, for their own protection.[57] Clearly, the scenario laid out by Schrader and Howk is a close echo of the Holt Report to U.S. Secretary of War Edwin Stanton, in which a *functioning* underground government of the South was said to be well under way in 1864.

Among the KGC's postwar leaders, according to *Jesse James Was One of His Names,* were not only Jesse James but Nathan Bedford Forrest, J. O. Shelby, Cole Younger, and, in a lesser role, former Confederate President Jefferson Davis.[58] They not only operated from Nashville, Canton (Texas) and then Colorado Springs, but had a network of affiliated leaders in Canada, Mexico and England. The KGC leadership placed moles inside telegraph operations, insurance companies and rail companies (some of those owned outright by the KGC)—each providing exquisite inside information for raids against trains, federal stage-coaches, banks and other targets.

The KGC plan often involved brutal actions. According to the book's authors, the militant order did numerous "violent and expedient" things in its complex history. On one hand, Dalton-James says that some of his dearest friends and most loyal protectors in his KGC circle were black; yet, at the same time, he acknowledges that the KGC formed the KKK as its militant and sometimes murderous arm to combat "unscrupulous Carpetbaggers" and to terrorize newly freed blacks in the South during Reconstruction.[59] The same KGC, he notes ever so candidly, was responsible for the disappearance of a number of black Union troops occupying the KGC hotbed of Van Zandt County, Texas, in the immediate aftermath of the war.[60] With such acknowledgments laid bare, there clearly was no attempt to canonize Jesse James in the book.

Concerning the KKK, Jesse admitted, "It was the secret military police of the Old South, but the Golden Circle really rode herd on their activities.

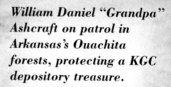

William Daniel "Grandpa" Ashcraft on patrol in Arkansas's Ouachita forests, protecting a KGC depository treasure.

1

The Brewer boys, Jack, Bob, and Dave, with their beloved uncle, Odis Ashcraft, son of W. D. Odis, killed in a timber accident a few years later, also knew the secrets behind the treasure signs.

2

W. D. Ashcraft, eyes rolled back, poses outside his cabin in a coded photograph, with a deer head, chalked-in numerals and other items in background serving as signposts for the local treasure grid.

William Martin Wiley (right) with armed colleague Feck Davis. Wiley, an ex-Confederate from Texas, stood guard for decades over a KGC treasure depository near Hatfield, Ark. W.D. Ashcraft later assumed Wiley's role as a KGC sentinel.

A coded photograph of a winking James Blalock, member of a clandestine KGC network operating in Arkansas's Ouachita Mountains in the early twentieth century. Among many KGC symbols in the photo: a U.S. Large Cent coin, a symbol of the KGC, or "Copperheads," on his lapel; an axehead atop Blalock's staff, also a symbol of the KGC; and in the instep of Blalock's right foot, an image of a Masonic, all-seeing eye.

Jacket of Edmund Wright, one of several intriguing nineteenth-century exposés of the Knights of the Golden Circle. It names some prominent officials, such as U.S. Vice President John C. Breckinridge, as affiliated with the clandestine movement.

*The Grand Seal of the KGC, from a nineteenth-century
KGC membership card.*

*George Bickley, the
quizzical frontman for
the KGC, who promoted
secession and was jailed
during the Civil War by
Abraham Lincoln.*

9

General John Anthony Quit-man, a pro-slavery ideo-logue with high status in Scottish Rite Masonic cir-cles. His pre–Civil War KGC affiliation is sug-gested by the star and crescent symbols on the horse's riding apron.

Masonic leader Albert Pike, who at various points of his career served as a Confederate brigadier general and the highest-ranking Scottish Rite Freemason in the world. Evidence suggests he was a KGC mastermind.

10

11

Nathan Bedford Forrest, feared Confederate cavalry leader, who later became a leader of both the Knights of the Golden Circle and the Ku Klux Klan.

KGC cipher and encrypted message written inside the cover of a prayer book once in the possession of George Bickley and now at the National Archives in Washington, D.C.

12

A B C D E F G H I J K L M N O P Q R S T U V W X Y

1 2 3 4 5 6 7 8 9

13

*Confederate cipher as discovered by
Union forces during the occupation
of Richmond in April 1865.*

*The KGC-encrypted
"Bible Tree," first shown
by W. D. Ashcraft to Bob
Brewer as a youngster in
1950. The carved beech—
here showing the horse or
mule figure, the J.A.S.
inscription and other
chalked-in markings—
served as a directional
road map for various
parts of the KGC's
Ouachita underground
treasure grid, as Bob
would later discover
over decades of
intensive research.*

14

15

Another ancient carved beech in Brushy Valley, showing the names of KGC associates W. D. Ashcraft and J. Avants, with dates ranging from the 1850s through the early 1900s.

16

Pages from the daybook of Isom Avants. The pocket note-book reveals the names of locals, including Will Ashcraft and James Blalock, apparently involved in some undefined business operation centered around Shady, Arkansas—the guarding of hidden caches of former Rebel treasure.

This page from Avants's "Memorandum" daybook, shows a spiderweb-like drawing that Bob Brewer would later discover to be a crude match for the circular "template" used by the KGC to lay out its treasure grids across the South and Southwest.

A spiderweb-like grid found on a "stone map" discovered in Texas and presumably outlining a KGC depository layout. Note the similarity to the drawing in Avants's daybook.

Large KGC coded inscription on beech in Ouachitas. The swaying palm, seagull and crescent moon formed a Confederate montage found in numerous emblems of secession, including the South Carolina flag.

Another heavily inscribed beech, serving as a road map for locating KGC treasure, in the Arkansas backcountry. Note the vertical snake figure and the egg-laying turtle figure to its right. The turtle is a key KGC sign for treasure. This tree map—in combination with other carvings and numerous items buried in the shallow surface—helped lead Bob Brewer to treasure.

Bob Brewer's lifelong friend and neighbor Bob Tilley, pointing to a carved snake. The snake form, in this instance, represents the course of a local stream.

Bob Smith, a treasure-hunting friend of Tilley and, for a short while, Brewer, holding up a large "heart rock" map that he dug up in the Brushy Valley. The rock is inscribed with numerous lines and dots. Hearts—carved into trees and rock faces or sculpted from stone or metal and buried in the ground—are key KGC markers for treasure. Brewer has identified more than a dozen such heart figures at suspected KGC depository sites.

22

Sculpted metal heart found jointly by the authors at a legendary Jesse James treasure site in Oklahoma, buried in an open field, about a foot deep, along a compass bearing that Brewer derived from nearby carved symbols.

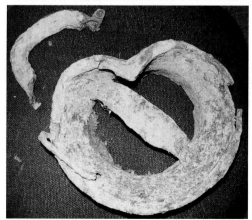

23

24

*A portrait of Jesse Woodson
James as a young man.*

*Front-page story in Lawton, Oklahoma, newspaper from the late 1940s.
The article sparked a nationwide controversy about the Jesse James
saga and associated rumors of buried Confederate treasure.*

Several telltale features, including a "JJ" for Jesse James and the date 1880, visible at a treasure site in Wapanucka, Oklahoma, where Bob Brewer and others located buried signposts and caches of coins.

Buried gun barrel as uncovered by Bob Brewer and Michael Griffith on a high ledge above Delaware Creek at the Wapanucka site. The gun barrel provided an important directional pointer for solving the treasure grid.

U.S. gold and silver nineteenth-century coins found by Brewer and Michael Griffith at sites in and around Wapanucka, Oklahoma. The newest coins in the batch are dated 1880, corresponding to the 1880 designation on both the Jesse James map and the "JJ" "1880" carvings found at the site.

The priest-templar stone map from the Superstition Mountain area of south-central Arizona. In broken Spanish, instructions advise to "Look for the Map, Look for the Heart." Bob Brewer was able to locate the topographic equivalent of the priest figure in the contour lines of a U.S. Geological Survey map of the Superstition area dating from the early 1900s.

Another artistically rendered stone map allegedly discovered in the Superstitions sometime in the 1940s. By deciphering the code on the tablet and deciphering clues from the field, Bob Brewer was able to discern the outline of the horse's body in topographic features of the area.

30

Tracing of horse tablet which shows the "behemoth" figure to the left of the horse's head. The figure is not shown in the photo of the stone tablet; it is possible that it was sanded off sometime after the tracing was made, which would explain the discrepancy.

31

Bob Brewer was able to show how each symbol in this tablet corresponded to a specific reference point on an enormous topographic grid of the area—ultimately defining the outline of a giant KGC depository and the solution to the "Lost Dutchman" mystery.

32

33

Elisha Reavis, a suspected KGC sentinel of the Superstition Mountain area.

These odd metal objects found in a 22-foot shaft on a private ranch in Arizona formed a KGC "waybill" or map. Standing in the background, from left to right, Brian MacLeod, Ellie Gardner, Bob Brewer, and Bob Schoose.

34

Five "beehive" huts near Gila River. Bob Brewer suspects that these odd-shaped structures had a symbolic and topographic significance—providing key lines of sight for one or several large and deeply buried KGC treasures in the Superstition region.

35

Giant skull-shaped boulder at Arizona site where Bob Brewer and Brian MacLeod were accosted by an armed interrogator who arrived by helicopter. The skull figure gazes into an area where a cluster of KGC markers were found.

36

Enormous carvings of five-pointed star (center) and jack-o-lantern face (above, right) on cliff in Superstition Mountains. These markers lie on key directional lines that Bob Brewer was investigating.

37

We began folding up the KKK a few years after the Golden Circle sealed its records in 1916. We oldtimers had absolutely nothing to do with the modern KKK, which is a different breed of cat."[61]

The KKK was but one of several lower-level, associated groups operating under the KGC umbrella. Others included the Knights of the White Camellias and the International Anti-Horse Thief Association, according to the Schrader-Howk account.[62]

9. John Wilkes Booth: An Associate of the KGC.

Could John Wilkes Booth have been a member or close associate of the KGC, and did he execute an order from his KGC superiors to kill President Lincoln? Dalton-James, through Howk and Schrader's telling in a chapter dedicated to the Booth saga, says that Booth was never a formal KGC insider but rather a member of the lower-ranking Knights of the White Camellias.[63] But the KGC sprang into action to keep Booth alive and out of government hands, following the assassination. The reason: "he knew too much" about KGC operations.[64]

It may never be known, beyond a reasonable doubt, whether J. Frank Dalton was Jesse Woodson James, the notorious "rebel" outlaw and averred head of the Knights of the Golden Circle. Despite being criticized on various levels by detractors, *Jesse James Was One of His Names* makes a number of intriguing assertions that merit further exploration and analysis.

No doubt, conflicting reports have been part and parcel of the Jesse James saga. Faulty memories, bad reporting, and indeed, *deliberate misinformation* play a role in the difficulty of sorting out such a complex, camouflaged story. Seen in that context, *Jesse James Was One of His Names* may prove a most revealing and vastly misunderstood book. It should be noted that Schrader and Howk were not the only ones drawn to J. Frank Dalton's story and to conclude that there may have been a darker, conspiratorial side of the Jesse James saga.

In *Jesse James "The Outlaw,"* author Henry J. Walker says that his independent research into the life of J. Frank Dalton convinced him that the old man was Jesse Woodson James and that he was a high-ranking member of a secret society for the Southern cause.[65] In his self-published 1961 book, Walker, who interviewed Dalton and his aged associates, says that Jesse Woodson James and KGC and Confederate guerrilla leader William Quantrill were "higher-degree Masons" and were members of an unnamed militant secret order "controlled by men in the high Confederate wing of the Democratic Party of that time."[66] Walker quotes J. Frank Dalton: "Quantrill was a thirty-third-degree Mason. We were all Masons, and attended Masonic Lodge meetings in various towns, using assumed names of course."[67] The order had gone around the country burying gold and other treasure for the cause. "Last year late in the fall I made the rounds, and we still have cached away in various places I visited $500,000 in gold money and an equal amount in the value of diamonds and jewels we hid in the 1860s and 70s and 80s," says one Dalton-James associate interviewed by Walker in 1949.[68] Walker's research led him to conclude—without ever mentioning the name Knights of the Golden Circle—that:

> ... the robberies and escapades they took part in were not actually of their own planning, nor the plans of their band of outlaws. The James boys were only a small part of a large movement of members of a "lost cause" in the South. Some of these members were even elected to government positions; some were employees of the express companies, and this secret organization was financed mostly by a foreign government to make regular espionage reports on the United States outpost forts, from 1865 to 1892. Not until this latter date did this spying movement collapse.[69]

The Hunt Extends to Oklahoma

8

AFTER pondering *Jesse James Was One of His Names* for a couple of weeks, Bob was convinced that he was searching for Rebel treasure—and on a large scale. He had little doubt that the mysterious signs he had been following in the Arkansas woods would lead to additional hoards—gold and silver coins, perhaps bullion, buried systematically—in other parts of the country. It all boiled down to locating the proper markers, deciphering their hidden messages and plotting their distribution on the topo maps. Someone, or perhaps some clandestine organization like the KGC, must have designed the elaborate, indeed ingenious, method used to mark the treasure-cache layouts. To think that a central player behind the conspiracy may have been the most infamous fugitive of them all, and a die-hard Confederate to boot!

Before he read the Schrader-Howk title, which he dubbed the "black book" for its black binding, Bob had wondered if there really could be as much hidden loot as the numerous markings and buried clues in the Ouachitas had suggested. Now, here were two twentieth-century co-authors telling him that an intricate subterranean patchwork did indeed extend over many state lines. Still, he needed to verify the scope of such a grand scheme, through his own methodical, step-by-step approach.

Setting aside the book's obvious yarns and hyperbole, Bob found that many of J. Frank Dalton's remarks about the code-makers' methods rang true. The abstract signs and symbols, the remote locations of the caches, the mining operations as potential cover for cache burials, the shoot-to-kill sentinels, and Jesse's "going into the woods alone," all sounded authentic. But parts of the book seemed hard to swallow. It was one thing to assert that the KGC's underground system was spread over more than a dozen states. But were there *really* hundreds of millions of dollars—*or more*—in hidden post-Confederate treasure, still untouched, as the book's authors assert? And what was all that about "the key" to those fabulous Confederate treasure troves?

While Bob weighed the latter question in the summer of 1993, a phone call came from a treasure hunter and Jesse James history buff in Oklahoma, a junior high school history teacher named Michael Griffith. Like dozens of other weekend treasure hunters who had obtained a copy of Bob's "Bible Tree" videotape that year, Griffith was probing for help on a pet project.

Over the phone, Griffith came across as cocksure about Old West history but deferential when it came to locating buried treasure. It was clear from that first call that Griffith was passionate about Jesse James history and lore, was a collector of James memorabilia and fancied himself an expert on the outlaw. Griffith suggested they meet and swap ideas. It was worth exploring, Bob thought, and he agreed to a visit.

He found the younger man congenial, if perhaps a trifle too gung-ho. Successful treasure hunting, like any good detective work, requires time and patience. Griffith, from those first face-to-face hours, seemed to be itching for a strike, despite a feigned nonchalance. Bob chalked it up to the amateur historian's passion for his subject, as much as to any pecuniary motivation. Any of Bob's initial misgivings were set aside by the fact that Griffith seemed extremely knowledgeable about the history of the Oklahoma–Indian Territory region; the middle-school instructor taught Oklahoma history on a regular basis to ninth graders.

Even more important, Griffith was well aware of the KGC: he had his own worn copy of *Jesse James Was One of His Names* and had conducted archival and field research of his own. It turned out that Griffith had been introduced to some of the local history by Bud Hardcastle, a Purcell, Oklahoma–based acquaintance of Bob's. Hardcastle, who had spent several years quietly investigating the J. Frank Dalton/Jesse James/KGC enigma, had provided Griffith with Bob's "Bible Tree" video.

But it was not just that Griffith had read the black book a dozen times. The Oklahoman told Bob he was convinced that rumors of the post–Civil War KGC and its hidden treasures were accurate: the trick was figuring out exactly where the caches were. He admitted that he had not had any luck recovering caches, despite several years of intermittent searching at a couple of suspected Jesse James hideouts in Oklahoma. Was Bob interested in visiting some of these, he asked. Bob was.

Even more intriguing was Griffith's assertion that he had photocopies of what he believed to be authentic Jesse James maps, and that one of the Oklahoma "locations" possibly was associated with one of the maps.[1] (These maps, Bob later learned, had been provided to Griffith by Hardcastle.)

His imagination stirred by the Schrader-Howk book, Bob was intrigued but still not convinced. He knew that in the ever-important getting-to-know-you period he would need to remain detached. Recalling his earlier unhappy experience with Bob Smith, he was not prepared to share all that he knew with a stranger. Specifics in the treasure-hunting world were disclosed sparingly, if at all, and then only at certain milestones in a relationship. He could not let his innate mountaineer wariness be overtaken by the thrill of the chase with this upbeat outsider.

After a series of late summer get-togethers at his home in Hatfield—mostly weekend visits by Griffith and his school-aged son—Bob concluded that he could do business with the enthusiastic schoolteacher. The two discussed a fifty-fifty partnership. Bob would bring his knowledge of finding treasure through decoding signs and symbols; Griffith would provide access to target locations and his collection of maps. Bob agreed, but he also reserved the right to work on his own projects and with others who might come forward with independent leads. Griffith shook on the deal and then asked to see some of Bob's fieldwork.

At the time, family obligations had narrowed Bob's window for tracking treasure. He and Linda had been sharing duties with other family members looking after Landon Brewer, who was stricken with Alzheimer's disease. Griffith, to Bob's surprise, nonetheless repeatedly made the drive to Hatfield to talk treasure during those drawn-out mornings and afternoons when Bob was housebound looking after his father. In the ensuing months, Bob carved out time to show his visitor a thing or two about "lost treasures" on the Arkansas side of the border.

On one occasion, while exploring along the banks of the Cossatot River, the two men responded to the faint calls for help from a teenage girl who had been swept downstream. The youngster was struggling for her life, half-submerged in the currents of the rain-swollen river. With another passerby, the men rescued the exhausted girl, who had been trapped in a whirlpool and was clinging precariously to a ledge. The incident would foster a growing trust and esprit de corps between Bob and Griffith.

Over several subsequent outings around Hatfield, Griffith grew impressed at the number of carvings and buried markers embedded in the forest—and how well Bob seemed to be able to link the signs and symbols together in a pattern. He kept asking whether there was a way to apply what had been accomplished in Arkansas to a possibly related site more than 130 miles away, in southern Oklahoma. The site, Griffith suggested, perhaps correlated to one of his photocopied treasure maps, which, he said, appeared to have been drawn up by Jesse James himself. (Among other indicators, the map contained the initials *JJ*.)

Not having seen anything to go by, Bob was noncommittal. He had worked a few Ouachita sites that extended just over the border into Oklahoma, but he had not ventured very far west into the neighboring state on any major cache hunt. But when Griffith got around to revealing the suspected cache site's general location—a wooded, hilly area of south-central Oklahoma—Bob became focused fast.

The nearest town of any size, Griffith said, was Atoka. Bob recalled that *Jesse James Was One of His Names* mentions Atoka "in the Indian Territory" twice: once where "Jesse and his friends were sitting around a campfire," and again as a site where Jesse had left behind one of his wives.[2] Griffith declined to show Bob the coded map, and Bob did not press the point. He was prepared to inspect the site on the basis of Griffith's word and on the few other promising leads, such as the site's proximity to Atoka.

But how could Griffith be sure that the site corresponded to a possible KGC depository, Bob asked.

The schoolteacher explained that a few years earlier he had heard about someone who had stumbled upon an odd series of rock carvings in the southern part of the state. When he asked to see a drawing of those carvings, he was struck by their correlation: the symbols appeared to be an exact match of the signs and code drawn on one of his "Jesse James" maps. He drove to the site, a hilly area near a limestone quarry. There, he was astonished to see an alphabet soup of chiseled signs and symbols. To his further amazement, the engraved symbols all appeared linked to those on his treasure map. While the grooved letters and symbols ultimately failed to lead to treasure in a subsequent three years of prospecting, he told Bob that he was persuaded there was Jesse James gold stashed on the site.

Griffith also disclosed how he and Hardcastle had discovered an inscribed rock ledge near a spring in north-central Oklahoma. After decades of built-up layers of soil had been removed, the engraved slab revealed the counterpoised names *Jesse James* and *Dalton,* with the letter *F* etched inside the *D* of *Dalton.* The ledge (originally found by Hardcastle through leads derived from documents dating back to the late 1880s) was full of KGC treasure carvings, making it a coded map in its own right. In preparation for their treasure-hunting trip, Griffith took Bob to see the cryptic slab—a sight that reinforced the possibility that J. Frank Dalton and Jesse Woodson James were one and the same.[3]

Over Thanksgiving weekend in 1993, Griffith and Brewer embarked on their first joint expedition to the southern Oklahoma locale.[4] After a five-hour drive and brief stops at suspected KGC sites along the way (including the remains of a probable KGC meeting house, with a large underground "bunker" and escape tunnel), they arrived at a wooded area near the small town of Bromide. The town was named for nearby sulfur springs, which, according to local lore, may have attracted a convalescing Jesse James.

Griffith parked his pickup next to a pasture fence blocking a dead-end road. There, he pulled out the Jesse James map for a few seconds to check his orientation, oddly refusing to let Bob see it. The Arkansan brushed off the slight, knowing how guarded treasure hunters can be about their "information." Bob mentally noted "strike one" in his silent strategy of testing his "partner."

Within minutes of passing through an old barbwire fence and arriving at a crossing on Delaware Creek, Bob spotted a characteristic set of axe-cut "blazes" high on a big, two-foot-diameter pecan tree. The engravings suggested an upside-down heart—two fishhooks facing each other at a slight westerly tilt. A KGC heart symbol, he thought. It hinted that something important lay nearby, to the west. Griffith apparently had no idea. Bob turned to his partner and asked if he had ever been to that exact spot and if he had ever dug treasure there. Griffith said no, on both counts. "Well, let's go dig it up then," Bob suggested, to the Oklahoman's astonishment.

Bob paced due west a few hundred yards until he spied a big red oak with characteristic carvings. The cryptic markings were similar to those that he had seen back in Arkansas. He told Griffith that he believed something was buried in the immediate vicinity and asked him to scan around the oak, near the creek bank. But the schoolteacher's rudimentary detector and his excited, ad hoc searching method hindered his ability to pick up a signal. Soon, Griffith was yards away, heading into a muddy cotton field.

Bob swung his own, more sophisticated detector over the area and, within seconds, received a strong signal. It indicated that an iron object was just inches below the black gumbo earth. The two men dug down about half a foot into the sticky soil. There, lying flat, was an old cap-and-ball revolver. Bob identified it as a .44-caliber 1858 Remington, a U.S. Army model. The rusty gun was in good shape, although the wooden grips had rotted off. Bob carefully and silently noted the compass bearing indicated by the tip of the gun barrel before plucking the "six-shooter" from its earthen mold. He had recognized the rusted artifact as a directional marker, one deliberately planted just beneath the surface—and thus an important clue to finding buried money.

Griffith, fondling the antique weapon, was at a loss for words. Within minutes of setting foot on the site, Bob had unearthed something significant by reading the tree carvings—coded markers all but invisible to the untrained eye. Griffith's elation and impatience for more, for shiny yellow metal, were palpable. Bob merely grinned and said that, because of an approaching snowstorm and the late hour, it was best to head back. They would have to plan for another day.

The schoolteacher could hardly argue. Bob held all the cards. When he and Griffith parted ways after the long drive north, the Oklahoman said he was going to keep the revolver because it was found on his site. To avoid confrontation, Bob said nothing. Besides, old guns and other trail markers already littered the grounds around his home. Access to new sites and to potentially valuable information was more important than quibbling over an old pistol, even if it had connections to the fabled Jesse James. Still, it was "strike two." When Bob told his old friend Bob Tilley about the incident, Tilley counseled him to leave the "snake" alone.

A month later, Bob returned with Griffith to the Delaware Creek site, this time accompanied by Griffith's father and son. He was amused at the sudden change in the senior Griffith: a month earlier, Charles Griffith wanted no part of treasure hunting; he said that he would rather stay home and watch football. But, following the discovery of the revolver, Michael's father had been transformed into a full-fledged "cache hunter," sporting a half-grown beard, a hunting cap and camouflage jacket. On the long drive to the site, the elder Griffith repeated nearly word for word what his son had told him about the possible Jesse James connection to the Bromide area.

Once on site, it took only minutes to find the covered-up hole where the Remington revolver had been recovered, and then a few seconds to obtain the correct compass bearing. Bob was set. He handed Griffith his Garrett metal detector and directed him to check along the creek bank, behind a large tree where the revolver had pointed. Almost immediately, the detector sounded its unique belltone, one familiar to Bob, who declared, matter-of-factly, "That's money!"

The men grabbed their shovels and dug a hole a little over a foot deep behind the tree. As soon as Michael reached in and said that he felt a glass jar, Bob announced: "It's payday." Michael handed his father the jar.

Charles Griffith could not believe his eyes. He kept repeating, "Golly, well, golly," as he counted out silver dollars, half-dollars and other silver coins dated from 1812 to 1880. Many were Morgan silver dollars from 1878–80. Michael Griffith, no less excited, grabbed his video camera and videotaped the scene in the minutes after the find.[5] "This was the location on the map. This was found right here at the one location on the map, where we found a pistol," he said while filming. "Just below where we found the ol' cap-and-ball pistol, we finally got one. And this worked out on the map," he continued, repeating himself amid the thrill of the find.

The muddied silver coins, totaling several thousand dollars in current market value and including a rare 1853-O half-dollar piece, were divided evenly between Bob and the Griffiths. The latter were stunned, this being their first recovered treasure. And it had been found by following a scavenger-hunt trail on the ground that, according to Griffith's own words, had corresponded to a general location indicated by the James Gang map of the area. Bob was convinced that the pint jar was a marker for a much larger KGC cache. To have a chance of finding it, he said, he would need to see all the symbols—particularly those that corresponded to the map, which Griffith continued to conceal.

Impressed with Brewer's work so far, Griffith agreed at the end of December that it was important for Bob to see everything. He finally showed him the copied map of the area, which had *JJ, 1880,* and a backward and misspelled reference, *FIND GUN BERREL NEAR CREEK,* in a schematic rendering. Although Griffith declined to give Bob a copy of the map, he handed him a copy of another probable KGC treasure map, this one far more complicated and obscure. It had a wolf or dog-like figure drawn in the middle, amid a flurry of lines, dotted lines and stick figures. Griffith said he had no inkling as to the map's geographic reference point but, after what had just happened, he expressed full confidence in Bob's ability to crack the code.

Months later, in April 1994, the Griffiths and Brewer returned to the area of their treasure strike. This time, the group set out about a mile and a half due east, in a remote section of wooded bluffs along the Old Leavenworth Trail. Known as Wapanucka, the picturesque area is named for a Delaware Indian chief. Its rugged limestone hills teem with wild boar, deer, duck, quail and wild turkey. Delaware Creek at the base of the bluffs is home to bass, perch and catfish. With its wooded bluffs providing long lines-of-sight over the surrounding flatlands, the area must have been ideal for crafting outlaw hideouts and mountain redoubts. From various promontories thick with buzzards and ven-omous snakes, Jesse James, Frank James, the Dalton brothers and other KGC "fugitives" would have been able to see oncoming lawmen well before any raid. As Griffith would point out, the initials *JJ*—resembling those in the black book and on Griffith's map—were inscribed inside the walls of a cave and on top of a cliff face in the area.

The sprawling property contained the ruins of the former Chickasaw Rock Academy, a school for orphan Chickasaw children built in the 1850s. The school, also known as the Wapanucka Academy, later served as re-gional headquarters for Confederate Brig. Gen. Douglas H. Cooper and his Chickasaw and Choctaw brigade. It then became a Confederate Army hos-pital. Cooper, who eventually rose to command all Indian troops, was a colleague of Cherokee KGC leader and Confederate brigadier general Stand Watie. He had been placed in charge of all Indian troops in the ter-ritory by Albert Pike. Once again, KGC symbols, Albert Pike, Confeder-ate Indians and the promise of buried gold seemed to intersect.

At the Wapanucka Academy site, near the line separating Johnston and Coal counties, the group arrived at the entrance of a large ranch. Noticing that the iron front gate appeared locked, Bob asked Griffith if they had permission to treasure hunt on the site. Griffith said yes, and then drove off to the home of an old-timer who seemed to be the over-seer. The man returned with the group and let the visitors in with a nod, after exchanging a few pleasantries with Griffith.

True to his word, Griffith showed Bob the mysterious symbols that had been chiseled into a bluff, near a quarry of bleach-white limestone. The

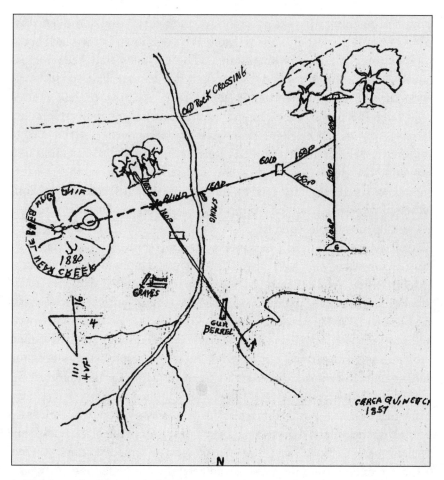

4. *This is a photocopy of what appears to be an authentic Jesse James treasure map. It led to the recovery of several KGC treasure caches in south-central Oklahoma. Bob Brewer and Michael Griffith located the various landmarks on the map, as well as specific symbols and captions (JJ, 1880, the turtle, gun barrel etc.) on site in Wapanucka, Oklahoma. These guideposts pointed to small caches of gold and silver coins. The original map is believed to have been found at another Jesse James/KGC cache site uncovered decades ago.*

view—atop the highest point in the area—was breathtaking. The carvings were no less dramatic. Bob ran his fingers over the grooves in the hard stone. The engravings included the letters *JJ*, alongside the numbers *1880* and *11,000* and a stick-figure turtle whose head pointed across the valley. Below the ledge was a box-shaped carving with a cross on top and two smaller, inverted crosses protruding from the bottom corners. This was powerful corroborative evidence: the apparent chiseled-in-stone signature marks of Jesse James, in the same mold as those shown in the black book.

Something troubled Bob, though. The carvings had been all but rubbed out, and it looked as though the vandal had acted fairly recently. On close inspection, it appeared as if someone had poured acid over the limestone etchings, hoping to obscure them. He could barely contain the thought that Griffith may have been the one to deface the delicate inscriptions, to keep others off the trail. Could that explain why the schoolteacher had insisted on keeping the treasure map and its representations of the symbols in his sole possession? When Bob asked what had happened to the signs, Griffith said that local kids must have done it.

Able to see enough of the symbolism to recognize the potential KGC orientation of the site, Bob moved on. The turtle alone was a well-recognized treasure symbol. Dating back to Spanish colonial days, the turtle symbol had appeared many times in the Ouachitas—and here it was juxtaposed with *JJ!* He recalled how Howk had made specific, albeit unexplained, reference to "seeing a turtle go by" to identify kin to Jesse James.

There was more to see, Griffith said, but it was best to head to a cleared hilltop on the other side of Delaware Creek to camp for the night. At the campsite, Griffith pointed out a few other chiseled symbols, including a large turkey track engraved in a slab just yards away from where the men had set up their tents. Again, images from the pages of the black book came rushing back to Bob. The phrase "turkey track," representing a known KGC directional treasure-marker, had been used as code to identify Jesse "Dingus" James—Jesse Woodson James's cousin—in the book. While Bob had seen several carved turkey tracks in the mountains of Arkansas, that distinct symbol's location among others possibly left behind by Jesse Woodson James was unforgettable. And there was more.

Near the campsite was the cave with a set of *JJ* initials cut into its limestone wall. Above the cave, a large boulder was inscribed with numerous KGC symbols. Some thirty yards from the boulder lay a slab with chiseled lettering. Bob carefully traced his fingers along its grooves and, after chalking them in, could read the following: *JW PicKeNS*. The *N* and the *S* were written backwards and the *K* had a weird arrow-like flourish. Bob interpreted the combination to mean "Jesse Woodson's Pickings." The *N* and the *S* were directional indicators, he assumed. Below was the lettering: *S. A. PARKER*. Bob was unsure of its meaning but noted that the second *A* was made out like a Masonic square-and-

compass configuration. To the left of *PARKER* could be seen a tiny turtle, its head pointing west while its crooked tail slanted southeast. Next
to the turtle was a carving of a hand, with its index finger aiming east
and its thumb pointing south—along the same north-south line indicated
by the *NS* in *PicKeNS*.

Heading south the next morning along the compass bearing indicated
by the rock carvings, Bob came to a disfigured oak tree about a quarter of
a mile away. Its bent limbs pointed north, toward Delaware Creek. On a
mossy ledge along the creek bank, Bob discovered a large neatly carved
arrowhead figure aimed at the ground. Directly beneath the pointer was a
large excavated hole—an apparent decoy or trick, Bob guessed, to make
one think that a cache had been buried there but was now long gone. Not
to be led astray by the spurious pit, he stayed put, closely examining the
ledge for subtle clues that might lead him through the maze. Hidden beneath a layer of slimy mineral deposits was a barely visible carving of a
turtle, about the size of a quarter. The head of the tiny turtle pointed back
toward the head of the larger turtle engraving that he had seen on the
other side of the creek, near the quarry. He knew then that he had discovered a major line, because terrapins ranked high in the pecking order of
KGC pointers for gold.

At the campsite later that day, Bob developed another line from a
large turkey track carving that the group had found on a nearby bluff.
The track pointed to a heavily engraved boulder, not more than thirty
yards away, in the direction of the creek. The continuation of the line—
from the combination of the turkey track and signs on the engraved
boulder—brought the group to the top of a bluff across the creek, northwest of the campsite. A careful search along an exposed limestone shelf
revealed a series of coded phrases and miscellaneous lettering. These
included an arched line of letters, yielding *LARCHDALE*. Near it were
two *I*s, a large number *4*, a large plus sign, and the letters *BHL*. In
LARCHDALE, the *C* was strangely constructed, with a small slanted
line attached to the bottom curve, perhaps suggesting that the *C* could
also be used as a *G*. The *D*, carved backward, was also part of a directional cipher or marker. Bob intuited a directional heading—running off
the back of the reversed *D*—indicating west-southwest.

Early the next day, at a distance of about one hundred yards from the
LARCHDALE inscription, along a line derived from the carvings, the
group carefully combed the area with their detectors. A few minutes
later, they unearthed a buried 1894 Winchester rifle, intact except for the

wooden gunstock. The gun barrel, as it turned out, lay on the same line indicated by the two turtle heads.

Griffith was elated. His map said, in backward writing and mis-spelled, *FIND GUN BERREL NEAR CREEK*. After a few days of searching, Bob had found the spot. Griffith had looked in vain for the "gun barrel" for over three years with treasure map in hand—a map that he still refused to share with Bob. (Having earlier deduced an important directional line running between the gun barrel and the academy, Bob guessed that *LARCHDALE BHL* contained the important anagram, BERL ACAD, which, if one adds the dual C-G letter, could spell, G BERL ACAD, as in "follow the gun-barrel/academy line." The ana-gram might also suggest, once having found the gun barrel, that the burial [read "berrel," using Southern phonetics] site was located on the same line! As Bob would later learn, Griffith's map did contain a key line running from the gun barrel through a rectangular figure—a seeming representation of the Wapanucka Academy—to a spot where another key line on the map crossed, near what appeared to be a row of three large trees. That spot on the map would later prove significant.)

For now, Griffith's selfishness mattered little to Bob. His mind was set on finding what he suspected was a master cache somewhere in the vicinity—and the rifle, he sensed, was a crucial orientation marker for the layout of what appeared to be a large KGC depository.

Yet the search for the bigger prize around Wapanucka during the spring of 1994 was not to be. Bob had returned to the campsite around dusk on their first day and was waiting for Griffith and his father to show up, when a couple of men unexpectedly drove on to the property with treasure-hunting equipment. One of them eventually introduced himself, saying he was on the property looking for treasure and had written per-mission to be there from the owners, the Gillespie sisters of Tulsa. Eyeing the metal detectors scattered around, he asked Bob what his group was doing. Bob readily admitted to treasure hunting, saying that his party had permission to be on the property as well. The strangers drove off, and some minutes later the Griffiths returned. Bob described his encounter with the other treasure hunters, but Michael Griffith said nothing.

Around noon the following day, just as Bob and Griffith were prepar-ing to attempt a second recovery based on the discovery of the rifle bar-rel that morning, the pair received a visit from a young man who said that he was the foreman of the Gillespie property. In a few curt words, the watchman told them that they were trespassing. He said that the sheriff had been notified and would arrive to arrest them if they did not immediately depart.

The group decamped, snatching up their gear and stacking it in Griffith's pickup. Once inside the cab, Bob scolded his so-called partner for telling him that they had permission to be on the property. Griffith threw up his hands and said that the old overseer had said it was all right. The truth, Bob later discovered, was that the old-timer had no authority to allow treasure hunting on site; he merely leased the cattle grazing rights to the 600-acre ranchland. Permission to hunt treasure had to come from the owners, sisters Ceci and Jo Anne Gillespie, who lived more than 150 miles away in Tulsa.

The whole affair embarrassed Bob and left him deeply disappointed in this junior-high school teacher who seemed to have a penchant for evasions. He knew, deep down, that this was probably a good time to part ways with Griffith, and he made no effort to contact him in the days after this latest excursion.

A short while later Bob received a revealing handwritten letter from Griffith.[6] He found it hard to believe, but Griffith had reconnoitered back on to the property, after being formally warned off the location just days earlier.

In his letter, Griffith greets Bob with an exclamation and says that he has news to tell about his "location" and his "latest find." He relates how he and his father "went down to the location about two days after we all had camped there." He describes how they had parked on a highway and then walked some two miles to get to the grave, an apparent reference to the tombstone of a pioneer schoolteacher buried on the Gillespie property. The letter goes on to detail how Griffith paced off in a southeasterly direction and eventually came upon three big trees, those apparently drawn on the Wapanucka treasure map. It then recounts how Griffith and his dad uncovered a buried old Colt pistol, with ivory handles. The pistol barrel, Griffith writes, pointed to another tree where they recovered a cache of $100 (face value) of gold and silver dollars, dating from the 1830s to 1880. One of the gold coins, from 1844, is "worth $700" alone. "Bob, I now have the map figured out and now know where to look for the big one. I know it's there. Just waiting to be found by us . . . with your help we can find it."

That turkey! Bob thought. Then Griffith called him, wanting to drive down to Hatfield to show off the newfound coins. Bob, undeniably interested in seeing Griffith's claim validated but disgusted by the man's conniving, reluctantly agreed to a brief visit. He suspected that Griffith was being less-than-factual about having used the Wapanucka Academy cemetery as a landmark to locate the second cache.[7] He believed that Griffith, in fact, had used the rifle barrel together with the map to acquire the directional line that led to the treasure, which had been in a ceramic spittoon. Now, over the phone, the Oklahoman was claiming the find as his alone. It would be interesting to see, Bob thought, whether there would be a cut for him.

Over the following weekend, Griffith and his son paid a visit. After a few awkward pleasantries at the door, Griffith placed a handful of gold coins into Linda Brewer's hand. Thinking it was Bob's share of the treasure, Linda thanked him—her surprise evident in the lilt of her words of gratitude. Immediately, Griffith grabbed back the coins, telling a now bewildered Linda that since Bob was not there when the cache was recovered, the Brewers would not get a share of the find. Adding insult to injury, he told them that the find was all on videotape. Bob ground his teeth. Strike three.

The visit left the Brewers with feelings of resentment. Linda felt that her husband was being grossly used, but Bob was not willing to terminate all dealings with Griffith. He was convinced that the small stashes were mere clues to much bigger treasures and that the small finds would sooner or later lead to a significant cache recovery, at which he would be present. Any dealings with Griffith, he knew, would be a Faustian trade-off: obtaining access and new insights into solving Jesse's puzzles from someone who shared a burning passion to "find the big one" yet who seemed callous to others.

There would be other costs involved, he knew. A silver lining was that the recovered antique revolvers, the old cap-and-ball gun and the Colt pistol, were known to be popular firearms during the James gang era.[8] And the gold coins, many dated to 1880 and consistent with the "1880" written on Griffith's map, meant that they probably had found part of "Jesse's Pickins!" Nevertheless, Bob suspected that the next strike was not going to be as easy. Indeed, he viscerally knew that the trail to recovering a master cache would be exceedingly complex and not without peril.

The Wolf Map

9

WAPANUCKA teased him. The carvings, the buried rifle and pistols, the coin-laden jar and spittoon had all hinted at some large treasure. So did Griffith's ephemeral map. But Bob was still at a loss as to what the "key" to the KGC's treasure troves might be and how solving that mystery might lead to a major cache. The cryptic "key" reference by J. Frank Dalton in the black book loomed ever large in his thinking.

It was around this time, in early spring 1994, that the answer started to take shape. For years, beginning in the late 1980s, Bob suspected that a geometric pattern had been laid out, topographically, at each major site, beginning with the Bible Tree area. The "pattern" was just that: a standard shape—indicated by carvings, buried clues and other markers providing directional lines—that could be replicated, from site to site, differing only in scale. In his fieldwork in Arkansas, he had seen how the pattern seemed to be formed around two major intersecting lines, shaped in an "X" configuration. These lines stretched northeast to southwest, and northwest to southeast across a large section of the topographical quadrangle map for a given region. And there was more to it.

He had discerned a pattern of lines radiating from the center of the "X" in every cardinal direction. This geometric hub, he imagined, marked the center of a circumscribed area where directional markers were distributed. Yet, he had also found other markers at equidistant locations *outside* the area of the interpolated circle. Like those key points within the circle, these outlying locations were found while he walked along magnetic-compass and Global Positioning System (GPS) headings. After he discovered one or two extraneous points, Bob found that he could project the approximate location of each subsequent outlying point via a series of triangulations. (Surveyors use triangulation to determine the relative position of three fixed points. By recording the known distance between two of the points and the measured angles of sight to the third, they can calculate the remaining sides and angle of the triangle formed by the points. Thus, triangulation is a preferred method to run lines and measure distances over mountains and across lakes and rivers.)

Ultimately, Bob came to believe that these extraneous marker points revealed an overarching pattern: a square formed around an inner circle.

His ability to envision this geometric layout stemmed, in part, from his Navy experience. Among his first assignments as a Navy metalsmith was painting aircraft, and one of his first tests was to paint the National Insignia—the five-pointed star surrounded by a circle—on a combat plane. (The original design of the circumscribed five-pointed star had been created using only dividers, a compass and a square, in a neat mathematical process known as the "squaring of the circle," by which the circumference is divided into five equal parts by bisection.)

The mathematically precise, grid-like system that Bob began to discern from the scattered forest carvings and buried metal markers was that of a neat circle bordered within a square, but with a multitude of bisecting lines within the figure. Adding to the complexity was that additional carvings or buried clues were found along eye-shaped elliptical lines, the end points of which extended beyond the square's perimeter on the north-south axis and east-west axis. As such, Bob's outlying square would need to be drawn with four identical D-shaped handles coming off each side.

For some time, Bob had a powerful hunch that the ubiquitous signs and symbols were not merely directional markers used for following lines to some random endpoint. Rather, he felt, they were data points designed to orient knowledgeable insiders to the centerpoint of a circle-within-the-square configuration.

He surmised that the learned elite of the KGC had employed centuries-old Masonic traditions in geometry to protect the secret society's hidden financial reserves. He recalled how Isom Avants's memorandum book from the 1920s had contained a hand-drawn spiderweb pattern of concentric circles that hinted at this overall design, but without the surrounding square. He also recalled the mysterious manner in which Grandpa Ashcraft and Uncle Odis had pointed out what later had proven to be specific parts of the geometric and topographic puzzle. And he further recalled how Isom Avants and W. D. Ashcraft were partners in "prospecting" and "mining" ventures in the Cossatot and Brushy region—the precise area where, as an adult, he had discerned the rough outline of the geometrical design.

For these and other reasons, Bob suspected that the two Ashcrafts and Isom Avants were deeply involved in twentieth-century KGC activity and that the center of this spiderweb of ghostly lines and dimly marked points would be found somewhere within the old Ouachita mining district. From his collection of field notes and marked-up topo maps, he began to sketch out a more definitive shape of the overarching pattern: the fixed geometry with its various lines and curves and specific ratios of distance. He had not yet assigned a name to the pattern, which was still, rather amorphously, floating around in his mind.

That all changed suddenly, during a visit from his out-of-town treasure-hunting associates Stan Vickery and John London. The men brought over a copy of a newsletter, *Treasure Hunter Confidential,* an entertaining flyer read by the cliquish treasure-hunting community. The back issue, dated April 1990, contained an intriguing article entitled "Knights of the Golden Circle." Drawing from an interview with a curiously named California-based treasure hunter, James J. Woodson, the article suggested that there were rumors of the KGC's having "had several major stashes throughout the South and West" and that some of those sites may have already "been cracked." As for the existence of the KGC in the post–Civil War era, the article said: "Depending on whose story you believe, the Knights of the Golden Circle (KGC) were either a short-lived group started by George Bickley in Cincinnati, Ohio, or a very well-heeled, powerful group who saw their destiny as that of saving the South. . . ." (Bob would later learn that Woodson's information largely came from a collection of letters and other personal effects from Orvus Lee Howk, a.k.a. Jesse Lee James.)

The kicker came in the final three paragraphs. These served as a long caption to an accompanying drawing that showed a tilted square superimposed on a circle, with numerous dotted lines connecting various opposing points within the circle and square. There was also an inner circle, denoted by a dotted line. The drawing was, in short, the master "pattern" that Bob had already begun deciphering from the field—with the exception that the large circle shown was not fully encapsulated by the square.

Moreover, the drawing showed numerous shaded boxes and shaded circles within the zone. The article claimed that the boxes represented large gold caches and the circles small stashes. It described the boxes as being along the circumference of the circle at the ends of the designated north-south and east-west axes and at the precise center of the pattern:

> Each square denotes a large treasure. Each circle represents small caches of gold, silver or money buried. Of course, the large, dark box in the center represents the treasure that in Woodson's words is "so fabulous, it would stagger the imagination." Usually these are in less than 30 feet of soil.
>
> The significant point about the circle is that if one can find one or two of the treasures, all the rest come easy. Everything is done on a north/south, east/west axis, so if you stumble across one of the treasures, you should be able to follow in a straight line until you come across the other treasure. Based on that heading, the rest of the treasures should stumble into place.
>
> The original scale of the KGC circle is one inch to the mile, so you should find a comparable scale if you were to find treasures that fit the general pattern seen in the circle. If you can locate two of them, then you know the approximate distance of the rest of the targets.

Although seemingly oversimplified, the article resonated powerfully. Coming on the heels of the Howk-Schrader book, which provided a loose historical context, the published interview offered a generalized, schematic rendering of something that Bob intuitively knew to exist in some form or another at a couple of sites. (As it turned out, John London brought over a second template-like geometric pattern that resembled the one shown in the *Treasure Hunter Confidential* article. This other pattern, which London had acquired from a treasure-hunting colleague, had been in his possession for almost fifteen years, well before he began his friendship with Bob. London, however, had never understood the grid's significance and thus decided that it was worth Bob's taking a look.)

Intrigued by the article, Bob began to search for other clues in print. He had only a few names to go by, other than the two authors of *Jesse James Was One of His Names*. While little turned up under Jesse Lee James (Orvus Howk), he did manage to find an April 22, 1973 newspaper article by Del Schrader in the now defunct *Los Angeles Herald Examiner*.[1] Schrader's sensational feature, "$100 Billion in Treasure— The Search for Rebel Gold," grabbed his attention.

While the headline and other outlandish monetary figures cited in the article cast some doubt on the story, Bob was fascinated by several key points made in Schrader's piece, which had been published two years before Schrader and Howk's book. The article was based on interviews that Schrader had conducted with "sons, grandsons and great-grandsons of the elite Knights of the Golden Circle," reportedly at an outdoor meeting of KGC descendants in California. The sources were not named, but initials were given, including J.L.J. (for Jesse Lee James, obviously). One of the old-timers—someone with the initials R.R.L.—told Schrader that there were a handful of depository maps in existence. (Schrader states that he, in fact, was allowed to make "Xerox copies" of some of these.) The KGC descendant cautioned, however, that "they won't do anybody much good. The maps are accurate, as far as they go, but you'd need the two or three *transparent overlays* [italics added], which each fill in a landmark, for the specifics. In most cases, a vital point of reference is carved on a nearby rock."

Bob's mind reeled. The Schrader article had revealed the "key" so cryptically referred to by J. Frank Dalton in *Jesse James Was One of His Names*. The key was the geometric pattern—in the form of a transportable "transparent overlay," several in fact, that had to be placed over a topographic map to orient oneself to the correct layout of any given KGC treasure depository. The key, as Bob would call it from this point on, was a "template." (The transparent overlay was probably—in the days before plastic—an oiled animal-membrane cloth.)

How ingenious. The rare illustrated maps, the obscure carved signs on trees and rock faces, the text waybills—they were all small but significant pieces of the puzzle. In isolation, they were not valuable. They had to be used in combination to orient the template, to determine the one topographical focal point in the middle of the designated circle that lay inside the square in a particular geographic area. By placing the center of the fixed template over a specific "centerpoint" on the topo map, one theoretically could locate the discrete KGC mother lodes buried in the large depositories. These would lie in a constant position relative to each other, as marked by cutouts in the template, along master lines.

Bob now had a theory, which might not be that easy to confirm. But it was a titillating concept. Adding to the thrill from reading the Schrader article, an accompanying photograph showed a template-like engraving on a rock face in New Mexico. The caption: "$40 million here? Master Compass Treasure in New Mexico is reported near this guide rock."

What Bob found most noteworthy was that the unnamed KGC sources in Schrader's *Examiner* article apparently had wanted to get their story out; nonetheless, they opted to hold back the *precise* whereabouts of the KGC treasures. Bob sensed from the engrossing article that the KGC descendants possessed a general idea about the treasure locations but not much more than that. One of them, J.D.J., was quoted as saying: "We have all the aces, kings, queens and jacks. We know how to get at the treasure—Washington doesn't." The article concluded with a bold assertion from a man with the initials J.L.J.: "Are the old-time Confederates trying to 'blackmail' the U.S. government into a deal? No, not at all. The gold can just lie down there until doomsday, I guess. With our devalued dollar and poor balance of payments situation, Washington could use this long-forgotten gold. We'll give it to them—but we believe we deserve 10 percent for a finder's fee if nothing else."

With that, something clicked. Behind J.L.J.'s (Jesse Lee James's) braggadocio, Bob sensed a certain desperation. Orvus Lee Howk–Jesse Lee James had been given the key—the template—by Dalton-James. But Howk-James did not know how to use the template! Applying its specific geometric pattern to locate KGC treasure might be straightforward if one knew how to find the centerpoint of a topographic layout.

That was the rub. Not only did one need to have experience in accurately deciphering the field symbols, buried metal objects and various codes, one also had to understand how to navigate over land using triangulation, trigonometry and other techniques. And one needed to define scale and understand how to adjust for scale; the template was useless if the wrong scale was used. Finally, even if one were to get close to the centerpoint within the depository, the pinpointing and recovery of a large, deeply buried treasure would almost certainly require high-tech detection equipment (electromagnetic induction tools or advanced ground-penetrating radar) and expensive, heavy machinery for excavation. Spades, shovels and horse-and-mule teams were good, but only to a degree.

For a number of years, Orvus Lee Howk had lived in the footsteps and shadows of an enigmatic man who undoubtedly knew where innumerable secret caches were buried; how frustrating must it have been for him not to have been able to find the precise spots! (Bob would later obtain copies of several letters written by Howk to family, friends and associates, some of them penned under the name Jesse Lee James or JJ III. The letters contain sketches and rough outlines of maps—ostensibly dictated by J. Frank Dalton to Howk. In some cases, it seems that Dalton-James may have taken Howk to the surrounding environs of the various depository sites themselves. The letters reveal a palpable frustration at not knowing precisely where the KGC money was hidden. The documents, distinct from those obtained by Woodson and which came to Bob from various treasure-hunting sources, leave little doubt that Orvus Howk–Jesse Lee James had some pecuniary motive in finding the buried loot.)[2]

As for his own prospects, Bob had no idea whether he would be any more successful using the tools at hand. But he was determined to give it his damnedest, wherever the trail might lead.

In the wake of Wapanucka, he knew it was only a matter of time before Griffith would call. He did not have to wait long. Griffith phoned in late April to say that he wanted to come over to discuss the other map—the one that he had given Bob in December with the wolf image and the complex series of lines and stick figures. Little did Griffith know that Bob had been working intensively to decipher it.

Back in December, when he had held the photocopied map for the first time, Bob had recognized that he was gazing upon a crude masterpiece. The level of sophistication and abstraction was several orders of magnitude greater than the Wapanucka drawing. Resembling a doodle-sheet of some crazed mathematics professor, the presumed treasure map presented a matrix of intersecting horizontal, diagonal and vertical lines (several of which terminated at what looked to be an obscure mathematical equation written in Confederate code). It was clear that someone had invested a great deal of time and effort into this treasure chart, not only in transcribing hidden pointers to ostensible cash hoards but in creating a kind of linear work of art, with calculated symmetry and balance.

From his initial cursory inspection, Bob had sensed that the detailed map was authentic. In the upper right-hand corner was a radiant sun, a KGC marker. Then there were several characteristic stick-figure animal renderings, as well as an abstract Indian pictograph with three-toed, bird-like (turkey-track) feet. There were also recognizable "vice-versa" symbols (a small circle with a slanted line running through it), telling the reader to interpret directions in a designated part of the map in reverse.

His experience with treasure signs prepared him to expect the unexpected, to consider new theories regardless of how odd they seemed when they popped into his head. Moreover, he was well aware that the creators of these hieroglyphic-like maps were expert at mind games and had packed their rare directional charts with a full bag of tricks.

True to the clandestine society's custom, the map left no ready clue as to the depository's location. That was the ultimate challenge: to find landmarks (some of whose names undoubtedly had changed over the past century or more) indicated by the code that was embedded in the scrambled letters, numbers and symbols drawn on the map. And just how old was the map? He could not tell for sure, but it appeared to be dated 1889, based on vertical and horizontal renderings of those numbers at the top of the photocopied page. Next to *1889* were the letters *DAT.* The period, he thought, dovetailed with all his previous work on KGC activities.

Bob was drawn to the map's most distinct and prominent illustration. Sketched at the top of what appeared to be a pyramidal or triangular configuration, the central figure was that of a wolf-like creature with a long snout. Right above it, in block lettering, was the word *TIME* and, above that, five capital *T*s grouped in an arch. For lack of a better name, Bob dubbed the apparent KGC treasure chart the "Wolf Map."

He had never seen anything as mind-boggling in his treasure-hunting career. Once he had set his eyes firmly on the rendering, the analytical side of his brain would not let go. Indeed, his fascination with the treasure hunt—and with this particular map—overwhelmed his dislike for its provider, Griffith. For the moment, he had to shake himself out of his mental daze: Griffith was asking what the chances were of breaking the seemingly indecipherable chart, which had been in circulation some sixty years among a coterie of treasure-hunters. Annoyed by Griffith's pestering, Bob curtly said that he would let him know when he had completed the task. Under all circumstances, Bob declared, the take would be "fifty-fifty" upon recovery, no questions asked. The two men shook on that.

For the next couple of months, Bob did little else than work on the Wolf Map. He was able to concentrate on the blizzard of lines and jumbled letters without much interruption. (By May 1994, Landon Brewer had been placed in a nursing home. Bob still devoted time to his care, but he no longer had to commit twelve out of every forty-eight hours to looking after his bedridden and increasingly senile father, who, months earlier, had nearly burned down the house. Landon Brewer would die at the nursing home in 1999. His parting words to Bob were: "Well, have you found the mother lode yet?")

Hunched over a table littered with drafting instruments and an assortment of pencils and colored pens, Bob spent hundreds of hours poring over the encrypted map, attempting to determine its precise point of reference in the continental United States. In the fog of information shown on the cryptogram, he sensed something significant and yet painfully elusive. His excitement would turn to frustration and sleepless nights as he mentally navigated into blind alleys.

Linda had never seen her husband so engrossed. He would come out drenched with sweat, his eyes red and his stomach growling from hunger. And he would often complain of pounding headaches from concentrating without end on the baffling treasure grid. She recalled how much effort he had put into solving the Bible Tree in the nearby Ouachita woods, but this went far beyond. She knew that her husband was nothing if not disciplined, yet his immersion into the Wolf Map approached a kind of obsession. She did her best to leave him alone during his code-breaking marathons in the study, silent twelve- to twenty-hour episodes broken only for short meals.

Eventually, Bob's self-declared "stubborn hillbilly" persistence began to yield some light. He had resolved to isolate all the letters, numbers, abstract symbols and Confederate Code characters on the map as a step in breaking this KGC depository cipher. There were about one hundred such letters and characters jumbled throughout the page. Some were in

5. (Overleaf) The Wolf Map. This extraordinarily complex Jesse James treasure map gives no indication as to its precise location in the United States. Bob Brewer spent over 1,000 hours cracking the code and determined that it was an authentic KGC-ciphered depository map for a site located in Addington, Oklahoma. Key features—in addition to the Masonic and KGC radiant sun symbol—include: the wolf figure in the upper middle section, the scrambled word "Beaver" in the upper-right quadrant, and the vertically written "Stink" in the upper-left quadrant. These all correspond to names of creeks in southwestern Indian Territory (latter-day Oklahoma) in the second half of the nineteenth century. Bob determined that the letters "KC" in the lower-left quadrant referred to Kiowa-Comanche territory, and "IC" in the lower-left quadrant referred to Indian Camp, an important landmark.

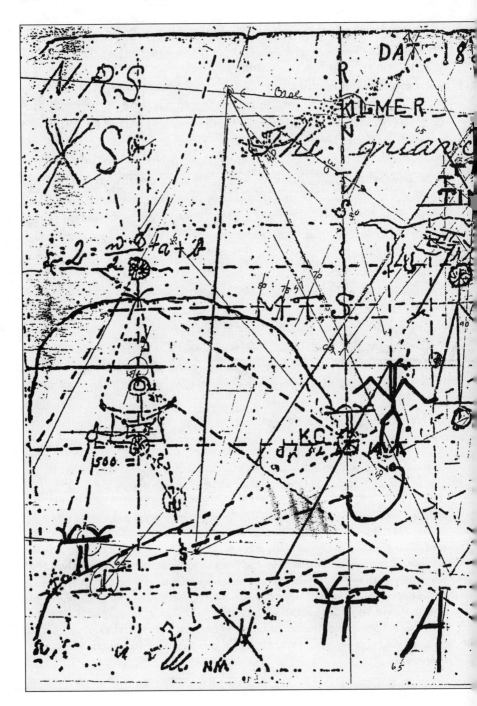

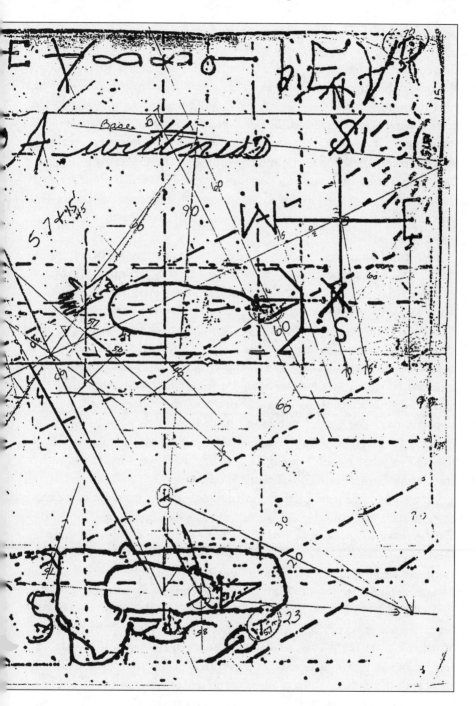

plain sight; others hidden within the contorted shapes of adjoining letters or figures, while still others were written upside down or backwards
or were merely suggested by a partial form that demanded interpolation.
Whatever their representation, the characters and letters all seemed to
have meaning. To solve the puzzle Bob would have to arrange them in a
certain sequence, he believed. The decoded "text" would then have to be
interpreted along with the information provided by the geometry and
visual imagery on the map. Gradually—through the anagrams (the peculiar arrangement of random letters into a known word or phrase) and
the replacement of the Confederate cipher with plaintext translations—
Bob developed a series of individual words or phrases that began to
make some sense.

The first anagram assembled from the scattered lettering was
ARBUCKLE, a name closely linked to the history of Indian Territory
and latter-day Oklahoma. Fort Arbuckle and the picturesque Arbuckle
Mountains, named for a decorated general in the U.S. Army, were two
important landmarks in the rough-and-tumble southwest frontier of the
mid- to late-nineteenth century. The *A* of the "Arbuckle" anagram was
clearly visible at the bottom of the map's midsection. Next to the *A* was
a dotted *R,* which was hidden behind a *K.* A small lowercase cursive *b*
had to be gleaned from the right side of the mathematical equation mentioned above. The *C* could be found turned on its back, just below the
Indian pictograph, and the *L* was written upside down just to the left of
the *A.* But what of the missing *U* and *E?* These were to be found by
translating Confederate code written on the map.

(The secret code used by the Confederate State Department and exec-
utive branch was found on April 6, 1865, in Richmond by Union officials. Assistant U.S. Secretary of War Charles A. Dana found the code in
the Confederate State Department archives after the evacuation of the
Confederate government. The code was not made public until *Century
Magazine* published it in its June 1907 issue. A copy of the code was also
printed in a 1946 U.S. Army publication, "Historical Background of the
Signal Security Agency," Volume 1, "Codes and Ciphers Prior to World
War I, 1776–1917."[3] The code comprises six distinct sets of cryptic letters, numbers and figures. Messages written in the code used different
subsets of the cipher, which made it extremely difficult to break.)

A merged *HE* figure at the top midsection caught Bob's eye. It looked
like a form of Baconian cipher (named for Sir Francis Bacon, the English
scholar, philosopher and Rosicrucian adherent, 1561–1626), in which

text written in slightly different fonts or styles—in this case, touching or merged letters—contains hidden meaning. Such enciphered characters are clues for the knowledgeable that appear to the average reader to be mere lapses in penmanship, grammar, spelling or the like.

Referring to his Confederate code matrix, Bob found that Confederate code subset #3 used an *H* for the plaintext letter *U*. He then found the required *E* in a merged *EAN* configuration in the top right corner of the map. The strange *A*-like figure appears in Confederate code subset #6 as a plaintext *E*. Unclear whether the now complete *Arbuckle* referred to the old fort or to the nearby mountain chain in south-central Oklahoma, Bob at least had a starting point as to the possible target area for the suspected KGC depository. The question was, what other landmarks could be discerned from the patchwork symbols on the Wolf Map?

On the heels of *ARBUCKLE* came *BEAVER*. The name appeared in distorted form in the upper right-hand corner, just above the radiant sun figure. The *b* was in lowercase and scrambled, as mentioned, with the ciphered *a*. The *E* was in uppercase and scrambled in the ciphered *EAN* combination that yielded the uppercase *A*. The *V* was represented as an adjacent upside-down *A*. The second *E* was missing, while the *R* was clearly visible, in uppercase, next to the upside-down *A*.

Bob reasoned that "beaver" was related directly to "wolf," two animal clues that suggested some common feature in the local geography. He then managed to isolate *STINKING* as his third key anagram. Found in a partly obscured vertical column of text at the top of the page was *STINK* (the *T* being concealed as part of the fishhook curve of the lowercase *g* from the misspelled phrase at the top of the map, *The greave is a wittnesd*).

All three names—Beaver, Wolf and *STINK* (or *STINKING*, if one includes another *I* and an *N* in an apparent *KIN* character-combination, as well as the connected lowercase *g* from *greave*)—referred to local Indian Territory creeks southwest of Fort Arbuckle!

Consulting U.S. government-issue maps of Indian Territory from the 1800s, Bob could see the outline of a Stinking Creek running between Fort Arbuckle (some sixty-five miles to the east) and a Beaver Creek (which ran a few miles to Stinking Creek's west).[4] Another Indian Territory map showed a Wolf Creek, just north and west of Stinking Creek. A comparison with contemporary maps showed that Stinking Creek had become Mud Creek; Beaver Creek—or a tributary thereof—had been renamed Cow Creek; and Wolf Creek had become Dry Creek.

Bob was struck by the alignment of the three creeks on the Wolf Map. Their natural geographic relationship to each other was implied by the considered placement of the words Stinking and Beaver and by the drawing of the wolf figure, standing, as it were, above and in between the anagrams for the two creeks.

At this point, Bob began to believe that the confluence of three creeks in the hill country of southern Oklahoma suggested a large KGC cache burial. His heart pounded with anticipation, yet he knew the beast—the elusive Wolf—was not fully cornered. He had taken the search for the Wolf Map depository from a "this could be anywhere" blank slate to a specific region of the country, home to Anadarko Basin oil patches and vast cattle ranches. It was an enormous advance. Still, he had to narrow his target zone to a sufficiently precise spot, say within a hundred square feet.

Bob badly wanted to share his moment of discovery with Linda, but he held back. There was more decipherment, map reading and archival research ahead, and he wanted to be sure of his detective work before saying anything to anybody. In this game of locating the lustrous needle in the haystack, precision was everything.

The sunburst was perhaps the most important factor for solving the Wolf Map and locating pay dirt. From his time spent roaming the Arkansas hill country and rummaging through dusty archives, Bob realized that the rising sun symbol was central to the solution of the obscure treasure chart. The beaming sun depicted in the upper right corner of the Wolf Map threw off a long dotted line—a symbolic ray—that intersected a small circle in the lower-left quadrant of the page. The line extended to a point near the lower-left corner, where two initials, *IC*, were barely visible. Bob sensed the letters' importance, for along this same line, in the upper right quadrant of the map, was a hand pointing in the direction of the *IC*, about one-third of the way down the slope from the rising sun symbol. Halfway between the hand and the *IC* were the neatly drawn letters *KC*. These were positioned next to a circle that had several lines running through it. On the other side of the circle was a large Indian pictograph (the figure with the turkey feet).

Bob, versed in Native American history (his mother's parents were of Cherokee and Choctaw heritage), had a hunch that *KC* stood for the Kiowa-Comanche Nation bordering the Chickasaw Nation to the west. His mind raced with excitement as he realized that the *KC* might designate the line where the two nations abutted each other, not far from the

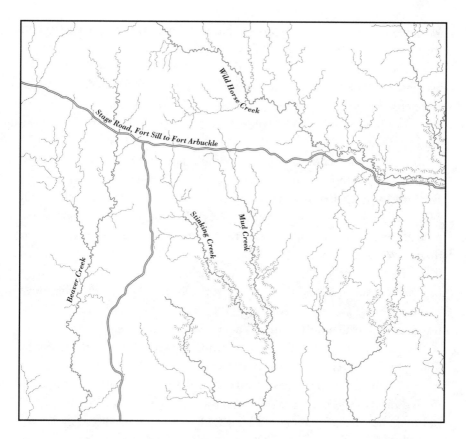

6. *U.S. military survey map of the Oklahoma (Indian) territory, produced 130 years ago and showing the old Stinking, Beaver and Mud creeks. Bob Brewer determined that this map, and others of the period, formed the geographical basis for the Wolf Map treasure grid.*

Chisholm Trail. The famous old cattle trail—where Texas longhorns were herded up to Abilene, Kansas, and other points north—ran alongside, and at times across, the north-south boundary line running between the Kiowa-Comanche and Chickasaw lands.

Bob thought that this would fit logically with the KGC's modus operandi, given the group's close association with the Chickasaws and other Indian nations during and after the Civil War. Unlike the information provided by the general location of the three creeks, this was a specific, vertical line: a documented border.

The Wolf Map would yield three more critical lines that would lead Bob into the cache zone. A second anagram combination, involving the

M in *MTS* and two dotted-circle symbols shown in the upper left-hand corner of the map, provided *MOO*. This, paired with a second decoded word *TRAIL* (whose letters derived from *The greave is a wittnesd* and a floating *L*), had given him the Cattle Trail, or "Chisholm Trail." Thus, three creeks and two north-south running lines (the KC Indian boundary line and the Chisholm Trail) were indicated for those able to follow the hidden messages.

The geographic coordinates, if one could detect them, were even more specific in defining the correct acreage. One of the most important, and certainly among the best-camouflaged directional clues on the Wolf Map, was *R7W*, short for Range 7 West. Bob derived this from subtle indicators appearing in the upper right-hand corner of the map. The *R* flowed from the double *R* indicated in *BEAVER*. The *7* was gleaned from the top deck of the *E* (the east indicator in a compass-rose, shown below the rising sun and the *R*). Lastly, the *W* proved a fascinating twist on that same *E:* an attached *3* on the bottom deck of the *E* was a KGC reversal sign, thus implying that East must be made West.

Range 7 West, part of a baseline grid for what is known as the Public Land Survey System of ranges and townships, was precisely where Stinking Creek and Beaver Creek straddled a divide, according to the antiquated map of the area that Bob was using. (The so-called "rectangular" public land survey system was launched in the late 1700s. The survey township—typically a six-mile-square grid—forms the basis of the system. Such "townships" are numbered in "ranges"—vertical, north-south running columns—that lie east or west of a designated "principal meridian." They are also measured in horizontal tiers that lie north or south of a designated "baseline." Townships can be further divided into thirty-six "sections," each one square mile or 640 acres. Taking it one step further, sections can be carved into quarters [160 acres], eighths [80 acres], sixteenths [40 acres] and so on.)[5]

On close examination, Bob could see that the Chisholm Trail passes over the ridge dividing Beaver and Stinking Creeks, very near where the baseline appears to cross those two streams. Moreover, he realized that the *DAT* inscription at the top of the Wolf Map was not solely intended as an abbreviation for "date" as the KGC cryptographer might have wanted the uninformed to believe. It was more likely an indicator for the Dona Ana Trail, a lesser-known route running parallel to the Chisholm Trail in the same general area.

Inspecting a modern map of the region, Bob noticed that there was a

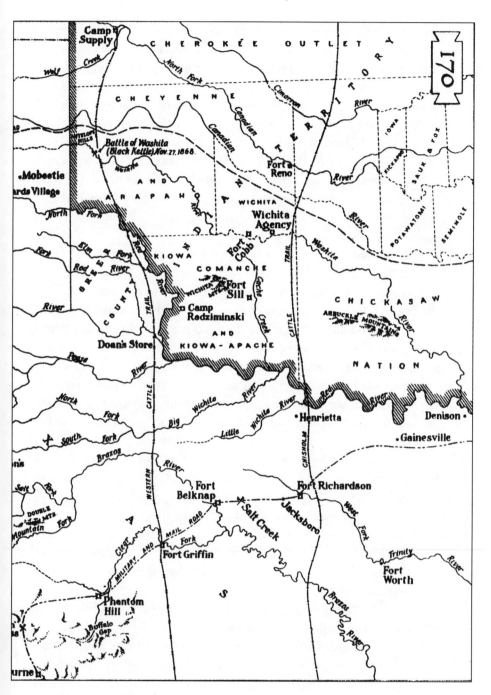

7. *Another map of Indian territory, showing the important Kiowa-*
Comanche/Chickasaw border, as well as the Chisholm Cattle trail—all
determined by Bob to be key landmarks denoted in code on the Wolf Map.

Chisholm Trail Lookout Monument erected on a hill. The hill appeared to overlook a valley where all of the key landmarks and lines seemed to merge.[6] This would be the starting point for his field investigation.

Bob spent the next few days reviewing his library of books on Oklahoma history, particularly those relevant to treasure hunting. One volume proved especially valuable: *Oklahoma Treasures and Treasure Tales,* by Steve Wilson, published some two decades earlier.[7] In the chapter titled "Jesse James's Two Million-Dollar Treasure," Bob was captivated by a hand-drawn diagram for buried treasure, one of the more alluring maps that he had seen. The map, according to Wilson, had been in the possession of a Wells Blevins, who allegedly had inherited it from a "member of the outlaw band" of Jesse James.

At the top of the map, written in uppercase, were the words *MADRUGADA ESTRELLA MAPA ORO,* which translates loosely to "Early Morning Star Map of Gold." Below the Spanish lettering was a childlike rendering of a fort with a flag on top and a dotted trail extending down from the fort and along the right side of the page. At the top of the trail was written, *3J loDS 2020#goLD.* The trail led to a point at the lower right-hand corner of the page that had the words *CAMP, SPRING, goLD,* and *DER,* written in a cluster next to two identical symbols: isosceles triangles with a small accent mark coming off the top of each.

A second trail, running from the word *CAMP* to a spot designated by *200.000 GoLD* and by a group of three small circles, flowed up the left side of the page and formed the other side of a large U. Running vertically through the U was some kind of divide, shown by two narrowly spaced parallel lines. On each side of this dividing line was a bust profile of a man wearing a hat, with each gazing at the other (a dotted line running from head to head seemed to indicate that the two figures were connected in some way). Using a magnifying lens, Bob noticed that one of the figures had what appeared to be shoulder-length hair or braids, while the other did not.

The cunning author of the map was making the ever-so-subtle distinction between the Civilized Tribes (Chickasaw) and the Plains Tribes (the braided-haired ones). Here in abstract pictorial form was confirmation that the two reputed treasure maps—the Wolf Map and the Madrugada map—corresponded! The divide running north-south on the Madrugada map was the KC line: the Kiowa-Comanche border with the Chickasaw Nation in south-central Indian Territory.

It all framed up powerfully: The fort in the upper right-hand corner of

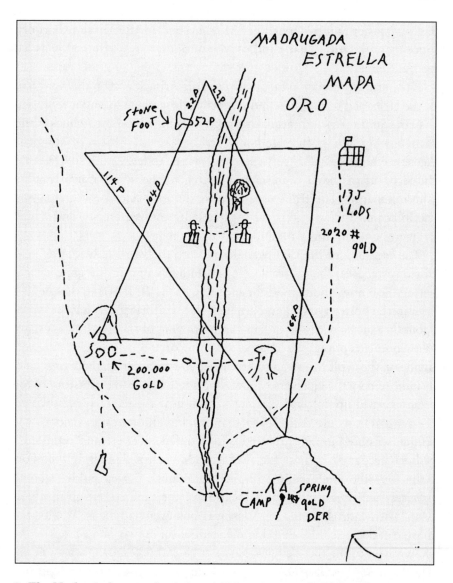

8. *The Madrugada map shows in primitive pictographic form clues to an Oklahoma gold cache marked by three boulders. This map is a microcosm of the site identified by Bob through his decipherment of the Wolf Map. It comes from Steve Wilson's* Oklahoma Treasures and Treasure Tales.

the Madrugada map, Bob surmised, was almost certainly Fort Arbuckle. That would make sense as the source for the gold. He had read, in Wilson's book and elsewhere, the story of a stolen Fort Arbuckle military payroll. The freshly minted coinage reportedly was nabbed from a federal paymaster unit by "a band of Missourians" in 1869, just a short distance from the fort. That band of Missourians, many assumed, was led by Jesse James.

If the crude drawing in fact depicted Fort Arbuckle, then the right half of the U-shaped trail designated on the Madrugada map might represent the Fort Smith (Ark.) stagecoach trail. The trail led to Fort Arbuckle and then further along into Indian Territory to the Kiowa-Comanche Agency, where the U.S. Army's Fort Sill stands today. And it follows that the left half of the U represents a stretch of the south–north-running Chisholm Trail. The trails crossed near the KC-Chickasaw divide and the indicated Indian camp, as suggested by the symbolism and coded drawings on both the Wolf and Madrugada maps.

The meaning of the two triangles next to the word *CAMP* was now obvious: teepees, the centerpiece of an Indian camp in the area, near a spring. Bob now understood the meaning of the *IC* lettering that he had seen in the bottom left-hand corner of the Wolf Map and how it corresponded exactly with the Indian camp drawing of the Madrugada map. With one exception, the relative position of the camp *IC* to the *KC* divide on the Wolf Map had to be viewed in reverse or as a mirror image, as indicated by the vice-versa code. (Bob's research into the history of the region turned up an old Comanche camp near the exact site shown on the map. He would later learn that the Indian campsite, next to the spring, was used in the early 1900s for Confederate veterans' reunions!)

Bob recognized that the Madrugada map's rendering of Fort Arbuckle—the likely source of the "luminous" buried gold—equated precisely with the topographic location of the radiant sun on the Wolf Map. The Madrugada map in Wilson's book even had the *R7W*, albeit in masterful disguise. Bob detected the symbolism in two small checkmarks shown next to the three circles, near where *200.000 GoLD* was written. The *M* in *MADRUGADA* (which is actually an upside-down *W*, if one notes the long extension of the middle line) points to the upside-down *7* that is depicted just outside the left corner of the triangle's base. The long leg of this upside-down 7 points back to the *R* in *MADRUGADA* at the top of the page. These three points combine to yield *R7W*, the same placement marker as on the Wolf Map and an essential vector point for anyone seeking the treasure.

He had critically narrowed the search.

The two treasure maps complemented each other beautifully. The Wolf Map was on a much larger scale, perhaps a couple hundred square miles, and provided clues for perhaps multiple treasures within an extensive KGC depository. The Madrugada map, on the other hand, was a specific sketch, likewise rendered in code, cipher and other abstraction, but pointing to a small area that appeared to hold a specific cache. The map indicated that $200,000 in gold coins (at face value, that is—but perhaps as much as $10 million to $15 million in current numismatic value) lay buried just east of the old Chisholm Trail next to three circular figures. The circles, Bob guessed, were some topographic feature in triplicate. Moreover, according to the Madrugada map printed in Wilson's book, the treasure's location was due west of the KC-Chickasaw divide.

Here was the opportunity: the Wolf Map—if properly deciphered—brought one to the correct stadium; the Madrugada map put one in the end zone. Bob knew the near exact location of the gold and which group had put it there. Their intellectual signature was unmistakable.

Without any real ability to determine whether the stories were apocryphal, Bob by this time had learned a thing or two about the Wolf Map's provenance. The original map, according to local historical accounts and the research of Bud Hardcastle, had been buried in a cast-iron teakettle north of a geological oddity—a solitary hill called Buzzard's Roost, near Cement, Oklahoma. The teakettle, allegedly buried by Jesse James in the late 1800s, had been unearthed in the 1930s by Joe Hunter, a former city marshal from Rush Springs, Oklahoma, according to the *Lawton Constitution* and other newspaper reports in the late 1940s.[8] Hunter, an avid treasure hunter, was said to have obtained—via suspicious circumstances that may have involved foul play—certain other reputed Jesse James maps before the teakettle discovery. These had led him to the Buzzard's Roost find. In the Buzzard's Roost teakettle were a handful of rolled-up maps, including *both* the Wolf Map and the map to the Wapanucka site, according to Hardcastle.

The original Wolf Map reportedly was etched on a soft, elongated copper sheet rolled up to fit neatly inside the teakettle. But it was not just the map that was found inside the rusted teapot: gold bullion and signature KGC symbols were discovered there as well.[9] Among the symbols: a large U.S. copper penny, dated 1841 (the big pennies were worn as emblems by KGC members and so-called Copperhead supporters); a small, nickel-sized five-pointed bronze star (the official KGC emblem, as found in the Bickley paraphernalia at the time of the KGC frontman's capture by federal forces); a large key-winder watch.

What precisely had led Bob to the Wolf Map's probable location, he did not know: experience, intuition, stubbornness, or some combination thereof. What he *did* know was that if the buried money were still there, he was going to find it.

The thrill of discovery was almost too much to handle. He came out of his room in a daze that night, in early May 1994, after weeks of incessant study and gently awoke Linda. It was after midnight. "It's done. I know exactly where it's buried," he whispered. He told her that he would set out the next morning to prove he was right.

Linda could sense her husband's hunger for the hunt, and so she helped pack the car that night. They were on the road before dawn. In the five-hour drive to the small town of Addington, some twenty miles south of Duncan, Oklahoma, Bob said little, his mind working over the complex formulas from the two maps.

When the couple arrived at the suspected site, near the Chisholm Trail Monument, just east of Addington, Bob's adrenaline was pumping. He and Linda climbed to the top of Monument Hill, where the memorial pillar stood atop the highest point in the surrounding grassland. Built in the 1930s, the memorial had an odd, smokestack shape and was adorned with plaques telling the colorful history of Jesse Chisholm and the thousands of other cowboys who herded longhorns to market until 1880. Below, rutted grooves from the old cattle trail could be seen running in a northerly direction through the bucolic expanse. Some several hundred yards due north the sloping prairie met a tree line bordering a small creek. Bob pointed to a tree-lined spot in the valley below, where the erstwhile Beaver Creek intersected the Chisholm Trail.

"That's the place."

On the way down the dirt road from the monument, Bob was stunned to see a large boulder leaning against a barbwire fence. It had three large pick-driven holes carved into its smooth surface, like a jack-o'-lantern. He recognized the sculpture as a KGC line marker. Was it suggesting that the three circles on the Madrugada map lay directly ahead, on that specific bearing?

Through a deliberate method that was part science, part art, he had found what he was seeking. He had intended to find two major trails that crossed at the headwaters of the erstwhile Beaver and Stinking Creeks. The trails and creeks had to be near the old Kiowa-Comanche/Chickasaw Indian boundary line. Moreover, the location should be found in Range 7 West, a short distance south of the baseline. He had discovered all of these physical landmarks, as well as the survey lines on the topographical maps, and they neatly conformed with the two abstract treasure maps.

Bob was euphoric. He had begun to think like the grid makers. The code breaking had clicked. Nonetheless, he and Linda could see that a huge hurdle lay ahead of any recovery: the location of the suspected cache site was in the middle of a private, fenced-in ranch and several hundred yards from the access road. He wanted to call Griffith and tell him the news—but at the right moment and place.

For an instant, Bob contemplated the alternative: telling Griffith that his map had proved too difficult and that he was abandoning the effort. For an instant, he envisioned going down the slope and recovering the gold himself. But he set such painfully tempting thoughts aside. The first order of business was to prepare to meet the landowner to seek permission to dig up the suspected Wolf Map cache.

10

The Wolf Emerges

IT was with a mix of pride and dread that Bob readied himself to tell Griffith about breaking the Wolf Map. The pride came from a quiet satisfaction at having delivered on the task: unlocking the seemingly indecipherable code and arriving at a precise location in the vast United States of America. No one other than Linda knew that he had taken on such a challenge. Having succeeded, he wanted to share his victory with someone who could appreciate the effort in this highly confidential, and thus lonely, pursuit. Griffith, whatever his faults, was one such person—someone who knew something of the diabolical ingenuity of the KGC and the background to its hidden riches.

Still, Griffith had his clear shortcomings as a "partner." Bob believed that Griffith had misled him about having the owners' permission to be on the Wapanucka property—and then had apparently circled back to the site shortly after eviction. Moreover, Griffith had denied him any claim to the ill-gotten gold and silver coins found during the Oklahoman's secret return trip to what appeared to be the Gillespie property. Not that Bob would have wanted treasure obtained that way, but the point was, Griffith simply had claimed it as his own.

Nevertheless, Bob felt morally obligated to tell Griffith that he had solved the Wolf Map because Griffith had provided the map as a starting point for the investigation. But precautions were in order. To protect his claim to any cash that might be found, he resolved to tell Griffith about the map's solution in front of witnesses. This way, Griffith could make no plausible assertion that he had independently discovered this out-of-nowhere spot—culled from the 3,678,890 square miles that constitute the United States.

Bob decided to set his plan in motion at a treasure-hunting conference in Wear's Corner, a small town in the Smoky Mountain region of Tennessee. He had been invited to speak on treasure-sign interpretation and the possible connection between the KGC and suspected treasure sites in the South and Southwest.[1] He would attend this once-in-a-lifetime conference with his friends, John London and Stan Vickery. They could serve, he thought, as witnesses to the revelation that had to be made to Griffith.

Bob invited Griffith to the show, and the history teacher wrote back to say that his classes would be over by May 26 and that he eagerly awaited the trip to Tennessee in June.[2] In the letter, Griffith mentioned that he wanted to sell a booklet at the show—a collection largely of photocopied published references that he had put together on the KGC—that, he hoped, would offset the expenses of attending.

With London and Vickery present on the eve of the conference, Bob told Griffith that he had solved the Wolf Map after putting in more than a thousand hours on the job. Griffith, caught off guard, was all ears as Bob announced that he knew the precise location of the Wolf Map treasure. "Linda and I have been to the general area and seen enough to give me a precise line to the spot," he said to a small group that had gathered on the front porch of the cabin where he was staying with London, Vickery and Griffith. Flushed with anticipation, Griffith urged an immediate trip to the site, which Bob had yet to name or describe. A trip was in order, Bob acknowledged, but on his schedule and only to meet with the ranch owner. As a starting point, he stressed, they would offer the rancher a one-third stake of the find in exchange for signed permission to attempt a recovery. What was clear to all was that Griffith had no knowledge as to where the Wolf Map pointed.

By this time, Bob's knowledge of the map's hidden location had grown exponentially. For one, he had discovered that, among his collection of photocopied letters from Howk, one illustrated waybill stood out. The site map drawing, signed by Jesse Lee James, contained a detailed sketch of what looked like the prominent hill—Monument Hill—at the suspected KGC depository site. In the background was a gradually sloping valley, a match for the pastoral environment of Addington that Bob and Linda had observed during their recent outing.[3] The sketch did not include a rendering of the Chisholm Trail monument nor, for that matter, any mention of any kind of geographic location. It did indicate that the area in question contained one or more KGC treasures (one of which apparently had been buried deep in a tunnel-and-shaft network on the central hill, where a house had evidently stood). When combined with the other information he had gleaned, Bob had little doubt that the letter pertained to the Wolf Map's precise location. In effect, this was the third map of the site.

Even more exciting than the visual corroboration provided by the drawing was the notion that the material depicted in Jesse Lee James's letter had been dictated from memory by J. Frank Dalton (or, perhaps, J. Frank Dalton had taken Jesse Lee James [Orvus Howk] to the site itself). The centenarian had disclosed privately to his understudy that there was a major treasure buried at the exact spot that Bob would independently locate decades later. Bob had relied upon both the Wolf Map (found independently in the Buzzard's Roost kettle said to have been buried by Jesse James) and the Madrugada map (said to have trickled into the public domain through someone formerly associated with the James gang). If the Wolf Map site in the Addington area proved a KGC cache location, would the waybill from Jesse Lee James/Orvus Lee Howk—confidant of J. Frank Dalton—not go far in proving that J. Frank Dalton was the real Jesse Woodson James, or at least someone high up in the hierarchy of the KGC?

There was yet another potential source of corroboration. After obtaining topo maps of the precise spot near Addington, Bob managed to begin orienting his version of the KGC depository template on the basis of the handful of clues that he had seen. He did not have much on-site information to go by, other than the carved boulder with its three circular grooves, as well as a disfigured pointer, or "hoot owl," tree that he had spied along another line. Any directional target indicated by the template at that early stage was merely suggestive, given the lack of additional information. To align the template correctly would require an extensive field survey.

Bob felt prepared to return to Addington to seek landowner permission and, with that in hand, to attempt a recovery with Griffith. In fact, he was so confident that no one else could figure out the overall layout without specific instructions that he decided to write to Griffith to tell him a little about his plan.

In an exchange of letters, Bob explained how he had arrived at the general location through the decipherment of such landmarks as Arbuckle, Stinking Creek, Beaver Creek, Wolf Creek, Kiowa-Comanche, Chisholm Trail and others. Griffith enthusiastically wrote back, noting that, according to his own research, Frank James reportedly had been looking for a James gang treasure near the Chisholm Trail. "So, I think we're on to something that no one else has figured out. Frank [James] said it was just to the side of the trail and not buried very deep. I think all we need is some luck to get to the spot. Am looking forward to getting a chance to go and check it out. Keep in touch and let me know how you are doing on your layout. Keep up the good work!" Griffith closed his letter, "Your Old Buddy, Michael." A subsequent letter from Griffith contained a page full of "Notes About Monument Hill," based on an interview Griffith had with his neighbor, a Mr. Allen, who reportedly had grown up seven miles from Monument Hill. "Mr. Allen said he was told by his grandad in the 1930's that Frank and Jesse James was at Addington and Monument Hill area several times. They stayed and had conversation in Grandad's house," the letter said.

But Bob knew that getting "to the spot" of the cache-burial in Addington was not a matter of "luck." It was a matter of science and math, of cryptanalysis and geometry, and he did not want to rush into it. He first wanted to decompress, and the best way he knew to do that was to return to the surrounding Ouachitas at home.

It had been nearly a year since the bizarre spectacle of the headless effigy in the Ouachitas. Yet his curiosity kept pulling him back to the same general area, in a densely wooded valley some ten miles from home. That earlier freakish incident, in October 1993, had deeply impressed Bob. But it did not prepare him for what transpired in late July 1994, within firing range of the spot where the suspended, bullet-ridden dummy had hung.

While investigating some partly developed leads, Bob noticed that his fiercely loyal guard dog, Lady, was agitated. The rottweiler was letting loose a low, deep growl and the hair on her back bristled. Bob immediately turned off his metal detector, and the dog's continued growling confirmed what he thought he had heard: a tire slowly rolling over gravel. The noise came from the ridge above him. Lady suddenly began to snarl. Crouching low, Bob could see two physically fit men, sporting short military-style haircuts, patrolling the ridge with their handguns held high. His heart pounding, he grabbed Lady and slid under a fallen oak tree that had settled at the bottom of the ravine. For several minutes, he kept one hand over Lady's muzzle, the other on his .357 Magnum. He was prepared to use the weapon if the two men approached with weapons brandished and failed to identify themselves. As it turned out, he could see the pair confer atop the hill after patrolling both sides of the valley. They left shortly thereafter.

Crawling out from under the foliage, he was shaken, and it took a while for his heartbeat to settle down. Nothing like that had ever happened. Who were those guys? What were they doing with their weapons drawn, not saying a word, not calling out? Were they a government counter-drug unit, or some special-ops military team in training? A local militia? Could their presence be connected to the effigy incident?

Such thoughts rushed through his head as he drove to the sheriff's office in Mena to report what had happened. The sheriff was at a loss to explain what Bob described. No, there would have been some notification if the Drug Enforcement Administration were conducting training exercises or real-time operations, Sheriff Mike Ogelsby said. The same for the military, he added.[4] In any event, Bob did not tell Linda, not wanting to frighten her.

Bob resumed his focus on the Wolf Map. Around the first week in August 1994, he telephoned the ever-anxious Griffith to announce that the hunt was on. On their long drive to the as-yet-undisclosed site, Bob made perhaps the biggest mistake of his life. He showed the school-teacher the page from Steve Wilson's *Oklahoma Treasures* book, the one that contained the Madrugada map under the heading "Jesse James' $2 million Treasure." In that naively unthinking moment, Bob let the rabbit out of the bag.

The equation was fairly straightforward. If one knew the reference point for the Madrugada map (with its three circles drawn next to the "200.000 gold") it would not take a mathematics PhD. to find the buried money. It would take someone who had been trained to follow KGC symbolism.

In a matter of hours, Bob stepped out of the car with Griffith in the trail-veined area that he so painstakingly had discovered. Standing atop Monument Hill, he described to Griffith the matrix of intersecting paths and creeks below. He showed him the grooved pumpkin-faced boulder propped up against the barbwire fence. Pointing due north along the line running from Monument Hill through the boulder, he said that the treasure should be just a few yards to the east of the Chisholm Trail, near the tree-lined gully. He also noted that the target area was in plain sight of the ranch foreman's house, which stood just a few hundred yards due north.

Griffith, by this point, was full of nervous energy. Bob, wanting to temper his partner's raw enthusiasm, stared at the younger man sternly. He emphasized that nothing was going to happen until they had written permission from the landowner to go onto the property. Any treasure found would be split three ways, with the rancher getting his share. Following Bob's lecture—and nods and expressions of agreement from Griffith—the two headed off to find the rancher. But they were disappointed to discover that the owner was away for the weekend.

Back at the car, the two men discussed what to do. Bob proposed that since Griffith taught school relatively close by he should take the lead: he would return with a contract for treasure recovery and obtain the rancher's signature. Griffith readily agreed and promised to keep Bob posted.

When they shook hands, Bob peered into the schoolteacher's eyes and wondered if he had made a terrible mistake. His stomach was in knots all the way home.

The phone call never came.

Over the next several months, Bob received a handful of letters from Griffith, each one saying how things around home and school had tied him up and prevented him from going to Addington.[5] Subsequent letters said family problems were keeping him from doing any treasure work for the time being: first it was his brother being injured, and then his mother-in-law having health problems. In one correspondence, Griffith went so far as to say that he had determined that J. Frank Dalton could not be Jesse James and that the whole treasure theory was probably a hoax—thus completely abandoning his long-cherished beliefs. And then, to top it off, Griffith wrote another letter with an illustration of what he claimed was a stone map with Confederate code inscribed. Bob could tell that the "code" was fake; for one thing, it did not include the required keyword for such codes or cryptograms to work between sender and receiver.

He had a raw feeling that Griffith had backtrailed him—that he had returned to Addington, raided the site and recovered the treasure.

In the fall of 1994, Bob made a couple of return trips to the Oklahoma ranch but still failed to connect with the owner. Once, he was told that the rancher had gone to Dallas on business but that he might be home that evening. Bob slept in his car waiting for him to return. When the man had not arrived by two o'clock the next day, it was time to pack it in. He phoned several times over the next several days, but the owner was never there. The whole Addington experience left him uneasy and restless for months.

To try to dispel the sinking feeling in his gut, Bob hit the trail close to home. He desperately needed to put Addington and Michael Griffith out of his mind. On a frosty morning in April 1995, he set out with Linda along a key directional line that ran for four miles past Smoke Rock Mountain. It was marked with a bewildering array of buried clues, tree carvings, blazes and disfigured oaks. The compass bearing happened to run toward the site where the effigy had been hoisted and near to the area where Bob had encountered the armed heavies—so he led the way with a mix of caution and anticipation.

At one point, the couple arrived at a spot laden with clues. Linda walked ahead with the detector as Bob took various readings off a marked beech and then off a large diamond-shaped rock.

Pointing to an open area that appeared extremely promising, he directed Linda to scan near the base of several large pines. In front of one of the trees, she quickly uncovered a semi-buried muleshoe that had been anchored to the ground. The muleshoe's placement suggested that a directional line ran up the incline. On that indicated tangent, some forty yards away, Linda received a strong signal: an iron rod, twisted into the shape of a snake, was buried about six inches deep. The place was hot; Bob knew it, viscerally.

It was not long before Linda found something significant on the line indicated by the head of the metal snake. It was a rusted, rectangular frame, but beyond that, she could not identify it. She called excitedly for Bob, who immediately recognized it for what it was: the blown-apart top of a Wells Fargo strongbox.

On close inspection, the couple could discern a subtle, discreet trail of rusted scrap leading off from the frame. The pattern and the spacing of the small parts were too linear to be a coincidence. Walking a few yards beyond the end of this line of "scrap," Linda received a powerful signal. Something large was buried below. Bob's quick probe of the soil indicated a big metal target at about eighteen inches down. When he dug deep, he discovered the rest of the strongbox, turned upside down.

Had he not become wise to the ways of the KGC, he may have taken the feint and headed home. No, the upturned box was designed specifically for the uninformed, to throw "cowans" off the trail, to make them think that whatever treasure might have been there was now long gone. As it happened, one of Howk's letters specifically mentioned the need to keep shoveling when encountering a buried upside-down container.

Bob felt complete confidence as he began to dig deeper. He waved the detector over the exposed site, and it all but honked its odd-sounding electronic signal.

At five feet, he hit metal. This was it. A big cache, buried deep, he knew it.

Peering down into the hole, he could see the outline of a large iron teakettle. He lifted its lid and his heart raced: pounds of pristine gold coins, many of them $20 double-eagles! He took a deep breath to settle his pounding chest.

For a few minutes, he stood there motionless, head bowed, trembling slightly, with Linda at his side. Neither uttered a word. The moment of victory was almost religious, a time of reflection and awe. There was no giddiness. No outburst of emotion. For Bob, there was just the supreme satisfaction a scientist feels when a hypothesis is shown to be valid, repeatedly.

The system had worked, once again. First fruit jars then teakettles, all filled with gold coins from the previous century. All methodically recovered.

His mind galloped ahead, his thoughts aswirl with the notion that he was on to something of mind-boggling proportions. The immense thrill was hard to pin down, but it went beyond the valuable coins and their promise of material comfort. To him, the spectacular glistening currency was powerful confirmation of something bigger, a complex ciphered net-work that had yet to be fully explored and understood.

Collecting their wits, Bob and Linda were confronted with the ques-tion of what to do about the found money.

It had happened so fast—they did not know quite what move to make. Bob felt queasy. He did not know if the area was safe from armed interlopers, who might arrive at any time.

The pair elected to do what was prudent and the least disruptive to their modest way of life.

In a few crisp seconds of deliberation, Bob and Linda resolved to take several handfuls of the gold coins with them. The rest would be reburied in a new, concealed spot. It would be their secret, theirs alone. They quickly found a fresh location in the woods, buried the container and departed.

11 The Empty Pit

IN June 1995, the Brewers visited the Griffiths at the Oklahoma family's residence, a white trailer home, in Poteau. Griffith immediately showed Bob and Linda the stone "treasure map" that he had described in his letters. In a few seconds, Bob realized that his hunch about Griffith's rock map was correct. It *was* bogus: the rock seemed to have been engraved with a high-speed rotary tool. The stone was covered with thick lichen and moss; the carving was new and clean. The power tool had cut through the lichen covering without a hint of damage to the surrounding vegetation, and the bottom of the grooved lettering was as smooth as machined metal. Bob suspected that Griffith was trying to set up a recovery (or, perhaps, had already completed one) such that it would appear that the schoolteacher had executed the recovery on his own—with the spurious rock "map."

Yet, what should he do? Should he call Griffith's bluff? Or should he meet with the rancher and warn him that someone was about to undertake a treasure hunt there (or may already have done so) without his knowledge? To do the latter, he worried, would appear to others that he was the one trying to cut his associate out of a deal with the landowner. That was out of the question. Then again, what if Griffith had contacted the rancher and the two had decided to cut *him* out of the deal. Not Griffith's style, he concluded. It was a confusing mess. So he resolved to take the high road—to wait for Griffith to make his move.

The wait was not long. In mid-September 1995, Bob received a letter from a dentist friend of his from Oklahoma City who knew of Bob's passion for the Old West, Jesse James and treasure hunting. Enclosed was a newspaper clip, a feature article by local reporter Tamie Ross, entitled "Jesse James Remains Mysterious," from the back pages of the September 4 issue of the *Daily Oklahoman*. To the right of the headline was a large photo of Michael Griffith holding up some Jesse James memorabilia.

It was almost as if something told him not to read the article, for he hesitated before starting at the top. The story began innocuously enough, relating Griffith's large display of collectibles and books associated with the Jesse James saga. It then described the "history teacher" and "amateur historian" as a supporter of the view that Jesse James had faked his death and that J. Frank Dalton's paper trail lent credence to the theory that Jesse had escaped capture. But, for Bob, everything boiled down to the last brief paragraphs of the article.

> The history buff's love for all things related to James has brought financial gain, as well. In December 1993, Griffith said he and two others decoded one of Frank and Jesse James' maps and unearthed a Wells Fargo safe full of gold coins. He won't say where because other excavations are planned near there.
>
> "I could talk for days about what I've learned and what I plan to do in the future to find out more," Griffith said. "I've never seen anything so complicated in my life."

When Bob let the article fall to the table, he felt numb. That someone could do a "friend" so wrong, and without remorse, was beyond comprehension. He wanted to confront Griffith. Yet his rage was largely directed at himself for having given Griffith the full benefit of the doubt. He did not quite know where to direct his anger and frustration. At a minimum, he decided that he must not let himself slump into deeper despair. As a first step, he resolved to verify that the recovery of the Wolf Map treasure had occurred exactly where he said a cache would be found.

There were so many unanswered questions. How could the reporter have failed to press Griffith for more details? How could the story suggest that the recovery occurred in 1993, and not 1995? (Griffith had given a copy of the map to Brewer for decoding at the end of 1993.) Where was the follow-up story? Finally, why did the *Daily Oklahoman*'s editors allow such a tantalizing tidbit—a bold claim of a safe full of Jesse James gold being found, most likely in their state—to be buried at the bottom of a story in the back of the newspaper?

The unpublicized story-behind-the-story was one man's life work— the cracking of the KGC's code and its cash-and-arms burial system. The article made the recovery of the "Wells Fargo safe full of gold" sound almost as if it were an everyday occurrence.

In the unsettling wake of the *Daily Oklahoman* article, Bob phoned his friend Bud Hardcastle. He liked Hardcastle because the used-car salesman and Jesse James researcher had been true to his word in all their dealings. Also, Hardcastle had invested much time and energy into tracking down the unconventional possibilities behind the Jesse James saga, as a fellow uncredentialed historian. The occasional pieces of information provided by Hardcastle over the years seemed to hold up in Bob's own grassroots research. (As Bob later learned, Hardcastle had given the ever-acquisitive Griffith a copy of the Wolf Map, as he had a copy of Bob's Bible Tree videotape. It must have been Griffith's calcula- tion all along, Bob realized, that if Brewer could uncork the Bible Tree code, then Brewer could probably unravel the cipher of the Wolf Map. Griffith, sadly, was not only persistent but also unabashedly resourceful, even at the expense of two alleged "friends," he concluded.)

During a brief phone call, Bob asked Hardcastle if he would be inter- ested in accompanying him on a trip south to Addington. Explaining what had happened with Griffith, Bob said that he had some on-site investigating to do. Hardcastle said that he understood and would make arrangements.

When the two men arrived in Addington, they managed—to Bob's amazement—to hook up with the ranch owner. He turned out to be a pleasant fellow in his late sixties or early seventies. After introducing themselves, Bob and Hardcastle asked if they could have permission to go on to the property, specifically down to the creek area, to do some historical research on the Chisholm Trail. (Bob knew that his statement was not completely truthful, but he felt that it was the best he could do to confirm whether Griffith had gone to the spot.) The ranch owner, whose family had owned the sprawling property for generations, con- sented with a firm handshake and a nod. In response to a question from Bob, he confirmed the existence of an old Indian camp, near a spring, in the valley below.

Heading down a ravine toward the target site, Bob spied a hoot owl tree that suggested where to proceed. At a ford crossing along the Chisholm Trail, Bob and Hardcastle headed north and spotted a grouping of three large boulders. The three circles on the Madrugada map, without a doubt! How easy it must have been for Griffith to have tracked everything from this point, he thought. The waybill's three circles equaled the trio of boulders.

Bob could feel the veins in his forehead pulse as he walked to the geological formation—a perfect topographical match with the crude schematic representation drawn on the Early Morning Star Map of Gold. A stone's throw from the three boulders, at a spot next to the creek and just thirty yards east of the Chisholm Trail, Bob glimpsed what he did not want to see: an empty, freshly dug pit, about eighteen inches deep and a couple of feet wide. The hole was exactly where he thought it would be.

With Hardcastle at his side, Bob knelt down beside the hole and reached in to touch the packed reddish soil. In the handful of dirt, he could see numerous flakes of rusted iron. "Yep! He found it!" Bob exclaimed in a hoarse voice. Hardcastle, seeing the anger in his friend's expression, said a few comforting words—to the tune of "That bastard screwed you and me both."

Before they left, Bob decided to take a GPS reading of the coordinates of the Wolf Map cache hole. He took note of several KGC symbols in the area, including a triangular shaped "map rock" that had been neatly engraved with coded directional markers. With this information, he could better determine just how well his system—and the use of his modified template—worked on a large-scale depository, say one as large as one hundred square miles or more, with dozens of symbols involved.

What Griffith appeared to have found was a sizable treasure but one that probably ranked as an easily detectable marker cache, he thought. That is, it was not an enormous master cache, which would have been buried very deep, thirty to forty feet down. Thus, there might be other larger treasures in the area. The thought gave him little consolation.

The only silver lining was that the Wolf Map—and its arcane symbolism, geometry and geography—had worked. He had, on a bigger scale this time, matched wits with the mapmakers and penetrated their veiled, underground secret. And this, in light of all the other tracking he had accomplished to date, provided growing confirmation that a large and efficient post–Civil War organization was behind these seemingly inexplicable burials of hard currency. It also suggested that Jesse James might have been more than just an itinerant bank and train robber.

Bob was too upset that day to talk with the rancher about what had transpired. But two days after returning to Hatfield, his thoughts collected, he called up the landowner. This time he reached him.

Bob explained that someone had taken a safe full of gold coins from the property, by the creek, and that a story to that effect had made the papers but had not mentioned the precise location. The man's reaction was immediate. He simply hung up the phone. No questions asked. Nothing. Bob's subsequent attempt to correspond—by letter this time—went unanswered: to say the least, he was mystified by the silence. (As it turned out, despite a few additional attempts, Bob never did speak again with the property owner, who died not long after. Could the rancher have known all along that treasure was on the property? The notion had crossed Bob's mind since he first discovered the locale. But it was unanswerable.)

His fury untamed, Bob decided that he had to confront Griffith directly and with a witness. He drove to a town not far from where Griffith taught junior-high history. From his motel room, he called Griffith at his weekday residence and, as if nothing unusual had happened, asked that they meet at the motel to discuss a couple of important matters.

When Griffith showed up, he was surprised to see Bob's friend Stan Vickery in the room. Bob said that Stan, who had come to Oklahoma for some dental work that week, was there as an observer.

Without preliminary conversation, Bob asked whether the "safe full of gold" mentioned in the *Daily Oklahoman* had been found at the Addington site—the place that he had deciphered from the symbolism on the Wolf Map and that he had taken him to see. Griffith, who seemed surprised that Bob had learned of the article, paused but then categorically denied the proposition. No, it came from the Wapanucka area and was found using the Rebel-code rock map, he declared, in turn claiming the proceeds all his own. Bob told Griffith flatly that he did not believe him. He said that a recovery had taken place at the exact spot that he had described to Griffith, standing atop Monument Hill in Addington. He said that he had just been to the exposed cache hole with Hardcastle, and that he was now owed a third of the recovered money and the rancher the other third. Griffith shook his head in denial.

How much, in fact, was recovered, Bob demanded, leaving the question of the locale aside. "$2,200," Griffith replied, noting the face value only. Bob again growled that he did not believe him. "$2,200 in coins does not come near the 'safe full' of gold that you claimed to have found in the article," he said. The Madrugada map, he reminded Griffith, referred to $200,000, or as much as $10 million to $15 million in current numismatic rates.

He could not help but ask what Griffith had done with the recovered coins in the interim. Griffith said that he had sold some to coin dealers and private collectors, putting income from those discreet sales into certificates of deposit in his family members' names. With that, the schoolteacher got up and left, saying that he looked forward to working with Bob again!

It was the last time Bob Brewer spoke with Michael Griffith.

In the months that followed, a psychologically painful stretch toward the end of 1995 when thoughts of physical retribution crossed his mind, Bob mailed a package to the Gillespie sisters of Wapanucka, owners of the property where Jesse James's gold had been found. He enclosed a copy of a videotape that Griffith had shot of the recovery of the two small caches in the Wapanucka area, including one (in which Bob was absent) on the sisters' property itself that had numerous glistening Golden Eagles among the coins recovered.[1]

Bob knew that he was late in sending the package, but he hoped that the Gillespie sisters, whom he had not contacted until this point, would take up the matter. Delivering the videotape to the sisters was, without question, an act of revenge against Griffith. Yet it was also a sincere attempt to warn the Gillespies that Griffith still had hopes of finding additional treasure on their property, as he had mentioned Wapanucka a number of times in the motel room. In his accompanying letter, Bob explained how he and Griffith had been kicked off their property and how Griffith had then boldly returned with family members soon thereafter; and how on that return trip, according to correspondence and videotape footage that he had received from the schoolteacher, Griffith had found a cache of gold and silver coins in a spittoon. Bob concluded his note with an apology for having been on the property without permission and with regrets that Griffith had led him to believe that it had all been cleared ahead of time. On a final note, he said that he would be open to work with the sisters—on an equitable basis—in the search for more Jesse James treasure at Wapanucka.

On December 20, 1995, Jo Anne and Ceci Gillespie sent a fax "for immediate delivery to Mr. Michael Griffith," at Griffith's school. It said:

This is official notification that you are not to enter our property in Johnston County at any time or for any reason. If you do set foot on our property again, you will be arrested as will your father, brother or anyone else remotely connected to you. You have never had permission to be on our property, have been asked to leave and have had the sheriff remove you. We have a copy of your KGC video taken on our property and will press criminal charges if the guns and 2 caches are not returned to us immediately.[2]

The women received a hostile letter in response from Michael Griffith. He denied trespassing on their property and said he had received permission to be on the property "to camp with my son" from Ray Hackworth (the local cattleman who, at the time, held a pasture lease on the property). Until the time that he and Brewer had been warned off the property, he "didn't know who the owners were, until this matter was brought up."[3] The Gillespies took no further action. They have since been in touch with Bob, who, with their support, has made some initial attempts at discerning the larger depository layout in the area—with further joint efforts under consideration.

Griffith recently put together a KGC informational package, with a videotape and reference booklet, priced at $50 and advertised on his home page on the Internet. In the introduction to his sales package, Griffith writes:

I have known of treasure hunters, who, without doing the research necessary, and not actually knowing how to hunt, that have spent thousands of dollars and, as yet haven't found a single real's worth of treasure. Yet others, by quietly doing the necessary research, and knowing how to conduct the search, have, not by accident, managed to "bring home the bacon."

It is a matter of record that around fifteen to twenty million dollars are admitted by the treasure hunters willing to put forth the necessary effort to scientifically search out and trace down the clues and information readily available. . . .[4]

In April 2002, Griffith said in a telephone interview that he had "retired" from the treasure-hunting circuit. He acknowledged that he had, in fact, recovered four small caches related to the Wapanucka Jesse James treasure map: the jar full of silver coins, along Delaware Creek in the direction of Bromide, with Bob; the spittoon filled with gold and silver coins near three tall trees shown on the map (which appear to be on the Gillespie property), as well as two subsequent caches of similar size and value on surrounding property. All four, he said, were in a precise, geometrically defined pattern at equal distances from each other. Griffith said that, unbeknownst to Bob at the time, he not only possessed the relatively detailed Wapanucka treasure map but a copy of a KGC "overlay," which seemed to fit the map in question but was indefinite as to scale. Griffith acknowledged that while he initially had a general idea where a cache might be buried from the map-overlay combination, it took Bob's ability to interpret clues on site to find that first treasure. Once the initial treasure—the jar with the silver coins—had been found, Griffith said he then was able to determine the precise scale and distance measurements for the "layout," the map-overlay combination. He said that he used the precise scale to easily locate the three other spots, which were indicated as distinct points on the inner circle of the overlay, or template. He noted that the Wapanucka treasure map—with its clearly defined landmarks—was unusually detailed and made such a multicache recovery far less challenging than most KGC depository layouts, that is, once the requisite information from the field had been revealed.

Griffith, in the interview, reiterated his denial—as stated to Bob in the motel room with Stan Vickery, back in 1995—that he had recovered a big cache at Addington. In fact, he said repeatedly, he had "never been to Addington" and had "never been to the site" near Monument Hill. He claimed that the large treasure recovered in the Wells Fargo strongbox, as cited in the *Daily Oklahoman,* came from a location "in eastern Oklahoma," near his hometown of Poteau. This, however, contradicted what he had said to Brewer and Vickery in the motel room in Oklahoma. Then, he had said the safe full of Jesse James gold was found at the Wapanucka site.

The Michael Griffith episode—and the apparent betrayal at Addington—shook Bob deeply. It made him cynical, and that, perhaps, was what he hated most about the whole affair.

Bob sank into depression during the holiday season at the end of 1995. Linda did her best to lift his spirits. She tried to keep him focused on the larger quest: his need to satisfy his curiosity about the history and hidden truth behind all this buried treasure. She told her husband that while Griffith may have snatched the Wolf treasure (and recklessly trampled on friendship and private property rights in so doing) Bob adhered to an ethical code. Besides, she said, he still held the key to unlocking the larger mystery of the hidden gold . . . and more prospects surely would beckon.

Her prediction materialized within weeks. Just after the New Year, Bob's spirits revived when a major new piece of the puzzle presented itself in a phone call from a stranger. This time, the geographic focal point was more than a thousand miles away, in Arizona, at the fabled Lost Dutchman treasure site in the Superstition Mountains. If he could solve this, perhaps the biggest treasure riddle in U.S. history, he would confirm his greatest suspicion: that the KGC had built an underground Federal Reserve stretching across the country.

The Lost Dutchman Legend

12

THE legend of the Lost Dutchman Mine is by far America's best-known tale of underground treasure. Its account of an improbable, fabulously rich gold mine in Arizona's Superstition Mountains is also America's most *enduring* yarn about hidden gold or "lost" mines. A dozen or so treasure seekers have died over the past century trying to find the rumored mine: their deaths attributed to the effects of brutal heat, snakebite, heart failure, high-elevation missteps, rockslides and, in a handful of cases, bullets fired by unknown assailants.

Scores of mostly self-published books and hundreds of newspaper articles have been written about the Lost Dutchman mystery, which first emerged at the end of the nineteenth century.[1] The initial reports—a colorful mix of limited facts and ample speculation—spurred a perennial wave of die-hard "Dutch hunters" in search of the elusive "gold mine" of prospector Jacob Waltz. (Some accounts refer to him as Jacob Walzer, but "Waltz" is the version more widely used for the quirky German immigrant, posthumously and affectionately known as the "Dutchman.")

An ailing eighty-one-year-old Waltz, the story goes, described the general location of the mine from his deathbed inside a Phoenix boardinghouse, in October 1891. The fading fortune seeker reportedly made the disclosure—via a cryptic verbal message—to his caretaker and neighbor Julia Thomas. Upon Waltz's death, Thomas set out with a few friends to try to pinpoint the site containing the mother lode, but to no avail.

Exhausted and broke, she abruptly ended her search around a prominent 4,500-foot peak, called Weaver's Needle, and went home. She would let others take on the crippling heat, the lethal Mojave and western diamondback rattlers and Centruroides scorpions—not to mention tarantulas and black widows—all in the otherwise magnificent Superstitions, with their towering saguaros and flowering prickly pears.

From that moment on, amid a handful of turn-of-the-century newspaper articles about Thomas's dedicated but fruitless search in the unforgiving Superstitions, a mythology developed around the Dutchman's alleged missing bonanza. Countless, often conflicting, versions of the tale have swirled through oral and written histories ("hearsay" might be the operative word) up to the present day. The *Wall Street Journal* carried this front-page headline in 1971: "Did the Old Dutchman Leave a Big Gold Mine or Merely a Legend?: Many Still Work—and Fight—To Find Lost Dutchman Mine Fabled for a Century or So."[2]

Fueling the controversy are certain largely undisputed observations. Each winter, from about 1868 to 1886, Waltz was seen wandering off to undisclosed locations deep in the remote Superstition canyons. (Winter is the only period that a sane person would endure—over long periods—the heat from the surrounding Sonoran desert, where temperatures can soar above 120 degrees in mid-summer.) Waltz was also known to have cashed in small quantities of rich gold ore and, some say, gold nuggets in the frontier towns of Phoenix, Florence and Mesa. Shortly before his death, he reportedly hid a small hoard—weighing some fifty pounds—of gold-bearing quartz under his boardinghouse bed.

Such accounts support the notion that the gritty old-timer may have known of, and had access to, a highly productive hidden mine or gold-bearing vein in the Superstitions. An alternative theory is that Waltz had stolen, or "high-graded," fine gold ore from mines outside the Phoenix/Superstitions area in his earlier life as a miner/prospector. Waltz, according to this scenario, hid the high-grade material in a secret recess in the Superstitions and had been cashing in over time, as he grew older and more infirm.

But arrayed against such tantalizing leads are some hard facts. Expert geologists have ascertained that no large, naturally occurring, commercially viable deposits of gold exist in the once-volcanic eastern Superstition range, where Waltz was said to have wandered. Second, no one has come forward with evidence that a mine or a cache exists, at least since Thomas embarked on her abortive search. A limited amount of gold ore was extracted at Mammoth Mine at Goldfield, a short-lived desert boomtown that sprang up to the west of the Superstitions in the 1890s, just after Waltz's demise. But no one to date, at least for the record, has limped out of the craggy Superstitions weighed down with sacks of gold nuggets. Consider, as well: no mining company has shown any interest in the general area in a very long time!

Perhaps, as some have said, the Dutch-hunter phenomenon is nothing but blind optimism. Whatever the precise motive, something powerful continues to drive hundreds of zealous gold hunters to nearby Apache Junction.

The closest town to the 200-square-mile Superstition Wilderness, some thirty-five miles east of Phoenix, Apache Junction hosts a cottage industry of hope. Its various hotels, RV parks and stores minister to those on a mission—ranging from the obsessive to the mildly curious—to find Dutch Jacob's fabled gold mine. They come from all over America and from abroad, undeterred by the widely reported story of the macabre, unsolved murder of Adolph Ruth, an elderly retired federal civil servant and Dutchman-seeker whose decapitated corpse was found deep in the Superstitions in late 1931. (Ruth's skeleton was discovered a month after his bullet-riddled skull was found several miles away and months after he was reported missing.) Then there are the subsequent reports, in 1948, of a second decapitation murder of a solo Dutch seeker, James Cravey, who also may have been hot on a Lost Mine lead. More than five subsequent, albeit less gruesome murders have also been reported and gone unsolved, and there have been other incidents of apparent foul play.

Fueling Lost Dutchman interest, the mainstream media every so often will return to the Southwest's most publicized mystery and generate dreams of quick fortune all over again. The "Lost Dutchman's Mine" was listed in *U.S. News & World Report*'s "Mysteries of History" issue in July 2000. On a map of the world showing a "Lost and Found" of rumored unfound treasures, the "Dutchman Mine" was the only land treasure site to be noted in the United States. The caption reads:

In Arizona's Superstition Mountains in the 1840s, the Peralta family discovered a mine with some of the purest gold ore ever found. Indians killed most of the family, but in the 1870s a descendant told Jacob "the Dutchman" Waltz where the ore was. He mined it for a time and died in 1891, leaving a pile of gold beneath his bed.[3]

The original version of the story, whether fact or legend, says that Waltz stumbled on the hidden mine during an 1870 excursion into the Superstitions from nearby Florence, or possibly from what was then the even smaller frontier hamlet of Adamsville, in Arizona Territory. (Arizona, which became part of New Mexico Territory after the Mexican-American war, became a "Territory" in 1863. It attained statehood in February 1912.) Another version, believed to have begun circulating in the early 1900s, was that knowledge of the mine originated with a fairly wealthy Spanish-Mexican mining family of northern Mexico, the Peraltas, who, through various coincidences, passed on the decades-old knowledge of the "mine" and its vast riches to Waltz. (This scenario, cited in the *U.S. News* brief, was described as one of several popular Lost Dutchman versions in the *Wall Street Journal* feature.)

No one knows for sure whether the rumored Peralta family existed in northern (Sonora) Mexico or, if it did, if the family had any link to the alleged gold mine, or mines, in the Superstitions. No documented evidence exists to establish a firm connection. Nonetheless, there is a twofold significance to the unverifiable Peralta version of the Dutchman legend.

First, it establishes a storyline involving marauding Indians—the Apaches. The nomadic tribe had made the Superstitions a sacred stronghold in the 1800s. According to legend, the warlike Apaches had ambushed a Peralta mining expedition's return trip to Mexico in 1848. All the miners allegedly were killed, except for a handful of Peralta family members who managed to escape to Mexico and whose descendants later informed Waltz (and possibly an undocumented partner, Jacob Weiser) of the secret mine.

Second, the Peralta version serves as a possible link to a set of mysterious carved stone tablets, the so-called Peralta stone tablets, or Superstition stone tablets, allegedly found by a visiting hiker in the Superstition foothills in 1949. The cryptic tablets were the subject of a June 12, 1964, *Life* magazine story, "Mysterious Maps to Lost Gold Mines."[4] The four exquisitely carved "maps" of reddish-gray sandstone—containing indecipherable signs and symbols, broken Spanish inscriptions and jumbled figures—do not mention gold, treasure, mines or the name "Peralta," for that matter. (Curiously, numerous engravings on the stone slabs were covered up by black tape in the photos that appeared in *Life*.)

That said, the stone maps have been associated loosely with a patchwork of abstract carved symbols on rock faces and on giant saguaro cacti spread throughout the Superstitions. Experts have not been able to determine whether these carvings in the field—some call them "petro-glyphs," from the ancient Greek for rock-writing—are Spanish "treasure signs" or Indian picture writings or a mere hoax.[5] (The Conquistadors, followed by the Jesuits, explored the area beginning in the mid-1500s; the ancient Hohokam Indians had settled in the surrounding Salt River Valley more than two thousand years ago, followed by the Pima and Maricopa Indians.) No doubt both outsiders and indigenous cultures left carved messages behind, but to what end? Today, the ledger-sized stone maps—each weighing around twenty-five pounds and extending some sixteen inches long and nearly a foot wide—are housed in the Arizona Mining and Mineral Museum in Phoenix.

The origins of the stone tablets aside, much of their symbolism is noteworthy. One tablet contains an inset (concave) heart, with the date *1847* inscribed. It also reveals a carved dagger next to the heart. A separate, three-dimensional valentine—a smaller heart-shaped stone tablet in its own right—fits neatly inside the inset, with inscriptions of its own. On the reverse of the main heart tablet is a large cross. A second tablet has a carving of a large draft horse, with the phrase, in broken Spanish, *YO PASTO AL NORTE DEL RIO,* or, loosely, "I pasture to the north by the river," engraved next to it. On the flip side of the horse tablet is a priest-like figure holding what appears to be a cross, with a caption, again in broken Spanish, that reads: *ESTA BEREDA ES PELI-GROZA . . . YO BOY 18 LUGARES . . . BUSCA EL MAPA . . . BUSCA EL COAZON,* or, "This trail is dangerous . . . I go 18 places . . . Look for the map. Look for the heart." Floating next to the "priest" is a menagerie of symbols, including what appear to be crescent moons, circles and a small heart. The fourth tablet contains a flurry of numbers, letters and a dotted line pocked by smooth drill-holes. On the flip side of this trail tablet is the word *DON.* Placing this last tablet alongside the heart tablet with the latter's superimposed valentine creates a neat trick: the dotted lines link up to form a trail leading to the center of the removable heart.

Did Mexican "Peraltas" of the mid-1800s leave behind these stone "maps" as guideposts for finding their way back to a hidden mine? That titillating concept has ardent believers, yet there is no evidentiary foundation to it. Moreover, the colonial Spaniards who discovered gold and silver deposits in *northern* Arizona in the late 1500s were not likely to have left behind engraved rock maps with the apparent date 1847 and coded messages written in fractured Spanish. No, someone or some organization went to great lengths to create the abstract inscriptions, with their deliberately misspelled words and odd phrases with potential hidden meanings. Although the tablets' age and provenance might never be fully known, they do seem to possess a certain authenticity.

While many aspects of the Lost Dutchman Mine story appear apocryphal, the Dutchman himself left behind a paper trail. That trail corroborates Waltz's long residence in America and his professional pursuits as a miner and prospector. From immigration and census documents, mining claims, tax rolls, deeds, county register listings, correspondence and other primary source material, a consensus "history" about Waltz has emerged. Tom J. Kollenborn, an Apache Junction historian and an administrator of the local school district, has compiled well-researched, documented "facts" about Jacob Waltz, which most Dutchman researchers support. The Kollenborn consensus pivots on the following historical profile, which includes information provided by other diligent researchers, such as T. E. Glover.[6]

The mysterious German immigrant, who lies buried in an unmarked grave in a downtown Phoenix cemetery, spent his youth in the Black Forest region of what is now southwest Germany, near Stuttgart. Born in 1810, Waltz emigrated to the United States around 1845, arriving first in New York City. What Waltz did before emigrating has not been documented, although there is speculation that he was born to a farmer and schooled as a mining engineer. Once in the United States, he headed for the country's first known commercial gold fields, established in North Carolina and Georgia in the late 1820s. He then moved to Natchez, Mississippi (the adopted home of pro-slavery secessionist and Mississippi Masonic leader, Gen. John Anthony Quitman), where on November 12, 1848, he signed a declaration of intent to become a U.S. citizen. Citizenship would bolster his case for staking a mining claim, and he was soon off to the gold bonanza just getting under way in Sacramento County in northern California. The discovery of significant amounts of placer gold at John Sutter's Mill along the American River in Coloma, California, had occurred at the beginning of that year. (Smaller amounts of panned gold had been found some forty-five miles north of Los Angeles in 1841, but nobody seemed to notice.)

Between 1850 and 1859, based on census records and other official documents, Waltz prospected for gold in the most productive regions in the Sacramento Valley. (A "J. W. Walls" shows up in an 1850 census taken in Sacramento, which most Dutch researchers believe is a mis-spelled reference to Waltz.) But by then the northern California Gold Rush in the Sierra Nevada foothills was largely over. By 1860, Waltz apparently had moved to the Los Angeles–San Gabriel Mountains area, where he again worked as a miner and prospector, according to an 1860 census in Los Angeles County that lists a "Jacob Walls." On July 19, 1861, Waltz successfully applied to become a naturalized U.S. citizen in federal court in Los Angeles, under the correct spelling of his name. It was during this stay in the Los Angeles–San Gabriel region that Waltz apparently met Elisha Marcus Reavis, who would later become known as the "Hermit of Superstition Mountain."

Reavis, who headed west to California from Illinois during the Gold Rush, prospected for placer gold along the San Gabriel River east of Los Angeles. He later taught school in El Monte, a mean mining town in the region, where he is believed to have met Waltz. The two may have met while working placer claims along the San Gabriel banks, where American, European, Mexican, Chinese and other prospectors lived in close-quartered mining camps. Or they might have met in one of the many KGC castles in the area. In any event, both men headed to Arizona Territory sometime in the early 1860s, at a time when limited gold strikes had been reported in the north of the territory.

(Elisha Reavis was a cousin of James Addison Reavis, an assumed KGC operative, who, in the 1880s, attempted to secure a great swath of Arizona and New Mexico Territory, including the Superstitions and points east along the Gila River watershed. J. A. Reavis did so through a grandiose fraud known as the "Peralta Land Grant" involving a slew of forged documents.[7] The scheme by the Missouri-born ex-Confederate involved attempting to grandfather nearly 20,000 square miles of federal property as privately deeded land. He fraudulently claimed that the "deeds" stretched back to noble Spanish families that in fact never existed. The bogus claims were exposed in a well-publicized federal court case that landed J. A. Reavis in jail during the 1890s. Coincidentally, Reavis was known to have marked some of the boundaries of the "land grant" with star figures and other symbolic KGC carvings in rock faces. To date, no historical account has explained how one man nearly pulled off such a coup to "steal" a chunk of Arizona overnight, or how he could have obtained the funding to carry on his outlandish exploits over more than a decade. In the end, it appears that the KGC hung J. A. Reavis out to dry, much as it had George Bickley, after his usefulness had expired.)

Waltz, for his part, is known to have arrived in Arizona Territory sometime in 1863. In September of that year, he filed a mining claim with four partners in Prescott—the first capital of the territory—for a site in the nearby Bradshaw Mountains, where Elisha Reavis also wound up. Can it be chalked up to coincidence that one of Waltz's chief claims (1864) in the Prescott-Bradshaw region was named "Big Rebel"? After his 1863–67 stint in Prescott and its surrounding mineral-rich hills, Waltz migrated to the Salt River Valley in 1868. The valley's western edge abuts the Salt River Mountains, later renamed the Superstitions. There Waltz eventually settled in an adobe home in what would become Phoenix, on the north side of the Salt River, after having registered a homestead claim on 160 acres.

Elisha Reavis arrived in Phoenix around the same time, in 1869. But by 1874, for reasons unknown, he decided to decamp for the hills and live in a mountain hideout inside the high canyons of the eastern Superstitions, at some 5,000 feet above sea-level.[8] A thickly bearded loner who reportedly made a living selling vegetables grown in his garden at "Reavis Ranch," he died under suspicious circumstances on a remote trail inside the Superstition range in 1896. His corpse was found beheaded.

Reavis had always been on the move, hunting across the valleys, mesas and canyons, and selling vegetables to the surrounding towns of Pinal, Picket Post, Mesa, Florence and Tempe. Not much is known about his relationship with Waltz, the wandering "Lost Dutchman," other than that they knew each other. The ranch-owning Dutchman never moved into the Superstitions, but he certainly did not spend all his time cultivating his wheat crop and tending his chicken roost in Phoenix, either. Curiously, during the 1870s, Waltz had a group of laborers, many of them Mexican, residing at his Phoenix ranch, according to the local census.[9] What might they have been doing?

To see Jacob Waltz for what he was—a Southern partisan and KGC sentinel—and to see the Lost Dutchman Mine legend for what it was—a fabricated cover story for an enormous KGC depository of cached gold and silver stretching across the Superstition Range and beyond—required special knowledge: the type Bob Brewer had acquired by the mid-1990s, through decades of unrelenting research.

13

A Confederate Fort Knox in Arizona?

THE start of 1996 proved a tough time for Bob Brewer. Coming off a bout of depression from the Wolf Map fiasco, he felt physically and emotionally drained. He was already smarting from a shoulder injury caused when he stumbled over a bluff in Arkansas. The pain—an aggravation of an earlier injury suffered in Vietnam—eventually became so distracting that he decided to undergo surgery and receive a shoulder replacement. His defenses down, he wound up with a severe case of pneumonia. Although a massive dose of antibiotics killed the infection, both his lungs had been scarred, leaving him weak for an extended period.

His main concern during convalescence was not letting his health interrupt his odyssey. A big-boned man with a strong dose of Indian blood, he had always relied on a combination of intense mental focus and ample physical strength to get things done in a timely fashion, whether cutting and hauling logs, repairing tractors and automobiles, or excavating treasure caches. His diminished strength was something that he only grudgingly came to accept. The physical setbacks and the mental aggravation from the Michael Griffith debacle notwithstanding, his resolve to get to the bottom of the KGC mystery and its links to W. D. Ashcraft remained undiminished.

In early January, Bob received a letter from a wealthy individual in Florida, who said he had invested in a number of treasure-hunting projects and recently had heard about Bob's success in deciphering treasure carvings. He was seeking advice before putting money into what he described as an Arizona treasure venture, centered on the Superstition area of Lost Dutchman fame.

As a child, Bob read about the storied Lost Dutchman Mine and was captivated by tales of the missing "Spanish" mother lode. As an adult, he never gave much thought to researching the far-off locale or determining whether the story was anything but myth. In responding to the Florida investor, he said there was no possibility of offering counsel without knowing a great deal more about the target site.

After a series of phone calls, in which the Floridian made it clear he wanted to check Bob's qualifications as a treasure expert, Bob agreed that it would be worthwhile for the fellow to come up to the Ouachitas for a couple of days. A few months later, the mountaineer wound up taking the "flatlander" around to a few of his locales in the backwoods, and, by the third day on site, the man said he was well satisfied by what he had seen. He invited Bob to accompany him to Arizona to meet the principals of a group called the Heart Mountain Project (HMP), which, he said, was investigating large rock intaglios as well as clusters of smaller carvings in the Superstitions—all possibly tied to "Spanish treasure." The group, he explained, had been working on the project on and off for about two decades. Now it was out of funds and was seeking new investors.

For Bob to join the exploratory trip, he would have to get approval from HMP, the investor explained. After several weeks of correspondence, the HMP partners invited him out to their research site. For his own due diligence—before agreeing to drive to Arizona to assess the situation—Bob asked to see photos, videos, maps and other visual evidence of signs and symbols in the target area, as well as copies of historical documents.

Within a week, a thick package of documentary material arrived. It contained photos from what must have been dozens of forays into the tough terrain of the Superstitions—an area of the country in which he had yet to set foot.[1] From his sifting through the photos of rock carvings alone, Bob sensed there was substance to the rumors. He noted a remarkable likeness to the symbolism found at other KGC sites. He guessed, at this early stage, that the Lost Dutchman treasure trail might well have existed beyond the realm of folklore—albeit for reasons known only to a small group of men, whose job it was to protect and, ultimately, if so required, to retrieve buried wealth.

One set of photos included a series of close-ups of "stone maps." Bob had heard of the Superstition stone tablets but had never seen photos of the inscribed slabs. He knew that they were controversial: some people swore by their authenticity, while others thought them bogus, the elaborate work of brainy pranksters. He grinned at the bewildering smorgasbord of human and animal figures, drill holes, dots, lines, symbols, numbers, letters and garbled ungrammatical Spanish phrases neatly chiseled into the stone. The artistic lettering, he noted, suggested a Baconian cipher, with some letters incised in uppercase and others slightly offset.

He marveled at the tablets' recurrent thematic symbols: the heart, the horse and the priest, among them. How many times had he encountered man-made hearts in Arkansas and Oklahoma. So many of these—whether sculpted in stone or metal—had a diagonal line running through them. Perhaps, he speculated, the symbol represented the "broken heart" of the defeated South. Or perhaps it suggested Freemasonry's tenet of the third degree, that of the Master Mason, to be, as it were, "prepared in one's heart."[2] The horse and the priest had appeared prominently and mysteriously in the Bible Tree's menagerie of cryptic images. The entire look of the Superstition stone maps smacked of the KGC.

Then there was the inscribed date, 1847, which appeared twice on the tablets. Might it allude to the end of the fighting in the Mexican-American War, Bob wondered. (That war represented a milestone "victory" in the eyes of KGC expansionists, resulting in Mexico ceding California, most of Arizona and New Mexico and other territories to the United States the following year through treaty stipulations. It was not until December 1853, under the pro-slavery expansionist and pro-KGC President Franklin Pierce, that the southernmost section of modern-day Arizona—from the Gila River south—and southernmost New Mexico were acquired for $10 million under the so-called Gadsden Purchase. Pierce's envoy to Mexico, James Gadsden of South Carolina, had been a big promoter of the southern railroad routes to the Pacific, a key KGC goal, and was the central force behind securing the 45,000-square-mile purchase—more an ultimatum to Mexico—that completed the U.S.–Mexican border. Gadsden also was one of the largest slave owners in antebellum South Carolina.)

Of all the cryptic inscriptions on the stone tablets, Bob found himself drawn most acutely to the priest image—a hooded figure with a cross emblazoned on the sleeve of his robe. Was the priest a symbolic Knight Templar, a monk-warrior? At a minimum, the icon appeared to be some kind of holy man holding a staff. His robe, Bob thought, could well be a habit: templars wore long white habits adorned with a red cross.

To this point, Bob had seen firsthand that the KGC's underground depository system existed in Arkansas, extended east into Georgia and west into central Oklahoma. Now, he was witnessing tantalizing visual evidence that suggested its tentacles spread into the Far West, into the great Sonoran desert.

One of the more captivating visuals was a copy of a U.S. survey map from the mid-1800s. It showed the sparse settlements and forts of what today comprises south-central Arizona. The most intriguing elements were the longitudinal lines demarcated in degrees from a meridian of Washington, D.C., a modern-day anachronism. The HMP partners had shaded a quadrant in the northwest corner of the map—partly capturing the course of the Gila River and the Superstitions to the north—and labeled it "Search Area." This area formed a rectangle comprising the area within 33 degrees and 34 degrees "Long. West of Washington" and that between 33 degrees and 34 degrees north latitude. Was it a coincidence, or did the Masonic-dominated KGC deliberately choose to create a major underground repository for its wealth at such a symbolically fraught geographic coordinate? How clever, indeed, Bob thought. Little did the partners from HMP realize the potential significance of their shaded map.

Bob's mind raced back to William Dobson, Grandpa Ashcraft's summertime associate, whose home for much of the year was just south of the Superstitions, in Coolidge, Arizona. Was there a KGC link between the Superstitions and Hatfield, through, among others, old-timers William Wiley, Dobson and W. D. Ashcraft? Could this explain why Dobson, a native of nearby Cove, Arkansas, had relocated to a remote part of Arizona in the early 1900s, shuttling annually between the small towns of Coolidge and Hatfield for some twenty-five years? Bob held up a pair of strangely posed black-and-white family photos of Dobson and wondered.

Something else had come his way to support his growing theory that the KGC, in fact, had fanned out deep into the American West. A friend from New Mexico had sent him a remarkable clip from a Hatch, New Mexico, newspaper, the *Courier*. The article, dated October 6, 1994, was written by the paper's editor, Gene Ballinger.[3] Appearing two decades after Schrader's *Los Angeles Herald Examiner* article (which was, at best, a second- or third-hand "insider" account of KGC descendants and their once-removed knowledge of buried KGC gold), the loosely edited Ballinger piece in the small-town paper was a personal testimonial of a journalist (now deceased) whose family members were, in his own words, likely involved in the KGC organization.

The parallels to the lives of his own relatives—as possible KGC sentinels—riveted Bob as he read the article.

GHOSTS OF THE RED BLUFFS: WHERE IS $80,000
IN CONFEDERATE GOLD?

STATE—Shortly before the end of the Civil War, a well-organized effort was made to move all precious metals and many important records belonging to the Confederacy to safe havens.

Most gold and silver specie, bar stock, and coinage, along with a great many records were moved from Richmond, Virginia, and Atlanta, Georgia, to locations considered to be "safe" from Union confiscation.

The officers and men responsible for that removal were all members of a quasi-secret patriotic Confederate Organization known as the Knights of the Golden Circle. The organization should not be confused with the KKK, or any like group.

The Knights were very active during the Civil War and counted many of the highest ranking officials in the Confederate Government and Confederate armed forces among their ranks.

As an organization, the Knights and their families, disbanded in 1908, although it is still believed that in some manner, the organization still exists and is loosely tied to the Southern and Western Masonic Orders. Every male member of the Ballinger family has been a member of a Masonic Order since 1773 in America. And until 1932, every male member of the Ballinger family married into the Cherokee tribe, when a "few" outside influences changed that. Belonging to, and marrying into the tribe, was a tradition that started in 1733 when the first family members arrived from Switzerland, and Ireland, and settled in the Carolinas.

And every male member of the Ballinger family has fought in every war the American people have ever participated in, from the French-Indian Wars, the Revolution, to right now in Haiti, in some capacity. Family members fought on both sides of the Civil War, with most fighting on the side of the Confederacy.

We have a very vested interest in the future, and the history, of our nation.

Very little of what most experts say may have been millions of dollars in gold and silver specie, bar stock and coin has ever been found, since it was moved out of Richmond and Atlanta.

The very purpose for moving and hiding such a hoard was known only to a select few.

That purpose [was] to continue the Civil War, or start a new one, according to KGC records.

Neither ever happened.

Some of that gold is believed to have made it to New Mexico in 1866 or early 1867.

There were many Confederate sympathizers living in the Territory of New Mexico and West Texas, several of them well-known ranchers whose families still live and ranch in the state. . . .

Immediately recognizable names from the days of the Civil War, and years following the war, were associated with the Knights, and the movement of missing gold, silver . . .

All are best known in history as outlaws in one manner or another. Yet, all fought with distinction for the Confederacy. A fact that might be challenged by some historians, yet true.

History shows that members of the James gang were in New Mexico, and more than once, after the war, in-between train and bank robberies attributed to them.

What they were doing here is not known, at least generally. They did not participate in any known criminal activity, they were seen publicly in a saloon and/or gambling hall or two, particularly in Silver City, but they never stayed anywhere very long.

It is known that Jesse spent several days, on more than one occasion at the John (Chisum) ranch, but no one knows why.

The link to New Mexico was of extreme importance to the Knights, and Jesse James was a major player.

As a trusted Lieutenant in the Knights, it had been Jesse's responsibility to see that an estimated $80,000 (at 1866 valuation) in Confederate gold coin and bars (the coin was a mixture of Spanish, English and French, with a small amount of U.S. gold coinage), was transported from Georgia to a safe haven in New Mexico. The bars were mostly from the New Orleans Mint, which had been seized by the Confederacy at the start of the war, along with gold obtained elsewhere, and locally smelted in the Georgia gold fields.

That part of the transport assigned to the James brothers, the Youngers, and several other die-hard southerners, passed through Atlanta less than a week before it fell to Union forces.

Other convoys headed south into Florida, one went into Mexico, another into Canada, after traveling west into Kansas and going north, to avoid Union troops.

Made up of wagons and pack animals the James convoy moved northwest of Atlanta to outside of Rome, then in a westerly direction through Alabama, Mississippi, Arkansas into the Indian Territory (Oklahoma) to New Mexico.

Where they went in New Mexico is pure speculation.

None of the wagons, or pack animals, ever appeared with the James brothers when seen in New Mexico, therefore, it is assumed that the equipment and gold was disposed of before they made any public appearance then, or in later years. . . .

I became personally interested in the Knights when I found out that there was a firm family connection between the Ballinger, James and Younger families . . .

When I found out that my grandfather George, a deputy U.S. Marshal, had moved from Missouri to Oklahoma, to secure tribal rights to family tribal land (Cherokee) in 1902 and then on to New Mexico with his brother, and homesteaded in Lincoln County in 1907, I became more than a little bit curious about what that was all about.

The Southern Cherokees fought for the Confederacy and were among the last to lay down their arms at the end of the conflict.

I understood (his) moving to Oklahoma—that was necessary to protect tribal land rights for each member of the family, which are still in family hands.

But when family records indicated that he moved on to New Mexico, and into Lincoln County, and he and his brother homesteaded there, my curiosity peaked.

My father John was one year of age when Grandpa homesteaded in New Mexico with his brother and other family members, and built the family ranch. . . .

Grandpa continued his duties as a deputy U.S. Marshal including service on the Texas/Mexico border, in Oklahoma, the Dakotas and in New Mexico. He died in 1940. I had only met him twice, and then as a very small boy.

But in tracing the history of the Knights of the Golden Circle, and tracking our own family's possible involvement in that organization, I finally came to the conclusion that my great-grandfather, and my grandfather, both were in some manner associated with the organization.

And furthermore, that my grandfather came to New Mexico, and homesteaded here for more than one reason in 1907. One was to make very sure that the cargo that the James boys brought to New Mexico for safe keeping, was indeed, still safe, and to secure additional family property.

Although Grandpa worked for the Federal Government as an officer of the law, I honestly believe that in his heart, he was still with the Confederacy, as was his father.

The answers to many of the questions I have had for years may have been lost in 1940 when two steamer trunks belonging to Grandpa were lost while being shipped by train from New Mexico to Missouri. In those trunks were all of his personal records. The trunks were never located.

The only hint of what Grandpa was most interested in came from my aunt Ora, my father's oldest sister. Ora passed away three years ago at the age of 96. She was 11 years old when the family came to New Mexico from Oklahoma in 1907. She was also the family historian.

She told me many years ago that Grandpa, George Ballinger, made it a point of riding south and east of Carrizozo to look at some "red bluffs" several times in 1907 and 1908.

Aunt Ora said there was something important about those bluffs to her father. She thought maybe a cave or something, but he never said anything, and eventually stopped making the trip. The bluffs were not homesteads owned by any family members at the time.

I do not know where those red bluffs are. I am not certain that my great-grandfather, or grandfather, were members of the Knights of the Golden Circle, although I believe so.

I do know that the Knights of the Golden Circle disbanded officially in 1908.

But we do know that there is no record anywhere that indicates that any part of the missing Confederate Treasury entrusted to the Knights of the Golden Circle, with the exception of two boxes of small gold bars that were accidentally found in Atlanta in the 1970s during construction excavation, and a few scattered, but unconfirmed reports of small caches found elsewhere, has ever been recovered in the United States, Canada or Mexico.

The worth of $80,000 in gold bullion and coin at 1866 valuation would be somewhere in the neighborhood of $5 million today. . . .

The Ballinger article, with its references to Jesse James and associated KGC operations in New Mexico, and the package of material sent by the Arizona-based Heart Mountain Project, made for a powerful combination. Bob retreated to his "war room" and, with the amassed material laid out in front of him, stayed put for the next three months. No visitors. Minimal phone calls. Even trips to the bathroom were made with old maps and annotated reference books in hand. The mission: to resolve whether the KGC field engineers did, in fact, burrow under the sands and buttes of the Far West, leaving ample treasure there. If the photos, maps and other material sent by the Heart Mountain Project did not add up to a KGC layout, he was not going to be interested. If the material did, in fact, point in that direction, then he was not going to stop until he had unraveled the tablets' code.

Bob wanted to know whether the teasing figures and symbols on the stone tablets connected in any way to the surrounding topography and to the carved symbols cut into canyon walls in or near the Superstitions. He could only go so far in operating remotely, with the photos in hand. But then again, he would only venture to the broiling Arizona desert if he knew, without a doubt, that he would get physical confirmation of such a connection.

Linda did not know what to make of Bob's return to full immersion. His was a disappearing act that required her to keep her spouse tanked on gallons of hot coffee and a steady flow of sandwiches. She again started to worry about his state of mind, given his total focus on "the maps." But, as with his earlier stint with the Wolf Map, she could tell he was on to something enormously challenging. At times, he would remain in the study for sixteen hours uninterrupted, prompting her to inquire, politely and with a smile: "Are you going off the deep end?" He would stare back, glassy-eyed, but with a grin splitting his broad face: "Not yet. Depends if I can figure out these maps." He explained that, as with the Wolf Map, the stone tablets were full of dead ends and false leads. Yet, he declared, he knew deep down that they were genuine treasure maps and most likely KGC.

To solve the stone maps (and assuming they were KGC waybills), he first had to connect their carved images and hidden messages to precise topographic features (as to location, date, scale, contour intervals) on U.S. Geological Survey topo maps of the target area. By now, he had learned that KGC waybills often were based on information contained in official maps. Logically, the government maps came first, with the encrypted waybill being created around specific features on the government maps—features that pointed to caches or cache-marker sites when incorporated into the ciphered KGC equation.

Bob knew that the U.S. government produced its first detailed topographic "quadrangle" maps of the Far West in the decades following the Civil War. USGS topographic teams headed out (and risked their lives) to chart the American hinterland during a peak period between 1879 and 1890.[4] These labor-intensive general purpose maps—designed to provide precise information about the natural resources and terrain in the so-called Western Country—were produced with fairly crude instruments and a lot of exertion. But the massive effort by the government's backpacking cartographers, at least from Washington's perspective, would pay huge dividends. The maps contained valuable data for military planning (in the wars against various Indian nations) and for the economic development of the interior (for agriculture, forestry, mining or the building of railroads) as pioneers migrated westward after the Civil War. The topo, today a wilderness hiker's best friend, is distinguished from other types of maps by portraying not only man-made "cultural" features, but also in providing "by some means the configurations and elevations of the terrain—the shapes into which the Earth's surface is sculptured by natural forces."[5]

Bob also knew that finding subtle clues hidden among the multitude of contour lines, trail lines, creeks, rivers, canyons, roadways and other calibrated markings on the quadrangle maps of the expansive West was going to be an unforgiving endeavor. Even more so, if the correct scale were not known.

Map scale—the mathematical relationship between the measurements of the features designated on the map and the physical features themselves as they appear in the terrain—is expressed as a ratio. Thus 1:1,000,000 scale represents one unit of map distance equal to one million of the same unit on the ground, that is, in horizontal geographic distance. Greater scale translates to greater detail, or magnification. Most modern-day topographic maps (whose production has been made vastly more efficient through aerial photography) are a standard 1:24,000 scale, where one inch represents 2,000 feet, or 24,000 inches. Many of the older topos are of a smaller scale, 1:125,000, for example, and as such were designed for comprehensive views of large undeveloped areas.[6] The USGS topographic "quadrangles" range from 1:20,000 to 1:250,000 in published scale.

Bob recognized the importance of having maps with the same scale as those used by KGC cryptographers and cartographers. Also, he knew to look for alphabetic and numeric hints (usually free-floating characters or anagrams) that revealed specific range or township numbers. He recalled the impact of deciphering the veiled free-floating components, "R," "7" and "W" (for Range 7 West) shown on the Wolf Map. These two elements—scale and potential township/range indicators—were crucial starting points.

To ensure that his painstaking effort was not a waste of time, he began researching the Superstition stone tablets and the Lost Dutchman's Mine legend. He knew that many of the rumors surrounding the stone maps and the Lost Mine fit the profile of a KGC depository cover story. As such, the elements of a rudimentary, straightforward tale had been designed to mean one thing to average readers yet convey an entirely different hidden message for the informed elite. These stories typically included a revelation about a fabulously lucrative lost mine or lost cache; a threat from hostile Indians; the encryption of information about the mine or hidden caches prior to the impending massacre by Indians; or an eventual rash of suspiciously timed newspaper articles indicating a "gold rush" in the area.

Bob had also recognized early on that the character and behavior patterns of Jacob Waltz fit the modus operandi of a KGC sentinel. Rather than secretly returning to his hidden mine (or aimlessly wandering about to find the alleged shaft, as some versions would have it), Waltz may just as easily have been on patrol *guarding* KGC cache sites from intruders. Moreover, Waltz may have been assigned the task of moving the caches and updating the treasure markers with the help of others, such as his resident Mexican laborers. Perhaps the gold ore that Waltz allegedly used as legal tender was, in fact, his "paycheck" from the KGC.

Bob surmised that carefully stoked bits of "folklore" may have created the desired impression among townsfolk: that Dutch Jacob did, in fact, have a mine. If almost everyone in the region believed a lost mine was at stake—and not a labyrinthine network of buried Rebel caches— the invisible KGC hierarchy would have been well served.

When Bob began to delve deeper into Waltz's migratory trail within the United States, two of the Dutchman's addresses—Natchez, Mississippi, and El Monte, California—sprang out as potential KGC markers. He knew, for instance, that Natchez—a southwestern Mississippi haunt of Anthony Quitman and Jefferson Davis (Davis's plantation was some forty miles north at Davis Bend)—was a stronghold and recruiting ground for the KGC between the late 1830s and 1860. While the roots of the KGC were deeply set in Charleston, Natchez attracted numerous

KGC sympathizers. These adherents would fan out and spread the secret society's expansionist mission, not only across the Deep South but also out West, all the way to the California coast. During the height of KGC expansion, wealthy Northerners and owners of Caribbean island plantations flocked to the rich Mississippi bottomlands, such as Adams County, where Natchez was the capital. Through both legal and dubious means, these outsiders obtained title to thousands of acres of the rich black soil and created powerful plantation-based empires—eventually becoming the core political and financial support structure for the KGC.

Could German immigrant Jacob Waltz's alighting in Natchez—after stints in the gold fields of North Carolina and Georgia—be chalked up to mere coincidence? Not likely. Waltz's trail from Germany to Natchez did not make much sense at all to Bob until he came across a couple of intriguing references. The first derived from J. Frank Dalton in Orvus Howk's (Jesse Lee James) first book, *Jesse James and the Lost Cause*; the other from an informative thirty-eight-page historical-society booklet, "The Knights of the Golden Circle: In California with Special Emphasis on Southern California and San Bernardino County," by Leonard B. Waitman.[7]

In *Jesse James and the Lost Cause,* J. Frank Dalton is quoted:

[KGC] Agents at work in Europe recruited German, Austrian, French and Italian tradesmen, and ex-soldiers who had served well in their own countries were persuaded to move to America. The Knights of the Golden Circle financed them, but first they had to take a blood oath of utter secrecy. They came over and were put on probation for a period of perhaps three years, more or less. After the probation period, they were then moved, as demand existed, into good jobs, such as brew-masters, distillers, stagecoach drivers, stagecoach relay station operators, livery stable operators, dairymen, truck gardeners, doctors, blacksmiths, shoe-cobblers, boot-makers, bakers, cabinet makers, jewelers, engineers, surveyors, geologists, and scientists. Each man brought with him his own specialized, specific trade.

Over in Europe most of these high type craftsmen, artisans and scientists would have had a very meager existence at best, but over here in America they had every opportunity to expand, live and profit, so we encouraged them to do their best for us. They were already trained and educated soldiers. All we had to do was caution them to keep their mouths shut, keep a level head, and follow our orders.[8]

Could Jacob Waltz, rumored to have been trained as an engineer, have been a KGC recruit from Europe? Might agents have met him in New York, sent him on probationary training to the gold fields of the Southeast, then on to full indoctrination in Natchez before being shipped with other KGC recruits to California?

Bob learned that many KGC initiates participated, for whatever reason, in the Gold Rush, digging and panning in the Sierra Nevada foothills. Others, in a later wave, headed to southern California following that unforgettable 1849–50 mother lode period. California, it seemed, would become an increasingly attractive target for KGC activity.

The militant secret order made significant, albeit unsuccessful, efforts—through subversion and the activation of its sleeper cells—toward bringing the state into the Confederacy before and during the Civil War. California possessed huge mineral wealth, big seaports and a large population of pro-slavery Confederate sympathizers. As such, it would have been an ideal western anchor for the expanding Golden Circle empire had the KGC-led uprising there been successful. The state, with its 1860 Census population of 380,000, remained badly divided before the Civil War and then for its duration. At one point, it nearly split in two because of KGC political mobilization efforts within its predominantly pro-South southern counties. And, in key cities and towns of the north, including San Francisco, KGC agents and their "secesh" supporters occupied influential positions in government and the local press. They also held prominent posts in the mint, navy yard and local army quarters, according to Waitman and other researchers. These undercover agents— operating under a password RABE (an anagram for BEAR, as in "Bear State," and a play on the term Rebel)—resorted to burning, plundering and stealing pro-Union assets in California as the war gripped the nation back East.

After obtaining a copy of Waitman's paper and archival references from the Civil War era, Bob was able to speculate on why El Monte, California, wound up as a principal stopover on Waltz's American exodus. (He also recalled how Del Schrader—in his *Herald Examiner* article about the California-based KGC descendants' reunion—quoted somebody as saying that El Monte was a KGC headquarters.) Waitman noted:

The KGC began infiltrating California in the late 1840s. By 1850, there were some 100,000 southerners in southern California, and perhaps

18,000 were KGC agents. The KGC wanted to be ready to move when the secession movement began. . . . It is easy to see why the Knights had such an easy time infiltrating California. They came by way of well-known routes and in many disguises: as miners, traders, settlers, and in various professions, such as doctors, lawyers and teachers. They usually traveled in small bands, rarely numbering over five or six in number. After reaching California, these groups divided into smaller units, spread out and set up organizational headquarters throughout the state.

The most active of these secessionist centers were in El Monte, San Bernardino, Los Angeles, San Luis Obispo, Mariposa, Stockton, Marysville, Sacramento and San Francisco.[9]

El Monte, a KGC hotbed, was singled out at the time by a pro-Union newspaper editor who found himself engulfed by hostile secessionist sentiment in the San Bernardino County community that his paper served. As editor of the local *Weekly Patriot,* Edwin A. Sherman wrote confidentially to the commander of the U.S. Pacific Division, Army Gen. E. V. Sumner, on June 3, 1861:

> There exists amongst us through all these southern counties a secret organization of secessionists, and in a settlement near Los Angeles there is an organized cavalry company which is ready at almost any moment to break out, holding an inveterate hatred toward the citizens of this place, and it is at this point they would make their first attack, and there are some in our midst who would receive them cheerfully and help them in their treacherous designs. . . . The secessionists of [El] Monte are only waiting the withdrawal of the troops from Los Angeles before they commence operations.[10]

Was it sheer chance, Bob wondered, that Waltz left El Monte for Arizona in 1863, settling in the Superstitions? Wanderlust and visions of gold could have played key roles. But there may have been a more complex explanation.

Southern Arizona, in the early phase of the Civil War, was home to large numbers of Confederate sympathizers—and, by extension, underground KGC operatives. The foremost goal of these pro-Southern westerners was to link with like-minded operatives in neighboring California and then to usher that strategically important state into the Confederacy. While the KGC's underground units likely remained active as fifth column operators in Arizona Territory throughout the Civil War, the Confederacy formed a formal, albeit short-lived, Arizona Brigade fighting force. It fought briefly in Arizona Territory—in the April 1862 Picacho Pass skirmish—before being driven from the territory by federal troops early on in the war. The seemingly insignificant Arizona–New Mexico engagements might have had significant repercussions for the Union if the Rebels had proven victorious and forged a viable link throughout the Southwest with their secessionist brethren in California.[11]

An intriguing hypothesis crossed Bob's mind. While Waltz was not known to have served as a Confederate soldier, he may have provided intelligence on the movement of Union forces occupying the territory. He also might have served as a sentinel for Rebel caches—treasure secreted both during the conflict and after the conclusion of the war.

Waltz's paper trail led Bob to his third avenue of attack for solving the Lost Dutchman riddle: searching for clues in the names of local landmarks. Two immediately stood out: Grayback Mountain and Dromedary Peak. He knew that Grayback was a nickname for Rebel soldiers and that Confederate notes were dubbed graybacks as a twist on President Lincoln's new fiat money, greenbacks. As an anagram, the word spelled out "KGC RAAYB," or a phonetic version of the KGC password, RABE.

As for Dromedary Peak, it likely was a tip of the hat to Jefferson Davis and his pre–Civil War plan, as U.S. Secretary of War, to use Egyptian camels as pack animals in the U.S. Southwest. Davis's bold 1855 proposal—to have dromedaries haul supplies and serve as mobile cavalry across the American deserts, including the brutal Sonoran in Arizona—received a $30,000 appropriation by Congress. But the U.S. Camel Corps quickly foundered for a host of reasons, including the fact that the seventy or so imported Egyptian camels had trouble adjusting to the rocky soil of the American deserts. Further, the Saharan imports frightened local pack animals, and their powerful odor proved too much for the olfactory sensibilities of American troops. Yet it was a noble effort, and a memorial to the dromedaries' Middle Eastern–born handler, Hadji Ali, a.k.a. Hi Jolly, was erected in Quartzsite, Arizona. J. Frank Dalton, in *Jesse James and the Lost Cause*, makes specific reference to Davis's "Camel Corp" and its denouement: wild, snorting camels inhabiting wide sections of the West, "especially Arizona" and intimidating the local fauna.[12]

There were other conspicuous place names, such as Price, as in Gen.

Sterling Price, the Confederate commander and participant in the Knights' postwar exodus to Mexico. Bob also could not help but notice the mining town of Reymert, a ghost town since 1891 lying just south of the Superstitions. The town, he discovered, was named after James DeNoon Reymert, a lawyer/entrepreneur of Scotch-Norwegian descent. In the late 1800s, Reymert owned several mines—Reymert Silver Mines, five miles north of Heart Mountain and the Gila River—and was the editor of the Pinal Drill mining newspaper. Reymert also happened to be a close friend of Caleb Cushing, an early leading light of the KGC who had mining interests of his own in various parts of the country, including Minnesota, where Reymert had been professionally active earlier in his life.

Reymert, who owned a law practice in New York City, corresponded extensively with Cushing. In an October 6, 1861 letter to Cushing, Reymert wrote cryptically: "I am anxious to lay before you some plans, which, if I can execute, will be of very great benefit to your interests in the Southwest, and, shall they meet your approval, I must hasten back to carry them out."[13] Reymert and Cushing also wrote to each other about plans for recruiting Scandinavian and other European engineers via a company called The Great European-American Emigration Land Co.

These and other "coincidences" among strategically relevant place names led Bob to suspect that KGC agents somehow participated in naming key landmarks in the Superstitions area. In the back of his mind, he had begun to wonder whether the Knights may have placed moles inside the U.S. Geological Survey.

Another clue—again, embedded in the name of a local landmark—emerged during his months of off-site investigation. He had noticed a "Hewitt Ranch" as one of a handful of residences along the remote western end of the Superstition Range. Hewitt Ranch happened to be located near "Reavis Ranch," named, of course, for Elisha Reavis, whom Bob suspected of having been a KGC sentinel. But what of this Hewitt, for which a canyon, a large ridge and a mountain road were named?

In *Jesse James Was One of His Names,* Col. Roy Hewitt is listed as one of the aliases of Jesse Woodson James.[14] In *Jesse James and the Lost Cause,* a photo of a rifle-toting, thickly bearded horseman carries the caption, "A rare photo of Jesse James when he was using the alias of Col. Roy Hewitt."[15]

Bob had no way of knowing if there was, in fact, a Jesse James connection to the Lost Dutchman, and, if so, whether it could hinge in part on the Hewitt Ranch. The notion of Jesse James's involvement in the Superstitions' enigma was compelling, particularly after Ballinger's fairly strong statement that Jesse and Frank had traveled at least as far west as New Mexico (Arizona) Territory—and on KGC-cache business!

There was one additional piece of potential "evidence" that might link Jesse with the Superstitions, although it was a long shot. Among his collection of photocopied letters, waybills and other documents from Howk (nearly all of which are signed JJ III or Jesse Lee James) was one particularly detailed waybill entitled "Arizona Desert Treasure."[16] It named the state that the alleged treasure was buried in, but, of course, omitted the location. No counties, no towns, no streets, no latitude-longitude coordinates . . . nothing. The waybill *did* contain, however, a drawing of a set of abandoned adobe buildings near the alleged buried treasure. Moreover, it presented a detailed account—however reliable—as to how the money ($440,000 in gold coins) was shipped to the region by rail, confiscated from the train and then buried, all part of an "inside" job involving Jesse Woodson James.

Bob did not doubt the authenticity of the Arizona Desert Treasure map. The waybill, with its illustrations, apparently had been dictated by J. Frank Dalton to Howk. The telltale Howk signature "JJ III" appears twice on the map. The handwriting and the overall look of the pictogram closely resembles other photocopied waybills from J. Frank Dalton (via Howk) that Bob owned. Could this suspected Jesse James treasure site lie near the Lost Dutchman Mine? The thought seemed a stretch but not beyond reason. Bob resolved that finding the coordinates of the site would be one of his top, if not *the* top priority, on any scouting mission to Arizona.

Yet he was not going anywhere until he made substantive progress cracking the stone tablets' code. After weeks of concentrated effort, nothing definitive seemed to emerge. He simply could not develop the overall theme and flow of the multifaceted cryptogram. In search of fresh leads, he called up the Heart Mountain Group and asked for maps from a different period. As it turned out, these would help a great deal, for certain place names had changed over time. But the core problem remained: finding the all-important starting point to begin the step-by-step process of decoding.

Frustration was building. The intermittent flashes of insight that had propelled him through the Wolf Map were stalled. Was his intuition failing him, or was something missing from the puzzle board itself?

During those aggravating spells in the spring of 1996, Bob would take a morning break and head to McLain's to unwind. While sipping coffee one morning, he bumped into a family friend, the widow of George Mitchell. Bob had known Mitchell, a veteran treasure hunter, only briefly before the local man died. He had met him at the very same coffee shop, in 1975, during a visit just before the Brewer family moved to Hatfield. The two men had chatted about local treasure lore, and Bob had come away impressed with the older man's knowledge. He was particularly interested in Mitchell's research into the so-called "Spider Rocks of Texas," a mystery centered on web-like patterns chiseled into stone slabs.[17] Now, more than two decades later, Bob realized that the Spider Rocks were likely symbolic representations of the circular KGC template—surrounded by jumbled text and numerals—carved into three stone tablets found at three separate locations near Abilene in the early 1900s. Was there a link between the Texas and Arizona stone tablets, he wondered.

When Rita Mitchell asked Bob what he had been up to, he said that he had been spending far too much time working his way through a stubborn treasure knot, one centered in Arizona. He hesitated before saying any more—not because he feared giving anything away, but because he knew the woman hated the very mention of treasure hunting. There was no other word for it: she *despised* the vocation. Her husband's all-consuming passion for treasure left her struggling to support young children when he died (a not uncommon experience in the hard-core treasure-hunting community). Yet, for some reason her hostility toward the topic seemed somewhat tempered that morning, and she volunteered that George had spent some time in Arizona looking for the Lost Dutchman gold mine.

Bob's heart jumped. He tried his best to stay cool. After he collected himself, he leaned forward and gently asked Rita if George had left any documentation of his work on the Dutchman. He expected a tongue-lashing, but surprisingly, after looking over her shoulder to see if anyone was eavesdropping, she said that she would rummage through George's files.

A week or two passed and, as it turned out, Bob and Rita Mitchell somehow managed to miss each other at the coffee shop. When they finally did connect, at Bob's usual table, she told him that she had been carrying around a small file of papers in her car. After a few minutes of small talk, she suggested that they step outside. She asked Bob to climb into her car so that no one would see what they were doing. She said that she didn't want anyone to know that she had anything to do with treasure hunting. But to Bob, it seemed as if she were particularly nervous about these papers. He didn't press the point. Reaching under the front seat, she produced a coffee-stained manila folder entitled "Horse Maps." In the folder were several sheets of carbon-copy paper, dated 1955, each one showing tracings of the original Superstition Mountain stone maps.[18]

Bob's reaction was gracious but low key at seeing the decades-old drawings. After all, he already had the set of professional photographs of the maps sent by the Heart Mountain Project. He had expected more. He asked if he could get copies of the papers made and then return the originals. She said she'd rather have the copies made herself and not let the originals out of her sight, but realizing that she already was late to work, she impulsively handed the stack to Bob and pleaded their speedy return. Bob made copies, returned the originals and hurried home to compare them to the photographs of the Arizona stone tablets. Right away, he saw dissimilarities.

Back in his study, his pulse raced at the sight of a small, elephant-like figure on one of the carbon tracings. The weird creature—with oversized feet, an extended belly and floppy ears—stood upright. The image, inscribed to the left of the draft horse on the horse tablet, was not visible on the photographs. Either someone had altered the tablets or there was another set stored somewhere. Either way, the small rendering appeared to have special meaning.

Attuned to the subtleties of the KGC's hieroglyphic-like cipher, Bob guessed that the elephant's importance was most likely to be found in some metaphor or allegory. He knew that the organization was fond of incorporating figures from the Old and New Testaments, the Jewish Kabbala and other tradition-bound sources, including the occult, into its encrypted messages. He theorized that the odd little creature was Behemoth, a giant animal—possibly a hippo or an elephant—mentioned in Job 40:15–24. He surmised that somewhere on the map of the area—in the physical topographic features—a giant beast was to be found. And it was not meant to be the well-known Elephant Butte landmark: an oddly shaped outcrop in the Superstitions that appears, in physical profile, to be an elephant's head. No, that would be far too obvious, and such a conspicuous target would have been more a deliberate diversion, a decoy. It would serve to send the uninformed cache hunter or lost-mine seeker running off with picks and shovels on a quixotic mission to . . . dry holes.

With this new variable, Bob experienced a burst of intuition. Behemoth—its trunk pointing east, directly at the horse's head—was signaling for the horse to be made large, in fact, mammoth. Find the giant horse to the right, or east, of Elephant Butte. But where?

All that night he hunched over the topos, looking for the outline of a horse in the hundreds of contour lines and marked trails, washes and streams of the eastern Superstitions. Bob took a clue from the ciphered Spanish text on the horse tablet—"I pasture north of the river"—to help narrow the search. Perhaps, he thought, north of the Gila River. But there was also lots of opportunity even further north, above the east-west running Queen Creek. He noticed that Hewitt Ranch was located where the north-south running Hewitt Canyon Road connected with Queen Creek. Was this a hint? Was the connection to the horse to be found in the immediate area of the Hewitt (Jesse James) ranch? (There was a *JJ* carving inscribed on the horse stone tablet, with the two *J*s placed upside down and back-to-back to the right of the horse's tail!)

Adrenaline surged through his body. He realized that *RIO,* Spanish for river, in *YO PASTU AL NORTE DEL RIO* (inscribed to the rear of the carved horse), was a wonderful cover for the second *RIO* found on the horse tablet. The second *RIO* carving was inscribed in front of the horse's head, near its right ear, and between two wavy lines that appeared like rivers or creeks. But the lettering was slightly different: the right leg of the *R* extended downward and the *I* hinted perhaps of the numeral 1. Only because he had spent months decoding the Wolf Map, with its *R7W* (Range 7 West) camouflaged coordinates, could he have figured out that something fundamental, related to the horse, was located in Range 10—or *R10*—on the century-old Florence topo. Range 10 East happens to be where Queen Creek traverses east to west, paralleling the boundary line between Maricopa and Pinal counties. The Superstition Mountain stone tablets, like the Wolf Map before, were narrowing the search in a way that was quintessentially KGC.

But Bob still could not see a horse in the 1:125,000-scale map. He was drained. Setting down his drafting pencil and dividers, he shuffled into the kitchen at dawn to get a cup of coffee. When he returned, he ran his eyes up along Hewitt Canyon Road on the topo. There, just to the west, he saw the downward-sloping oval of a horse's eye. It was visible in the contour lines for a prominent peak in the area, Hewitt Ridge, near Mill-site Canyon. "My God," he whispered to himself. "This is good!" Suddenly lightheaded, he dropped into his worn-out swivel chair, overcome with the same feelings of nausea he experienced when he broke the Wolf Map.

"Amazing, amazing," he repeated. After a few minutes, he was able to run his finger over the now traceable outline of a giant horse's head. Hewitt Ranch formed one nostril along the horse's muzzle that was created by the undulating line representing Queen Creek. Gently winding Hewitt Canyon Road defined the left upper jawline; Milk Ranch Creek Road the right upper jawline. Two upright ears also were visible, as was the slope of the neck, formed in part by Reavis Trail.

Now not only could he see the nose, eyes, ears and neck but also the front legs and midsection. All this in the myriad squiggles and punctuated open spaces of a near century-old U.S. Geological Survey map—one that covered more than three hundred square miles! The only parts of the giant horse missing were the hind legs and tail. This was because the animal's now penciled-in body ended at the east side of the topo grid, with its rump running off the page.

Bob sensed that the engraved stone slabs were composed entirely from information shown on the 1900 Florence topo. Thus, the stone tablets could not date back to Spanish Colonial times or even to the mid-1840s era of the "Peraltas." Topo surveys of the kind laid out on his drafting table were not made that long ago. The "Peralta" makers of the stone tablets would have had no such reference points to draw upon for their encrypted artwork.

And what extraordinary art it was! The topographically rendered equine conformed beautifully to the shape and proportions of the artistically rendered horse on the stone tablet. He marveled at the clandestine ingenuity of the mapmakers and the men who carved the stone slabs. They had left behind their signature system of symbolism, too subtle for most to recognize and perhaps too clever for those in the know to be able to follow the encrypted signposts. The fabricated story of the "Peraltas" had been attached at some point as a smoke screen to throw off outsiders.

He now faced the KGC draftsmen, surveyors, cartographers and cryptologists at their most masterful, if not brazen. Their esoteric purpose was to guide the informed, the initiated, back to the secret location of something immensely important. Such markers had to endure over an extended period, when the effects of weathering, erosion and vandalism might obliterate key signposts. The tablets, he guessed, were not absolutely required to solve the treasure trail mystery but at least seemed designed to make the job easier for cipher-literate insiders.

For a while that morning, Bob walked quietly along the perimeter of his property, strolling past the vegetable garden and down to his stocked catfish pond. He questioned the validity of the intuitive leap that he had made. It seemed almost too much of a stretch. Only a short while back, the stone tablets appeared unsolvable, forever inscrutable. But now he felt confident of his analysis.

In the days that followed, his intuitive floodgates opened wider. Having transposed the stone tablet horse to the old topo map, he repeated the process using other symbols from the tablets: the dagger and the priest-templar. A solitary stone-map/topo-map alignment might have seemed an anomaly. But three such associations in succession made the connection convincing. The carved dagger had its physical doppelgänger in an isolated knife-shaped mountain (seen topographically, it might also be described as a meat cleaver) lying west of the horse's head and due south of Superstition Mountain. The symbolically represented priest had its look-alike image anchored in various topo features well to the southeast, below the Gila. Along with a peaked hood and a cross emblazoned on its sleeve, the priest-templar's key topo features were his watchful eye (composed of the elliptical lines of a lone hill) and long nose (formed by contour lines running east-west below his hood). The giant figure was looking west, through Grayback Mountain and thus near the center of Bob's initial zone of interest.

Bob had found—through a mix of analysis, intuition and raw trial and error—the signposts that he needed to proceed.[19] With the coded messages of the tablets seemingly resolved, he felt certain that he had defined the general parameters of the search area. Now all he had to do was follow the rules set down by the KGC and pray that there was a connection to the "Arizona Desert Treasure" waybill. Otherwise all the hard work—the unraveling of the symbolism—might amount to nothing.

Off to Arizona

14

AFTER a long two-day drive, Bob arrived in south-central Arizona in July 1996. The heat was predictably intense. A bright scorcher, climbing to 110 degrees by noon, had enveloped the greater Phoenix area. Way too hot, he thought, for an Arkansas mountain man. At best, he would be able to hunt but a few hours a day with the principals from the Heart Mountain Project, Elwin "Ellie" Gardner, then of Phoenix, and Gardner's brother-in-law, Brian MacLeod, of Seattle.

On the road to Apache Junction, he saw signs for Florence, a former frontier town just south of the Gila River. Having arrived a day early, he decided to see if he could pick up a few leads. Jacob Waltz, according to the legend, had launched some of his clandestine treks into the Superstitions from nineteenth-century Florence, so it was worth asking around. He chatted with a few locals about the town's history and fished for rumors of buried treasure. The woman at the gas station kidded him about looking for "that damned Dutchman's mine." Bob joked that, no, he was looking for something a lot harder to find.

Exiting Florence, home to a giant POW camp during World War II, he noticed a historic plaque for Adamsville. The sign said the stamp-sized hamlet had been wiped out by the Gila's floodwaters in the late 1800s. However brief its existence on the map, Adamsville, if he had to bet, was going to be central to solving the Dutchman puzzle. Its geographic location, at 33 degrees north, seemed well suited for a pivotal role, if, indeed,

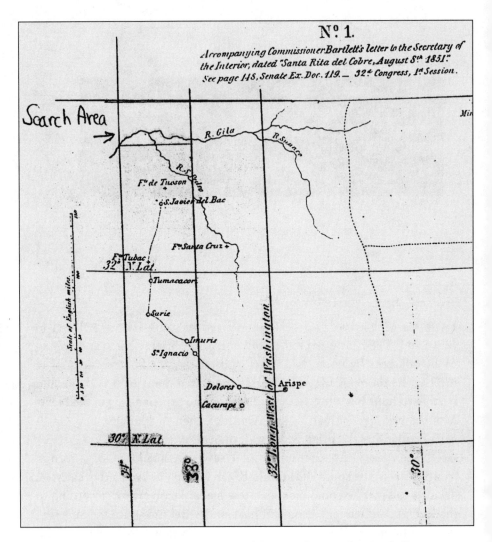

9. Historic map of southwestern United States, showing longitude lines west of Washington, D.C. The KGC treasure search area of the Superstition Mountains falls within latitudinal and longitudinal coordinates involving the key Scottish Rite Masonic number 33.

the Scottish Rite of Freemasonry were associated with the Dutchman's Mine.

As he approached the small plot that was once Adamsville, some three miles southwest of Florence along Old Adamsville Road, he could not resist investigating a powerful hunch. He pulled over and spread a copy of the old Florence topo on the hood of his car. The USGS quadrangle was now full of precise directional lines that he had drawn in pencil: each tangent delineating a compass heading indicated by the code on the stone tablets. Two of the key lines—one running down the middle of the south-pointing topographic dagger (shown as "Dinosaur Mountain" on current maps), the other running down the end of the topographic priest's contoured nose via Grayback—intersected *precisely* at Adamsville! If the past were any guide, the spot where two major lines converged yielded some critical dividend. He trusted that the Arizona lines would prove no different. Lying next to the unrolled topo map was the other key document: the J. Frank Dalton waybill to an "Arizona Desert Treasure," as illustrated—with its adobe buildings—by Howk (signed JJ III).

Bob drove to the spot where his two conceptual lines intersected. There, on the north side of Old Adamsville Road, stood a cluster of three adobe buildings, apparently abandoned and in disrepair. Next to one of the buildings was a wooden fence that had once perhaps formed the perimeter of a corral. The open area was not posted, so he briefly strolled around the roadside cluster of idle structures. As he walked over to inspect a large adobe to the south, he noticed an exposed floor foundation of what must have been another crumbled home or building. Running past the ruin was a faded dirt trail leading off to the west. It seemed somehow familiar.

Seeing the exposed foundation within the context of the three adobes made Bob's head reel. He was overcome with a dizzying sense of déjà vu. After a moment, he hurried to his car and grabbed the J. Frank Dalton waybill. He ran his forefinger across each sketched structure on the map in sequence, looking up each time to confirm the waybill's fit with the buildings before him. It was a match. An exact match! This was the place; there was little doubt. Adamsville was *the* bull's-eye location for the "Arizona Treasure Map."

On the waybill/map, he could see the same general layout of the buildings—the kicker being the slightly elevated, rectangular floor hardpan with a caption that read, "Adobe burned by Geronimo 1884." Just

10. (overleaf) Arizona Desert Treasure waybill, a pictogram to an unde-fined spot where Jesse James is alleged to have hidden treasure. Bob Brewer located the ghost town, Adamsville, as the likely target for the map, based on code-breaking efforts. The structures shown on the waybill appear to correspond to old adobe buildings still standing on the site. An excavation on the property led to the discovery of a 22-foot shaft filled with an odd assortment of carefully laid metal and porcelain objects, as well as a horse skull.

ARIZONA   O.E

This chest said to contain 2 said $140,000

York City Railroad office by Jesse Woodson

four thriving RR-Express Companies fast

about 15 miles of a new RR Spur-line

Old JwJ, left his RR office over

winter of 1896-97. JwJ, went on ahead an

Timothy James, Jesse F.B.James, and his twin

and two Indian guides. A hole was dug

the train the chest was on was due to

Lo, and beheld a gang of fierce

reported to have robbed the Express car

The chests never even left that train— m

car—The chest was delivered in person to

Adobe barn
Geronimo

Old Adobe Bldg

Ruins of Adobe Building

Elevation 20ft above the
River Stage

Hard-Gravel Here

T   TREASURE
...cked with the said $440,000 Gold coins at the New
himself and was to be shipped by one of three or
d—to be paid to a RR Grading contractor for
Mexico. A Connecticut Insurance Company carried the Risk.
...ks before the Fire, occ...was to be shipped in the
...is men, Butch Cassidy Sundance Kid, Bill Barnhill, Ora D,
James the Negroes, Sam Skates "Lucky" Johnson, Geo Robertson,
...mately as shown 12 ft, deep five days before

...ty Train Robbers, ...
...hest and one for 65,000 of a ...ted hospital
...to another express Ruins
...nd buried as shown in

Water Stand Pipe Tanks
& Well dug by hand
Also on this
Tombstone

...town was almost
...abandoned by 1896-97
The other chest said to
be $65,000 was buried
...ent around the town in the corner of a Corral

Legend on this Tombstone Jack
...died Geronimo p... & Jack
Train load of Gold + Money 19
$58 for horses, Guns, etc etc

N   W   S

8 ft deep

$65,000
more or less

...was an "Inside Job", so Jw J, got
...against a former Union Army General who
...ager of a leading New England Insurance Co—
...to the tune of over Half Million Dollars,
...less.

below was written, "stage road." (The destruction of the adobe must have taken place in the first weeks of 1884, for Geronimo is known to have surrendered—and not for the first time or the last—to federal troops in January or February of that year.)

His pulse racing, Bob felt an enormous thrill—a heady mix of elation and relief. The reference point of an indeterminate treasure map—one that well could have fit anywhere within many thousand square miles of "Arizona Desert" territory—had been found with reasonable certainty by using coded messages devised by the KGC. From this point forward, he proceeded on the now plausible premise that the Lost Dutchman, the stone tablets and Jesse James–KGC operations were somehow linked in what appeared to be an enormous KGC depository covering many hundreds of square miles.

As for the buried gold indicated on the Jesse James map—two caches, one put at $440,000 in coins, the other at $65,000—any attempt at recovery would have to wait. For starters, he had to solidify his relationship with the Heart Mountain Project and then contact the Adamsville property owners. Such a recovery no doubt would require substantial resources: the waybill indicated that the treasure cache was buried "12 feet deep" in "hard gravel" and that the surrounding soil was at an "elevation 20ft above the river stage." According to the pictogram, one of the chests seemed to be buried near or on the stage road, the other was buried in the "corner of a corral." The loot, it said, came from "an inside job" in which "JWJ got revenge against a former Union Army General who was manager of a leading New England Insurance Co." The Connecticut-based firm, it said, had insured the money chests on a western-bound train from New York in the winter of 1896. There was an ironic twist: the waybill stated that Jesse James and his KGC cohorts had robbed the train, stealing Jesse's own gold and making the insurance company pay for the theft!

And there were other hints pointing to an Adamsville-KGC link. The Adamsville-Florence Masonic cemetery down the road contained numerous graves of ex-Confederates and an odd formation of rocks in the shape of an eight-spoked wheel. There was no explanation for the man-made monument. Bob guessed that it represented the KGC template and, thus, the likely overall shape of the depository layout. The spoked-circle pattern reminded him of the Texas stone spiderwebs and the mysterious drawing in Isom Avants's diary. Within hours on site, he was convinced that his trip out West would not be in vain.

Bob's first order of business was to meet the two men from HMP and examine the giant intaglios. His primary task had nothing to do with the Adamsville site; it was to evaluate prospects for his Florida investor acquaintance at what HMP called "Heart Mountain," an intaglio-laden peak some fourteen miles east of Florence and just north of the Gila. Certainly, after all those long months of map work, he was eager to examine the "rock art" and decide whether that far-off site could be developed.

When he met Gardner and MacLeod the next day, along with the Florida investor, he found the two men congenial. They seemed to be soft-spoken, understated types. He sensed they were devoid of the "I know better" arrogance that he quickly recognized in some members of the treasure-hunting community and that he so despised. Physically, the chubby, garrulous Gardner and the rail-thin, pensive MacLeod resembled Laurel and Hardy.

The pair, in turn, sized up Bob as an unassuming straightforward character with a certain "worldliness" that they had not expected. They made it clear how eager they were to hear his impressions and interpretations, particularly of Heart Mountain, which, like proud parents showing off their child's creative scribblings, they dubbed "a thirty-six-square-mile work of art."[1] Their world revolved around solving the puzzle behind five man-made earthen signs—three giant hearts, a horse and a large arrow—which they had discerned on Heart Mountain's slopes.

Gardner, a mechanic turned insurance salesman, said that his father had spent tens of thousands of dollars over two decades investigating the "Heart Mountain" mystery but had died before any concrete results were produced. The project's aim was to recover any Spanish treasure associated with the location and to preserve the Spanish Colonial site for "future generations and research." There was a hint of impatience in his voice as he recounted how he had taken up where Elwin Gardner, Sr., had left off, about nine years earlier, and how, after nearly a decade, he was hoping for a breakthrough. The notion of Ellie's continuing a legacy appealed to Bob.

The conversation then turned to how the Heart Mountain Project had been working with the state of Arizona and the Arizona State Museum to obtain "special land use" permits for historical research and for "treasure trove" recovery.

[Treasure-trove recovery is traditionally defined as discovering money, coin, gold or silver bullion buried by an unknown owner—as distinct from recovering antiquities and artifacts, or, a separate category altogether, recovering minerals through prospecting or mining. In fact, treasure-trove hunting and recovery, if done under the guise of mining, is illegal.

A treasure-trove recovery attempted on state property, according to Arizona law, must be overseen by the Arizona State Museum's archaeological division and by a consultant in possession of a state antiquities permit. Any recovered treasure trove in HMP's project-specific undertaking would have to be turned over to the state. Subsequently, HMP would need to go before the state courts to appeal for their share in the "disposition of the trove." All costs involved—including the archaeological work and the restoration of the land—would need to be assumed by HMP, according to state procedure.

A similar, more involved permitting process would be required for any recovery being planned on federal land, where treasure-trove hunting and recovery is technically allowed—in certain limited areas—with proper paperwork. National Park land is strictly off-limits for treasure-trove recovery. Depending on the prospective site's location, permitting would need to be undertaken with the Bureau of Land Management; part of the U.S. Department of the Interior, for any site on BLM property, or with the Forest Service, part of the U.S. Department of Agriculture, for sites on National Forest property. (Wilderness areas within the National Forest program are the most restrictive within the USDA. Indeed, the last time such a permit was granted within the 124,000-acre Wilderness Area in the Superstitions was more than fifteen years ago. Mining for gold ore within the Superstition Wilderness Area was banned in 1984.) Finally, the U.S. General Services Administration would have the final say in any agreement to recover the suspected treasure on federal land: the GSA would issue a contract to carry out the search, including provisions on safety, safeguarding of recovered items, and division of proceeds between the treasure-hunting party and the government.[2] Final disposition of recovered treasure would also be subject to various claims.]

Whatever treasure might exist at Heart Mountain (which lies south of what is considered the Superstitions proper and outside the Wilderness Area supervised by the U.S. Forest Service) dated from the Spanish Colonial occupation, or so Gardner said. Bob listened to every word, nodded respectfully and asked to see the sites.

With the Florida investor at the wheel in a rented four-wheel drive, the four men began a three-day off-road tour of some of the most rugged terrain in the Southwest. As they headed into the canyons in the cool early-morning hours, Bob was struck by the natural beauty of the place: wildflowers, prickly pear and giant saguaro cacti dotted the landscape; pungent sagebrush scented the air; the cackle of cactus wrens and the warble of desert doves echoed off the exposed cliffs. As a woodsman and naturalist, he felt at ease and inspired. Yet he realized that the desert and the looming mountains could kill mercilessly just the same—simply by swallowing the unprepared in their vastness, under the broiling midday heat.

He soon recognized that finding physical clues to the larger puzzle was going to be both physically taxing and mind-bending. Ironically, his investor acquaintance from Florida, sitting next to him in the Jeep's driver's seat, seemed to think that it was just a matter of going out and digging one up—all in a day's work!

Not his style at all, Bob thought. He realized, then, that he might have erred in getting involved with the strike-hungry character. For the moment, he could much more easily relate to Gardner's more measured refrain that this was the land of elusive Spanish treasure—and that as a team, they were bound to figure it out in good time. Well they might, Bob said diplomatically.

Later that day, he and the others examined multiple rock carvings in two remote arroyos known as Box Canyon and Martinez Canyon. "Spanish treasure signs," Gardner asserted. Bob quietly scrutinized each incision in the cliff face and made quick sketches in his journal. He registered each location's GPS coordinates and marked the spots on his topo. He then videotaped every chiseled sign and symbol with his small hand-held video recorder.

Finally, the group arrived at its prime destination: a wide valley surrounded by long, sloping hills. Halfway up one of them, Bob recognized the giant landscaped heart intaglio that he had seen in the photos. The subtle figure on the slopes of Heart Mountain covered thousands of square feet of soil and vegetation. At first blush, the earthen valentine appeared unquestionably man-made.

While walking the lines of the mysterious intaglio, Bob could see that the shape of the heart was created by removing boulders, rocks, trees and other large objects from the interior of the pattern. Some group must then have replaced whatever had grown inside the perimeter with a particular form of fast-growing, nonnative vegetation. The result: with summer rains, the interior of the landscaped heart, arrow and horse figures quickly become bright green, in contrast to the surrounding parched-brown terrain.

Gardner explained that the enormous stick-horse pattern measured some eight hundred feet long, tail to nose; the largest of the three landscaped hearts extended some eight hundred feet along the slope of the hill; and the arrow stretched some five hundred feet from stem to tip. He said that he could not be sure of the intaglios' origins (a mystery, as well, to local scientists brought in to evaluate their authenticity).[3] But he held out the possibility that the patterns predated the Spanish. Again, Bob kept his opinions to himself. Yet his guess was that the hallmark ciphers and symbols of the KGC had been magnified in an almost unimaginable way in these Arizona mountains.

Back at Apache Junction, Bob spent hours alone, quietly analyzing what he had seen. He had brought along his transparent template and had begun to use it with limited initial success atop the old topo maps. His hosts marveled at his ability to go off for hours at a time (and there was lots of downtime because of the broiling heat) and simply stare at his topos and plot points.

The group repeated the early-out, early-return pattern on the second day of the expedition, which allowed Bob to take additional field data. After a third full day of reviewing HMP's sites, he told the group that the signs on the canyon walls and the giant intaglios on Heart Mountain's slopes showed promise. Nevertheless, he added, he was not prepared to say whether the project merited large-scale investment on such short notice. There was no way of predicting whether this was a lucrative high-risk venture or a "money pit"; it was best to opt for caution. (Speaking privately to Gardner afterwards, Bob explained that he was reluctant to proceed especially because the fellow from Florida seemed to have unrealistic expectations about the time involved to recover a treasure that had eluded everyone else for more than a century. Gardner and MacLeod, with whom he had developed a rapport, heartily agreed.) The Florida investor took Bob's counsel, declined the opportunity and thanked everyone for the adventure. The next day, he headed back east, with Bob driving him to the Albuquerque airport on his way back to Hatfield.

It was only a matter of weeks before Bob heard from Gardner and MacLeod by phone. They chatted for a while. Bob said that he would like to keep in touch and had enjoyed their company. The two HMP partners reciprocated by saying that the group seemed to have bonded and that one of the things they liked best was Bob's coolness to the idea of rushing out to dig up an improbable, quick fortune. For all three, it seemed more a question of determining whether they could put together the pieces of an elaborate historical puzzle—and prove, to begin with, that a puzzle even existed in the desolate mountains. They also appreciated Bob's declining to ask for payment for services.

Bob, in turn, said that they were on to something big: they unfortunately had no idea what they were chasing! It wasn't Spanish; it was Rebel, post–Civil War treasure. And the treasure was not likely hidden near Heart Mountain but elsewhere, miles away, in various locations in and around the Superstitions.

Gardner and MacLeod were stunned. They had never heard of the Knights of the Golden Circle, much less the notion that this clandestine group had hidden gold and other fortune in coded underground depositories, not just in the old South but in the Far West. Bob had anticipated their response and told them that the best way to begin to grasp what he was attempting to explain was to see his sites in Arkansas. He liked the duo's modesty, their passion for history and their "underdog" status. So he invited them out. They took up the offer, visiting Hatfield in fall 1997, another step in what would become an ongoing friendship and partnership.

On Bob's return trip to the Superstitions in January 1998, he made clear that his was not some farfetched scenario that he was chasing in Arizona. Gardner and MacLeod were still not entirely convinced and maintained a "show-me" posture. But they were open to suggestions, and if "Hillbilly Bob" had proof to back up his claims, they were ready to participate in his quest, and on his terms.

Unlike the first trip, in July 1996, in which Gardner and MacLeod had taken the lead, showing what they had discovered in and around the Superstitions, Bob now took charge and directed an intensive search for points of interest, based on *his* mapwork. If they could get to certain remote spots—seemingly inaccessible places that he had plotted with the use of his intersecting lines—they would stand a good chance of encountering other highly important carved symbols, he predicted. He placed a current topo map on the hood of Gardner's Jeep Cherokee and pointed to four spots that he had selected. They would be looking, he said, for distinct symbols on site: a large cross, a double *J* (back-to-back fishhooks), an elephant head, and a figure eight (infinity symbol), all indicated on the stone tablets. "These are the four locations. Can you get me there?" he asked. "Sure thing," Gardner nodded.

To Gardner and MacLeod's astonishment, Bob was right, on all four counts. He found the cross carved into the side of a canyon, an incision stretching some eighty feet; he spotted the *JJ* about a mile and a half to the east of the spot, also engraved in hardrock bluffs; he discovered the elephant profile on a butte a quarter-mile west of the *JJ*; and, lastly, he spied a small infinity symbol carved into an old saguaro cactus, about 1,000 feet west of the elephant. (Saguaro are known to live 150 or more years and to grow fifty feet tall.)

Gardner and MacLeod didn't know how Bob came up with this stuff, but they had become believers. They were, at a minimum, open to the theory that something extraordinary—beyond the usual suspects of the Spanish or the Lost Dutchman himself stashing away gold—had taken place in the arid mountains of south-central Arizona.

The evidence kept building. The following day, while the three were driving out into the flats south of the Gila, Bob suddenly asked Gardner to stop. They had driven about a quarter of a mile from a dirt-road intersection, with Bob watching the odometer and his GPS unit over the entire distance. (He always insisted that Gardner and MacLeod drive slowly so they wouldn't miss anything, otherwise they might as well "just pack it in.") His request to stop seemed to come out of the blue; there was nothing around. Using his compass and GPS handset to confirm his location, Bob asked the other two to keep their eyes peeled for an unusual object or sign in the barren dusty expanse, distinguished, as it were, by one out-of-place white boulder. Within thirty feet of the parked Jeep, the group discovered a five-pointed star formed out of unused shotgun cartridges. The shells had been neatly arranged in the desert floor. "That's a KGC sign right there—definitely not left by the Spanish," Bob said.

"That's plain weird," Gardner opined.

At yet another stop, on a high-elevation trail near Grayback Mountain, Bob alerted the others: "There's supposed to be something here. We need to look for a sign." Gardner burst into a laugh, saying that he had just seen a Halloween "pumpkin face" carved into a cactus leaf. When Bob blurted excitedly, "Where, Ellie? Where did you see it?" Gardner realized that it was no joke. Bob recounted how a similar face, albeit carved in stone, had led to the recovery of a safe full of gold coins back in Oklahoma. The spooky face on the prickly-pear leaf, found just off the trail amid an enormous cactus cluster, corroborated their line of investigation—a welcome relief after hours of back-and-forth searching.

The next day, the group headed for the northeastern section of the Superstitions. On a large outcrop known as Buzzard's Roost (no relation to the Oklahoma site), Bob detected a colossal carving—measuring thousands of square feet in area—in the shape of a five-pointed star and, next to it, a massive ever-familiar jack-o'-lantern face. He had been focusing his video camera's zoom lens on the distant crag when the enormous carvings came into focus. The crag lined up precisely with a recently discovered clue.

This was no mere landscaping on a sloping hill, as with Heart Mountain: this was the product of hardrock drilling and chiseling on a sheer cliff—most likely done by men dangling from long ropes—and on a monumental scale. A fascinating aspect was that the huge star and skull images (signature markers of the KGC) showed up best as shadow signs—distinct against the backdrop at a certain time of day and visible from several miles away.

Up close, Bob noticed that the Buzzard's Roost outcrop resembled a horse's rump. Perhaps this was it, he thought: the missing rear of the horse on the Florence topo map, which, in turn, was the draft horse figure sketched on the first stone tablet. Further, might the star incised into the cliff represent the five-pointed star shown on Mitchell's tracing of the horse stone tablet? "My God," he said to Gardner and MacLeod, as they stood next to him with expressions of awe and bewilderment. "What kind of organization goes to that much trouble to mark their treasure?" The group agreed that it would have taken a skilled crew many months to create such designs. Perhaps, Bob thought, this was where Waltz's resident Mexican laborers had been spending much of their time.

By that evening, the pair from Heart Mountain was dumbfounded: How could Bob predict where carvings and buried markers would appear in the desert, not to mention in the mountains, and at distances of up to twenty miles away? They had just witnessed pieces of what Gardner described as a "gigantic unbelievable puzzle."

The men asked Bob to become a full partner in the Heart Mountain Project, something which they had discussed only in general terms before. Bob agreed, but refused to move out to Apache Junction. Too hot to think, and thinking is what he liked to do best, he quipped. In the spirit of the new partnership, he disclosed that he had already found a site on private property, the day before their first meeting, which seemed promising. It was far from Heart Mountain, in fact from anything related to the areas that they had been exploring under HMP state permits. The prospective recovery site was not in the Superstitions proper. Without going into details, he told the two men that he would be delving into the data acquired on this second trip and would keep them posted. Nonetheless, it would be a while before he could return to Arizona. In the interim, he suggested that they work over the phone and the Internet: Gardner and MacLeod would be the eyes and ears, confirming the exact location of new signs and symbols that he would project from topo lines developed remotely.

Gardner and MacLeod agreed: setting aside differences about the origin of the rumored treasure would be no big deal, they laughed, after twenty years or more of chasing the wrong rabbit! Gardner still insisted that the Heart Mountain site was possibly of Spanish origin, while the other sites in the region were perhaps KGC. Not impossible, Bob replied. (The KGC was said to have made significant efforts to recover—through the use of financial incentives to informants—older Spanish and Indian treasure buried in North America. Golden Circle agents, according to J. Frank Dalton, were said to have traveled to Spain to investigate leads in dusty archives for that purpose.)[4]

Back in his hotel room, Bob realized that he had just launched perhaps the greatest hunt of his career. The desolate range out West, with its enormous vistas and extended lines of sight, resonated with KGC-Masonic intrigue. He had plotted points along transit lines that ran twenty to thirty miles. Where Brushy Valley back home had a depository or two on a scale of fifty square miles, and Addington, Oklahoma, say, 100 square miles, the master depository surrounding the Superstitions appeared to be on a scale of 1,000 to 1,500 square miles. Moreover, if the Wolf Map had some one hundred symbolic pieces to sort out for that Oklahoma-based puzzle, the stone tablets/Lost Dutchman riddle appeared to involve well over double that amount. In fact, there could be as many as four or five interlocking depositories in the surrounding area!

The scale and ingenuity of the layout made it clear to Bob that his early suppositions were correct. The remarkable grid-like "system" laid out before him was no small feat; it appeared a massive undertaking by a disciplined army of devoted men—engineers, surveyors, miners, mathematicians, cryptologists—working in secret over what must have been many years, if not decades. And the esoteric "cause" behind it all, he recognized, must have been bigger than a revived Confederacy . . . something extending beyond politics and the nation-state into the realm of philosophy or, perhaps, religion and spirituality.

Moreover, the vast size of the depository suggested that the treasures could be much larger than anticipated and, therefore, hidden far deeper by industrial-scale feats of engineering: long shafts leading to voluminous chambers or bunker-like structures. (Bob, in fact, had several unidentified sketches of deep burials, all from his set of Howk–Jesse Lee James documents. The locations, of course, were not provided on the waybills.) He wondered: If this were an underground KGC depository on a grand scale, could this explain why so many Dutchman hunters had disappeared or been murdered? Did their deaths result from some burnt-out, rifle-toting desert rat protecting what he swore was the true lost Dutchman mine; or were these homicides something different, something resembling professional hits, with sworn-to-secrecy sentinels pulling the trigger?

15 Threats from Above

IN the final few days of their January 1998 expedition, Bob, Gardner and MacLeod encountered something for which they were wholly unprepared: aerial reconnaissance.

As a gesture of goodwill, Bob had promised to investigate a few areas on or near Heart Mountain for signs of cache markers. He managed to discover a cluster of interesting carved symbols just a short distance outside the HMP permit zone, to the east. When he suggested that the trio spend the next morning exploring the area with metal detectors, Gardner and MacLeod jumped at the chance.

At the site, Bob switched on his detector and began scanning behind a few large boulders that had been inscribed. Within fifteen minutes of activating his device, a helicopter with civilian call signs appeared overhead, made two low-altitude passes and flew away. One passenger seemed so intent on monitoring the activity below that he nearly fell out the bay door on the chopper's second pass.

The scene reminded Bob of his months as a Navy helicopter gunner in Vietnam. But it also reminded him of the threatening incident with his dog, Lady, back home in the Ouachitas, where, within minutes of activating his "Two-Box" detector, the vehicle with two armed snoopers had moved in to reconnoiter. This fly-by in Arizona had made him apprehensive, but he stayed cool. There was no flinching now.

Gardner and MacLeod were in a cold sweat. They had never encountered something like this before. Bob's advice was to pack it in and stay away from the area, at least for a while. On the drive back to town, he told the pair that it could have been a mere coincidence: the helicopter might have been on a flight path over the site and simply turned around for some unrelated sudden change of plans. Far more likely, he said, was that the trio had entered a hot spot—triggering a response.

Without sounding too sure of his hypothesis, he suggested that some of this treasure—if it existed—might still be guarded. Moreover, it was possible that remote sensors had been placed near the target zone and had picked up the electronic signal emitted by the metal detector. When Gardner and MacLeod pressed him for *who* might have sent the chopper, he threw up his hands.

A few days later, at a site thirty miles north, a second incident occurred. Exploring with MacLeod in a ravine thick with KGC symbols, Bob discovered a sculpted white boulder set on top of a rock ledge. In profile, the boulder resembled a large human skull, with deep-set eyes, brooding eyebrows, an aquiline nose and jutting chin. There was no doubt that the big spherical rock had been carved to look like a skull under the right sun and shadow conditions. It gazed directly into a rocky area, across a creek, flush with other treasure signs. These included a large three-pronged arrow (turkey track) figure made of stones and a big, heart-shaped hole in a protruding bluff: a man-made window. The combination of the skull, heart and turkey track sent a familiar adrenaline rush through Bob's body.

Bob turned to MacLeod and said that he wanted to switch on his detector to scan the dense menagerie of clues. As he went to retrieve the gadget from the car, he gently warned his friend to be prepared for visitors, based on what had happened a few days earlier. He had a powerful conviction that they were about to breach a sensitive area.

Taking his detector out of the car, he braced for another strange encounter. His .357 was loaded.

It was not more than twenty minutes from the time he activated his detector that a blue Bell helicopter came shooting over a hilltop. Like the one before it, the chopper came from the northwest, from the general direction of Phoenix, Tempe or Mesa. With Bob and MacLeod looking up from the small ravine, the low-flying aircraft cruised right over the pair and then shot past the next butte, out of sight. Bob heard the chopper's blades transition from forward-motion to hover; he knew for sure that it had landed behind the nearby cliff. This could get interesting, he thought. Unfazed, he continued to hunt for metal clues with his detector for some fifteen minutes until he heard MacLeod say, "Hey, look, there's a guy and a woman coming our way." A few minutes later, two strangers appeared in clear view through MacLeod's binoculars, and, from the bright reflection off a metal object, it was obvious that the man had a large handgun in his shoulder holster. "They're coming right at us," MacLeod said, a slight tremble in his voice.

MacLeod suddenly felt his palms go sweaty. Bob, now somewhat nervous himself, could sense MacLeod's rising anxiety. "These guys could be watchers," he cautioned, adding in a calm assured voice: "Let me do the talking. We'll just tell them we're out rockhounding."

MacLeod, his lips and throat parched from a combination of fear and the scorching midday heat, nodded. He was carrying a handgun, and he checked to see if his pistol strap was off and his weapon ready.

When the stranger—a clean-cut, muscular fellow in his late fifties—approached, he got right to the point. He displayed no badge. He didn't identify himself. He made no mention of the helicopter. He simply asked Bob and MacLeod what they were up to—the whole time keeping his right hand loosely at his side, in easy reach of his .44 Magnum. The woman, in her late thirties or early forties, stood some ten yards away.

Bob replied that he and his friend were just out "rockhounding a bit," and mentioned that they had been collecting desert agate. He and MacLeod held out handfuls of the semiprecious stones and a few pieces of quartz in their sweaty palms.

The stranger ran his cold blue eyes up and down the length of the barrel-chested, thickly bearded Brewer and the lanky, close-shaven MacLeod. Bob guessed their interrogator was either preparing to see who might make a move or, more likely, mentally recording physical descriptions. Then, out of the blue, the stranger asked, "Have you seen a window rock?" He stared intently at both men, as if to detect the slightest body language.

Bob took it in stride, but MacLeod was unnerved. He felt almost physically knocked off balance. It seemed a strange kind of question to throw at a stranger, and it conveyed, "This is a trap. Watch how you answer." MacLeod casually moved a few steps away from Bob, thinking it best to avoid being taken out in a single line of fire.

Bob, fully prepared to shoot in self-defense, answered the question in his best, unflappable "hillbilly" way. "No, can't say we seen anything like that. What the heck is a 'window rock'? We're just out here rock-houndin', picking up these desert opal-like stones." Without further chatter, he and MacLeod moved nonchalantly toward the parked Jeep.

They politely nodded their caps at the couple, who nodded back. The man and the woman then wandered over to the symbol-rich area that Bob and MacLeod had been inspecting, and then disappeared into the ravine.

On the drive out to the main road, Bob could see no sign of a second automobile. The interrogators had come by helicopter; there was no doubt.

This second encounter shook MacLeod, who said little for much of the trip back to Apache Junction. He was looking for answers about the identity of the interlopers—answers that Bob could not provide with absolute certainty. But the older man took a crack at it, admitting that he, too, had been sweating it back there.

Had such incidents happened only once or twice, they could be chalked up to coincidence, he explained. But over the years he had been approached a number of times—directly or covertly by armed, unidentified men—while investigating suspected KGC cache sites. He recounted the story of the effigy. This, fortified by what had just happened, seemed to suggest that certain KGC depositories—containing big, deeply buried master caches—were guarded.

But by whom? Bob had two theories.

One possibility, he surmised, was that the "guards" are treasure hunters themselves who know only the approximate location of the treasures (perhaps through having deciphered some but not all of the clues themselves, or through sophisticated remote-sensing technology). This group theoretically might allow others to get just close enough to identify the exact location within the target zone.

A more likely hypothesis, he suggested, was that the guards are modern-day "sentinels," members of an organization with ties to the Masonic-influenced KGC or a related organization. If that were the case, then some of the KGC cache locations may have been forgotten over time by the ultra-secret group that kept few, if any, written records. Those "lost depositories" obviously would not be guarded, nor would smaller sites with shallow buried caches (i.e., fruit jars, kettles, washpots, strongboxes and safes stuffed with coins) that could be picked up relatively quickly. However, the bigger "master" depositories—where deeply entombed stacks of bullion and containers full of coins, jewels and arms were stored in thirty-to-forty-foot-deep shafts—would present a huge logistical challenge to any outsider. A lone sentinel might be all that was needed to call in the necessary resources to prevent a known "big one" from getting away. A quick visit by helicopter and the inter-jection of a polite, armed "heavy" might be enough to deter intruders, "cowans." Just theories, Bob said to MacLeod, who slowly had regained his color.

The helicopter incidents provided an unsettling send-off for Bob's return trip to Arkansas. Still, he regarded the excursion as highly pro-ductive, not least because he had cemented a friendship with Gardner and MacLeod. He liked the pair for their character, energy and curiosity. A few weeks after his return to Hatfield, he received e-mails from the two men about other strange encounters on the Superstition trail. In one incident, while exploring a new prospect on directional lines provided by Bob, MacLeod and Gardner came across a beheaded rabbit. The head was neatly severed, by a knife. The body was placed on the crumbled stone wall of an old house they were investigating. With thoughts of Adolph Ruth's macabre fate, the men lost no time returning to Gardner's four-wheel drive.

The Template:
Walking
the Lines

16

BOB spent the rest of 1998 and most of the following year in the Ouachitas, pondering the Dutchman puzzle much of the time. From the
brightly lit confines of his war room, he tried to determine whether his
methodology in Arizona was sound and whether it was getting him
closer to finding the centerpoint of what he suspected was an enormous
KGC treasure depository. He put his fieldwork results through rigorous
cross-checks to prove that the symbolism decoded had a solid basis in
fact. Had the physical landmarks matched up with the topographic layouts, as well as with the messages on the stone tablets?

Everything had to mesh: plot points and compass bearings generated
from clues found on cliffs, boulders and century-old cacti. Topographic
lines drawn by government surveyors, with curious place names established by locals—most likely by "KGC" affiliates and transient "prospectors." Finally, conceptual lines conveyed in code by the stone tablets.
These tangents—indeed, the overall geometry—had to connect exactly,
not approximately. There could be no fudging, no self-justifications for
adjustments of a fraction of an inch, of a degree, on the precise, standard-
ized topos.

To the best of his judgment, his lines and the tablets' images *did* correspond. There was a distinct overlap. The next question: Was any of
this coincidence? Was it nothing more than a mere sequence of loose
associations, with some of the pieces given more heft to make the puzzle
fit? Now, more than ever, he needed to be skeptical and scientific. Yet,

each time, he seemed to get confirmation from the interplay of the stone tablets, the topo maps, the field markers and the directional lines.

Ultimately, he asked himself, was it possible to put the clues into a geographic-geometric equation that might reveal the centerpoint of an extraordinarily complex KGC depository? If so, he knew he stood a chance of aligning the template and solving the century-old mystery of Dutch Jacob. There was little question in his mind: the stone tablets provided a valid, albeit partial, road map to the KGC layout. Even more certain, the Superstition Mountain stone "maps," other than providing a convenient cover story for the KGC, had nothing to do with the apocryphal Peraltas.

As a starting premise, Bob was convinced that the ciphered tablets must be used with those topo maps made at the time of the depository's organization or reorganization. Specifically, to reveal the full layout of the system would require layering those lines derived from the stone tablets and those from field clues onto the 1900 Florence topo (and onto any contemporaneous surrounding quads).

From this point forward, the process was one of trial and error. The only way to know whether his compass-line-of-sight and GPS-acquired tangents were in proper alignment would be to find the grid's centerpoint. This was the ultimate, if perhaps unattainable, solution. If his translucent template—a circle-in-square pattern cut into a Lucite slab—was correctly aligned on top of the topo, the full range of the encrypted stone tablets' messages would become apparent in some coherent whole, he theorized.

Bob sensed that his work over the past quarter-century had been building to this challenge: the opportunity to draw on all that he had learned to unveil an above-below nexus of unparalleled intricacy and ingenuity. Perhaps Egypt's Giza plateau, with its pyramids and Sphinx, or that ancient nation's Valley of Kings and its pharaonic tombs, were each connected in some ciphered network and through some as-yet-undiscovered subterranean tunnel system. That was for the PhDs—the Egyptologists, archaeologists and geophysicists—to discover.

This was different. What encoded information lay before him, in an obscure corner of the United States, bordered on "arcanum": mysterious knowledge known only to the initiate.[1] It was not merely weaving together the geometry, the hieroglyphic-like symbolism and the cartography. It was also knowing the interplay of historic names, places and dates over a wide spectrum—outlaws, Rebels, Freemasons, Rosicrucians, Knights Templar—all thrown down on a bewildering set of maps of south-central Arizona! But who would believe it, who could grasp the full picture? For a start, one would have to walk the lines and examine the evidence on the ground.

Armed with fresh visual information from HMP, Bob's overarching goal at the start of his 2000 trip was to determine the size and shape of the giant depository, leading, in the end, to the centerpoint. The tablets' horse, dagger and priest-templar images—all by now neatly transposed onto the 1900 map's topographic features—had given him a lead. Whether he could locate the hot zone—the potential hub for aligning the circle design of the template and, consequently, for finding potential cache burial sites, as denoted by circular notches cut into his template— was an open question.

Bob strongly suspected that the centerpoint lay somewhere south of the topo horse's head, between Queen Creek to the north and the Gila River to the south, and, on the east-west axis, between ranges 10 and 11. The hints thus far indicated that the template's centerpoint could be found somewhere near the middle of the 1900 Florence quad. He felt positive of that.

Providing inspiration were directional lines that intersected just south and east of Dromedary Peak. Several tangents ran up through that area from the top of Grayback Mountain in the southeast. (A northeasterly line intersected the second *I* in Millsite Canyon on the topo, which lay near the bottom of the sloping "eye" of the topo horse and was a key factor in Bob's detecting the face of the behemoth horse in the contour lines.) These lines radiating from Grayback led toward an enormous topographic heart shape, which Bob discerned in the center of the north-west section of the Florence quad. The contoured valentine ran from a place called Bark's Ranch across to Randolph Canyon, down to Whit-low Canyon and then on a roughly symmetrical track to the west, to form the heart's left lobe, and then, similarly, winding around another peak and canyon for the right lobe. But was it *the* heart?

The stone tablets had hinted at a centrally important heart or, in fact, multiple hearts: a prominent textual clue on the priest-templar tablet instructed one, in broken Spanish, to "look for the map" and then "look for the heart."[2] A small heart-like figure had been engraved to the left, or northwest, of the horse's head on the horse tablet. Hidden inside that petite valentine were the numbers 7 and 5. These numbers provided what turned out to be distance measurements that Bob used to find this

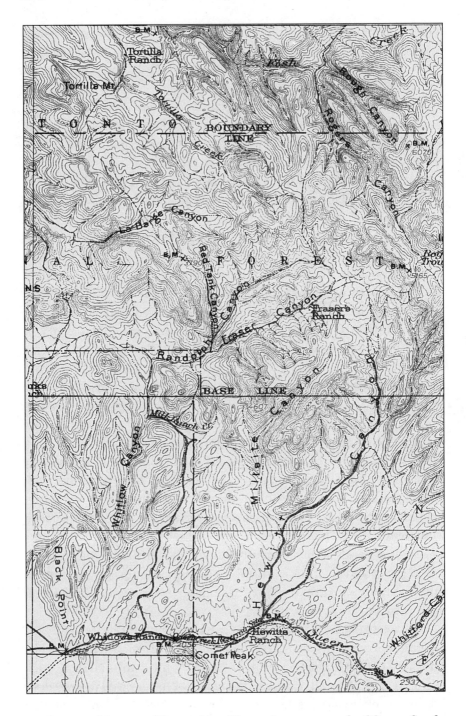

11. Topographic map of Superstition Mountains area, north of Queen Creek.

initial topographic heart and its surrounding diamond-shaped border.

There seemed to be value in searching for the heart—perhaps the overarching theme of the puzzle. A heart theme would be both consistent with KGC symbolism (as in the fight to restore the broken heart of the defeated South) and with symbols of Freemasonry and the Knights Templar. (In Templar legend, the heart represents "the Heart of Bruce" or Robert the Bruce, progenitor of the Stuart line of Scottish and English royalty.[3] In Masonic lore, the Scottish-independence stalwart Bruce was "one of the patrons and encouragers of Scottish Freemasonry."[4]) In the advanced degrees, the heart represents the heart of a mythical character by the name of Hiram Abiff, the supposed master builder of King Solomon's Temple.

The topographic heart provided a line that ran through a mountain called Comet's Peak, on through the near-center of the 1900 map. Bob saw a symbolic parallel: one of the stone tablets had a large incised heart pointing directly at a carved triangle that, in turn, was intersected by an engraved comet-like squiggle, à la Comet Peak.

The trail was playing itself out. Bob had been directed—through the tablet's arcane code—to make the horse into a behemoth and to find that oversized horse "pasturing" north of the river. He had done just that, all above Queen Creek and the Gila River. He also had been told to find a giant heart; again, that he did, the equivalent of a mile or so west of the topographic quadruped's head. He knew, from experience with the Wolf Map and other KGC ciphers, that important symbolic figures pointed to the next critical steps. The heart had a directional tip-point of its own. That much was clear. But what about the gargantuan horse? Was it providing a clue?

Knowing the resourcefulness of KGC cryptographers and their penchant for clever flourishes, Bob surmised that the textual clue *DON* (taking up one whole side of a stone tablet) was intended to be read in reverse, as *NOD*. If the giant horse's head were to nod—"to let fall slightly forward when sleepy"—it would be facing the zone of interest, directly south. The stallion would be peering down somewhere between the long-abandoned mining hamlet of Reymert—put on the map by Caleb Cushing's friend—and Picketpost Mountain.

The area near Reymert is dotted with old mines and, as denoted on the topo, is traversed by a long stairstep surveyor-line running northwest. Reymert was one of the first places that Bob had asked to see on his initial trip to the Superstitions two years before. Now he wanted to

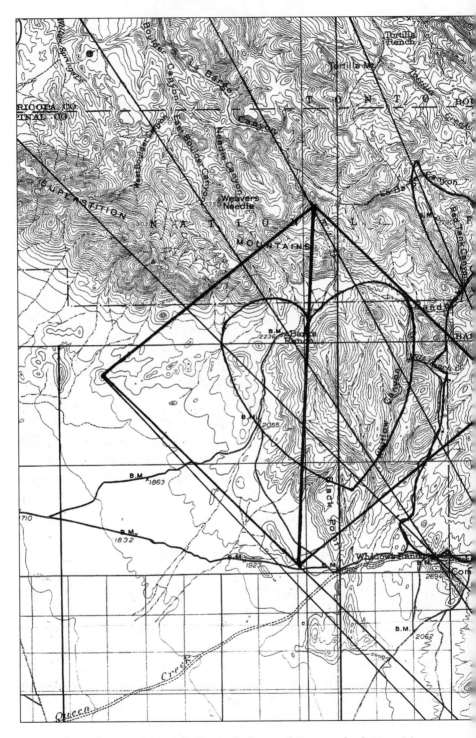

12. Outline of horse's body (the Santa Fe horse shown on the Superstition stone tablet) and priest figure (shown on page 227) superimposed on contour lines, as discerned by Bob Brewer after hundreds of hours of map

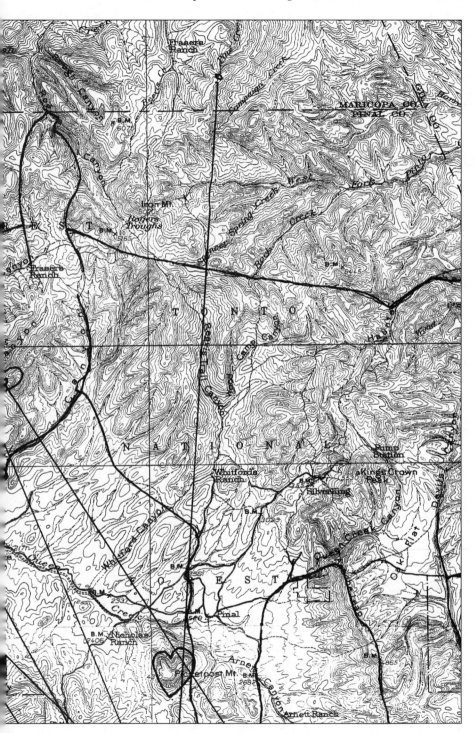

work. The four quadrants of the entire map (upper left, upper right, lower left, lower right) are shown here separately.

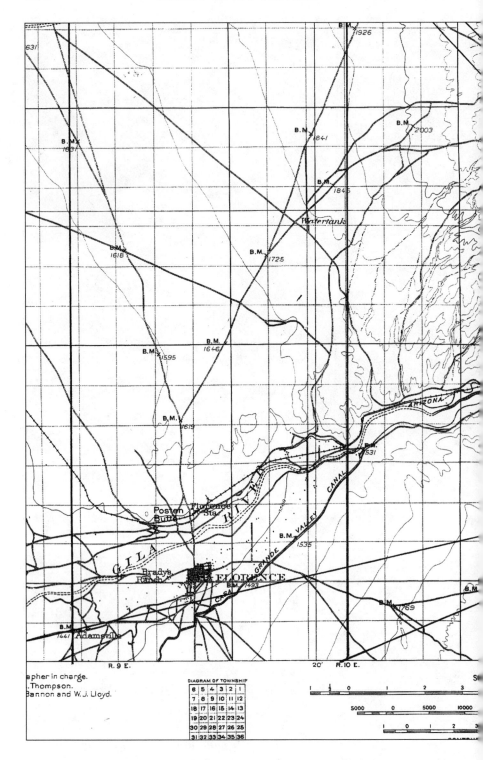

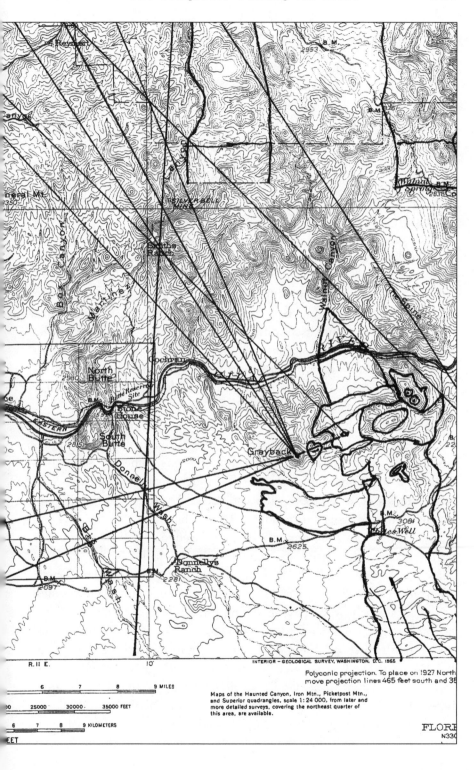

return with Gardner and MacLeod, to confirm that key directional lines pointed toward Reymert—and to understand why. The priest figure, he felt, might tell him that.

Bob had sensed that the priest figure represented a hooded medieval Knight Templar. He presumed that such a venerated icon—the soldier-monk—would hold further clues toward finding a starting point to on-site investigation. Simply delineating the priest-templar in the contoured mountain elevations and trails in the southeast corner of the Florence quad had been an enormous challenge.

In his analysis of the 1900 topo and associated USGS maps, he had discovered two potentially significant landmarks: a Crozier's Peak, lying just beyond the southeast corner of the map, and a ravine called Ripsey Wash tucked inside the southeast corner. When he looked up the defini-tion of "crozier" (also spelled "crosier"), he discovered that the word derived from the old French, "crossier," for "staff bearer." In modern parlance, the term stands chiefly for the staff of a bishop, abbot or some other holy person, but its traditional meaning was "the carrier of the staff." The KGC cryptographers appeared to be instructing him to search for the cross-carrying priest-templar in the topographic features near Crozier's Peak. And there were other subtle hints to follow: select place-names pregnant with meaning.

Bob had been struck by such names as Hewitt's Ranch and Hewitt's Canyon, with their possible ties to Jesse Woodson James. He also had suspected that the name "JJ Fraser Ranch" was coined to serve as a deliberate directional indicator. Was it, in fact, a shrouded reference to Jesse James and to the medieval Scottish clan leader Simon Fraser, who fought alongside Scots national hero Robert the Bruce?

According to an 1896 obituary that appeared in a local Arizona paper on the death of Elisha Reavis, rancher John J. "Jack" Fraser had pur-chased the Reavis Ranch soon after Reavis's passing.[5] The article reported that a "Billy G. Knight"—an "English cowboy" and foreman on Fraser's ranch properties—had cautioned Reavis a couple of weeks before his mysterious death to "see a doctor." Reading between the lines, the "English cowboy" could easily pass for a medieval Knight Templar, Bob thought. The G could well be a nod toward the hallmark symbol for "Geometry" (some say, "God") in Freemasonry. And, he speculated, based on related clues uncovered in Arkansas and Oklahoma, "William" could suggest William Wallace, the heralded Scottish freedom fighter who sought to help Robert the Bruce gain the throne. The thematic Scots place-names appeared themselves to be a form of cipher: a way to tell a story within a story that would be noticed and understood only by those deeply versed in knowledge of the code.

In his youth, Bob noticed Grandpa Ashcraft and Uncle Ode engaging in such mysterious wordplay. Now those double meanings started to come sharply into focus.

Assuming "Fraser" to be a deliberate anagram, Bob derived *FAR SE R*, as in, find the "far southeast R" on the Florence quad. His best guess was the *R* in Ripsey Wash, an arroyo represented in the lower right-hand corner of the Florence topo. Ripsey, itself, was a possible anagram for Priest, with a *y* replacing the *t*. Using the trio of Crozier's Peak, Ripsey Wash and Grayback Mountain as ciphered reference points for triangulating the approximate location of the hidden priest-templar figure, Bob eventually found the face of the holy man. The priest-templar's silhouette, topographically speaking, stared directly into Grayback.

What other tricks did the priest-templar figure have up his sleeve? A number of things, each seemingly designed to direct the informed into a target zone between Reymert and Picketpost, Bob perceived. For a start, the priest-templar inscribed on the stone tablet appears to be standing on a three-tiered pedestal. Was this not a metaphor for the stairstep dotted-line configuration on the Florence quad that runs northwest—beginning near Silver Bell Mine, then passing Reymert onto Dromedary Peak and ending near Comet Peak?

The leads did not end there. Bob deduced further messages in the charm-like figures falling from the "cross" held by the holy figure, the last of which was a heart.

Assuming that the cross represented a crozier, as in Crozier's Peak, and that the heart alluded to the large topo heart in the northwest quadrant near Fort McDowell, Bob guessed that the priest-templar was instructing him to align the template along a tangent that ran from Crozier's Peak to some point inside the northwest quadrant's heart. On close examination of the topo, he could see the following pattern: Crozier's Peak, the *R* in Ripsey Wash, the highpoints of the stairsteps, and Comet Peak were all in a line leading to Fort McDowell. That same line intersected the giant topo heart just off center, in its left lobe. He recalled that, on the sculpted three-dimensional valentine that fits into the heart stone tablet, a large *X* had been inscribed in the same relative position . . . on the left lobe.

At this point, Bob took out the Lucite template and placed one of its two sloping "master lines" along the Crozier's Peak tangent running northwest.

Significantly, at a spot where the inner ring of the template intersected both the important reference point *R* in "Ripsey Wash" and another key reference point, the template's center appeared directly over Reymert.

Bob sensed a sweet spot. Reymert was a *possible* centerpoint—the master-line X intersection or "cross"—of the template, insofar as it corresponded to key bearings and landmarks on the 1900 Florence quad. The engraved stone templar figure hinted at it with his cross and spilled charms; the carved horse on the flip side of that tablet seemed to be "nodding" at it; and the inscribed heart from another slab appeared to be pointing at it.

But why Reymert? It could not all be reduced to the Reymert-Cushing connection, however important that historic friendship to the overall scheme. For days Bob searched for an answer. Could it have been a clever play on "Outremer"—the Templars' term for their monastic-Crusader stronghold in the Holy Land? Outremer (Palestine) was the "Land beyond the Sea."[6]

Was Reymert the place where Waltz, Reavis and other likely KGC sentinels centrally patrolled, starting their treks from Adamsville and Florence, the nearest towns? Were the old abandoned Reymert "mines" really mines or just operational cover for cache-burial activities on a massive scale? The similarities to Brushy Creek, Arkansas, and its "mines" claimed by the likes of Bill Wiley, Grandpa Ashcraft, and Bill Dobson seemed powerful.

In the spring of 2000, Bob returned to the Superstitions. His most pressing task was to search for landmarks that would give him confidence that his interpretation of the maps, carved symbols and stone tablets was correct for aligning the template on the 1900 topo. Most of all, he wanted to know if he needed to make precise adjustments, topographic fine tunings, that would force his hand and move the template's X-spot to someplace new, perhaps not far from Reymert.

He suspected that the KGC masterminds would not have been content to settle for a direct "linear" solution to the puzzle. Perhaps they had simply thrown him a bone with Reymert [a potential scramble for TRY (OUT) REME (R)]. But only the very persistent and open-minded would think that more attempts at alignment were required to crack the maps,

13. A computer-assisted rendering of the KGC's circle-in-square template, overlaid on an early 1900s topo map of the Superstition Mountains. The centerpoint of this grid is Reymert, but Bob decided upon further analysis that this was not correct.

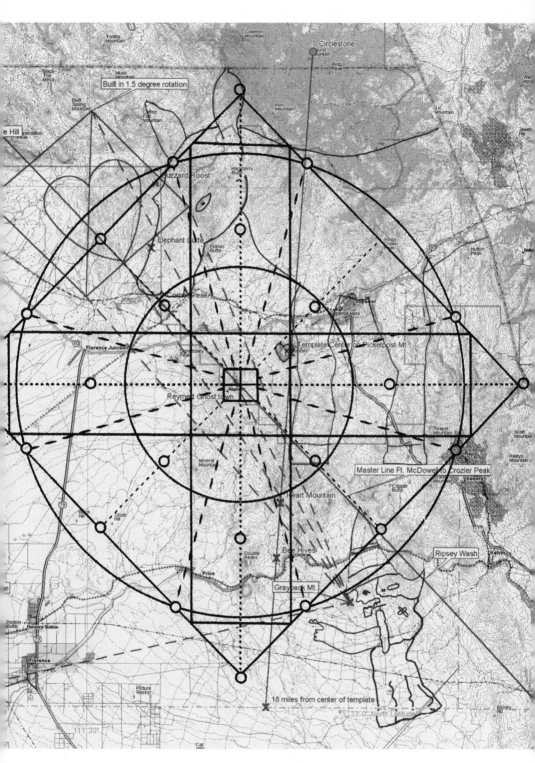

to resolve where the KGC had built its underground storehouses within the inner circle of the fixed geometry of the template.

Bob remained convinced that key symbols on the stone tablets would get him tantalizingly close to the template's precise positioning. Yet, to solve the overall puzzle, those symbols had to be placed in proper context and in some logical sequence with other abstract markers found in the field.

One of the tablets' small, yet seemingly important, symbols was a circle carved behind the neck of the stone-tablet horse. Projected onto the Florence topo, the "circle" showed up near the old Reavis Ranch in the eastern end of the Superstition range. Perhaps the circle, which had a dot at its center, was meant to symbolize a particular mountain peak, he thought. But, without any numeric distance or directional marker provided, it could be any one of a dozen buttes in the area.

Fortuitously Bob had come across a crucial clue on his last trip, while visiting a treasure-hunting supply and bookshop in Apache Junction. Thumbing through a booklet written by two local historians, *Circlestone: A Superstition Mountain Mystery,* he had been drawn to an aerial photograph of a large circular rock monument. The monument's layout appeared remarkably similar to the design of the KGC template.[7] Up to that point, he had never heard of the "Circlestone," a flat-lying stone-wall geometric arrangement built just northwest of an extremely remote peak called Mound Mountain. Coincidentally, the mysterious (some say prehistoric) Circlestone "monument" lies in Section 33 of the local grid. It also lies at 33 28′ 35″ North latitude.

From then on, Bob was aware of the potential significance of the site described in detail by Apache Junction authors James Swanson and Thomas Kollenborn. The Circlestone, he guessed, was the topographic reference point for the circular symbol carved on the neck of the stone tablet horse. Little did the two local authors know that they were outlining the secret geometry of the KGC's template. The site's location—in Section 33, due north of Reymert and very near what was the full-time residence of assumed KGC sentinel Elisha Reavis—was highly suggestive. Bob wondered if it was a coincidence that Grandpa Ashcraft and Bill Wiley also had lived in Section 33 back home in Brushy Creek?

From the photos in the book, he could see that several stones appeared to have been deliberately removed from the pattern—most likely to prevent the Circlestone from being readily recognized for its true significance. Nonetheless, simply from the topographic information provided by the detailed booklet, Bob felt that the scope of the depository was becoming apparent. The Circlestone was in the north sector, and with Reymert near or in the center, there would need to be something south of Reymert to anchor the bottom of the outlying square perimeter of the circle-in-square template.

Among the first things Bob did upon returning to Arizona was to ask whether his HMP partners knew of any strange man-made structures lying south of Reymert, toward the Gila. Gardner said that, in fact, there was a mysterious row of beehive-like huts just west of a ghost town called Cochran. He had a file folder with a few photos of the "beehives," locally known as the Florence coke ovens. The file material described some of the lore behind the weird, thirty-five-foot-tall stone structures. They allegedly had been built by Welsh engineers as a place to convert local wood to coke, the latter being a more efficient fuel for smelting ore. But a close reading of the documents revealed that no one really knew the true origin, age or purpose of the peculiar domed structures. "We need to go there, tomorrow," Bob declared, pointing at the photos.

The next day, the group headed out on a jarring four-wheel-drive expedition that required fording a section of the Gila from the south. The spike in blood pressure and rattling of kidneys was worth it. When Bob saw the ornate hives, he immediately sensed that these "smelters" were much more than what they seemed. They were too well built, too perfectly aligned, to be mere charcoal ovens for local miners of the last century. Moreover, he noticed that the structures were largely free from creosote stains around the vents. If the "ovens" had been used to make charcoal over any length of time, the light-colored stone would have been stained permanently. No, the ovens were built more for symbolic purposes than for actual use, he concluded.

Bob knew from his research that the beehive was a key Masonic symbol for industriousness.[8] He surmised that the Florence coke ovens were KGC-Masonic in origin. Whatever their precise provenance, the row of domed structures anchored an important topo line, a centrally placed geographic clue to the overall puzzle, given their precise linear presentation.

A line-of-sight reading of the ovens' path revealed what he had anticipated. They were aligned on a 4-degrees–true-north compass heading, pointing directly at the Circlestone! (If one took a protractor and measured the angle of the ovens, denoted as a short line with five dots on the modern topo of the area, 4 degrees true would show as the bearing. Topographic and other surveying maps are laid out on a true-north grid. True north is a constant, whereas magnetic north, which a compass reads, can vary, depending on where one is located.)

Bob's beehives-to-Circlestone line, as measured by his GPS unit, ran due north through a thumb-shaped ridge of Picketpost Mountain (which has a heart-shaped topographic configuration around its peak and lies some four miles to the northeast of Reymert). The line's southerly extension, he noted, ran through the center of Heart Mountain, at exactly the tip of the giant landscaped arrow that Gardner and MacLeod had studied for so long.

Back at Gardner's residence that night, Bob broke out his marked-up 1900 Florence quad. He asked his two friends to take a look at the plot points from the day's findings. Noting the vertical alignment of key landmarks—the beehives, the Circlestone and Heart Mountain—Bob showed how this tangent most likely was the true central north-south line for the template, as opposed to the one running north-south through Reymert.

This was the fine tuning, the subtle shift, that he had suspected was required for the proper solution. Now the question was: how to find a point on that vertical north-south tangent to center the two sloping northeast-southwest, northwest-southeast master lines of the template? That three-line nexus, he believed, would mark the true centerpoint of a master KGC depository in the barren Superstitions of south-central Arizona.

When Bob shifted the Lucite grid's centerpoint to Picketpost Mountain nearby—a logical first choice among nearby landmarks on the new vertical line—one of the dots on the circumference of the template's outer circle aligned directly over Grayback Mountain. That, he knew, was a good sign. Grayback, by name alone, suggested KGC and Rebel intrigue.

And there was other corroboration with regard to Picketpost, including a key hidden message from the stone tablets. Suddenly, the meaning of the odd equation, $18 = 7$, which had been chiseled into one of the tablets, was clear. If Bob placed the template over Picketpost, the heart-

14. *The solution of the Lost Dutchman mystery: an expansive KGC depository, with a centerpoint at Picketpost Mountain. Notice the location of the horse and priest-templar figures from the stone tablets as seen in specific contour lines and suggested by KGC cipher. The priest-templar gazes through Grayback Mountain to Adamsville; the beehives align with the centerpoint at Picketpost up through the Circlestone.*

Built in 1.5 degree rotation

Knife Hill

Buzzard Roost

Base Line

Elephant Butte

Peak

Florence Junction

Template Center on Picketpost Mt.

Ghost town

Master Line Ft. McDowell to Crozier Peak

Heart Mountain

Bee Hives

Ripsey Wash

Grayback Mt.

Poston Butte

sville

18 miles from center of template

33° 0' North Latitude

111° 20'

Approximate 33' 0" West Latitude from Washington, D. C. using old method of survey from 1851 map

ME

TN
MN

shaped mountaintop was entirely enclosed by the cutout square at the center of the transparent overlay. The north side of the square fell exactly on the boundary line between Sections 18 and 7. The peak of Picketpost Mountain happens to lie precisely where the two sections border each other on the 1900 Florence quad!

Bob was now persuaded that the southwesterly sloping master line of the properly aligned template no longer ran through Adamsville but instead shot just to the north of Adamsville. The initial northeast-southwest line had run through Adamsville and exited the 1900 Florence topo a few miles short of the spot representing the southwest corner of the old map. The new line, running southwest from Picketpost, not Reymert, jumped off the map at precisely 33 degrees latitude. That was also the case with the line connecting the priest-templar's nose to Adamsville: it crossed precisely at 33 degrees. This was not a coincidence; it was cunningly neat.

This was what Bob had expected would result with the proper overall alignment: all the clues would begin to make sense within a KGC-Masonic context. Perhaps the most fascinating (albeit certainly obscure) revelation was that the Circlestone proved to lie topographically at the top of an equilateral triangle or pyramid design. The two intersecting lines forming the apex of the triangle derived from the corner of the outer square of the template, properly aligned. It was not left to chance that this geometry had come together to make the KGC conspirators' greatest symbol: the all-seeing eye atop a pyramid.

The Masonic eye of the pyramid was, in fact, the Circlestone monument, which, in turn, was the physical circle-within-the-square representation of the template. The vertical line running through the center of the north-south pyramid was the Beehive–Heart Mountain–Circlestone line.

Here was the total solution—he could do no better. The full menu of symbols on the stone tablets had been solved. Picketpost Mountain was the vortex of the template, from which all main lines radiated and intersected. Moreover, this peak as the centerpoint simply made good sense, not only on the basis of the esoteric geometric/topographic solution that he had developed from the cipher but also in practical terms. The peak of Picketpost provided a vast line of sight in many directions. This must have been an extraordinarily important factor when laying out the far-flung lines of a master KGC depository.

Picketpost was not chosen arbitrarily. The need to construct the master depository layout as an exact duplicate of the KGC's "key"—the template—required the utmost care in surveying the lines. Standard methods of surveying were adequate for land-division purposes and might well have sufficed for surveying a sprawling depository over hospitable terrain. But hostile Indians made travel through the canyons of the Superstitions extremely hazardous, and a KGC survey party large enough to accomplish the legwork and defend itself would have drawn unwanted attention from the U.S. Army, in control of Arizona Territory at the time. (Whether an undercover KGC unit would have been vulnerable to any such attack from indigenous Indians—with whom they may have been secretly allied—is uncertain. U.S. Army commanders in the region at the time would not have felt comfortable with any organized party of white men marching off into the mountains.)

Compass headings for master and sub-lines throughout the depository needed to be accurate to within tenths of a degree to ensure that buried treasure could be recovered by retracing the exact method used for the cache burials. Errors of even a few feet between distant points might result in a true "lost treasure." Since many of the reference points lay atop steep mountains separated by dozens of miles, the KGC most certainly sought a shortcut to design the depository grid for its major stockpiles. It so happens that there was an ideal tool for the job in Arizona Territory.

In 1886, a novel overseas invention was imported into the American Southwest to aid Brig. Gen. Nelson A. Miles in his war against Geronimo and other renegade Apaches.[9] The "heliograph," which used large mirrors to flash messages between signal stations on mountain peaks separated by great distances, was meant to change the battlefield calculus of the Far West. (The term derives from the Greek *helios* for sun and *graph* for writing.) This innovative apparatus had been invented in France and used to some effect by the British Army overseas. It achieved some limited utility for the U.S. military in the mostly sunny Superstitions and their far-flung, often-impassable canyons. But rather than being helpful in capturing Geronimo and his followers (who quickly became wise to the system's purpose and thus stayed away from specific areas), the mirrors were useful in other ways: in conveying information about friendly troop and supply movements, weather patterns and other workaday matters. Using reflected sunlight, the heliograph stations certainly were more efficient in the mountainous terrain than the traditional flags used by the Signal Corps. Yet, as an Army historian noted, the best method for communicating urgent intelligence about hostile Indian movements was the use of friendly Indian scouts in combination with the invisible telegraph![10]

After studying the history of the heliograph in Arizona, Bob had difficulty discounting its probable use by the KGC for its own clandestine purposes. It was a natural tool for setting up extensive depository lines in the years immediately after 1886. (Of course, use of the system would not have precluded KGC individuals or small groups from having hidden and guarded smaller caches within the same target area prior to 1886, when the initial design may have been sketched out.) Personnel likely would not have been a problem. The postwar KGC was believed to have placed agents in all branches of the U.S. government, including the Army. It would not have been difficult for the KGC to have planted a few men in the local Heliograph Corps to shoot the depository lines, say, under the pretense of sending official messages, or under the guise of conducting practice drills. As it turned out, the heliograph was employed through the 1890s, with at one point more than fifty relay stations active in the West.

With Picketpost as the centerpoint, Bob conducted an analysis (later corroborated by a topographical-mapping software program) of unobstructed lines of sight between various mountain peaks. It quickly became obvious that a heliograph stationed on top of Picketpost could have been the solution for surveying the template's lines with absolute accuracy. In the handful of places where direct line of sight was precluded, simple triangulation between three stations would have generated survey lines almost as accurately. Moreover, the average distance between the referenced peaks is well within the range of the heliograph's capacity. Even Adamsville, south of the Gila, is plainly within direct line of sight from Picketpost, as are Dinosaur Mountain, Comet Peak, Grayback Mountain, Dromedary Peak, Crozier's Peak, Ripsey Hill, Buzzard's Roost, the Circlestone atop Mound Mountain and Hewitt Ridge (where the highest point marks the pupil of the topo horse's left eye).

Thus, while identifying Picketpost as the centerpoint remained a matter of informed conjecture, Bob recognized a simple fact: Picketpost Mountain, which had a heliograph station, is the only prominent spot in the region with a direct line of sight to each of the points on the circumference of the KGC's topographical circle. And, with the power of the heliograph operating in such panoramic conditions, a forty-mile line could have been established in a matter of minutes. It might have taken weeks or months to survey the same line overland using traditional methods.

The ever-resourceful KGC may have used another "basic" tool to survey its lines from peak to peak: fire. Near the middle of the zone of interest, Bob came across a lone hill called Poston Butte that lies near

Florence and is visible from many miles in every direction. It once was the scene of a strange, long-standing fire ritual.

Kentucky-born Charles Debrill Poston (sometimes called the "Father of Arizona" as he had served as the Territory's first delegate to Congress) was a lawyer, explorer and entrepreneur who settled in Arizona (then part of New Mexico Territory) in the 1850s as the head of a mining enterprise. Poston was also a self-proclaimed "Sun Worshipper." (Old photos of the eccentric businessman dressed in exotic garb recall the anachronistic attire worn by high-ranking members of the Scottish Rite's Supreme Council.) As a tribute to the sun, Poston announced that he would keep a perpetual fire burning on the peak that would later be named after him. He built a road up the steep hill and had firewood hauled up the slope by the wagonload. A large blaze was set, and it burned continuously for several months.[11]

Could Poston's fire have served as a surveying beacon during nights when men worked on distant promontories to establish key lines for the KGC's grid? Today, atop Poston Butte, stands a stone memorial to the enigmatic and widely traveled Poston, who reportedly died in abject poverty in 1902. It is in the shape of a pyramid.

His mind churning with pride, tribulation and exhaustion, Bob late one night turned to Gardner and MacLeod and apologized for the complex hypothesis laid out before them. He said there just might be a big chunk of "Jacob Waltz's lost mine"—U.S. mint gold coins confiscated by die-hard Rebels—stored in vaults underneath Picketpost Mountain and a handful of other sites. But, as far as he could tell, all were on government land or on posted mining-company property. Putting his pen and protractor down, he threw out a caveat: "It's only map work. And who's to say whether my call's right, or whether the money's still there."

Whether they could get to dig on site at Picketpost—whether such sites were accessible in terms of permitting, deep-excavation technology or other factors—were open questions. For the time being, he suggested, it was best to focus on Adamsville—a viable location on private property with an apparent Jesse James connection.

17

Evidence in the Ground

THE mystery of Adamsville loomed large. It was time to lift the lid on possibilities there, and Bob resolved to do so with the participation of his HMP partners. Their information had helped generate lines to the ghost town, and his guiding principle was that if others had materially contributed to the solution, they were to participate in any recovered treasure. His collision with Griffith had not shaken his belief in doing others right—that is, if they proved straightshooters over time.

Near the end of his spring 2000 trip, Bob surprised Gardner and MacLeod by showing them the KGC treasure waybill of what he now knew to be Adamsville, with its neat sketches of the adobe structures. Their curiosity grew when he revealed how several key lines cut through the center of that former stage post. Bob then demonstrated how one of the overlaid template master lines—from his initial alignment of the template—led precisely to the site from the northeast section of the 1900 Florence topo.

Once on site, Gardner and MacLeod endorsed Bob's hypothesis that the adobe remnants of Adamsville were the subject of the illustrated "JJ III" waybill. Their enthusiasm notwithstanding, Bob refrained from telling his two friends exactly where they should look. That small detail would have to come later, after efforts were made to see what the property owners' response would be to the idea of a dig.

Back in 1998, Bob had told Gardner and MacLeod that there might be something of historical significance buried in, or near, old Adamsville. At the time, he had been deliberately vague. He had asked Gardner to keep an eye on the general area and to try to find the owner of a stretch of private property on the north side of Old Adamsville Road, where the stage depot and post office had once stood.

Gardner obliged, and, after making discreet inquiries and combing the Pinal County Recorder's Office records, he found the owners. In a brief telephone conversation with one of them, he explained that there could be something of historical interest buried on the property. He asked whether a small group could do some initial probing with non-invasive detection tools. The owner said that he would ask his brother, a co-owner, and get back. Gardner waited for weeks, then months, for a call—to no effect. After the initial frustration wore off, he simply put Adamsville out of his thoughts.

Bob's trust in Gardner and MacLeod had solidified over the subsequent two years of adventure and discovery, and he resolved to put all that he knew about Adamsville on the table. Before any major move was undertaken, he wanted to be kept informed and, preferably, to be on the property. He would leave it to Gardner to arrange permission to get on the property for a possible recovery. Gardner immediately took up the challenge of trying to reach the owner, but with no more success.

After several months awaiting a response, Gardner resolved to have a friend—a certified geologist—walk onto the property and do some above-ground surveying of a target area. The target was a section of the old stage road that Bob, by interpreting the information on the "Arizona Desert Treasure" waybill, had projected as the hot zone. The goal during those late summer weeks of 2000 would be to locate any major iron concretion (a safe, strongbox, metal chest) and then to estimate the depth of the target. If they received a positive reading, they would move to a higher level of planning.

Using remote-sensing equipment, Gardner and his geologist friend conducted a quick survey of the area in front of two adobes and near what looked like an irrigation-pipe storage facility. The scan produced a definitive reading for a significant metallic target. Wanting to confirm its characteristics, Gardner decided to bring in a small vacuum drill to probe the soil below. The machine pulled up pieces of red brick, charcoal, broken china and scraps of rusted metal. Given these indicators, Gardner decided to bring in some heavy equipment.

Not long after the preliminary survey (and unbeknownst to Bob in Arkansas) Gardner arranged for a team of trusted friends to come to the site to dig. The timing was coordinated with underground repair work being conducted in the immediate area. Gardner thought that his team would blend in. They did just that, working through the night, as the El Paso Gas team dug away, down the road, installing a new underground valve system.

Gardner and his team dug with picks and spades, working in shifts, in the cool autumn night air. One person would pick and shovel, another would grope for objects and a third would secure the sides of the deepening hole in the gravelly soil. It was slow going: each digger was trying to be meticulous, recording anything encountered in the subsurface and showing its approximate alignment.

At just over a foot down, the men heard the clang of a pick striking iron. The metal target was an antiquated road-grader blade, about eighteen inches long.[1] (Coincidentally, the Knights of the Golden Circle waybill to the site mentioned that the stolen money was meant to have been payment "to a RR grading contractor.")

Next, the diggers uncovered a couple of bricks, each cut in half, and some pieces of fine china pottery. (In an exquisite detail going unnoticed at the time, one of the distinct half-dollar-sized pieces of porcelain had a glazed circle of gold, a Golden Circle. Another piece of china was found with petite rose petals.)

At three feet, the group struck a cross-pattern of two lengths of rusted cast-steel steam pipe, each three feet long. (The symbol of the third degree in Craft or basic Masonry, that of a Master Mason, is a skull and crossbones.)

After six hours of hard effort, the men were both exhausted and exhilarated. They were mystified by their strange findings. Some swore that they had burrowed into an old junkyard.

The group returned the next day, but this time with a mechanized post-hole digger. The experiment proved short-lived: exhaust from the machine reached dangerous levels inside the pit and made the diggers dizzy at their peril. With safety the priority, the group abandoned the approach.

The following night, to Gardner's delight, an eighteen-wheeler arrived carrying a Bobcat and a new backhoe. The excavating machine—owned by a friend who had volunteered for the adventure—was a four-wheel drive model, with floodlights and with an extender that allowed its bucket to dig deeper than a standard backhoe. After the digging resumed, a combination of handiwork and mechanized scooping, it became apparent to all that this was no random pit filled with contemporary debris. Old apothecary bottles, fine china, and horse bones were part of the eclectic haul.

In excavating down to the machine's maximum depth, some twenty-two feet, the group gradually uncovered a carefully laid out, vertical column of man-made objects placed at calibrated levels. At one point, they found five large wagon steering pins laid out in pattern; then four such pins were discovered a foot lower, then three more a foot lower, then two in sequence. At ten feet, the group discovered a lone horseshoe. At twelve feet, they encountered a sculpted metal heart, bent into form from a band of steel. Then the diggers uncovered a vertically implanted crowbar, its point heading down at a slight angle.

At just over thirteen feet, the skull of what later was determined to be a Percheron draft horse was found, facing northeast—toward Grayback Mountain. It was lodged upright between a shovel head and a door from an old iron stove. (An ancient French breed from the Normandy region, the Percheron historically was used by medieval knights and crusaders as they rode into battle; around the 1880s, the modern draft-horse version of the breed became a popular import into America.)

The propped-up horse skull was the clincher for Gardner: this was no accident but some relic of a strange plot, he thought. Still, he was befuddled by being so close to what appeared to be a spot associated with treasure, and yet finding none. Gardner and his team got a laugh when they discovered two pairs of decomposed cowboy boots (soles were all that remained), each pair found in a separate foothold in the shaft's wall.

After they had excavated to the limit of the earth-moving machine (at one point they nearly lost the backhoe and the operator to the precarious pit), the men covered up the hole and went home. With a bunch of rusted metal, tinted medicine bottles, pieces of china, bricks, animal bones and other miscellaneous items stacked in their pickups, they were not exactly whistling all the way to the bank. In fact, they didn't know what to make of the experience.

When Bob received a call from a weary Gardner shortly thereafter, he could not believe his ears. "What! You dug the site!" he exclaimed. He spent the next few minutes rebuking Gardner for not informing him about the dig. After a pause, he asked whether Gardner had finally heard from the rancher. "No," the Arizonan replied. "Well, that's your call," Bob said, adding: "So, what the heck, tell me what you found. Did you record where everything was and where they were pointing?" Gardner said that they had dug within a few feet of where Bob had determined something could be buried. He said that they had done their best to be careful: plucking each piece out by hand, then using the bucket of the backhoe to clear the next exposed layer, and attempting to plot everything on paper in what turned out to be a difficult dig. Before launching into a long list of items recovered, Gardner explained that it at first seemed that they might have stumbled upon an old trash heap. But on closer inspection, he recounted, he could tell that everything uncovered had been carefully laid out—a feat of engineering that involved finely spaced footholds along the rim of the shaft. Then he ticked off the list of recovered "junk": the crossed pipes, the china, the charcoal, the propped-up horse's head, the metal heart.

"You've found a map, perhaps *the* map, of one of the big depositories," Bob said.

After a few seconds of letting it all sink in, he explained to Gardner that on a number of occasions in Arkansas, he had run into buried metal clues involving similar cross-laid pieces of metal. The horse, he said, appeared to be a widely used KGC symbol perhaps suggestive of the Knights Templar and certainly a possible connection to the stone tablet horse figure and its double, the topo horse. That horse was stout, robust and suggested a draft animal. He reminded Gardner that the horse tablet, priest tablet and heart tablet all had contributed to his having found Adamsville in the first place, as the target site for the "Arizona Desert Treasure" map.

"Ellie, think hard about this. You said the horse's head pointed northeast. Do you remember . . . was it pointing at anything?" he asked. Gardner, pausing for a moment as he recalled the exposed layer with the horse skull, said, yes, it did. "Grayback. Grayback Mountain."

"Reinforces my lines," Bob replied, without taking the discussion further. He knew that he had to appraise the situation in person.

Bob told Gardner that it was impossible to assess the significance of the shaft now that its directional signposts had been removed. He conveyed his lingering annoyance about that fact and about Gardner's jumping the gun. Still, out of fondness for his friend and his desire to see

the KGC trail revealed, he promised that he would return to the Superstitions to inspect the recovered pieces. Perhaps in the minutiae he would
find a directional gem in the rough. In the meantime, he suggested that
Gardner try contacting the property owner to secure permission to
attempt greater depths of excavation—this time with better equipment
and proper safety precautions.

When Gardner finally did manage to reach the rancher, he was
stymied by the man's reaction, or rather, lack of reaction. In the first few
minutes of the call, Gardner acknowledged that a team of locals had
conducted some probes on the property and that they had dug a pit and
found all sorts of strange odds and ends. The rancher simply wanted to
know: Were they digging in his crop fields? Gardner assured him that
they were not. He explained that they had dug a narrow shaft in the old
dirt trail running in front of the fenced field; had restored the site to an
even better condition than before; and now wanted to complete the project and document it. The laconic owner said that he was not interested,
for the time being, in any joint venture: all he cared about was running a
successful farm. "Even if this project could earn you millions of dollars
in possible buried treasure?" Gardner asked. The man said, no, he was
not interested at the time, but said he would leave the door open for further talk. So ended the conversation, leaving Gardner perhaps more
bewildered than ever.

When Gardner described the conversation to Bob, the Arkansan was
unfazed. Bob recounted the not dissimilar reaction of the rancher in
Addington, Oklahoma, the suspected site of the Wolf Map treasure.

In the wake of Gardner's surprise dig in Adamsville, Bob sought out a
famous treasure-hunting book by J. Frank Dobie, a legendary Texas and
Southwest chronicler. Dobie's classic *Coronado's Children,* which held a
prominent place among his library of treasure-hunting books, contained
a fascinating and curiously relevant passage. In a chapter entitled
"Down the Nueces," Dobie relates a search for hidden gold by a Texas
treasure-hunter named "Peg Leg Tumlinson." According to hearsay cited
by Dobie, Peg Leg was told by a Spanish Don to find a specific spot near
an old corral, where a "burro load of gold money is buried."[2] Peg Leg
was then advised to "dig down two feet and there he should find some
charcoal; two feet under that he should find a saddle blanket; two feet
under the saddle blanket, burro bones . . ." Peg Leg and his friends dug
a ten-foot diameter pit, found what they were told to expect and then

burrowed down to twenty-two feet, where they paused before digging all the way down to a depth of thirty-four feet. Ultimately they "struck a vein of water and quit."

Not only was the story from the early 1900s eerily parallel to what had just transpired in Adamsville; there were other odd "coincidences." In *Jesse James Was One of His Names,* Schrader and Howk note that J. Frank Dalton was an avid reader of Dobie's books and had earmarked pages of Dobie's works "with strange symbols." Additionally, the person who allegedly found the Superstition Mountain stone tablets in 1949 was a man named Travis Tumlinson.[3] Some suggest that Travis Tumlinson was directly related to Peg Leg Tumlinson.[4]

Bob thought this fascinating but didn't know what to make of it. Was it a means of conveying insider knowledge of the depository burial system? Perhaps, he thought.

In spring 2001, Bob returned to the Superstitions to meet with his HMP friends. He was eager to see the recovered items from Gardner's Adamsville probe, and he was particularly interested in examining the smaller bits and pieces that no doubt had escaped the attention of the diggers. When he saw the material, stored neatly in a shed, he immediately focused on the seemingly insignificant finds: the glazed porcelain, the apothecary bottles and the rusted metal heart. The group had completely overlooked the significance of the small porcelain handle with the delicate Golden Circle glaze, as it had the piece with the rose petals.

The emblematic Golden Circle shard was, for Bob, everything. It was the most explicit signature of a KGC depository that he had ever encountered. Holding the small piece of china in his hand, he could only smile at the mapmakers' ingenuity.

Little could the others have known that the helter-skelter pile of junk laid out before them, in the same layer-by-layer pattern in which it was found, served as an esoteric, subterranean map. One had to know where to look for the clues within. They were arranged as subtle visuals: some as anagrams, some as hieroglyphics, some as pictograms—all related to the surrounding topography in the Superstitions and its environs. Among the esoteric indicators: one of the apothecary bottles was half-filled with mustard seed. The lettering on the bottle's label yielded "BIBLE" as an anagram. The Bible (Matt. 17:20) contains a parable in which Jesus says: "If ye have faith as a grain of mustard seed, ye shall say unto this mountain, Remove hence to yonder place; and it shall remove, and nothing shall be impossible unto you."

Was some secret society telling the discoverers of this "junk heap" that they needed to find the right mountain, shift it and then most of their worries on Earth would vanish?

The answer, for Bob, was yes. The all-important horse skull had pointed to Grayback, along a northeasterly tangent. That strange, buried signpost had confirmed the critical directional line discerned at the outset of his Superstition investigation: the one running from the priest-templar's face (from the eye down along the extended nose) through Grayback Mountain, on to Adamsville and exiting at the corner of the Florence 1900 topo map at 33 degrees latitude.

Studying his Florence quad, he could see that between the priest-templar's nose and Grayback was an inconspicuous topographic feature, depicted in the shape of a small heart with a circle in each lobe. If one were standing in Adamsville, this topographically heart-shaped hill to the northeast could be seen if Grayback were moved off the line, as in a mountain removing "hence to yonder place." But that was only part of the equation. The priest-templar stone tablet had urged one to look for the map and look for the heart. Taking that lead, Bob envisioned drawing a line straight to Grayback from the priest-templar's silhouette and, in so doing, piercing the small heart-shaped ridge shown on the old 1900 topo.

Knowing that the heart theme was central to the overall puzzle, as it had been in numerous other KGC sites, Bob felt strongly that he was being directed into one of several important cache sites: the heart-shaped ridge, jutting off Grayback and lying in front of the priest-templar's nose. The ridge lay at the intersection of two key lines, one involving the priest's eye and the other incorporating the jack-o'-lantern-cutout in the cactus leaf. Perhaps most important, Bob recalled that when he had placed the translucent template over Picketpost, one of the key cutout circles on the Lucite grid had fallen directly over this same ridge off Grayback. If Woodson's article in *Treasure Hunter Confidential* were correct, this would correlate to one of the shaded circles on the template's key lines, or, in other words, a probable KGC cache site.

When Bob took his HMP partners to the suspected Grayback cache site, the group encountered indicative signs along the way. At one point, they noticed a stack of colored stones set atop a large boulder, which

Bob interpreted to be a rock monument of sorts, serving as a line marker. Atop the ridge, reached after a twenty-minute hike, the group came across a spot that appeared to have been disturbed long ago.

Faintly discernible in the discolored soil was what looked to be the filled-in top of a deep shaft, some twelve feet wide. The surface area was dome-shaped and devoid of vegetation, while all around the soil plug was fairly thick brush. Another noticeable feature was stains from the last rains, indicating seepage into the apparent filled-in shaft. Finally, there was the faintly visible trace of a wagon trail running up to the top of the ridge and then disappearing altogether.

After confirming with his GPS unit that the spot was precisely where the two directional lines crossed, Bob briefly switched on his metal detector. It responded with a marked deflection of the needle. He kept his emotions in check for he knew that whatever generated the signal was far too deep for any kind of definitive reading.

Whatever lay below—perhaps a natural fault, perhaps a man-made burial shaft or an abandoned mine—would take a massive effort to identify. But there was an even bigger issue: the possible treasure shaft lay in the middle of federal land overseen by the Bureau of Land Management.

The group had known about that before setting out to find the possible master-cache site at the location. Moreover, they all had recognized that even if they were to find something tantalizingly suggestive on site, it might be for naught. Attempts to obtain BLM or National Forest Service permits for a treasure-trove recovery on federal land in Arizona fall through in most cases.

Most of Bob's projected sites in the surrounding area were on federal land and thus would require an extensive permitting process that might or might not yield a green light.

In addition to the daunting regulatory gauntlet, Bob and his two partners, Gardner and MacLeod, would have to confront the large expense of bringing in sophisticated devices for detecting objects buried twenty to fifty feet below the surface. And there was the even greater cost of introducing heavy excavation equipment into the difficult terrain. Someday, they agreed, if everything lined up, they would set the process in motion for permitting and a recovery attempt.

Nonetheless, atop Grayback's ridge, there was a sense of victory. The puzzle had come into sharp focus. The clue-laden shaft uncovered in old Adamsville—found by intersecting lines developed from the stone tablets and cryptic clues from the field—had yielded a collection of symbols and markers that in turn had pointed to yet other prospective sites, such as the promontory where they currently stood. For now, it would be left an open question whether sealed stores of gold coins and bullion lie buried deep underground in the Superstitions, part of a multicache KGC master depository in south-central Arizona.

Bob was convinced that, unlike so many tales of treasure that ultimately lack foundation, the "lost gold" of the Dutchman was more than a figment of an overheated imagination. The KGC had been there, planted its flag and buried its riches.

18

Arkansas: The Sentinel's Treasure

BOB BREWER'S education as a Confederate code-breaker had come full circle. As much as any outsider could, he had begun to lift the veil on the KGC. He had come to appreciate why some had described the secret organization as the most powerful subversive group in American history. Over five decades, beginning unawares with his great-uncle in the Ouachitas, he had uncovered numerous trails and unearthed certain treasures left behind by the conspirators. Along the way, he had encountered a number of snakes—some garden variety, some human. And he had made some good friends, among them Tilley, Fretz, London, Hardcastle, Gardner, and MacLeod.

To a man, these friends at first did not know what to make of Bob's quest, his unbending effort to expose unwritten chapters of American history. But eventually they realized that his hunt was grounded in reality. It was not starry-eyed, but systematic; not unproductive, but enlightened and enlightening—and potentially lucrative. They had seen the evidence at the end of the trail and were awed, unlike others who, behind his back or to his face, had scoffed at his "obsession."

Bob had felt no real animus toward the naysayers, some of whom were kin. Even when faced with the cool-to-the-touch reality of the gold and silver coins, many found the dizzying story behind his finds just too much to follow, much less accept. Perhaps, in some cases, it was just jealousy, or a reluctance to eat one's words when shown to be wrong.

As for Michael Griffith, Bob had not completely purged the bitter memory of his dealings with the Oklahoma schoolteacher from his mind. On one occasion, he drove through Griffith's hometown of Poteau, near the Arkansas border, and pulled within sight of Griffith's residence. On the hillside above Griffith's modest mobile home stood a new, large modern Victorian-style house, surrounded by a high fence. This obvious "lifestyle change" was particularly notable, Bob thought, for someone on a schoolteacher's salary and for a treasure-hunting hobbyist who had worried about not being able to afford attending a treasure symposium.[1] Disgusted, he whipped the car around and headed home. As best he could manage, he put the past behind.

Back in Hatfield, there were new forces pushing his investigation forward, into new locales. Through TreasureNet.com and other treasure-oriented websites and chat communities, word had gotten round that "Hillbilly Bob Brewer" was not the typical blowhard with nothing to show for his wisdom. Buzz on the Internet among veteran cache hunters was that "HBB" was a straightshooter who could "read the signs" and had found verifiable treasures.[2]

Eventually, hundreds of curious folks from around the country—people who had never met Bob—started contacting him by email about possible KGC markers seen while hiking, hunting, fishing, logging, treasure hunting or simply working in their own backyards. Digitally transmitted photos, some showing century-old symbols possibly etched by Jesse James, started flooding into the computer in his war room.

Bob was not used to being called an authority, and he got a kick out of the interest and curiosity expressed from far off corners of America. Sometimes, he would volunteer free advice on specific questions from newcomers to the treasure-hunting world. Other times, he would establish a working relationship and selectively agree to consult for a fee on specific projects. But there were instances when he would not respond, mostly out of disdain for the correspondents' "need to know yesterday" approach or, at times, the presumptuousness of those who might simply have held a small piece of the KGC tiger by the tail. He had no truck with those who failed to respect the camouflaged and potentially dangerous beast that he had been dealing with nearly all his life.

Still, in a sense, the correspondence was all a sideshow. He had a bigger mission to fulfill: closing the loop on Grandpa and Uncle Ode's mystery, right there in his backyard.

Just twelve miles west of his home in Hatfield stood Smoke Rock Mountain and its Bible Tree: critical landmarks to an enigmatic grid.

That grid, he now realized, was a microcosm of the astounding puzzle that he had uncovered in Arizona and elsewhere across the South and Southwest.

Bob settled down to assemble pieces of the Arkansas puzzle that he and Linda had diligently acquired from dozens of sources and hundreds of sites. There was little doubt, after his years on the trail, that the Brushy and Cossatot valleys were the setting for extensive KGC depositories. Jesse James likely had set it all in motion. Bill Wiley, Will and Odis Ashcraft, Isom and Ed Avants, J. P. Smith, Will Dobson, Jack Hicks and others, possibly including Goat Brown, had protected the layout for decades under supervision from unnamed higher-ups. All this, it appeared, was a part of a KGC master scheme initially sketched out by Albert Pike, Caleb Cushing and other powerful behind-the-scenes men of intrigue.

So much had pointed in that direction, albeit in an indecipherable jumble, during his boyhood. With the wisdom that he since had acquired, he could analyze much more of the encrypted evidence for its true meaning and significance. The signs certainly were there: the difference was that he now had the computational lens to bring them into focus, to read between the lines, as it were. Moreover, years of conducting background checks into Jesse James, Albert Pike and others had paid dividends in his fieldwork. Of no less import were additional copies of Orvus Howk's letters, waybills and other documents that had come his way from treasure-hunting associates.

The textual and visual information in Orvus Lee Howk–Jesse Lee James's letters and maps had worked! These, along with the general guidance provided in Schrader and Howk's book and his own personal archive of historical and familial material, had helped propel him to the *systematic* recovery of treasure and other buried items in carefully laid, geometric grids.

The Howk letters had provided crucial insights into the tricks that the KGC employed in burying its caches. They also had shed light on some of the most important strategic decisions made by the clandestine group's top echelon. Perhaps the most fascinating example was the suggestion that the KGC—responding to intelligence reports that maps for key depositories in several states had fallen into the hands of "some thugs"—had ordered particular caches moved.[3] These reburials, according to Howk, were said to have occurred in the 1930s and 1940s. This might explain the camouflaged activity of W. D. Ashcraft, Dobson and others in the backwoods around the Brushy and Cossatot valleys during that period, Bob surmised.

Another case—one that helped persuade Bob that the James brothers and their KGC comrades had designated the Hatfield–Brushy Creek area for "master depository" status—was a cryptically written article in the *Mena Star* of May 21, 1931.[4] If Bob Tilley's wife Wanda, an avid genealogist and researcher of local history, had not scoured reel upon reel of microfilm, Bob and his lifelong friend might never have seen the embedded KGC waybill describing the layout of the local treasure grid.

The story presented, on one level, an uncorroborated account of a second Jesse James stagecoach robbery just east of Hot Springs in the fall of 1874.

Every James gang historian knows that the notorious outlaws robbed the Hot Springs stage in January 1874, but few have heard about the second time the gang allegedly hit the same stage, in September of that year. What caught Bob's attention was the alleged escape route, from Hot Springs west to the Choctaw Nation in Indian Territory. If the account were taken at face value, a running gun battle had ensued while the outlaws rode west through Caddo Gap and then into the precise area where Albert Pike's cabin had stood. The chase carried on toward Bill Wiley's cabin, over a thickly wooded area known as Long Ridge, and then on to Brushy Valley to within a few hundred yards of the log cabin where Will Ashcraft spent most of his life. The outlaws' reported route also would have taken them to the doorpost of Isom Avants's homestead and within half a mile of the Brewers' future home.

Bob found it notable, as well, that the author quoted someone who said that "it had all been planned out well in advance . . . to follow an almost straight westward route towards the Choctaw Nation."

Bingo. Bob had no way of knowing whether the event had occurred. But, in applying this newfound knowledge to his fieldwork, he recognized the critical subtext. These "robbers" had traversed the KGC depository at almost its exact east-to-west centerline. To ride at a gallop through the remote system of streams and valleys of rugged west-central Arkansas is no small challenge: it would take a prescribed path marked by knowing scouts, the likes of Bill Wiley and, later, Will Ashcraft. The article ended with a sidebar describing a dashing "Capt. Smith"—a self-proclaimed associate of the James gang—arriving in the area with a horse named "Wild Bill." The latter happened to be Wiley's nickname.

Bob was convinced that the article was meant to be read as a territorial marker and potential road map for those who knew the basics. Its real purpose was to inform members of the secret order of the depository's general location and to mark its approximate center. At best, it was an "establishing" document: impenetrable to most and yet too general to show precisely where to retrieve a KGC cache.

That indispensable knowledge—seldom if ever spelled out in text— would be passed on in the most mysterious of ways. It had everything to do with a rifle, a deer and the two larger-than-life characters from Bob's boyhood adventures under the Ouachita canopy, Grandpa and Uncle Ode Ashcraft.

When Aunt Bessie, Ode's widow, had bequeathed Grandpa's prized 1899 Savage rifle to Bob in the late 1980s, little did he realize how symbolically important the heirloom was—particularly as it was being handed down to someone outside the Ashcraft bloodline.[5]

As a boy, Bob had been wildly impressed with the power and accuracy of the weapon. (It could shoot through thick pieces of metal with its high velocity cartridge, while the more common Winchesters could only dent the dangling metal squares.) As a grown man inheriting the well-oiled gun, he originally viewed the rifle merely as a fond keepsake. He felt a piece of history was being passed on: the weapon had belonged to Bill Wiley, who had given it to W. D. Ashcraft as a token of their friendship, who then had passed it on to his son, Ode.

But now Bob was aware of something larger: the story of the rifle was somehow a symbolic link between members of a secret clan that lived in the Brushy and Cossatot valleys. It was a vital key, he realized, to Grandpa's devotion to the woods, to the coded layout of the grid and to the old man's attention to him as a youth. The gun was the shoot-to-kill weapon of a KGC sentinel, of W. D. Ashcraft, who had lived in Section 33, and who had been assigned to kill cowans on sight, questions asked later.

The rifle's arcane relation to the treasure grid would become apparent by chance. Bob had seen, in Wapanucka and numerous other sites, how the KGC had buried rifles, pistols and other firearms as pointers to important treasure markers or to the smaller caches themselves. The sleek 1899 Savage, however, had not been employed as such: it would not be left behind under inches of topsoil. Instead, it had been elevated to icon status in Brewer-Ashcraft family lore, in the oral tradition so important to many Arkansas backwoods families.

Ode, according to family narrative, had used the rifle to fell the "biggest buck ever seen in the Ouachitas." The woodsman, according to family tradition, had made a remarkable shot through stands of tall white oaks that wounded—but did not kill—the robust deer, sometime in 1932. The badly crippled buck, its shoulder shattered, had managed to clamber over three mountain crests before being tracked down by dogs and killed with a second shot from the Savage. In the end, the buck had traveled over three miles—on a route that passed known streams and watering holes—before succumbing. The story had seemed too elaborate to Bob when he first heard the tale as a kid. But the account, repeated a number of times by Grandpa and Uncle Ode, stuck in his memory because it was so unusual for an animal to wander so far after being hit by a bullet fired from such a high-velocity gun.

Bob had not given the deer story much thought until some fifty years later. While visiting Jeff Ashcraft, a great-grandson of W.D., he came across a strange, carefully staged photograph of Grandpa sitting next to the trophy-head of Ode's sturdy buck. The photo was among the contents of the old woodsman's mysterious padlocked box—the same chest that Bob had sat upon as a child when visiting Grandpa in the Ashcraft cabin.

The antiquated box, which Jeff Ashcraft had recovered from a barn owned by a relative, contained an assortment of W. D. Ashcraft memorabilia: a shoebox stuffed with photo negatives, a set of worn brass drafting tools and a brass pocket compass. The tools were nearly identical to the set Bob used for doing his precision map work.

The drafting set and compass spoke to W.D.'s true profession, or at least to one of many. Grandpa was a mapmaker and a surveyor. Will Ashcraft—and most likely Bill Dobson—were not only assigned to protect the buried KGC gold in the region; they were also trusted operatives assigned the task of moving the caches! Why else, other than for measuring and placing lines on maps with absolute accuracy, would someone (no less an uneducated woodsman) keep such expensive drafting instruments locked up as prized possessions? The more Bob thought about it, the more sense it made. Moreover, this might explain why he had encountered so many dry holes where the old markers had told him to go.

And, he learned, under the floorboards of the old cabin there was more evidence throwing light on Grandpa's past. The curious assortment of artifacts also included two heavy, rusted ingot trays. Could it be that the secretive sentinel was not only in charge of overseeing the revised layout of a master KGC depository but perhaps also of making sure that incoming coinage be melted into bullion, stripped of all vestiges of its official origins and mintage?

What caught Bob's attention most of all were the box-camera negatives stacked in the shoebox. The old film should not have been there: he had been told by older Ashcraft relatives that Grandpa did not own a camera and thus did not leave behind any visual record of his activities. As it turned out, Bob found scores of photo negatives, possibly from the 1920s and 1930s. The negatives appeared to be mostly of outdoor scenes of the Ouachitas, although it was hard to be sure without having the prints in hand.

Jeff Ashcraft later offered to convert a number of the negatives into black-and-white prints. As it turned out, they *were* mostly landscape shots: showing Will Ashcraft, his sons and various unidentified men standing with rifles in front of mountain outcrops, tunnels and other landmarks deep in the wooded hills.

Bob noticed an uncanny pattern to the photos and soon found himself lost in the images. When he took the prints into his war room and scanned them into his computer for higher resolution, his fascination grew. He had been to nearly every location as a youth! He soon began to recall things about which he had thought little in decades. He remembered how, for instance, at nearly each location Grandpa or Ode had told some anecdote or another—about a hunting feat or the like.

Now it was becoming clear why he had been the recipient of all this oral history in his boyhood and teens. He was being groomed to become a custodian of secret knowledge, for that day when the old-timers would be gone . . . when he well might be the only one around who knew the "story" about the designated sites. And there they were in the old photos, inconspicuous spots on trails, as snapped decades earlier: White Hole, Doe Hole, Blue Sky, Spanish Gold Mine, Blalock Fields, Jack Hicks's homestead. Places frozen in his distant memory, all stemming from those cherished, youthful outings with his favorite pair of mountaineers.

The strangest photo was that of W. D. Ashcraft grasping the deer mount from Odis's grandiose hunting story. The "portrait" was taken in front of the stone chimney of the Ashcraft cabin. The old man's eyeballs are rolled back, showing only the whites—the first thing to indicate that there might be something significant about the photo. Using a magnifying glass, Bob could see a strange but now oddly familiar set of symbols drawn on the chimney in the background: numbers, letters, hearts, triangles and a jack-o'-lantern face. He also could see that Grandpa's left foot rested on a flat piece of metal with a hole in it. A small heart-shaped rock lay in the foreground, and a pyramid-shaped rock rested on a ledge between the mountaineer's legs.

It was a map, a *photographic* waybill!

The KGC had resorted to all available means for conveying critical geographic information. On the receiving end were those who knew how to read the visual code and those with an aptitude for written and spoken allegory. An ultra-secret organization that dared not leave behind incriminating or revelatory texts (Orvus Howk's mid-twentieth-century letters being a rare exception), it sought vehicles for ciphered correspondence, including abstract carvings on trees, rock faces, cacti and other landscape features; oral and written stories meant to serve as allegorical road maps; illustrated waybills that corresponded with topographic contour lines and directional lines marked by buried metallic clues; and finally, the overlying template, the indispensable element for integrating the depository system and locating the deeply buried master caches at specific sites. Now, adding to this extraordinary mix of esoteric nontextual communication, came a fascinating series of photographs, rich in content, with no captions attached.

Over several days of analysis, in which he compared the new photographic data to information that he had already plotted on the old topos, Bob realized that the photo-map in Grandpa's deer portrait was a symbolic rendition of the template. The site where the deer allegedly was first shot with the Savage was the approximate center of the template grid, and the allegorical trail taken by the deer over the three mountains was the centerline—all demarcating the revised layout anchored around Smoke Rock Mountain. He could well imagine that the Ouachita sentinels—Bill Wiley (who would die in 1930), and his sworn successor, Will Ashcraft—devised the plan under orders from the organization's top ranks.

Now Bob understood the importance of the gun. It was not the rifle so much as the *deer*. That was the key to the cipher. The solution was to follow the path of the bullet: from its discharge out of the gun barrel, to its penetration of the robust deer, to its final resting-place inside the animal's carcass miles away. The photo-map was meaningless without the Ashcrafts' oral waybill—a legend whose details were known only by a very few, indeed by those close to the family of the designated sentinel.

The photo-map, no doubt, could also be used with the subtext of the 1931 *Mena Star* article, which was meant to create a lasting impression—a mental imprint—of the general location of the treasure layout. How brilliant, yet how obscure! Obviously too obscure, he realized, for a then-ten-year-old kid.

As a seasoned adult, Bob did what the allegorical map in Ode's hunting story—and thus in Grandpa's deer-trophy photo—told him to do. With Linda, he followed the topographic details symbolically indicated in the photo to the end of the designated trail, to a specific location in the woods where the deer was said to have been killed. It turned out to be the precise spot—at what would be the northern tip of the aligned template—where he and Linda had recovered the teakettle stuffed with gold coins from the blown-apart Wells Fargo strongbox in April 1995. Here was incontrovertible proof that Grandpa was, in fact, a sentinel, that he had used an intricately choreographed and symbol-laden photo of himself as a road map to one of the treasures that he had guarded!

The trail did not stop there. Grandpa's photos, combined with the countless clues and signposts that Bob and Linda had uncovered over the decades, provided a narrow target zone for the centerpoint of the template. Now, with Ode's deer story and Grandpa's deer photo deciphered, Bob was able to determine the precise alignment of a KGC treasure grid on the local topographic map. He obtained confirmation of this, in part, by revisiting the spot where earlier he and his brother Jack had found the metal rod seen under Grandpa's foot in the deer photo: they had discovered the rod embedded in a spring on a line that Bob only now realized helped reveal the full layout of the depository. This, he knew, could not be chalked up to coincidence.

The unraveling of the Ouachita KGC treasure grid was almost magical—indeed, automatic—from that point on. The properly aligned template indicated about a dozen spots where treasure caches would be buried, some along the key centerline indicated by the deer photo. At each indicated spot in the forested hills, all now on government property, Bob found an unmistakable burial marker. These were all but invisible to the untrained eye; yet he knew exactly what they were. Each time, it was almost as if he recognized the scribbled signature of family.

He realized that he had arrived at another milestone.

Directly below his feet, at each spot marked with a subtle distinct symbol, he knew that there was a sizable cache buried, no doubt similar to the coin-laden iron kettle that he and Linda had uncovered at the strongbox site. This time, he just walked away, empty-handed.

As he left the sites, Bob's mind veered back to the milestones in his quest. The Ouachita jars full of gold coins, the upturned strongbox, the Wapanucka and Wolf Map sites, the coin-filled teakettle, the innumerable carved and buried clues along the backcountry trails from Arkansas to Arizona, the Adamsville shaft and other burial locations—all these pointed to the bigger truth of the underground nationwide "system." Now he had become aware of the precise location of multiple moorings to one section of that subterranean financial network: a secret subsurface bank guarded, he now fully comprehended, by some of his forebears. The deer photo—with Will Ashcraft cryptically pointing the way through a symbolic maze—had capped it all. It miraculously allowed Bob to redraw the cache-burial plan exactly like the one Grandpa and others originally had used to plot their multiple interments of hard currency. But to recognize the photo-map for what it truly was took a lifetime of learning.

A huge calm flowed through him. He felt deeply satisfied. He had acted out a dream. Challenged as a child by a mystery, he had applied his physical, mental and emotional energy toward its solution and, in the end, he had achieved his goal. His true quest, he had always sensed, had been to solve the puzzle hinted at by Grandpa and Ode. It was not just a narrow search for gold; it was a much wider search for answers. In that exploration into the unknown, he grew to understand that the simple answer is not necessarily the most likely answer. He now knew that the Confederacy did not die in 1865; it went undercover.

Having come this far in the unceasingly complex process of decipherment, he felt a powerful respect for the machinations, the ingenuity, the dedication of the code-makers and their modern-day adherents—right or wrong in their obscure beliefs. And he knew that it was not right for him to take the money.

The incontrovertible knowledge that Grandpa, Ode and their associates had placed the treasure markers in and around Smoke Rock was worth far more to Bob than any amount of hard cash. After years of undiverted mental focus and physical exertion, he was in possession of the outline of an impossibly complex master plan used to harbor treasure in the mountains of western Arkansas.

Now, in his sixties, Bob realized the enormity of what had been going on, beyond his comprehension, in those days of adolescent abandon: it had been an unknowing, silent pre-initiation into an immensely powerful underground society. He realized why the old-timers had pointed out the carvings, had taken him to remote spots and recounted elaborate hunting tales. He now felt as if Grandpa and Uncle Ode were speaking to him from the grave, beseeching him to retrace the steps they had made before. Whatever the eerie, inscrutable purpose behind the secret treasure grid, he knew that he had linked the key pieces together in a coded calculus. Oddly, he felt almost as if he had become one of them, insofar as he had begun instinctively, if not automatically, to understand the layouts—as if there were some readily recognizable and eminently solvable mathematical equation.

He knew that the golden grid inside the Ouachitas was now *nearly* fully revealed. His discoveries along the deer trail were variables in a much larger equation—all hinted at by Grandpa's photo. The equation led, ultimately, to a *master cache*. Not only did the symbolism in the photo (and in other prints of Grandpa's) correspond to the many carved and buried directional markers that he had long since found, but it was also consistent with the location of mining claims held by Wiley, Grandpa, Dobson and others. Most significant, the cryptic photo-map and its associated clues from Bob's fieldwork corresponded with another photocopied J. Frank Dalton waybill (from Orvus Howk–Jesse Lee James's collection), one describing an apparently vast "Solomon's Temple" treasure.[6]

The cryptogram, of course, did not mention a state or specific location. But it did prove—through Bob's investigation—to be a dramatic KGC and Masonic connection to Arkansas and the backcountry woods of his youth. (As mentioned, one of the core Masonic legends is that of Hiram Abiff, the mythical architect/builder of Solomon's Temple.)

The "Solomon's Temple" waybill, which specifically refers to the "Knights of the Golden Circle," contains a sketch of the template. The scale is one inch to one mile—far different from that of most of the coded maps. The illustrated waybill states:

> The Confederate Government leaders were powerful, rich influential men of the deep South who saw that the War Between the States did not settle all of the issues or problems of that era. So finances were raised, Gold Bars, Gold Nuggets, Gold Dust, coins, silver, platinum, diamonds, were hoarded then buried in what they termed to be Military-Strategic locations all over North America. . . .
>
> The bulk [of Solomon's Temple] treasure was said to hold a few tons of gold, plus over $1,000,000 in old coins—Buried less than 30 feet deep.

The Confederate Government leaders were Powerful, rich, influential men of the Deep South who saw that the War Between the States did not settle all the issues or problems of that era. So finances were raised, Gold Bars, Gold Nuggets, Gold Dust, coins, silver, platinum, diamonds were hoarded Then buried in what they termed to be Military-Strategic locations all over North America.

The Worshipful Master sits in the East, The Senior Warden sits in the West

These Treasures were hauled into this wild area between the years 1869/1890

Scale: 1 inch = 1 mile

This survey pattern fits in with USGS maps of This particular area

W — E

The bulk treasure was said to hold a few tens of Gold plus over 1,000,000 in old Coins - Buried less than 30 ft deep. Twelve other Treasures of less value represents 13 Southern States of USA - These Sympathetic toward the Cause of the Old South

We learned that There was no Temple. North door in King Solomons Temple you to enter the secret chambers of the secret workmen - we should by any and all means commune in the South and work our way Toward the Northwest. Jesse James saw to it That cleanfolk are on guard - watching over These great Treasures

Knights of the Golden Circle

And other powerful organizations.

15. *Textual waybill for King Solomon's Temple Treasure depository, located in Brushy Valley, Arkansas and protected by Bill Wiley, W. D. Ashcraft, Odis Ashcraft, Isom Avants and other KGC "sentinel" families dating back to the late nineteenth century. (Note the turtle figure.)*

Twelve other treasures of less value represents 13 Southern states of USA—Those sympathetic toward the cause of the Old South. . . . These treasures were hauled into this wild area between the years 1869–1890.

This survey pattern fits in with USGS maps of this particular area. . . .

We learned that there was no North door in King Solomon's Temple. So to enter the secret chambers of the secret workmen, we should by any and all means commence in the South and work our way towards the Northwest. Jesse James saw to it that dead folk are on guard—watching over these great treasures.

The Worshipful Master sits in the East. The Senior Warden sits in the West.

Methodical fieldwork eventually led Bob to the location of the Solomon's Temple layout. In a remote corner of the Ouachitas, he and his friend Tilley found a cluster of coded engravings and buried clues that suggested construction of a rectangular grid, forty yards by sixty yards. The layout was cornered by a small pine knot, which had been splotched with red paint and carved subtly into the shape of a horse's head. The durable pine marker—full of pitch that provides protection from rotting and pests—was disguised to look like a land-surveying corner marker. Yet it was in an area where the land had never been subdivided. Inside the conceptualized rectangle, the two men found carefully placed stone markers, which Bob interpreted to represent the stations of a Masonic temple. (The temple lodge is said to replicate the architectural design of Solomon's Temple. In a Masonic Lodge room, the Worshipful Master sits in the east, as do the treasurer, the senior deacon and the secretary. The senior warden and junior deacon sit in the west.)

They had found the symbolic intimation of a Masonic lodge hall along a trail suggested by clues gathered for decades and on a path subtly intimated by Will Ashcraft and his co-devotees to a cause. All these clues had provided the centerpoint for the alignment of the template, which, in turn, led to this precise spot indicating the burial of a KGC master cache. Solomon's Temple treasure, one of the KGC's master-cache sites, was in Arkansas, buried deeply and, as it turns out, on government land.

Those secreting the treasure left nothing to chance or coincidence. After all, "the Worshipful Master sits in the East," and none other than Albert Pike, the world's highest ranking Mason for decades, had lived due east of where the two men now stood.

The ultimate secret behind Grandpa and Uncle Ode's devotion to the woods was no longer a mystery. Bob, with his devoted friend by his side, sat down near the red horse marker. The two men had a good laugh:

even if they *could* recover the treasure from the deep underground, what would they do with it!

After fifty-odd years, Bob Brewer had fulfilled his quest. He felt wiser, and not without battle scars. He looked at his lanky, soft-spoken partner, whose forebears, likewise, had fulfilled the sentinel's zealous mission in privation and with no complaints. The two shook hands on a pledge: they might reveal the subject of their discovery but never its precise location. The pair of mountainmen then carefully replaced all of the clues they had found and restored the site just as they had found it, with one small exception. The markers were placed slightly below ground so that anyone looking for them would need to know exactly where they were.

After finishing their work, the two Bobs sat down on the forest soil and ate a lunch of Vienna sausages and cheese crackers. It was the same meal that they had eaten years ago, as young men working the timber on the slopes of the Ouachitas for seventy-five cents an hour. Now they were the old-timers. The other players in the game were all dead: the Ashcrafts, Isom and Ed Avants, Bill Dobson, the Hatfields and others, all gone. Men in whose shadow they had lived as youth, and whose names would show up in Isom Avants's cryptic illustrated diary from the 1920s. A diary that they both now realized was a work ledger for faithful members of the KGC, committed sentinels charged with protecting buried money over the course of their adult lives.

As a result of what might best be described as discriminating wisdom, Bob knew that he had found the final path to the sentinel's master treasure, to the gold overseen by W. D. Ashcraft. More than forty years after the old man had offered to "dig up" some "cash money," Bob realized that Grandpa had meant it. The gold, independent of its intrinsic value, was the anchor of the system, a system bound up, it seemed, in politics, philosophy, religion, sociology, math and science.

Despite all that he had read about the KGC and its rumored caches of gold, silver and arms, not to mention all that he had seen firsthand, it still seemed incredible that large quantities of precious metal had been left in the ground. It was even more incredible, Bob thought, considering that those involved lived at or below the poverty line. But KGC gold—ever more valuable since its interment—*was* hidden in a network of depositories stretching across the lower section of the country, just as J. Frank Dalton—via Orvus Howk and Del Schrader—had asserted. He just did not know how much. That had never been a concern of his.

The old mountaineers who guarded Solomon's Temple and other KGC sites gained no wealth or fame from their vigil; they all had lived hard lives and had little if anything to show for it when they died. But they each had appeared content. They were men who stood for a cause and were not tempted by the likely millions in gold they protected: men who could be trusted, who loved their families and neighbors but would unhesitatingly kill intruders should the need arise.

It was a difficult story to understand, but true. And, at this later stage of his life, Bob resolved to get the story out, realizing that he was perhaps one of the very few individuals alive who had obtained knowledge about this camouflaged segment of American history. While the Solomon's Temple treasure would remain sealed, he vowed that he would—for the sake of history—try to locate and aid in the recovery of a master KGC treasure, buried thirty to forty feet deep, either in Arizona, Arkansas, Oklahoma or one of the many other states where he had been on the trail. This recovery would have to be conducted under government supervision, with heavy equipment, and with a stipulation that all money recovered would be put toward a good cause, one supporting education for underprivileged children across the nation.

No doubt, some of the caches likely were "forgotten": lost in the telling from one generation to the next in an underground movement that relied almost entirely on oral tradition and unwritten communication. Others unquestionably were lost to natural forces: wind, fire and ice that would destroy engraved, centuries-old trees; and erosion that would erase chiseled KGC markings on outcroppings. But what about caches that were not forgotten, that were deliberately left buried—some apparently still guarded?

Whatever the motivation behind such lifelong devotion to a cause, Bob knew that the cause was bigger than the War Between the States, that it went beyond politics, beyond the Confederacy and a romantic notion that the South would rise again. There was no question that it went beyond the notion of state, period. If gold were knowingly left in the ground and protected well into the twentieth century, then the motivating force behind such concealment would have to verge on the religious—a higher calling, an article of faith.

Based on his intensive research into the roots of the KGC, Bob imagined a third-way belief system, lying somewhere between Catholicism, Protestantism, Judaism, Islam and mysticism. Indeed, he thought, nothing short of religion or some form of spiritual allegiance could have fused a bond among men that would endure for so many decades, if not centuries. The buried gold, perhaps, was meant to be the financial underpinning of that new "religious" order. Gold, unlike paper money, maintains its value as a world-recognized medium of exchange and serves as a safe haven in times of economic and political turmoil.

Soon after the men's return from the Solomon's Temple locale, Tilley received a visit from an ailing Bob Smith, his old treasure-hunting pal, who was near death from cancer and would soon spend his last days in Granbury, Texas, the same small town where J. Frank Dalton had died. Smith left behind a package. In it was a smooth, gray triangle-shaped rock. It had been neatly inscribed with a carving tool. In the salutation, the *o* in "to: Bob Tilley" happened to fall neatly into the uppermost corner, the apex, of the pyramid—the all-seeing eye. On the back was a silhouette of an Indian, wearing a necklace of sorts. The chain of the necklace, in fact, was nothing more than an inverted drafting compass: as in "compass and square," the other world-renowned emblem of Freemasonry.

Epilogue—
The European
Connection

FOR years, Bob had sensed a powerful European dimension to the KGC mystery. The links seemed to reach across a spectrum of shared symbolism, esoteric communication and, perhaps, an obscure anti-authoritarian philosophy. It was a bold, tantalizing concept.

There were some obvious pointers to a trans-Atlantic connection. To begin with, there was the Scots-Irish ancestry of many in his own family and that of die-hard former Rebels, such as Jesse James, who had formed the KGC's core. Then there was Pike's trip to Europe during the Civil War to attend a "Rosicrucian" conclave. At war's end, there were safe-haven flights to London and other European capitals by Breckinridge, Benjamin and other Confederate-KGC exiles. Further, there were abundant allusions in the KGC underground literature to "the chivalry" and, specifically, to the European Knights Templar.

What of these medieval Templars—monastic "bankers" to the world during their peak period of influence in the twelfth and thirteenth centuries? During their long-running confrontation with the Church of Rome, these monk-warriors allegedly moved "underground" and placed their vast wealth in subterranean vaults. In considering the longevity of the Templar saga, Bob wondered about the longevity of the KGC in America: What was the powerful force or idea that held it together? Was it fundamentally political, or was it something powerfully philosophical or theological, a faith-based secret creed imported from Europe?

Indeed, what should one make of the religious-spiritual-philosophical references suggested by the veiled scripture on the Arkansas Bible Tree, by the priest figures on that same tree and on the Arizona stone tablets, not to mention numerous other KGC symbols with Biblical connotations—crosses, hearts, skulls (as in Golgotha, the "place of the skull")—at sites across America's southern tier?

The best Bob felt he could do, as he had been told as a youth, was to follow the symbols and look for parallels.

By happenstance, the prospect of an intricate European connection to the KGC's underground grid came into focus in the spring of 1998. One of his sons, a former U.S. Marine firearms instructor who had taken part in one of his Arizona expeditions, sent him an intriguing book as a present that year. Living in San Diego at the time, the younger Brewer came across the title while browsing at a local bookstore, where he had been thumbing through a section of books associated with the Knights Templar. Little did he know how much impact his gift would have on his father.

Entitled *The Tomb of God: The Body of Jesus and the Solution to a 2,000-Year-Old Mystery*, and written by British authors Richard Andrews and Paul Schellenberger, the book describes a mysterious, geometrically defined grid in southern France that allegedly points to a hidden, buried secret of enormous import.[1] Their book is based, in part, on earlier research and analysis published in Michael Baigent, Richard Leigh and Henry Lincoln's *Holy Blood, Holy Grail*.

The provocative book engrossed Bob from the moment he opened it. He was startled to see vivid, graphic parallels to the geometric/geographic layouts that he had uncovered in America, though the book, to be sure, makes no mention of the Knights of the Golden Circle, has nothing to do with the United States and reveals no treasure recoveries. *The Tomb of God*'s photographs, maps, diagrams and other visual components were but half the story. The authors' evocative description of a strange sequence of events—following a widely reported discovery of ciphered parchments in a church in the historic village of Rennes-le-Château in southern France in the 1880s and 1890s—pulled Bob in and never let him go. The blurb on the front jacket caught his eye.

The parchments, the authors demonstrate, point toward a secret tradition—a hidden geometry of lines and angles apparent in certain maps, tombs and artworks over the centuries. . . . This geometry corresponds to a map of the region surrounding Rennes-le-Château, with the lines intersecting at a precise point. . . .

While rejecting the authors' speculation as to what lies at the core of the Rennes treasure grid, Bob sensed that a new window into his quest had been opened. There were striking parallels between the late-nineteenth-century intrigue in the small French village of Rennes-le-Château near the Pyrenees mountains—a former Knights Templar stronghold—and the late-nineteenth-century KGC intrigue in mountainous parts of the American South and Southwest.

Surrounding the Rennes was a pattern of encrypted markers, which, in turn, yielded conceptual topographic lines for some esoterically conceived geometric pattern. Moreover, the topographic/geographic pattern—based on a circular map of medieval Jerusalem—involved a master circle, a square, pyramids, and comet-like "fans" with required degrees of rotation! It looked like a blueprint for what Bob had painstakingly uncovered over five decades of investigation in remote parts of America, beginning in the Ouachitas.

Not only did *Tomb of God*'s authors describe an analogous integration of directional lines with landmarks and subtle features on topographic maps; they also showed how enciphered text from the parchments found by a local Rennes priest, François Bérenger Saunière, hinted at those topographic features, in both cipher text and allegory.

Further, the book's authors go into detail in explaining how paintings by the French master Poussin had served as deliberate visual waybills for locating components of the grid.[2] Andrews and Schellenberger demonstrate how key components of Poussin's pastoral "Arcadia" paintings provide lines of investigation toward the final target: a mountain, on government land, where, the authors speculate, a tunnel or tomb holding the Templars' ultimate secret is located. Yet the "practical" problems—of the tomb being buried under thousands of tons of rock inside the mountain "tunnel," and of needing "permission of the local authorities and, in view of the implications, perhaps the French government"—prevent any easily achievable move toward substantiation of their hypothesis.[3]

Had Nicolas Poussin (1594–1665) deliberately painted an idyllic road "map" to provide clues to the repository of some fabulously important and dangerous secret? Had the painter David Teniers followed suit in the same general period? If true, to think that the KGC may have carried on a practice of providing coded road maps through visual arts: encrypted 1920s black-and-white photography from the likes of Will Ashcraft had followed in the stealthy tradition of Poussin's cloaked masterworks in oil!

The Knights Templar, according to *Tomb of God* and *Holy Blood, Holy*

Grail and other popular texts, had absorbed many Jewish, Cabalist, Hermetic and Muslim traditions of the East during their long residence in Outremer, the Holy Land. As such, they may have sparked the beginning of a powerful *mixed-faith spirituality* movement—one that emphasized open-mindedness, individualism and a blend of religion, science and mysticism—giving rise to the seventeenth-century Rosicrucianism. With their emboldened foes of Vatican orthodoxy, their strident proponents of intellectual freedom and their mysterious symbol of the red rose, the Rosicrucians attracted many of the intellectual, scientific and cultural leading lights of the period.[4] Here, perhaps, was the beginning of an enduring link between the KGC and the Templar phenomenon in Europe, Bob thought.

He had come across a brief but perhaps significant sentence in *Jesse James Was One of His Names*. In their chapter "The Knights of the Golden Circle," authors Schrader and Howk state: "Some of the craftiest, finest brains in the South directed the activities of The Knights of the Golden Circle. . . . A couple were members of the Rosicrucians." It was almost as if, in the book's three hundred pages about the exploits of Jesse James, the offhand remark was meant to be an aside. But it most likely was not, he thought.

What might explain, he wondered, the odd timing of events occurring on both sides of the Atlantic in the late 1800s? That is, the KGC's designing vast and disparate depots for buried treasure and the discovery in France of encrypted parchments that ultimately revealed, according to *Tomb of God*, a "recurring system of symbolism" and an extensive topographic/geometric layout?[5] Clearly, the groups behind such carefully planned layouts—whether in the Superstition Mountains of Arizona, the Ouachitas of Arkansas, or the rolling terrain of south-central France—had expert knowledge of surveying, engineering, mathematics, "sacred geometry," Euclidean logic, geology, encryption. And they must have been powerfully motivated to go to such lengths. But why? Was there a religious connection?

Father Saunière, the priest who discovered the coded parchments in France during the late nineteenth century, inexplicably placed a demon-figure sculpture inside his Church of Mary Magdalene: the demon happens to be making the key KGC hand signal—the tip of his right forefinger touching the tip of his thumb to form a circle. Saunière's fantastic disclosure, coincidentally, resulted in his becoming quite wealthy—paid in vast sums of gold francs by unknown sources. Following his discovery the local priests affiliated with him suffered sudden, mysterious deaths.[6] All this occurred around the same time as the enigmatic activities of Jacob Waltz, the Lost Dutchman, who seemed to have come into certain wealth, appeared to have had some connection to encrypted tablets or signposts and who apparently had placed a curse on those trying to find his gold in the Superstitions.

Bob had no knowledge of a positive link between the events in France and the KGC. He speculated that they were connected through a Templar–Rosicrucian–Scottish Rite–KGC continuum. He found a connection in *Holy Blood, Holy Grail*. About halfway through the book, there is a specific reference to the Scottish Rite and to Rennes-le-Château.[7] Citing the 1979 French book *Treasure of the Golden Triangle* by Jean Luc Chaumeil, and its "privileged sources" of information, the *Holy Blood, Holy Grail*'s authors say that Chaumeil noted that "a number of clerics involved in the enigma of Rennes-le-Château—Saunière, Boudet, quite probably others—were affiliated with a form of Scottish Rite Freemasonry." They observe:

> . . . the Masonry M. Chaumeil describes would have been acceptable, despite papal condemnation, to devout Catholics—whether eighteenth-century Jacobites or nineteenth-century French priests. . . . Rome certainly disapproved—and quite vehemently. Nevertheless, the individuals involved seem not only to have persisted in regarding themselves as Christians and Catholics; they also seem, on the basis of the available evidence, to have received a major and exhilarating transfusion of faith—a transfusion that enabled them to see themselves as, if anything, more truly Christian than the papacy.[8]

Because the available evidence was at best sketchy, Bob would not draw any hard conclusions about shared philosophical or spiritual ideas behind the grid-making under way on both sides of the Atlantic in the mid- to late-1800s. At best, Bob concluded, both groups of grid- and map-makers seem to have borrowed from Templar tradition, ritual and lore.

Bob had spent decades exploring how the KGC employed Masonic ritual, imagery and symbolism: an effective means of communicating with an informed elite that left others in the dark. He had learned that where virtually no paper trail exists, as typically is the case with secret societies, analysis of symbols is the only substantive and effective way to investigate. That said, he recognized that there would always be ambiguity in interpretation.

He did not have to look far for parallels in symbolism in the seemingly overlapping pattern of events in Europe and America. Leaving the geometry aside, *Tomb of God* describes a large, carved horse's head observed in the side of a mountain. The book also refers to encrypted hidden messages translating as the "Horse of God." Were the shadowy players in France aware of the modus operandi of those in Arkansas who had inscribed the Bible Tree with its central horse figure? Were they in lockstep with those in Arizona who had engraved the stone tablets with a draft horse (and the misspelled caption "EL COBOLLO DE SANTAFE"—HORSE OF HOLY FAITH) or those who had buried the Percheron horse skull in Adamsville? Did the Latin cipher in Saunière's parchments have a direct parallel to the Spanish code in the Arizona stone tablets? Were the clues on both sides of the Atlantic indeed derived from the same symbolic set?

One particular description about the symbolism in the Rennes area was evocative. Henry Lincoln, coauthor of *Holy Blood, Holy Grail*, reportedly had come across a rock face, near the historic town, that had been inscribed with a heart shot through with an arrow, and with a symbolic name and the date 1891 chiseled below. In his 1998 sequel about the mystery of the surrounding topographic grid, *Key to the Sacred Pattern*, Lincoln says the circumstances overshadowing his discovery of the carved symbol were disturbing: "It is to be the first evidence that our movements are being watched. And the watching eyes, it seems, are unfriendly and even unscrupulous. Our return visit produces a shock. The inscription is no longer there. It has been hacked from the rock. My photograph is the only evidence that the inscription ever existed." [9]

There was little doubt in Bob's mind that the KGC depositories and the grid around Rennes-le-Château, as described in *Tomb of God* and *Holy Blood, Holy Grail*, were connected to Templar/Masonic tradition. He knew of other sites in England and Scotland that could be placed in the same category, again because of the recurrent symbolism and an implied geometry centered on a perceived circle-in-square template. And then there was Oak Island, Nova Scotia, where a suspected treasure—possibly associated with the Templars and Freemasons—had eluded discovery for centuries despite extensive excavation in a deep shaft known, yes, as the Money Pit.[10] That no gold or other treasure had been recovered on Oak Island mattered little. What did matter to Bob were the mysterious artifacts that had been retrieved and recorded over many decades from the Canadian site: sculpted heart-shaped rocks; slabs with inscribed hieroglyphic-like writing; slabs with the letter G, slabs with drill holes; boulders shaped like skulls, deep earthen shafts with layers of charcoal and broken porcelain laid down; rock pile formations in the shapes of circles, arrowheads and crosses; and cryptic carvings in trees.[11]

Were these signs and symbols—stretching from Europe to North America—all part of the unspoken, esoteric vocabulary of Grandpa and Uncle Ode? Perhaps. On his regular visits to Six Mile Cemetery, where his father and the two Ashcraft woodsmen lie buried in a hilly patch a mile from Hatfield, Bob thinks about such things, about unexpected connections. And he dreams about traveling, with Linda, to that mysterious village in southern France, to Oak Island and other places where such connections might exist.

Placing his hand over etchings of single-stemmed roses on the Ashcrafts' tombstones, he wonders about the hidden mission of the sentinels. He wonders whether the nation's brutal Civil War might have had undercurrents that went beyond slavery and states' rights. Each time he leaves the gates of Six Mile, he wonders whether the War Between the States might have been something far stranger in its genesis.

The pursuit of independence by these confederated States has a very different aim from the redress of such shallow griefs as these.

Whoever shall be able hereafter to reveal the secret history of these various conclaves which have held counsel on the repeated attempts to invade and conquer, —or, as the phrase was, liberate Cuba; whoever shall unfold the schemes of seizing Nicaragua, of aiding revolution in Mexico, of possessing Sonora, will make some pretty sure advances in disclosing the true pathway to the sources of this rebellion. The organization of the Knights of the Golden Circle, and their spread over the country; their meetings and transactions; who managed them and set them on to do their appointed work, —whoever shall penetrate into the midnight which veiled this order from view, will also open an authentic chapter in the history of this outbreak.

—From the 1865 book Mr. Ambrose's letters on the rebellion, by former U.S. Secretary of the Navy and Maryland congressman, John P. Kennedy.

Notes

1. THE EFFIGY

1. Phone interview with John London, Amarillo, Texas, July 2001. London, one of the participants in the outing with Bob Brewer and mutual friend Stanley Vickery, made these observations: "When we pulled up, it looked like they had hung the poor son-of-a-bitch and shot him. It made your heart hammer." London took the effigy as a warning: "There was a feeling of evil about the place. It was pretty clear someone was saying, 'Stay the hell away.'" Vickery, in a phone interview in March 2002 from his home in Alexandria, Louisiana, said he thought they had come across some kind of "occult ritual . . . it was spooky."

2. Polk County (Ark.) sheriff Mike Ogelsby and chief deputy sheriff Tommy Hubbard confirmed that the incident was reported by deputy sheriff Randy Gibbons. Interview, Polk County Sheriff's office, Mena, Arkansas, August 2001.

2. THE EDUCATION OF A CONFEDERATE CODE-BREAKER

1. See feature article about W. D. Ashcraft of Hatfield, Arkansas, in *Mena* (Ark.) *Evening Star*, November 15, 1967, in the "Around Polk County" column by J. C. Lawless.

2. Personal diary of W. D. Ashcraft in possession of his great-grandson, Jeff Ashcraft, in Texarkana, Arkansas. Don Ashcraft, Grandpa's grandson and father to Jeff, related the story of Delia Ashcraft's labor in an interview, Hatfield, August 2001.

3. See Albert G. Mackey's *Revised Encyclopedia of Freemasonry*, Volume I (Chicago: Masonic History Company, 1946), p. 249.

4. See George A. Mitchell, "Twin Springs Spanish Gold," *Frontier Times*, December–January 1969, pp. 32–33. The article contains a loose description of the Avants family and gold intrigue in the immediate Shady-Brushy Creek, Arkansas, area. A primary source indicator of a direct link in "mining" operations between W. D. Ashcraft and the Avants family is Isom Avants's memorandum book from 1920, in possession of Isom's nephew, Bob Tilley, of Hatfield. The record book contains Avantses' and Ashcrafts' names, as well as an illustration that appears to be a spider-like grid or map, with "Shady, Ark. Aug. 23, 1920," written below. Also, a list of multiple mining claims in an area

held jointly by W. D. Ashcraft and the Avants brothers is on file at the Polk County courthouse in Mena, Arkansas.

5. Wells Fargo stagecoaches transported gold and other valuables in large iron-hinged oak crates, known as strongboxes, that were bolted to the stage's floor with iron strips and padlocked for added security. Later versions were made of tempered steel.

6. Bob Brewer, "The First Motor Saw," *The Looking Glass Magazine* (Murfreesboro, Ark.), Winter 1995, pp. 42–45. The article describes logging outings with Odis Ashcraft and Brewer boys.

7. See article by Larry Rhodes, in the *Ouachita Mountaineer*, Looking Glass Press, Murfreesboro, Ark., Spring 1996, pp. 30–34, on the path taken allegedly by Jesse James after reportedly holding up a stagecoach southeast of Hot Springs, Arkansas, on September 17, 1874. Also see Rhodes's article in the *Ouachita Mountaineer*, Winter 1996, pp. 11–18, about an earlier, better-known Jesse James robbery in the area in January 1874.

8. Arley Woodrow, "After Gay Life in City Wiley Bill Retires to Mountain Cabin," *Fort Smith Southwest-Times Record* (undated newspaper clipping from the early 1900s). The article states: "Bill Wiley makes his living in the woods. His chief occupation is mining, but no one has ever known Wiley to strike 'paying' dirt. . . . This hermit of the hills knows every tree and trail of importance in this part of the mountains. When he goes hunting, he knows just where the game is most likely to be." In a 1993 interview with Bob Brewer, Wiley's daughter Carrie Wiley Winters (of Pomona, Calif.) states that Bill Wiley had served as a Texas ranger before becoming a Confederate soldier and then moved to Arkansas sometime in the 1860s. She said that her father (married to Julia Ward in 1902) at one point had been "supervisor for all the mining in Texas and Arkansas." Prior to living in the hut, Wiley had run a "mining" operation on another part of his property in the Ouachitas, known as Baby Ruth City, located near a large cold spring at the base of Hanna Mountain. A group of "miners," including Wiley, had lived there in a bunkhouse, which stood four miles from Grandpa's cabin, during the late 1880s. This was a time when local newspapers reported widely of a gold rush spreading through parts of the Brushy and Cossatot (Ark.) valleys.

3. KNIGHTS OF THE GOLDEN CIRCLE

1. See *Reports on the Order of the American Knights, Records of the Office of the Judge Advocate General*, National Archives, Washington, D.C. Also, see Joseph Holt Papers, Library of Congress, Washington, D.C., and "Official Report of the Judge Advocate General on the Order of American Knights," published in *The War of Rebellion: A Compilation of the Official Records of the Union and Confederate Armies* (Washington, D.C., 1880–1901), Ser. 2, Vol. 7, pp. 930–53.

2. An exception among mainstream Civil War treatments is the Pulitzer-Prize–winning book by Princeton University historian James M. McPherson, *Battle Cry of Freedom: The Civil War Era* (New York: Ballantine/Oxford Uni-

versity Press, 1988), which makes multiple mentions of KGC activity before and during the war. To be sure, McPherson does not suggest that the KGC had a huge membership, that it existed after the Civil War, or that it buried gold and other treasure to finance a second civil war. McPherson relies heavily on Wood Gray, *The Hidden Civil War: The Story of the Copperheads* (New York: Viking, 1942), and various works by Frank Klement (see below).

3. Frank L. Klement, *Dark Lanterns: Secret Political Societies, Conspiracies, and Treason Trials in the Civil War* (Baton Rouge: Louisiana State University Press, 1984). This narrowly focused academic book deals extensively with the prewar and wartime KGC in the Midwest, and its offshoots. Klement's analysis downplays the scope and power of the KGC, describing it as a movement largely restricted to a few states—Ohio, Indiana, Illinois, Iowa—and one at best with overblown potential. It also belittles another known and well-chronicled prewar and wartime KGC stronghold: the Republic, and then state, of Texas. The KGC's strength in Texas is described in the first chapters of Donald S. Frazier's *Blood & Treasure: Confederate Empire in the Southwest* (College Station: Texas A&M University Press, 1995). Also helpful on Texan and Southern expansionism as eventually expressed through the KGC's Southern strongholds is Robert E. May's *The Southern Dream of a Caribbean Empire: 1854–1861* (Baton Rouge: Louisiana State University Press, 1973). At the opposite end of the spectrum from Klement's dismissive treatment of the KGC is a speculative yet in parts compelling book, Anton Chaitkin's *Treason in America* (New York: New Benjamin Franklin House, 1984), which argues that the KGC was part of a powerful, internationally active, British-Swiss–masterminded conspiracy to bring about a divided United States. Such internal division, the theory goes, would keep America weak and thus beholden to certain European power elites.

4. For primary source overview on the early KGC and its goals, see a September 1859 pamphlet, *Rules, Regulations and Principles of the K.G.C.*, in George Bickley Papers, Reports on the Order of American Knights, National Archives. Bickley is the presumed author. Also, in Official Reports, see government intelligence on the KGC in the John P. Sanderson Papers. For secondary mid-nineteenth-century authored sources, see I. Winslow Ayer, *The Great North-Western Conspiracy in All Its Startling Details* (Chicago: Rounds & James, 1865); Henry Conkling, *An Inside View of the Rebellion* (Cincinnati: C. Clark, 1864); and Thomas Prentice Kettell, *History of the Great Rebellion* (Cincinnati: F. A. Howe, 1866). Among twentieth-century secondary sources, see Ollinger Crenshaw, "The Knights of the Golden Circle: The Career of George Bickley," *American Historical Review* 47 (October 1941), for an even-handed view of the controversial, figurative head of the public KGC. Also see George Fort Milton, *Abraham Lincoln and the Fifth Column* (New York: Vanguard, 1942), a well-researched analysis although limited by its focus on the role of Bickley and the KGC in the North.

5. For a sketch of KGC operations in California, see "K.G.C.—A Tale of Fort Alcatraz," *The Overland Monthly* (San Francisco, Ca.), March 1888.

6. See Conkling, p. 7, for an analysis of the KGC's aim of establishing an agrarian-based oligarchy or monarchy in the South and perhaps beyond. The author cites numerous editorials from Southern newspapers and various correspondences. He also cites a February 1862 address by Andrew Johnson (who would become the Southern Democrat vice president to Abraham Lincoln in Lincoln's second term) to the Third Minnesota Regiment, near Nashville, Tennessee. Conkling, p. 6, writes that Johnson had said that "he knew the leaders of this rebellion well, both personally and politically, and he declared it was the firm determination of the rebel leaders to overthrow popular Government, and establish a despotism instead of our present liberal institutions, and that the people of the South would not submit to a President who had sprung from the common people, as Abe Lincoln had." Compare this with Bickley's KGC manifesto: "We aim at the establishment of a great Democratic Monarchy—a Republican Empire, which shall vie in grandeur with the Old Roman Empire," as stated in *Rules, Regulations and Principles of the K.G.C.*, p. 57. Conkling's brief 23-page book was published just months before the April 14, 1865, assassination of Lincoln.

7. Ayer, pp. 15–16. Ayer is mistaken in saying that the KGC "dissolved" and was replaced by the Order of American Knights.

8. McPherson, pp. 560, 591–609; Gray, pp. 112–15.

9. Klement, pp. 23–33; Ayer, p. 20.

10. Klement, p. 25, cites *Indianapolis Daily Journal* and state governor Oliver Morton as sources.

11. JohnWarner Barber, *The Loyal West in Times of Rebellion* (Cincinnati: F. A. Howe, 1865), pp. 276–79.

12. Klement, pp. 26–33, 141.

13. See, for instance, reports from Brig. Gen. Henry B. Carrington and Lafayette C. Baker, Records of the Office of the Judge Advocate General, National Archives.

14. Charles G. Leland, "The Knights of the Golden Circle," *Continental Monthly*, May 1862, Vol. I, Issue 5, p. 574.

15. Ibid. Leland refers to quote in piece cited above.

16. Ayer, p. 18.

17. McPherson, p. 597.

18. None of the Union's intelligence reports have any substantive information on the KGC's core Southern-based operations.

19. For a nineteenth-century account of the riot, see John Benson Lossing, *Our Country: A Household History for All Readers* (New York: Johnson, Wilson & Co., 1875), pp. 1630–32.

20. Ibid.

21. Conkling, p. 16. The dogged author provides evidence of this view in a Sept. 21, 1863 letter from James Murray Mason, a Confederate diplomat and KGC operative, to the British foreign office's Earl Russell. The letter notes that Confederate President Jefferson Davis had, by that time, written off British intervention as a non-starter, following several years of "overtures" by Mason.

4. COMING HOME: A GOLD-FILLED LEGACY

1. Polk County Circuit Court Records, August Term, 1884, Thursday, August 28, Case #133 Against T. A. Hatfield, for Murder.

2. *Fort Smith* (Arkansas) *Elevator*, July 18, 1884, p. 2; and *Daily Arkansas Gazette* (Little Rock), July 11, 1884, p. 6.

3. Mining claims, Polk County Courthouse, Mena, Arkansas.

4. Letter to Bob Brewer from J. Michael Howard, Arkansas Geological Commission. "There has been manganese mining in this area, but despite a great deal of prospecting for gold and silver, to our knowledge, none has been discovered, much less mined," Howard wrote.

5. A number of articles appeared in the *Mena Star* in 1896–97, boasting (erroneously) of gold being found.

6. Interview with Jim Harris, Hatfield, August 2001.

7. Death certificate, William Chambers Dobson, Beasley-Wood Funeral Home, Mena, Arkansas. Cause of death cited is heart attack and stroke.

8. *The Illustrated Book of Trees and Shrubs* (London: Octopus Books, 1985), p. 15.

9. For an insightful analysis of the origins of American surveyor terms, see the recently published book by Andro Linklater, *Measuring America: How an Untamed Wilderness Shaped the United States and Fulfilled the Promise of Democracy* (New York: Walker & Co., 2002).

5. THE KGC: THE HIDDEN HISTORY

1. See *Joseph Holt Papers*, Library of Congress, by far the most trenchant analysis in the government's files of the prewar and wartime KGC.

2. Ibid., pp. 7–8. Holt gives credence to Vallandigham's own estimate of 500,000.

3. Ibid., pp. 14, 16.

4. Ibid., p. 16.

5. Ibid., p. 29.

6. Ibid., pp. 26–27.

7. For a detailed history of the Scottish Rite of Freemasonry in America, see William L. Fox, *Lodge of the Double-Headed Eagle: Two Centuries of Scottish Rite Freemasonry in America's Southern Jurisdiction* (Fayetteville: University of Arkansas Press, 1997).

8. Robert Penn Warren, *The Legacy of the Civil War* (Lincoln: University of Nebraska Press/Bison Books Edition, 1998), p. 87.

9. See C. Hugh Holman's introduction to *Partisan Leader: A Tale of the Future* by Nathaniel Beverly Tucker, 1836, as reprinted by the University of North Carolina Press, 1971. Tucker's "fictional" story is a thinly veiled account of KGC-type subversive activity in Virginia during the antebellum period, replete with descriptions of codes and secret grips. Originally "secretly" published in Washington, D.C., the novel clearly has John C. Calhoun as a disguised philosophical protagonist, in the view of Holman and others.

10. See Stephen Joel Trachtenberg's foreword to Fox's *Lodge of the Double-*

Headed Eagle. Trachtenberg is president of George Washington University in Washington, D.C.

11. This is an unanswerable question and the subject of lively debate. One informative contemporary source on Templar history and possible Freemasonic associations is John J. Robinson, *Dungeon, Fire and Sword: The Knights Templar in the Crusades* (New York: M. Evans, 1991), pp. 470–76.

12. See Laurence Gardner, *The Illustrated Bloodline of the Holy Grail* (New York: Barnes & Noble Books, 2000), p. 207.

13. For a solid analysis of the origins and modern influence of Freemasonry in Europe and America—and its possible Knight Templar connections—see John L. Robinson, *Born in Blood: The Lost Secrets of Freemasonry* (New York: M. Evans & Co., 1989). See, in particular, pp. 181–84 on Ramsay, and for other references to the order's ill-defined origins, see pp. 185, 281, 287, 288 and 291. Also, see Fox on Ramsay, pp. 8, 25 and 26. In addition, see Michael Baigent, Richard Leigh and Henry Lincoln, *Holy Blood, Holy Grail* (London: Dell, 1983), pp. 145–50, for a discussion of both Radclyffe and Ramsay roles.

14. See brochure, *Presenting the Ancient and Accepted Scottish Rite of Freemasonry,* The Supreme Council (Mother Council of the World), Southern Jurisdiction U.S.A., House of the Temple, 1733 Sixteenth St. NW, Washington, D.C., 1998.

15. Jonathan Blanchard, *Scottish Rite Masonry Illustrated* (Chicago: Ezra A. Cook, 1944, reprinted 1957), pp. 34–35.

16. Leland, *Continental Monthly,* p. 573; Winslow, p. 5.

17. Holt Report, p. 12.

18. *An Authentic Exposition of the K.G.C., Knights of the Golden Circle, or, A History of Secession from 1834 to 1861* (Indianapolis: Perrine, 1861). (Hereafter, *Exposition.*) The anonymously written exposition served as the basis for much of the official information passed on to President Lincoln and other Union officials in the early stages of the war. The authors of this book are convinced that its author is James M. Hiatt, author of *The Voter's Text Book* (Indianapolis: Asher, Adams & Higgins, 1868). Both texts are published in Indianapolis and there is significant overlap in prose and subject matter. See, for instance, *Exposition,* p. 15, on the expulsion of 25,000 Germans from Texas by the KGC, and then p. 151 of Hiatt's book on the same subject. Hiatt, the authors believe, was a former Southern-based KGC member who fled the organization and sought refuge in Indiana during the latter part of the war. There he became a journalist/historian. Moreover, the authors believe that Hiatt is the author behind the pseudonym "Edmund Wright" in the book cited in endnote 23 in this chapter. The reasoning is similar: subject matter, specific turns of phrase and in-depth knowledge and observations of the inner workings of the KGC.

19. Ibid., p. 5.

20. Ibid., p. 9. In addition, for early KGC pro–slave trade polemics see James B. D. De Bow's *Commercial Review of the South and West* (De Bow's Review) on "The African Slave-Trade," July 1857, pp. 47–56; March 1855, pp. 297–305; and January 1855, pp. 16–20. Also, on slave trade, see McPherson, p. 103.

21. For a thoroughly researched and footnoted analysis of Quitman's role in overseas expansionism and possible Scottish Rite Masonic motivations, see Antonio de la Cova, "Filibusters and Freemasons: The Sworn Obligation," *Journal of the Early Republic* 17, No. 1 (Spring 1997), pp. 95–120. De la Cova, a professor of Latin American studies, does not mention the KGC. For a solid biography on Quitman, see Robert E. May, *John A. Quitman: Old South Crusader* (Baton Rouge: Louisiana State University Press, 1985). May does not mention the KGC.

22. The engraving, from a portrait, is on display in the Gratz Collection of the Historical Society of Pennsylvania in Philadelphia, Case 4, Box 38.

23. See *Narrative of Edmund Wright: His Adventures with and Escape from the Knights of the Golden Circle* (Edmund Wright—pseudonym; J.R. Hawley Publishers, 1864), on file at the Library of Congress. This book (hereafter, *Edmund Wright*) is valuable for any scholarly analysis of the KGC in that its insider-type account by an anonymous author goes into a great deal of credible, visual detail—corroborating other visual accounts of KGC symbolism and regalia. There is some probability—given similar turns of phrase and data provided—that the author is the same for the 1861 *Exposition*. The overall credibility of *Edmund Wright* is buttressed by several key historical observations in the narrative. For example, on page 137, the author describes being in New Orleans in early 1860 and hearing about a coup within the KGC ranks in which "Bickley was deposed, and an entirely new government inaugurated." As Klement points out in *Dark Lanterns*, pp. 10–11, Bickley was all but tossed out by KGC operatives in New Orleans after his failed 1860 raids in Mexico and then, subsequently, managed to recover some of his status by calling for a KGC convention in Raleigh, N.C. in May of that year, which served to restore his pro-forma authority. At that May 7–11 convention in Raleigh, Bickley asserted that the KGC would, if well managed, "lead to the disenthrallment of the cotton States from the oppressive majority of the manufacturing and commercial interests of the North." Such comments marked a clear departure from filibustering (vis-à-vis Mexico) and toward the bigger, more salient issue of secession at home. See also Crenshaw, p. 39.

24. Quitman's rise to Supreme Council (33rd-degree) status reported in *Freemason's Monthly Magazine*, February 1, 1848, as cited in Ray Baker Harris, *History of the Supreme Council*, p. 236. Also see May, *Old South Crusader*, p. 373 endnotes on Quitman's being Grand Master of the Mississippi Grand Lodge, 1826–36 and again in 1840 and 1845–46.

25. Harris, ibid.

26. May, *Old South Crusader*, pp. 60–63.

27. McPherson, p. 4.

28. De la Cova describes Order of the Lone Star intrigue in New Orleans. Also see Milton, p. 66.

29. *Exposition*, pp. 6–12.

30. See *Exposition*, p. 23, which states, as far as the armed KGC strength in the North was concerned: "At no time previous to the bombardment of Fort

Sumter was it presumed that the number of men to be counted on from the North would fall below 100,000."

31. There is little reliable independent biography on Cushing. Voluminous primary source material is available through Caleb Cushing Papers at the Library of Congress.

32. De la Cova, p. 98. Caleb Cushing Papers, Correspondence: George W. Sargent to Cushing.

33. *Franklin Repository and Transcript*, December 5, 1860, p. 4.

34. *Exposition*, p. 21.

35. Milton, p. 33, notes: "In December 1861, the former president was charged with having had a hand in the organization of the Knights of the Golden Circle in New England. The undiplomatic (U.S. Secretary of State) Seward wrote him of these charges and asked him for an explanation."

36. *Exposition*, p. 36, provides detailed analysis of how Floyd, as U.S. Secretary of War under Buchanan, managed to order the shipment south of more than 100,000 weapons before the outbreak of war. These weapons, all stored at Southern-based U.S. armories, for the most part were absorbed or seized by Confederate forces when those armories were abandoned by U.S. troops.

37. Cushing correspondence in Cushing Papers at the Library of Congress includes letters he exchanged with Jefferson Davis, Franklin Pierce, Albert Pike and others likely associated with the KGC. Cushing's behavior is somewhat reminiscent of the much better known, earlier intriguer and conspirator, Aaron Burr, the former U.S. vice president under Jefferson. Burr played various sides of the political aisle against each other in an opaque strategy apparently aimed at dismemberment of the young Union. His machinations in the early 1800s involved various plots to seize territory in the trans-Mississippi West, the Ohio Valley/Old Northwest, the Deep South and Mexico—a possible forerunner scheme for the KGC, some might argue. Burr's son-in-law, Joseph Alston, was a prominent plantation owner and defender of slavery in South Carolina, eventually becoming the state's governor. Burr and Alston were known to be close. It might also be noted that Burr was given to encrypted correspondence. For a recently published, intriguing exploration of Burr's treasonous plotting, see Buckner F. Melton's *Aaron Burr: Conspiracy to Treason* (New York: John Wiley & Sons, 2002).

38. *Vanity Fair*, March 30, 1861, New York. See column entitled "Philp, His Hand-Book."

39. See Cushing Papers, Library of Congress, Letters from Albert Pike, March 2, March 14, May 25, 1843, as pointed out by Chaitkin, p. 185.

40. *Continental Monthly*, May 1862, p. 576.

41. See Fox, who dedicates several chapters to Pike and his history with the Scottish Rite. Also, for a largely tongue-in-cheek overview of the Scottish Rite, see "Men in Hats: Secrets of Freemasonry Revealed. Fezzes, Sphinxes and Secret Handshakes," in Peter Carlson's cover-story, *Washington Post Magazine*, November 25, 2001. The article makes the point that the popularity of Freemasonry in America has fluctuated, and that it is now in a downswing: from a peak

of more than 4 million members in 1960 to less than 2 million today. A lack of interest in ornate ritual among younger Americans is cited. The article does not mention the role of Pike in the Confederacy or in the KGC, nor does it mention the Scottish Rite's mooted association with the original Ku Klux Klan.

42. Fox, pp. 10–22.

43. Ray Baker Harris, *History of the Supreme Council 33rd Degree, Mother Council of the World, Ancient and Accepted Scottish Rite of Freemasonry, Southern Jurisdiction, USA, 1801–1861*, Washington, D.C., 1964, p. 277.

44. Fox, pp. 74–75.

45. Ibid., p. 69.

46. Harris, p. 271.

47. *Edmund Wright*, pp. 54–55.

48. Conkling, p. 8.

49. *Edmund Wright*, p. 56.

50. Harris, p. 271.

51. See *Exposition*, p. 30; Kettell, p. 32; Conkling, p. 8.

52. For Pike's role in recruiting Indian Nations to the Confederate cause, see Walter Lee Brown, *A Life of Albert Pike* (Fayetteville: University of Arkansas, 1997), for detailed treatments. Also see Fox, as well as Frank Cunningham, *General Stand Watie's Confederate Indians* (San Antonio: Naylor, 1959, Reprint, Norman: University of Oklahoma Press, 1998).

53. Brown, p. 318.

54. Robert L. Duncan, *Reluctant General: The Life and Times of Albert Pike* (New York: E. P. Dutton, 1961), p. 159.

55. *Arkansas True Democrat*, August 29, 1861, newspaper clipping.

56. Holt Report, p. 2.

57. The Cherokee connection might also explain the KGC's apparent use of deformed oak trees as pointers along their treasure trails in Oklahoma and other states. See the self-published *Cry of the Eagle: History and Legends of the Cherokee Indians and Their Buried Treasures* by Forest C. Wade, 1969, Cummings, Ga. Wade includes several pictures of "bent-knee" trees. He does not mention the KGC.

58. Brown, pp. 425–26.

59. In addition to the *Exposition*, articles appeared in July 1861 in *Louisville Daily Journal* and *Louisville Daily Courier*, as cited in Klement, p. 13.

60. *Edmund Wright*, p. 21.

61. See photo and caption of Pike's "jewel," in Fox, in photo section following Chapter 4.

62. *Edmund Wright*, p. 20.

63. Ibid., pp. 43–53.

64. See illustration of Scottish Rite symbolism chart in Fox (in photo section).

65. *Exposition*, p. 12.

66. Kettell, p. 31.

67. Ayer, p. 16.

68. Allen E. Roberts, *House Undivided: The Story of Freemasonry and the Civil War*, Fulton, Missouri Lodge of Research, pp. 10–20.

69. Letter from Robert Bethell to Abraham Lincoln, April 18, 1861, The Abraham Lincoln Papers, Topic: The Knights of the Golden Circle, Library of Congress.

70. Letter from Samuel T. Glover to Abraham Lincoln, Sept. 29, 1861, The Abraham Lincoln Papers, Topic: Relations with Mexico, Library of Congress.

71. Letter from Thomas Ewing to Abraham Lincoln, April 9, 1862, The Abraham Lincoln Papers, Topic: Loyalty of General McClellan, Library of Congress.

72. *Exposition*, p. 49.

73. Ibid., p. 75.

74. Francis Wilson, *John Wilkes Booth, Fact and Fiction of Lincoln's Assassination* (Boston and New York: Houghton Mifflin, 1929), p. 29.

75. *Exposition*, p. 57.

76. *The Great Conspiracy* (Philadelphia: Barclay & Co., 1866), p. 26. In Rare Book Collection, Library of Congress.

77. Ibid.

78. Ibid., p. 101.

79. Izola Forrester, *This One Mad Act* (Boston: Hale, Cushman & Flint, 1937), p. 118.

80. Ibid., preface.

81. See William A. Tidwell, James O. Hall, and David W. Gaddy, *Come Retribution: The Confederate Secret Service and the Assassination of Abraham Lincoln* (Jackson: University of Mississippi Press, 1989).

82. Robert D. Meade, *Judah P. Benjamin: Confederate Statesman* (New York and London: Oxford University Press, 1943), p. 300. Another biography worth exploring is Eli N. Evans's *Judah P. Benjamin: The Jewish Confederate* (New York: The Free Press, 1988).

83. Robert N. Rosen, *The Jewish Confederates* (Columbia: University of South Carolina Press, 2000), pp. 320–21. Rosen cites diary of former Lincoln confidant and U.S. senator, Orville H. Browning.

84. Ibid., p. 315.

85. Hines bore an uncanny resemblance to Booth and was mistaken for the actor while fleeing to Canada from Detroit in the days immediately following the assassination. Described by biographer Horan as "the most dangerous man in the Confederacy," the stealthy Confederate secret agent operated in high circles of both the KGC and Scottish Rite Freemasonry. Significantly, Hines was a close friend of KGC member and Confederate Secret Service agent John Yates Beall, who had been hung—despite repeated appeals to Lincoln for clemency following his capture in New York—by Union forces on February 24, 1865. According to Horan, the proud Virginian Beall had demanded that his hanging "be speedily and terribly avenged." U.S. Senator Orville H. Browning, a close friend and confidant of Lincoln's, made an intriguing entry in his diary (on file at the Library of Congress) soon after the assassination. "I am at a loss as to the class of persons who instigated the crime—whether it was the rebel leaders; the

Copperheads among ourselves, in conjunction with foreign emissaries; gold speculators; or the friends and accomplices of Beall, who was recently hung at New York," he wrote, adding: "I am inclined to the latter opinion." In the seconds after Booth shot Lincoln, the president's assassin had shouted, *"Sic semper tyrannis!"* The slogan, which translates to "Thus always to tyrants!" happens to be the motto of Virginia.

86. James D. Horan, *Confederate Agent: A Discovery in History* (New York: Crown, 1954), p. 13.

87. Edward Steers, Jr., *Blood on the Moon: The Assassination of Abraham Lincoln* (Lexington: University Press of Kentucky, 2001), p. 7.

88. Fox, pp. 77–79.

89. John L. Robinson, *Born in Blood: The Lost Secrets of Freemasonry* (New York: M. Evans & Co., 1989), p. 328.

90. Walter Lee Brown, "Albert Pike, 1809–1891" (Ph.D. dissertation, University of Texas, 1955), p. 783, as cited in Fox, pp. 81, 435.

91. Philip Dray, *At the Hands of Persons Unknown: The Lynching of Black America* (New York: Random House, 2002), p. ix.

92. Fox, pp. 81–82.

93. Ibid. Pike, indeed, is not made in the mold of the Southern fire-eater. He does fit the profile, however, of the calm, collected multifaceted powerbroker behind the hidden KGC.

94. Brown, *A Life of Albert Pike*, pp. 439–40.

95. See Mark M. Boatner III, *The Civil War Dictionary* (New York: Vintage Books, 1988), pp. 295–96.

96. Fox, p. 81.

97. Eric Foner, *Who Owns History?* (New York: Hill and Wang, 2002), p. 196.

98. See William C. Davis, *An Honorable Defeat: The Last Days of the Confederate Government* (New York: Harcourt, 2001). Davis makes numerous mentions of "treasure train."

99. Rosen, p. 351.

100. William C. Davis, *Breckinridge: Statesman, Soldier, Symbol* (Baton Rouge: Louisiana State, 1974), pp. 559–63.

101. McPherson, p. 763.

102. Horan, p. 295.

103. See Caleb Cushing Papers and Breckinridge Family Papers, Library of Congress, for mining claims.

104. *Exposition*, p. 50.

105. Brown, *A Life of Albert Pike*, pp. 464–65.

106. Ibid.

6. RETRACING HISTORY IN THE ARKANSAS WOODS

1. Interview with Bob Tilley, August 2001, Hatfield.

2. George A. Mitchell, "Twin Springs Spanish Gold," *Frontier Times*, December 1969, pp. 32–33.

3. Interview with Don Fretz, August 2001, Hatfield.

4. Bob Brewer interview with Mitchell Cogburn, 1992, Hatfield. Also see article by Ida S. Cobb, "Mountain Legend of Albert Pike's Two Years in the Ouachitas," in *Mena* (Ark.) *Evening Star*, April 22, 1939. Most of the Cobb observations correspond to Cogburn's recollections, but not all.

5. J. Mark Bond, "One Black Pot with a Yellow Fortune," *Old West*, Fall 1970, pp. 18–19, 54–55.

6. Del Schrader (with Jesse James III), *Jesse James Was One of His Names: The Greatest Cover Up in History by the Famous Outlaw Who Lived 73 Incredible Lives* (Arcadia: Santa Anita Press, 1975).

7. Ibid., p.187.

8. Ibid., p. 250.

9. Ibid., pp. 239–41.

7. JESSE JAMES, KGC FIELD COMMANDER

1. Biographies of Jesse James are too many to mention, but one of the best regarded is William A. Settle's *Jesse James Was His Name; Or, Fact and Fiction Concerning the Career of the Notorious James Brothers of Missouri* (Columbia: University of Missouri Press, 1966). For a period piece along the same lines, see Frank Triplett's original 1882 *The Life, Times & Treacherous Death of Jesse James* (with introduction in reprint edition by Joseph Snell), as reprinted by Konecky & Konecky/Swallow Press, New York, 1970.

2. T. J. Stiles, *Jesse James: Last Rebel of the Civil War* (New York: Knopf), pp. 6 and 99.

3. "Lost and Found . . . and Found . . . and Found," *U.S. News & World Report: Mysteries of History*, July 24–31, 2000, as shown on map, pp. 52–53, and as mentioned on p. 79.

4. The debate has even led to the inconclusive exhumations of bodies long ago buried. In the first instance, the remains of the professed "real" Jesse Woodson James (the one most historians accept as having been shot and killed in 1882) were unearthed in 1995 from their resting place in Kearney, Missouri. In the forensic examination led by George Washington University law professor James E. Starrs, a DNA test supposedly proved that the remains were those of JWJ. Some observers claim that the source of the genetic material tested for DNA—a tooth—did not come from the grave site in question but rather from a Missouri museum. A second exhumation, this time of the long-lived, self-proclaimed Jesse Woodson James (a.k.a. Frank Dalton), occurred on May 30, 2000, in Granbury, Texas, some forty miles southwest of Fort Worth. Those sponsoring the exhumation, notably Bud Hardcastle of Purcell, Oklahoma, wound up uncovering the skeletal remains of someone else, a one-armed man by the name of Henry Holland. The mishap, according to Hardcastle (interviews May 2000, March–April 2002), was the result of the tombstone having been placed incorrectly. Also see numerous articles, including Penny Owen, "Outlaw Won't Rest in Peace," *The Sunday Oklahoman*, May 7, 2000, Oklahoma Now section, p. 1. Hardcastle is awaiting a court decision to attempt to reopen the correct grave of J. Frank Dalton in Granbury.

5. John N. Edwards, *Shelby and his men: or the war in the West* (Cincinnati: Miami Printing and Publishing, 1867), p. 379.

6. See John N. Edwards, *Noted Guerillas or the Warfare of the Border* (St. Louis: Bryan, Brand, 1877).

7. Schrader and James (Howk), see pp. 97–132.

8. Ibid., p. 5.

9. Ibid., pp. 2–3.

10. Ibid., p. 5.

11. Ibid., p. 98.

12. Ibid., pp. 39–40.

13. Ibid., p. 6.

14. Ibid.

15. Ibid.

16. Ibid.

17. Ibid., p. 7.

18. Ralph P. Ganis, *Uncommon Men: A Secret Network of Jesse James Revealed* (St. Petersburg: Southern Heritage Press, 2000). See preface, pp. viii–xi, and 36.

19. Ibid., see preface, p. x.

20. Schrader and James (Howk), pp. 2, 7, 43, 44 and throughout.

21. Ibid., p. 189.

22. Ibid., pp. 2, 50, 51, 274.

23. In addition to Schrader and James (Howk), see J. L. James (Howk), *Jesse James and the Lost Cause* (New York: Pageant Press, 1961), pp. 87, 102 and throughout.

24. Schrader and James (Howk), p. 57.

25. Ibid., p. 254.

26. Ibid., pp. 66–80.

27. Ibid., pp. 70–79.

28. Ibid., pp. 1, 9–35, and throughout.

29. Ibid., p. 31.

30. Ibid., pp. 28–33.

31. Ibid., pp. 68–69.

32. Ibid., pp. 2–7, 51 and throughout.

33. Ibid., p. 44.

34. Ibid., p. 7.

35. Settle, p. 75.

36. Ted P. Yeatman, *Frank and Jesse James: The Story Behind the Legend* (Nashville: Cumberland House, 2000), pp. 209–10.

37. Schrader and James (Howk), p. 8.

38. Ibid., p. 275.

39. Ibid., p. 187 (Rosicrucian), p. 4 (alchemy). For an excellent historical analysis of these centuries' old themes, see Frances A. Yates, *The Rosicrucian Enlightenment* (New York: Routledge, 1972, reprinted 2000).

40. Fox, p. 76, cites an unpublished manuscript and correspondence of Hutchins.

41. Ibid. Also see Yates on Rosicrucians and alchemy throughout her academic analysis, including mentions of Isaac Newton.

42. See Chaitkin, p. 56, who cites R. Swinburne Clymer, *The Book of Rosicruciae*, published by the Rosicrucians, Quakerstown, Pa., 1946–49, Vol. II, pp. 70–71.

43. Schrader and James (Howk), p. 4.

44. Ibid., p. 207.

45. Ibid., pp. 186, 250.

46. Ibid., p. 241.

47. Ibid., pp. 240–41.

48. Ibid., pp. 240–59.

49. Ibid., p. 208.

50. Ibid., and p. 244.

51. James (Howk), p. 33.

52. Schrader and James (Howk), p. 209.

53. Ibid., p. 245.

54. Ibid., p. 250.

55. Ibid., p. 242.

56. Ibid., p. 210.

57. Ibid., pp. 188, 210.

58. Ibid., pp. 188–98.

59. Ibid., p. 207.

60. Ibid., p. 200.

61. Ibid., p. 207.

62. Ibid., p. 187.

63. Ibid., see chapter "The Odyssey of John Wilkes Booth," pp. 133–42.

64. Ibid., p. 135.

65. Henry J. Walker, *Jesse James "The Outlaw"* (Des Moines: Wallace-Homestead, 1961).

66. Ibid., p. 70.

67. Ibid., p. 155.

68. Ibid., p. 133.

69. Ibid., p. 18.

8. THE HUNT EXTENDS TO OKLAHOMA

1. Copy of suspected Jesse James treasure map in Brewer's possession, as provided by Bud Hardcastle. Hardcastle says the source of the original map was Oklahoman Joe Hunter, who in the 1930s and '40s reportedly came into possession of several maps, gold bullion and other items believed to have belonged to Jesse James. Griffith showed Brewer the photocopied map months after their initial acquaintance, but declined to give him a copy. The map is filled with sketches of trees, springs and trails. It also contains a drawing of a neat box, with the word *gold* written next to it: the spot being the top of an isosceles triangle drawn in the northeast quadrant. Other illustrations include a set of small rectangular *graves* and another rectangle designated as a "gun berrel" [sic]. But

by far the most captivating component of the map is a large circle, containing text and illustrations, on the left-hand (west) side of the page. In the middle lies a stick-figure turtle, with a dotted line extending from its head in a bee-line to the gold box. Below the turtle is what looks like a double fishhook—or two *J*s abutting each other, back to back—and the date *1880*. On the inner perimeter of the circle are the words, written backwards, *Find Gun Berrel Near Creek*. Next to the circle is a large *4* figure, with the numbers *4* and *16* attached, perhaps denoting some kind of surveyor mark.

2. Schrader and James (Howk), pp. 237, 273.

3. Videotape in Brewer's possession shows the inscriptions in detail.

4. In one of dozens of letters from Griffith in Brewer's possession, Griffith describes looking forward to working together, November 23–26.

5. Videotape in Brewer's possession.

6. Letter from Griffith to Brewer. The find is also recorded by Griffith on videotape, where he shows the gold coins recovered.

7. Brewer subsequently returned to the site with the Gillespie sisters, and, through his own map-decoding work, showed the Oklahoma women two small holes where Griffith apparently had dug up the pistol and spittoon filled with gold. As he had suspected, it lay on a line running from the gun barrel site through the academy, as the code had suggested. There was no "river" nearby, only a dry wash. Griffith apparently had tried to pull one over on him as to the precise location.

8. See photo of Civil War–era pistol in Walker's *Jesse James "The Outlaw"* (Des Moines: Wallace-Homestead, 1961). See preface.

9. THE WOLF MAP

1. Del Schrader, "$100 Billion in Treasure—The Search for Rebel Gold," *Los Angeles Herald Examiner*, April 22, 1973.

2. Jesse Lee James (Orvus Lee Howk) letters (copies) in Bob Brewer's possession.

3. See *The History of Codes and Cipher in the United States Prior to WWI*, edited by Wayne G. Barker (Laguna Hills, Calif.: Aegean Park Press, 1978). The source for the Confederate code is the History Section of the Army Security Agency, Washington, D.C., 1946.

4. Among the maps that show Beaver Creek and Stinking Creek is one on file at the Library of Congress, cartography division, "Chickasaw Country and Contiguous Portions of the Indian Territory," prepared by First Lt. E. H. Ruffner, chief engineer, military department of the Missouri, Fort Leavenworth, Kansas, November 1872. Another map used was G.W. & C.B. Colton's Map of Indian Territory, 1873.

5. Information on the rectangular survey system can be obtained from numerous sources. This background was provided by a 1969 Rand McNally map of the Township and Range Survey System of the United States.

6. The baseline used to locate the Wolf Map site appears to be very close to the head of Stinking Creek on the old, large-scale maps from the 1870s. How-

ever, on modern maps, the line and the old Fort Smith stage route are some twelve miles north of the Wolf Map's location. It is likely that those burying the treasure and making the map knew of the difference in distance but used it both as a generic reference point and as a small misnomer to keep any outsider from finding the exact place too quickly.

7. Steve Wilson, *Oklahoma Treasures and Treasure Tales* (Norman: University of Oklahoma Press, 1976).

8. See articles, *Lawton* (Okla.) *Constitution*, Feb. 29, 1948, and May 19, 1948. Among the discoveries revealed by Hunter were buried metal pick heads and wedges, all apparently clues on a Jesse James treasure trail. Notably, three months after Hunter first disclosed his finds in Lawton, in Feb. 1948, he received a visit from J. Frank Dalton.

9. See Wilson, ibid., p. 138. Wilson's book does not mention the watch's hand-setting. This information came to Bob separately.

10. THE WOLF EMERGES

1. The "Treasure Vacation Extravaganza '94" was—at the time—the largest-ever gathering of the U.S. treasure-hunting fraternity: a four-day camp attended by leading treasure-hunting personalities in America. Dorian Cook, a well-known treasure writer, organized the TVE event, at which the KGC would be a major topic of public discussion for the first time.

2. Letter from Griffith in Brewer's possession.

3. Letter written by Jesse Lee James (Orvus Howk) in Brewer's possession.

4. Interview with Sheriff Mike Ogelsby, Mena, Arkansas, who confirmed Brewer's reporting of incident.

5. Letters from Griffith in Brewer's possession.

11. THE EMPTY PIT

1. Videotape in possession of Brewer.

2. Copy of 1995 Gillespie fax to Michael Griffith, and extensive interviews with Gillespie sisters, 1998–2002.

3. Copy of January 8, 1996 letter from Michael Griffith to Jo Anne and Ceci Gillespie. Griffith's letter denies any trespassing occurred and asserts that he did not know that the Gillespies owned the property "until this matter was brought up."

4. Michael Griffith KGC sales kit, 2001, in Brewer's possession.

12. THE LOST DUTCHMAN LEGEND

1. See, for instance, Estee Conaster, *The Sterling Legend: The Facts Behind the Lost Dutchman Mine* (Baldwin Park, Ca.: Gem Guides Book Co., 1972). Conaster's book provides a straightforward and detailed assessment of the myth and controversy. Conaster asserts that a significant cache of gold was found secreted in a cave in the Superstitions in the late 1940s (pp. 51–52), but says there is no way of knowing whether the cache was related to the Dutchman legend. Also see T. E. Glover, *The Lost Dutchman Mine of Jacob Waltz* (Phoenix,

Ariz.: Cowboy Miner Productions, 1998). Glover provides a well-researched, comprehensive look into the Dutchman saga. Also consult short works published by local Apache Junction historian and Dutchman researcher, Tom J. Kollenborn. An excellent overview appears in *The Arizona Republic*, Sunday Magazine, October 20, 1991, in a feature by Charles Kelly, "Mine of Legend: Lost Dutchman Still Stirs Golden Dreams." The first newspaper article about Thomas's search for the lost mine appeared in the *Arizona Weekly Gazette*, September 1, 1892, under the headline, "A Queer Quest: Another 'Lost Mine' Being Hunted for by a Woman." The brief article was clearly skeptical.

2. James F. Carberry, "Did the Old Dutchman Leave a Big Gold Mine or Merely a Legend?" *Wall Street Journal*, October 18, 1971, p. 1.

3. "Lost and Found . . . and Found . . . and Found," *U.S. News & World Report: Mysteries of History*, July 24–31, 2000, p. 53. The Lost Dutchman's mine caption is printed directly below the same magazine's reference to "Jesse James's gold." This blurb is based on the description of the Dutchman legend provided by the official Arizona State Parks Website: http://www.pr.state.az.us/text/lostdutchlegend.html.

4. *Life*, "Mysterious Maps to Lost Gold Mines," June 12, 1964. Multipage spread begins on page 90.

5. One carving, shown in a photo in Glover, p. 294, depicts a sunrise with the word *ORO* (Spanish for gold) written underneath. Recall that the sunrise is a key KGC symbol and that the secret order deliberately camouflaged its symbolism so as to appear "Spanish."

6. See Glover, pp. 163–67, for helpful listing of "Official Records and Newspaper Accounts pertaining to Jacob Waltz."

7. None of the Reavis biographers mentions KGC involvement directly. For a solid review of the plot, see Donald M. Powell's *The Peralta Grant: James Addison Reavis and the Barony of Arizona* (Norman: University of Oklahoma Press, 1960).

8. For background on Reavis Ranch, see Kollenborn's booklet, *The Apache Trail* (Apache Junction, Ariz.: World Publishing Corp., 1999).

9. Glover, p. 128. Glover raises the issue of why a man of seemingly moderate means would list all these paid laborers resident at his ranch in the census.

13. A CONFEDERATE FORT KNOX IN ARIZONA?

1. Photographs, maps and other documents from Heart Mountain Project in possession of Brewer.

2. See Mackey's *Revised Encyclopedia of Freemasonry*, Vol. 1, p. 447, for heart reference.

3. Gene Ballinger, "Ghosts of the Red Bluffs: Where Is $80,000 in Confederate Gold?" *The Courier*, Hatch, N.M., October 6, 1994, p. 1A.

4. For a helpful review of the U.S. Geological Survey's topo production history, see Morris M. Thompson, "Maps for America: Cartographic Products of the U.S. Geological Survey," Third Edition, 1987, published by U.S. Geological Survey.

5. Ibid., p. 28.

6. Ibid., pp. 15, 109.

7. Leonard B. Waitman, "The Knights of the Golden Circle," *San Bernardino County Museum Association Quarterly*, Vol. 15, No. 4 (Summer, 1968). On file at the Library of Congress.

8. Jesse Lee James (Howk), *Jesse James and the Lost Cause*, p. 33.

9. Waitman, p. 14.

10. See *War of the Rebellion, Official Records of the Union and Confederate Armies*, Series 1, Vol. 50, Part II, Operations on the Pacific Coast, pp. 496–97, on file at the Library of Congress (or see "Making of America" digitized version on Internet) and cited by Waitman. *Official Records* is also the source for RABE reference, from correspondence of a Clarence E. Bennett to General Sumner, pp. 556–58.

11. See Robert Lee Kirby's *The Confederate Invasion of New Mexico and Arizona 1861–1862: The Civil War as Fought in the Far West* (Tucson: Westernlore Press, 1958). Kirby emphasizes the strategic significance of the Far West in the Civil War. He does not directly name the KGC in his references to guerrilla war in the state.

12. James (Howk), p. 26.

13. Letter on file under the heading "Land Speculation" in Caleb Cushing Papers, Library of Congress.

14. Schrader and James (Howk), p. 8.

15. James (Howk), p. 65.

16. Copy of "Arizona Desert Treasure" map (illustrated waybill with text, signed *JJIII*, as in Jesse Lee James–Orvus Howk) in Brewer's possession.

17. For a recent feature story on the Spider Rocks of Texas, see Evan Moore, "The Unending Quest for Coronado's Gold," *Houston Chronicle*'s *Texas* magazine, May 6, 2001, p. 8.

18. Photos and carbon copies of Superstition Mountain stone maps in Brewer's possession.

19. In the summer of 2000, Brewer would receive a copy of the April–May 1973 issue of *Frontier Times*, a small-circulation history and treasure-hunting magazine, which included a fascinating feature by Bernice and Jack McGee, "Are the Peralta Stone Maps a Hoax?" It was sent to him by his friend Bob Tilley, who knew that Brewer had been focusing on the Lost Dutchman mystery. Tilley's wife, Wanda, who worked at the local library, had brought home a stack of old treasure magazines that had been recently donated. To Brewer's amazement, the article showed the topographic outline of the horse's head. It did not discuss or reveal the topographic presence of additional stone-tablet images— the priest, the dagger, the heart and others. Brewer found the article cryptically written, at times seemingly infused with insider knowledge of the fuller picture. Significantly, the article made the tablets out to be a "hoax" as far as the chiseled slabs' link to the fictional Peralta family were concerned. The article made no mention of the KGC, the Confederacy or any other organized group. The thrust of the piece was critical: it sought to belittle the tablets, to show them to

be nothing more than the work of pranksters. Brewer thought otherwise and knew that the interpretations posited in the article hardly scratched the surface. In fact, he thought, a typical reader of the possibly ciphered article might just conclude, "Clever ruse these tablets, but no sense wasting any time trying to dig up a lost treasure or mine out in the deadly Superstitions." On the other hand, the highly informed reader might just notice a few uncanny observations and realize that there could be something significant embedded in the prose.

14. OFF TO ARIZONA

1. Interviews and correspondence with Ellie Gardner and Brian MacLeod, April 2001 through Spring 2002.

2. The legal guidelines for the U.S. General Services Administration to enter into such a contract are in the U.S. Code, 40 U.S. 310, under "Abandoned Property" provisions: "The Administrator of General Services is authorized to make such contracts and provisions as he may deem for the interest of the Government, for the preservation, sale or collection of any property or the proceeds thereof, which may have been wrecked, abandoned or become derelict, being within the jurisdiction of the United States, and which ought to come to the United States, and in such contracts to allow such compensation to any person giving information thereof, or who shall actually preserve, collect surrender or pay over the same, as the Administrator of General Services may deem just and reasonable. No costs or claim shall, however, become chargeable to the United States in so obtaining, preserving, collecting, receiving or making available property, debts, dues or interests, which shall not be paid from such moneys or shall be realized and received from the property so collected, under each specific agreement." Notably, as a "codification" to the provision states, property once in the possession of the "so-called Confederate States" and now belonging to the United States was omitted from the existing iteration of the law.

3. Some of the scientific interest in the HMP research project is expressed in a letter sent to Gardner, February 17, 1997, by Deborah H. Johnson, principal archaeologist, DSHJ Research Associates, Inc. of Phoenix. Letter in possession of Bob Brewer.

4. Schrader and James (Howk), p. 241.

16. THE TEMPLATE: WALKING THE LINES

1. As defined in *Webster's Ninth New Collegiate Dictionary* (Springfield: Merriam-Webster, 1990).

2. The broken misspelled Spanish says "BUSCA EL MAPA" and "BUSCA EL COAZON."

3. Templar's heart symbol, as described in Michael Baigent and Richard Leigh, *The Temple and the Lodge* (London: Jonathan Cape, 1989), p. 34.

4. Mackey, p. 157.

5. Kollenborn's article, "A Wilderness Mountain Resort," cites the *Phoenix Daily Herald*, "J. J. Frazier, Mayor of Bloomerville," July 16, 1898, and the *Florence Tribune*, January 6, 1900. Fraser's true identity is not known, other than

that he was allegedly born in Nova Scotia, Canada, came to the area around 1883 as a cattle rancher and got involved in mining interests. He reportedly sold the Reavis Ranch to William J. Clemans, owner of the Clemans Cattle Company.

6. See reference to Outremer in, for instance, *Holy Blood, Holy Grail*, pp. 72, 79.

7. James A. Swanson and Thomas J. Kollenborn, *Circlestone: A Superstition Mountain Mystery* (Apache Junction, Ariz.: Goldfield Press, 1986).

8. See Fox; photo section includes beehive on chart of the Scottish Rite, 1874, in Scottish Rite Museum, Lexington, Mass.

9. See paper by Army communications historian and former director of the Fort Huachucha, Arizona, Museum, Bruno J. Rolak, "General Miles' Mirrors: The Heliograph in the Geronimo Campaign of 1886," presented at the Fort Huachucha (June 1975) seminar on The History of the Indian-Spanish-American Southwest, 1598–1886. Also, see Report of Brig. Gen. Nelson A. Miles in *Annual Report of the Secretary of War for the Year 1886* (Washington: Government Printing Office, 1886), Vol. 1, pp. 173–75.

10. Ibid.

11. See Edwin Cole, *The Gila: River of the Southwest* (Lincoln: University of Nebraska Press), p. 208.

17. EVIDENCE IN THE GROUND

1. All recovered items in possession of Heart Mountain Project.

2. J. Frank Dobie, *Coronado's Children* (New York: Garden City, 1930), pp. 71–73.

3. See Glover, p. 336, for Tumlinson example.

4. Bernice and Jack McGee, *Frontier Times*, ibid., p. 13. The McGees write that Travis Tumlinson was directly linked to Peg Leg Tumlinson. Their article quotes alleged friends of Travis, the "Hansons," as saying: "The name Tumlinson apparently springs from an ancient ancestor. Travis told us that it came from 'Peg-Leg' Tumlinson, who is mentioned in J. Frank Dobie's *Coronado's Children*."

18. ARKANSAS: THE SENTINEL'S TREASURE

1. Griffith, in April 2002, telephone interview said that he "took a bank loan out," to purchase the house.

2. See TreasureNet.com's "Forum" section under "Treasure Hunting" heading. Go to archives and see references to Hillbilly Bob, HBB, Knights of the Golden Circle, KGC and Jesse James.

3. Copy of Howk letter in possession of Brewer.

4. Bob Berry, "When the James Boys, Famed Bandits, Visited Arkansas: Following Robbery in 1874 of Stage Coach Running between Malvern and Hot Springs, Band Said to Have Escaped by Way of Old Cove," *Mena Star*, May 21, 1931.

5. The rifle is in the possession of the Brewer family, as are old photos showing it in hands of associates of Wiley, Will Ashcraft and others.

6. Letter and waybill concerning "Solomon's Temple" treasure in Bob Brewer's possession.

EPILOGUE—THE EUROPEAN CONNECTION

1. Richard Andrews and Paul Schellenberger, *The Tomb of God: The Body of Jesus and the Solution to a 2,000-Year-Old Mystery* (Boston/New York/Toronto/London: Little, Brown, 1996). Also see Michael Baigent, Richard Leigh and Henry Lincoln, *Holy Blood, Holy Grail* (New York: Dell, 1983), cited earlier.

2. Andrews and Schellenberger. The many references throughout book include detailed decipherment of directional tangents depicted in paintings.

3. Ibid., p. 432.

4. See Yates, *The Rosicrucian Enlightenment* for names of Rosicrucian leading lights, such as John Dee.

5. See Andrews and Schellenberger, introduction.

6. Ibid., p. 183.

7. Baigent et al., pp. 196–97.

8. Ibid.

9. Henry Lincoln, *Key to the Sacred Pattern: The Untold Story of Rennes-le-Château* (New York: St. Martin's Press, 1998), pp. 33–34.

10. There have been a number of insightful and, to be sure, speculative books published about the Oak Island mystery. The one that seems most balanced and relevant—in terms of its analysis of a possible Templar/Masonic connection at Oak Island—is Mark Finnan's *Oak Island Secrets: The Treasure and the Treasure Hunters* (Halifax: Formac Publishing, 1997).

11. Finnan describes all of these artifacts as having been uncovered (and subsequently debated) by an assortment of Oak Island treasure hunters and history buffs.

Index

Photograph credits: 1, 3: Don and Jeff Ashcraft; 2, 8, 14, 19–21, 23, 25, 27, 28, 33, 35, 36: Bob Brewer; 4, 5: Bob and Wanda Tilley; 6, 11: Library of Congress; 7: Collection of Fain McDaniel; 9: Historical Society of Pennsylvania; 12: National Archives; 15: Bob Brewer and Bob Tilley; 16, 17, 22: Collection of Bob Tilley; 18: Collection of Jerry Eckhart; 26: Ceci and Jo Anne Gillespie; 29, 30, 32, 34: Ellie Gardner; 31: Bob Brewer

Map credits: 1, 13, 14: Designed by Bob Brewer with DeLorme TOPO 4.0, used with permission; 2, 11: U. S. Geological Survey, Library of Congress; 4, 5: Collection of Bud Hardcastle, used with permission; 6, 9: Library of Congress; 7: Atlas of American History, Revised Edition, *by Kenneth T. Jackson and John T. Adams, Charles Scribner's Sons, © 1978, Charles Scribner's Sons. Reprinted by Permission of the Gale Group.; 8:* Oklahoma Treasures and Treasure Tales *by Steve Wilson, used with permission; 3, 10, 12, 15: Bob Brewer*